Language
Acquisition
Made
Practical

This Lamp
Belongs to

This book is designed to lie flat when opened to any page. Prepare it by placing the binding flat on your desk with the edges of the pages upward. Hold the front cover (and this page) down on the desk and run your fingers firmly down the edge of the page, close to the binding. Be firm, but don't break the binding. Do the same with the back. Repeat the creasing procedures with the first, and last few pages. Continue folding down the pages, alternately front and back, until you reach the center of the book.

Language Acquisition Made Practical

FIELD METHODS
for
LANGUAGE LEARNERS

E. Thomas Brewster, Ph.D.
Elizabeth S. Brewster, Ph.D.

Published by: **Lingua House** • Pasadena, CA 91182
Order from: Academic Publications, Summer Institute of Linguistics
7500 W Camp Wisdom Road, Dallas, TX 75236

ISBN 0-916636-00-3

Library of Congress Catalogue Card Number: 75-43377

Printed in the United States of America

First Printing	April 1976
Second Printing	November 1977
Third Printing	June 1981
Fourth Printing	December 1982
Fifth Printing	June 1984
Sixth Printing	September 1987

There have been five men who have had a profound effect on the development of our sensitivity to cross-cultural communication. We would like to dedicate LAMP to them.

Leslie Mark *who continues to be a dynamic example of a sensitive cross-cultural communicator.*

Donald Larson *who has developed many significant innovations, some of which we have been privileged to help implement.*

Eugene Nida *whose guidance stimulated our first major retrieval of feedback from cross-cultural communication attempts.*

Paul Hiebert *whose non-threatening approach to anthropological issues has enabled us to evaluate and modify some basic presuppositions.*

Donald Smith *who has helped us recognize the significance of symbols in communication and the role of evaluative research.*

v

Illustrated by
Dick Williams
Colorado Springs, Colorado

The LAMP Demonstration Tape

The *LAMP C-90* cassette tape will be especially helpful if you have had no previous orientation to these techniques. The tape includes demonstration samples of the practice drills described in Chapter One, and also gives examples of the sounds described in Chapter Four. Whenever a section of the book is demonstrated on tape there is a miniature cassette drawn in the margin. The footage indicators of different brands of tape recorders don't consistently yield the same readings, so we have not indicated the footage on the drawings. You may want to note the footage from your own tape recorder and write it in the margin beside each demonstrated portion, so that you can more easily return to that recorded demonstration as needed. *LAMP* tapes are available from **Lingua House.**

Acknowledgements

Trail blazers we are not — few of the ideas of this manual are original with us. Dr. Donald N. Larson conceptualized the Daily Learning Cycle and, together with Dr. William A. Smalley, wrote *Becoming Bilingual* which we have used in the classroom for the past few years. We have taught phonetics using Smalley's comprehensive *Manual of Articulatory Phonetics.* Most of what we know about phonetics is therein contained. Larson's latest book, *Deschooling Language Study Through Involvement and Independence,* contains suggestions for nine months of self-directed language learning. We incorporated many of those ideas into our Chapter Two. Also, many of the cultural probing ideas for the Set 4 topics of Chapter Two were stimulated through reading *American Cultural Patterns* by Dr. Edward C. Stewart.

Dr. H. David McClure wrote his dissertation on Comprehension learning. His abundance of ideas contributed heavily to Chapter Three. We are also deeply indebted to the research of the Foreign Service Institute who developed the ''Self-Rating Scale for Speaking Proficiency,'' which we have modified somewhat for the Appendix.

Two colleagues who used the first draft of Chapter One and gave helpful suggestions were Daniel Brewster and Dwight Gradin. We want to express our appreciation to Joyce Flint of Igbaja, Nigeria, to Dr. John Oller (Chairman of the Department of Linguistics at the University of New Mexico), to David and Leilani McClure, and to Janet Kobobel for their careful manuscript evaluation and style suggestions.

The first draft of Chapter One was typed by the typing center at Campus Crusade for Christ. Judy Clark was the typist for the first four chapters of the final manuscript. Marilyn Heavilin typed the various drafts of Chapter Five and the Appendix, and helped proofread the typeset copy. We have greatly appreciated their careful, skillful typing and their consistently cheerful attitude.

A special thank-you to Mr. and Mrs. Clarence Kiphart and the entire staff of Via Type (La Verne, California) who gave the care required for typesetting Chapter Four. Other specialists also contributed beyond the call of duty: Artist Dick Williams, for his creative illustrations; Sally Stephenson, for her careful layout work; Jim Winchell for technical assistance with the cover; and Yancey L. ''Butch'' Busby, III — the recording technician who made the LAMP demonstration tape possible.

We also owe a great deal to our students of the past decade in overseas orientation courses (primarily at the Toronto Institute of Linguistics and in the AGAPE Movement). Helping them understand how to respond to language learning problems has helped us think through their needs. This book is a response to those needs.

CONTENTS

LAMP KEY

PART TWO
GOING ON!

111

xii

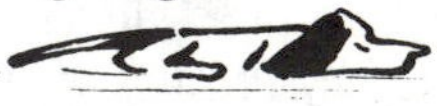

CHAPTER FIVE — HOW TO MASTER THE STRUCTURES OF YOUR LANGUAGE 313

It can be done!   And it can be fun!

You *can* successfully learn another language.

What does a child language learner know about language learning that enables him to successfully learn a language virtually on his own?

"I think I can . . .
Yes, I can!"

Successful language learners — both children and adults — begin with an underlying knowledge that *a language is learned* rather than *taught*. And they know how to take advantage of the abundant resources available to them. These resources are the *people* who speak the language.

In general, successful language learners *learn a little* and *use it a lot*. They get what they need, and practice it, and then use it in actual communication with people. They also spend time in reflection — consolidating their gains and identifying new felt needs — which in turn leads them to get and practice more material which is then also used. You were once a child and this is the way you learned your first language.

These steps of getting, practicing, using, and evaluating are probably employed spontaneously by all successful language learners. We call these four steps a Learning Cycle.

In this book we have carefully described the *techniques* and *activities* that you, the learner, can follow to complete a comprehensive Learning Cycle each day. Specific activities are presented in a step-by-step way which you can easily follow. As you practice the techniques of the Learning Cycle, you will learn to spontaneously use the different learning activities, and you will become increasingly involved with people who speak the new language.

Cycling

Before you start, here are some necessary bits of information about how this book has been arranged. The manual is divided into two parts. The first part carefully describes a methodology by leading you step by step in each of your daily activities. The second part gives you ideas for the content of your daily procedures. Part One deals with *how* to do it, while Part Two deals with *what* you can do. First you need to learn how, and then, when the procedures are second-nature to you, you need ideas for going on.

Part One leads you step by step through the detailed activities of a methodology called **The Daily Learning Cycle.** You are led through the Learning Cycle five times — once for each day of your first week.

Next, is a KEY. It serves as a working index to help you select from a variety of themes, ideas, drills, and activities of Part Two which you can plug into the methodology of Part One.

Part Two assumes that you no longer need to be led by the hand through the procedures of the Learning Cycle, and gives you specific ideas to guide you over the long term: topics for cycles (Chapter 2), drills for understanding (Chapter 3), plus help for pronunciation (Chapter 4) and grammar (Chapter 5).

The Appendix should be read early, for it will help you set your goals and evaluate your on-going progress.

SET YOUR GOALS
EVALUATE YOUR PROGRESS

To the individual learner

LAMP shows you *how* to learn another language. Of course, you must also *want* to learn if you are to become bilingual.

Motivation to learn a language is an *act of the will*. Some language learners make the mistake of equating motivation with enthusiasm. For them, when their enthusiasm is up, their "motivation" is up. But enthusiasm is an emotion. It ebbs and flows in relation to how you feel, or how the world is treating you. In reality, motivation is not an emotion, so don't tie it to your emotions. Motivation is a determination which results in a *decision of the will* — "I *will* learn." The "I will" is far more important in language learning than the "I.Q." (Your aptitude is fine since you already speak English like a native.)

This determination to learn can be both internally and externally stimulated. Sometimes a person's own personal goals will drive him to achievement in learning a language. Unfortunately, for many individuals this inner drive may be the result of initial enthusiasm, and be of relatively short duration. Language learners who have been placed in a field assignment by a sending agency may be encouraged to make a determined decision to learn because of an external stimulus — the agency can simply enforce a policy stating that if a certain level of proficiency is not achieved in a given amount of time, the individual will be recalled from the field assignment. (Agencies may decide to provide some external motivation by requesting field members to submit a monthly progress report like the one suggested on page 384.) Some agencies make language learning a condition for receiving full pay. This external stimulus can create a determination to learn which is frequently of longer duration than the individual's own initial internal drive — especially if his own determination is tied to how he feels.

This manual is a simple guide planned to help you, the learner, proceed without boredom or frustration, through manageable steps, so that you can become proficient in your new language.

A simple guide

The procedures are defined in a precise way, so that learners who have no opportunity to attend a language school will know how to proceed. However, if you are attending a school, this manual will help you determine the comprehensiveness of the language learning program of the school and will enable you to supplement any weak areas of the formal program. When you need to supplement the program, the manual can show you: (1) how to prepare materials you actually need to use in conversation; (2) how to practice systematically; (3) how to use the new language in communication with others; or (4) how to evaluate your daily progress. Even the best language school cannot teach you a language; it can only give you an opportunity to learn. By using the techniques outlined in this manual you can continue learning even after your formal study is terminated.

NOTE: Occasionally the authors are available for initial short-term supervision of groups of language learners in the field. LAMP procedures would be implemented. Address inquiries to the authors: 915 West Jackson, Colorado Springs, Colorado 80907.

Tom and Betty Sue Brewster

To the classroom teacher

What if Johnny studies French, Spanish or German now but ten years from now finds he needs to be able to use Swahili or Arabic or Mandarin? With the shrinking "global village," today's student living in tomorrow's world may be faced with the need to communicate with people in any of the world's thousands of languages. The student needs to develop a positive attitude about languages and language learning, for involvement in this linguistically complex world will be a future fact of life.

Modern foreign language education can prepare students to make a contribution and function successfully in such a world if two goals are adopted:

Train students in *how to learn* a language. Prepare students to be *communicators* in another language.

Often, language classes spend time studying *about* a language rather than learning to *use* the language in cross cultural communication with people. Courses are often taught as though *studying* a language were an end in itself. No wonder enthusiasm for foreign language study is declining! On the other hand, learning to use another language to *communicate* could open up a whole new world of potential relationships.

Learning *how* to learn, and learning to *communicate* in a given language are both objectives that could be accomplished in the classroom if the classes were oriented to those goals.

For the typical language classroom at the high school or university level, the Daily Learning Cycle technique offers a significant advantage over standard methods — students not only learn the language, but they also learn *how* to learn. They can continue learning after the course is finished. Furthermore, the ex-student will be able to proceed with learning any language he may encounter in the future since the "know-how" can apply to any language anywhere.

In **regular language classes** the teacher might fill the role of the helper. (An alternative would be to use an international student or a foreign neighbor who is a native speaker of the language being learned.) Students can rotate the responsibility for leading the Learning Cycle activities from day to day. The Communication part of the cycle can be simulated by having students on their feet to "be the community." During this time they talk with each other in the language in free interpersonal encounters. Where possible, homework assignments should include conversing with any available native speakers in the language.

In the university setting, this manual can be implemented in **anthropology** and/or **linguistics field-methods** courses. Both language and techniques are best learned while the student is actually carrying out the procedures in field work. The authors have taught language acquisition courses where these techniques and procedures were discussed, demonstrated and practiced in the classroom, then each student did his own fieldwork in the community with speakers of the language of his choice. We have had courses where as many as 15 different languages were being learned by the students in a single class. We monitored the development of their language learning skills through the Exercises described in Appendix B.

Language schools overseas can easily adopt these methods. Their adoption could result in improved student proficiency, while simultaneously reducing the operating costs. Schools can offer supervision (see Appendix B) and provide the external motivation for learners to maintain a disciplined learning schedule. Fewer professional teachers are needed, but a staff member should be responsible for checking the techniques and involvement of students, monitoring their progress, and helping with problems.

Introduction

When you travel in countries outside of the English-speaking world, you soon find that a large percentage of the world's population speaks more than one language — probably well over half! Multitudes of illiterates are multilingual without the benefit of a language school. They learned the language because they *used* the language. The main place for learning a language is in the streets and homes of the community. In contrast, many Westerners feel that they are not studying if their nose is not in a book and a pencil in their hand. They feel guilty about "wasting" study time by "just" talking with people.

Studying!

How often have native speakers of English studied a foreign language in high school or college, only to find that they cannot communicate when they meet a native speaker.

Monica had just completed her bachelor's degree with a major in French. Academically, she was qualified to be a French teacher, but she wanted to have some cultural experience before taking her first job. She decided to spend the summer in France. In Paris, everyone seemed to talk much too fast! She couldn't even follow conversations, let alone participate in them. You can imagine how chagrined and disillusioned she felt: "All those years studying French, but I can't even talk with anybody!"

It seems that language courses which emphasize the cognitive skills of learning grammar rules, memorizing conjugations and declensions, studying vocabulary lists, etc., all too frequently produce students who are unable to communicate in the language they have studied. The unfortunate result is that the student becomes convinced that he cannot learn a foreign language. Indeed, almost all native English speakers suffer from the "I-can't-learn-a-foreign-language" syndrome.

"I can't learn a language!"

But, speaking a language is more of a performance skill than a cognitive skill. Learning to speak a language is more like practicing basketball than studying history. Performance skills are learned by disciplined, consistent practice and use.

How does one practice language? The learner must learn to *use* the language, rather than just "study" it. Language learning can then be fun and natural. It can almost be a game.

The Fun of Language

Have you ever noticed how a child plays with words? No child learns to speak his language by memorizing grammar rules or vocabulary lists. Instead, he makes a game out of practicing language. He will stand, for example, at the edge of a fountain and say, "The water goes up in the air and falls down; it goes up and falls down, up and down, up and down." For quite some time he may stand there describing what is happening, completely occupied — practicing language. Or the child may play with a doll or a pet, always talking with it — experimenting with language. Sometimes he will corner an adult and "talk his ear off" — testing his own language skills.

Children talk — and talk

The adult is reluctant to act in "childish" ways. His self-image has been established, and restrains him from behavior which he interprets as childish. He doesn't want to make childish mistakes. But, to be an effective language learner, the adult must be willing to be child-like. Being "child-like" is different from being "childish." It is a voluntary act requiring a special kind of maturity. Some adults scorn child-likeness for fear that it will be interpreted as childishness. They are therefore unwilling to interact with people and to involve themselves in the community where their new language is spoken. They try to study the language in much the same way as they might study history.

Ed was studying Spanish in Guadalajara, and was self-conscious of the mistakes he made when speaking Spanish to other people. (He was being too severe with himself because of his pre-established self-image.) He decided he would learn all the grammar rules first, and then speak without making childish errors. So he put his nose in a book and isolated himself from opportunities to speak. Ed, like many other North Americans, found this grammar-first approach appealing. It was more in harmony with his educational habits, not to mention his self-image.

So he put his nose in a book

Ed should not have been so self-conscious about his mistakes. If a learner is making progress, most people will be more tolerant of his mistakes than he is himself. They are less likely to laugh at him than he is to think that they must be laughing at him. It would have been better for Ed to experiment and play with the language, making a game of it and using it at every possible opportunity. This approach can be fun, and is more like the way a child learns. It is also more effective.

The Role of the Language Learner

It is not uncommon for people who speak English to establish themselves in roles overseas which make language learning virtually impossible. For example, the person who goes as an administrator subconsciously puts on an administrator front, and acts in an administrative way. If someone goes as a teacher, or a medic, or a missionary, he has a high-status role. His self-image compels him to behave in ways which conform to that role. A person who wants to learn another language often has legitimate responsibilities to perform, and these should help motivate him to learn the language well. But in language learning, the attitude of superiority that often goes (subconsciously) with the sophisticated role, must be laid aside.

The superior role!

The learner must assume the role of a learner; he must act like a learner. He should view himself as a student of the language and culture. He is the one who does not know, and those around him are the ones who do know what he needs to learn. They know how to act as insiders in the culture, and he only knows how to act as an outsider, a foreigner. Every native speaker is potentially a person from whom he can learn. As he assumes the role of a learner, they will feel more comfortable in correcting his mistakes and helping him learn. On the other hand, if he takes on the role of an educated foreigner who has come to help "these people," then hardly anyone will feel comfortable in giving him the help he needs. He may never learn to communicate as an insider would, and he will frequently be misunderstood.

Swede is a good example of one who consciously assumed the role of a learner. He serves as a supervisor of the Latin American national leaders of his organization. Because of his responsibilities, he was highly motivated to learn to speak Spanish well. He practiced the language faithfully, even when with his men, and he laughed heartily with them at his own mistakes. Swede's role as a supervisor didn't make him too proud to accept correction from them. The men respected him as their supervisor. Yet he became still more effective as he fulfilled the role of a learner. His language ability steadily improved, and he was also becoming a cultural insider. Thus he has earned the deep confidence and warm devotion of the national leaders whom he supervises.

The role of the learner should be established from the very beginning. But how? By the second day of language learning, the learner could express something like this:

"This is
my second day here"

"Hello, how are you?
I want to learn to speak your language.
This is my second day here.
This is all I can say so far.
I'll be seeing you.
Good-bye."

PART ONE

GETTING STARTED

The Daily Learning Cycle

Putting it all together

PART ONE

GETTING STARTED

Our objective in Part One is to help you learn *how* to learn a new language. You should be able to master the procedures by the time you have completed a couple weeks of language learning. As you follow this guide, you will need to budget about six hours each day, at least for the first couple weeks. After you have learned the procedures, you should continue to budget six hours, gradually reducing it to about three or maybe two hours daily. Maintain specific hours each day for your learning program. With discipline you will make steady progress. Thomas Edison had little trouble making an electric light that burned — the challenge was to make one that didn't burn out. Decide now to stick to it; don't let your desire to learn burn out after an initial flash of enthusiasm.

The Daily Learning Cycle

Each day's work, whether for six hours or two hours, should contain four general activities. They may be thought of as four parts of a learning cycle. As the cycle is repeated daily, your language proficiency will spiral upward.

The four parts of each daily learning cycle are:

1. **Prepare** what you need for the day.

2. **Practice** what you prepare.

3. **Communicate** what you know.

4. **Evaluate** your needs and your progress, so you will know what to prepare for tomorrow.

There are four parts

The heart of the daily learning cycle is the third part — *using* what you have practiced and what you know in *communicating* with people in the community. From the first day, you should use your new language as a means of communicating and interacting with people. Language learning should not be simply lists of rules or things to memorize.

A list to memorize

Each day you will proceed through all four parts of the learning cycle.

Selecting a Language Helper

You will need the help of a native speaker who understands some English. It will be helpful if he can read and write his own language. (If no one speaks English, you must begin by acting out and mimicking — The Summer Institute of Linguistics offers excellent training for working with a monolingual helper. People with that type of training will be able to adapt these procedures as needed.) Your helper will work with you during the preparation and the practice parts of your daily cycle.

Your helper should be honest and open with you, and willing to consistently correct your errors. He should be more eager to help you learn his language than to improve his own mastery of English.

Your helper should probably not be a teacher, because teachers tend to have their own ideas about teaching techniques. Most teachers will teach about the language rather than help you practice the language with them. You should ask a native speaker to come and let you hear him speak his language and practice with him. Emphasize the fact that he does not need to prepare anything beforehand. Don't use the terms "teach," or "teacher," due to the possible conflicting concept of teacher. We encourage you to call him your helper.

You may want to offer to pay him for his time; however, you will probably not want to obligate yourself to long term employment until after you find you work together easily, and you are convinced that he is a satisfactory speaker of the language. At first pay for one day; then commit yourself to a couple days; then a week if you are satisfied; then longer as you see fit. We recommend that you find out the minimum wage and offer that for starters.

Before hiring a helper, learn what the normal working hours are in the community. If you fit into the local schedule rather than expecting your helper to fit your schedule, you will probably find your helper more alert and ready to work. (Expecting a helper to work during his normal rest time is a sure way to have a sleepy, uncreative helper.)

Another tip. When selecting your helper, ask around: "Who is a good speaker of your language?"

Let's call your helper **Kino Rikki**. (You will call your helper by his own name, of course!) Before Kino comes to help you for your first day of learning, you should read through "Monday" of Chapter One. That way you can plan what is going to happen, and will be able to avoid losing time.

Kino Rikki

As for supplies, we recommend that you have notebook and scratch paper, and that you keep a small pocket notebook and pencil with you at all times. We will call this pocket notebook your "data book." Three-by-five cards are helpful in keeping information organized — get a shoe box or something to keep them in. A small tape recorder will also be most valuable. If you don't have a cassette tape recorder you should get one — it will be well worth the investment. We highly recommend the use of recorders with the *Cue/Review* feature and a digital footage indicator. These features allow for instant return to any point for easy repetitious listening and mimicry. (Drills can be practiced without a tape recorder, but it is rare for a helper to have sufficient patience to give you all the repetitious drilling you really need.)

Ready?

Go!

CHAPTER 1

The
First Week

Time now to get down to the nitty-gritty of technique.

This chapter describes five days of language learning activities named for the days of the week, *"Monday"* through *"Friday."* Each day you will complete the four parts of the Learning Cycle: **Prepare, Practice, Communicate** and **Evaluate.**

"*Monday*"

Your objective today is to begin to communicate with people in your new language.

Cycle Part One —

Prepare What You Need

The Preparation part of the learning cycle is made up of six specific activities:

Obtain	— Get the phrases to express the message you want to learn to say today.
Check	— Make sure it sounds natural to your helper, and is suitable for your use.
Transcribe	— Write down the phrases.
Understand	— Find out the general meaning of each phrase.
Note and Classify	— Make careful notes of opportunities and problems. In Practice you can design drills to respond to the opportunities and overcome the problems.
Record	— Make a tape recording of the message, in various ways, for use in the Practice part of the cycle.

The remainder of this Preparation section explains the procedures that you will follow with your helper in preparing the message you will learn today. We will call this message a text. The word "text" refers to the message or material which you prepare to learn each day. The text should be a short story, or a conversation, or a short speech, or anything you want to learn to say. Early texts should be useful in a wide range of the common situations which you might be involved in frequently.

Obtain the Text

Explain to your helper, "Kino," that your objective is to begin communicating with as many people as possible. You will want to greet people; tell them you are learning their language but can't say more; then a leave taking.

Tell Kino that, in English, the basic idea you would like to be able to communicate might go something like this:

"Hello.
I'm learning (name of language).
This is all I can say.
Good-bye."

Ask Kino how this might be said in his language. Caution: Be sure he understands that you do not want him to give you a word-for-word translation of the English phrases. He should say the meaning in a way that sounds natural in his language. He should also understand that you want to learn to say it the way you should say it when *you* talk to others, rather than the way *he* would say it in talking *about* you to his friends. In other words, you want to tell people, "I am learning (language)," rather than, "He is learning to speak our language."

Your elicitation might proceed as follows. You could ask Kino, "How do I greet someone in your language?" (Have Kino write down this greeting, or put it on tape.) "How would the person answer my greeting?" (After Kino says it a couple times, again have him write it or record it.) Then ask, "How can I make him understand that I want to learn to speak his language?" "How can I tell him that I can't say anything else, or that this is all I can say?" "What should I say when I want to leave?"

What Kino has written may prove to be suitable for your first text. Have him say it out loud in his language one or two times and then have him say it again as you record it on tape.

NOTE: Some of the people who use this manual may have lived for some time where their new language is spoken, but are just now seriously beginning to learn it. In that case, the content of the message which would be appropriate for the first text, might be slightly different. Your text might say something like this:

"I want to learn to speak (language).
I am now beginning to study it.
This is about all I can say.
I will learn more tomorrow."

You should, of course, modify the text to meet your own needs and fit your own situation.

There is skill involved in asking questions so that your helper knows what you want to communicate and feels free to tell you how and when you can say it appropriately. Be careful not to overcontrol your helper, but make it clear that this is a *work* relationship. As you cultivate your helper-learner relationship, remember to be patient and to give compliments generously. Be a good host and be considerate of Kino's needs. Be careful about using English idioms and jokes as they could easily be misunderstood. Keep your instructions simple and clear. Rephrase them as needed, and take the blame for any errors made. Relax.

Check the Suitability of the Text

To check the suitability of the text, have Kino listen to the recording which you just made, and ask him if the text sounds smooth and natural *to him*. Will it be OK for you to say this to people on your first day?

You will also need to decide if the length and difficulty of the text are suitable *for you*. The sounds of the new language may all be strange to you. As you listen to the text, everything will probably sound like a series of nonsense syllables. Your reaction may be that it is too long and too difficult for you. If so, you might have your helper try to make the sentences shorter. If he is able to shorten it, have him record the shortened text and listen to it again to be sure it sounds natural.

Step C — Transcribe it

Transcribe the Text

Begin to keep a notebook of your texts, so you can have them all in one place. Have your helper listen to the recording of the text you are going to learn today, and write it for you in your notebook. It will be helpful for him to refer to this written text later on — in the recording step. (If you have had any training in phonetics, you may also want to transcribe it phonetically.) In a few days you will begin doing the writing yourself if your new language is written in a Roman script.

NOTE: If you are working in a language which is unwritten or has a non-Roman script, it is a disadvantage. But not a disaster. Carefully study Chapter Four, and adapt a phonetic writing system for your use in transcribing the language. A phonetics course would also be very helpful.

On your first day, it might be confusing for you to try to read what your helper has written. To learn the alphabet or writing system at this time would be outside the performance objectives for today. You should always beware of the temptation to learn *about* language, rather than learning to use language.

Understand the Text

Today you have told your helper what you want to say and therefore you have an idea what your text means. However, during the understanding step in future cycles, you may need to find out the general meaning of each phrase. After you get the gist of what the text says, you will also begin to learn how your language organizes the parts of the sentences.

Step D — Understand it

Check with your helper to confirm the general meaning of each phrase of today's text. Write it down with the text in your notebook. After this is completed, you will be ready for the next step of the Preparation part of today's cycle.

Note Opportunities and Problems

The new sounds and sentence patterns that you encounter each day present opportunities for growth in the language. Note and classify these new features. By preparing drills and practicing the new sounds and structures, you can make them your own and you can steadily advance in your speaking ability.

It is also important to know how to learn from mistakes. Note your problems and classify them. Problems you will first note will be pronunciation problems. Other categories for classification will include grammatical structures, needed vocabulary, and topics you want to be able to talk about.

Step E — Note
opportunities and problems

Make a note about the sounds that you say somewhat differently than Kino. Which ones does he correct you on? At what point do you stumble? Indicate these points of difficulty in the transcription of the text with a wavy line under the sounds.

On *"Wednesday"* you will begin to learn how to respond to your pronunciation needs.

Record the Text for Practice

To complete the Preparation part of the cycle, you and Kino will make a tape recording of the text in various ways for Fluency Practice. This will enable you to practice the material until you become proficient in it, and it will also spare your helper from undue boredom. Drills can be practiced without a tape recorder, but it is rare for a helper to have sufficient patience to give you all the repetitious drilling you really need.

Today you will record three simple exercises that will help you say your text with flow and confidence.

The following paragraphs describe how to prepare and record them. You will then use them in the next step as you practice the text. For the first drill today, your helper will simply record your whole text, and for the second one he will put a portion on the tape and then leave a pause so that when you drill you will have time to mimic or respond before he resumes.

Before recording each drill, it is particularly helpful to record the name of the drill and the directions for you to follow when practicing it. In this way, you will know what follows on the tape, and what to do as you drill it. The name of the drill and the directions for practice are given in quotation marks at the beginning of each of the drills outlined below.

Be sure to set the footage meter of your tape recorder at zero before taping the first drill. Make a habit of noting the footage at the start of each successive drill so you can easily find the beginning of it.

Proceed through the following steps as you prepare your recording. Record the name of the drill and the directions for yourself each time before you record the drill.

Name: **"Whole Text Listening Drill."**
Practice Directions: "Listen Only."

Ask your helper to say the whole text at normal speed while you record it.

Ask him to say it twice more, at normal speed, so that the complete message will be recorded three successive times without interruption.

NOTE: Remember that your helper is a person, not a machine. Try not to treat him in a mechanical way. Help him understand both what you are doing and why you need to do it.

The other drill for today is a sentence drill for mimicry. In Part A, the sentences are given *three times,* and in Part B only *once.*

Name: **"Sentence Mimicry Drill — Part A"**
Directions: "Mimic each sentence during the pause."

Ask Kino to record the first sentence and then pause long enough for you to be able to mimic the sentence when you listen to the tape. Then, ask him to repeat the sentence again followed by a pause. Repeat it a third time. Proceed through the text in this manner, sentence by sentence, recording each sentence three successive times with pauses.

For example, a drill on the English counterparts of today's sentences could be done as follows:

> "Hello."
> Pause
> "Hello."
> Pause
> "Hello."
> Pause
> "I'm learning English."
> Pause
> "I'm learning English."
> Pause
> "I'm learning English."
> Pause
> "This is all I can say."
> Pause
> "This is all I can say."
> Pause
> "This is all I can say."
> Pause
> "Good-bye."
> Pause
> "Good-bye."
> Pause
> "Good-bye."
> Pause

Taping!

In order for the pauses to be of satisfactory duration, you will need to *silently* mouth the sentences during the pause, and then indicate to Kino that you are ready for him to say the next sentence. (In Practice you will mimic the tape during the pauses.) You could explain the recording procedures to your helper by saying: "We are going to record each sentence three times. I'm going to mimic you in a whisper. Begin your next sentence or repetition as soon as I have finished mimicking you. Let's try doing it with this sentence three times before we actually begin recording." As soon as he gets the hang of it, record the drill.

Name: **"Sentence Mimicry Drill — Part B"**
Directions: "Mimic each sentence during the pause."

This time, have Kino record the text straight through, giving each sentence only once, with pauses. It will go like this:

> "Hello."
>   Pause
> "I am learning English."
>   Pause
> "This is all I can say."
>   Pause
> "Good-bye."

Looking Back at Preparation

You have now completed the Preparation phase of your first cycle. In this part, you have obtained a text in your new language. You elicited your text by describing your objectives to your helper, and having him give you the language material to handle your situation. You then checked the suitability of the text by making sure it sounded okay to your helper, and by having him shorten it, if necessary. The text was written down in your notebook. You checked to be sure you understood it, and then wrote down the general meaning. You noted problems for future pronunciation practice. The last step was to record it, in various ways, for Practice.

You are now ready for the second part of your first learning cycle.

Cycle Part Two —

Practice
What You Prepared

In Practice activities, the learner will be engaged in three progressive stages of involvement:

The first stage is **listening.**
The second stage is **mimicry.**
The third stage is **production.**

Fluency Practice With Your Helper

At this point in your learning, it is important to practice in person with your helper, before practicing with the recording. He will be able to give you suggestions for improvement which, of course, the tape recorder cannot do. Have Kino go through the practice drills similar to the way they were recorded in the Preparation phase.

First, *listen* as Kino says the text repeatedly, following the instructions given for the Whole Text Drill (page 18).

Then *mimic* him as he goes through the text sentence-by-sentence. Follow the instructions for mimicry drills (page 19). As you mimic, pay close attention to your pronunciation as described below.

If a sentence seems too long to mimic easily, do a **Build-up Mimicry Drill** with Kino. Have him say the last couple words of the long sentence, and you mimic him. Repeat this phrase two or three times. Then have him include another word or two. Mimic two or three times. Build up to the full sentence. You could explain the procedure to Kino, like this: "I don't think I can say this whole sentence in one try. Is it possible to break this into shorter phrases for practice? Where can it be divided? (Mark the divisions on the text.) I'd like to work up to saying this whole sentence. First, say *this* three times (point to the *last* phrase) while I mimic. Next, add this on (point to the next-to-last phrase) and say both of these phrases three times while I mimic."

1. LISTEN

2. MIMIC

Here's an example of how this drill could go:

<pre>
Kino: "I can say."
 You: "I can say."
Kino: "I can say."
 You: "I can say."
Kino: "all I can say."
 You: "all I can say."
Kino: "This is all I can say."
 You: "This is all I can say."
</pre>

Note that a build-up drill starts at the end of the sentence and moves to include the beginning of the sentence. This helps ensure a normal ending intonation. Otherwise you might be saying "This is" incorrectly dropping your voice on "is."

While working through the mimicry drills, ask Kino to point out to you the places where your pronunciation is inadequate. You should expect many of the sounds to be different from the sounds you are accustomed to in English. Listen carefully, and try to mimic as well as you can. Do not follow along in the written transcription as you practice; *it is important to train your ears.* There will probably be sounds that you are unable to mimic to your helper's satisfaction. Do not let this frustrate you or him. Assure Kino that you will keep working on it. Smile. Do your best. After about five minutes of focusing on an elusive sound, fatigue sets in. So if you don't get it within three to five minutes, note the specific problems and then go on — in a couple days you will learn drills to improve your pronunciation.

Also, pay close attention to the intonation (melody), emphasis, and rhythm of each sentence, and try to reproduce them as you mimic. Have Kino say the sentences at normal speed, as much as possible, so these features will not be distorted. Be careful not to say the sentences of your text with the questioning intonation that in English means "Did I say it right?" Be especially aware of this in tone languages, as you could completely change the meaning of the sentence by changing the intonation.

After working with Kino through the listening and mimicry drills described above, you are ready to begin the *Production* Stage of Fluency Practice. In the Production stage you are no longer just mimicking — you are producing the sentences yourself.

Here is a drill to help you in the Production stage; it is

called a **Completion Production Drill.** In this drill Kino says the first word or two of each sentence and you say the whole sentence. Kino then corrects you, like this:

Kino: "I'm. . ."
You: "I'm learning Swahili."
Kino: "I'm learning Swahili."
Kino: "This is ..."
You: "This is all I can say."
Kino: "This is all I can say."
Kino: "Good ..."
You: "Good-bye."
Kino: "Good-bye."

You are ready to practice your "speech" using the tape recorder. You can now let Kino go home for the day. Try to do so before he becomes overcome with boredom. Before he leaves, arrange a time to meet with him tomorrow.

Fluency Practice With the Tape

Your objective in practicing with the tape is to get the text down pat and to develop confidence in your ability to say it. You will have learned the text when you can easily say it without stumbling. To achieve this objective, you will want to start at the beginning of the tape and go through the listening drill, and the mimicry drills. It will probably be necessary for you to work through the drills three or four times, or perhaps even more. As suggested before, if your recorder has a digital footage indicator, it will be helpful to write down the footage number at the beginning of each drill, so you can return to the begin-ning of a drill more easily. Be careful to actively listen to each part of each drill, to be conscious of trying to reproduce it as accurately as possible, and to keep the meaning in mind as you say each sentence.

Digital footage indicator

As a production exercise, rewind the tape to "Sentence Drill B." Previously, you *mimicked* each sentence, repeating it after it was given on the tape. This time, however, *produce* the sentence in the pause *before* the tape recorder gives it. Repeat this **Sentence Production Drill** until you can give each phrase without hesitation during the pause.

Next, a **Simultaneous Production Drill.** Return to the first recorded drill (*Whole Text Drill*) which you have used for listening up to this point. Now, however, produce the text,

DRILLS: SENTENCE PRODUCTION — SIMULTANEOUS PRODUCTION

saying the speech *simultaneously* with the tape. As you do this repeatedly, pay special attention to rhythm and intonation. It'll be a challenge for you to keep up with the tape, but the extra fluency is worth the effort.

As a final production exercise, practice saying your entire speech without any reinforcement or help.

When you can say your speech with some degree of confidence, you will have completed the Practice phase of today's learning cycle. Confidence and fluency are, of course, relative. Don't prematurely set a standard of perfection which is unrealistic for you to reach at this point. Your fluency and confidence will continue to improve during the third part of today's cycle.

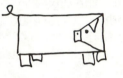

Looking Back at Practice

You have now completed the Practice part of today's cycle. The task has been divided into small, manageable units, and you were able to back up or slow down as you needed. In the next few days, you will be introduced to additional practice procedures.

You have practiced in three different involvement stages:

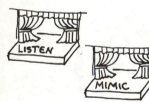

Three stages

> *Listening.* In the Listening Stage you listen only, with no attempt to mimic.

> *Mimicry.* In the Mimicry Stage you listen carefully and then try to imitate.

> *Production.* In the Production Stage you try to reproduce the sentences from memory.

These constitute the fundamental order for practice.

When practicing with your helper, you were focusing on accuracy of pronunciation and intonation. Then, while practicing with the tape, you were learning to produce the text fluently.

The Preparation and Practice phases may have taken you about a total of three hours today. In future cycles, this amount of time may be reduced somewhat after you have internalized the methodology.

You are now ready for the *heart of the cycle* — communicating what you know. You are ready to go and *use* what you have practiced.

If you feel you still need written reminders, put a few key words on a card. You can use it to help jog your memory. Don't write it all out, and don't read it as you communicate. What you can write is only symbols — it is not the real thing. What you have practiced with your helper is the real stuff. In other words, don't trust your written symbols as though they were completely accurate — learn to trust your mind.

Cycle Part Three —

Communicate What You Know

As soon as you finish reading this section, go out and begin talking with people in the community. During the next two and one-half hours you should give your speech to as many people as possible. As you communicate, you will be demonstrating that you want to learn the language. You may become the talk of the town, and the result will be that your role as a learner will become widely known.

> Give your talk to your landlord.
> Talk with children.
> Talk with people in the park or town square.
> Talk in the market.
> Talk with many vendors.
> Talk with the shopkeepers of many stores near your house.
> Every person you see is a potential individual to talk with.

Sure you feel reluctant. Plunge in anyway. Use your new language with thirty to fifty different people (or more). Of course, you will not have much time, or ability, to socialize. A pitfall of some, at this point, is to waste time talking English with anyone who is able to talk in the familiar tongue — but remember, practicing English is not your objective.

Plunge in

A good sense of humor is always helpful as you use your new language. You will be saying something in their language which they have probably never heard before. Some will smile, or even laugh at you. Others will begin rattling off some response to you. Others may be completely perplexed. Some may try to help you improve your pronunciation or even give you alternative things to say. Of course, you will probably not understand most of what they say to you. But don't get paranoid. Recognize that what you are doing is unusual and no doubt amusing. Smile, and be thankful you have this opportunity to add a ray of pleasure to their day.

Have a nice day

Okay — Go to it!

Cycle Part Four —

Evaluate
What You've Done

Welcome Back!

You now need to spend about thirty to forty-five minutes evaluating and wrapping-up your day. The Evaluation Part of the learning cycle is made up of four specific activities:

Evaluate
Procedures — Look at each part of the cycle methodology and at your strengths, weaknesses, reactions, and attitudes; with the objective of improving and refining your techniques, and adapting your attitudes to maximize efficient language learning.

Note and
Classify — Note and classify opportunities and problems so that you will know what features you should be responding to.

Decide on
Next Step —   Review our suggestions for each "day" (later, review ideas from the chapters in Part II), and evaluate your personal needs and problems, then plan your next day's activities.

Organize New
Material —   Keep your data and cultural observations organized and up to date so you have ready access to all accumulated information.

Daily evaluation will stimulate you to continually gather and analyze feed-back so you can improve your language learning procedures. It will also provide a record of the language needs that you feel and help you keep material organized. You will then be able to prepare texts and drills which will help you respond to these needs. In this way, your learning activities will be relevant to your own felt needs and to your level of learning. The daily evaluation will provide a record of your experiences, attitudes, and progress.

The following two pages form a record sheet for your evaluation. The remainder of this section explains how to fill in the record sheet and complete evaluation activities. Read it while you are filling in the record sheet. Write small and neatly.

I. *Evaluate Procedures*

Look at each part of the cycle methodology and at your strengths, weaknesses, reactions, and attitudes, with the objective of improving and refining your techniques, and adapting your attitudes to maximize efficient language learning. What did you learn about yourself as you participated in the different activities of today's cycle? What did you learn about the cycle?

A. **Preparation.** On the record sheet, space is given for you to write out the *text* you learned today. Do not refer to the text that Kino wrote in your notebook. Write it the way it sounds to you. Don't necessarily try to spell it as a native speaker might, but spell it so that you can read it yourself. You will notice some sounds which will be difficult to represent with the English alphabet. Write them as best you can, and indicate the difficulties with asterisks (*). These are sounds for which you will probably need to prepare pronunciation drills in future cycles.

"Monday" Evaluation Record

Date: _____

Day 1 — Objective: To begin to communicate with people.

I. Procedures

  A. **Preparation**

    The Text: _____

    _____

    _____

    _____

    Evaluation of Preparation: _____

    _____

    _____

  B. **Practice** — Fluency Practice

    Listening Stage:

      1. Whole Text Listening Practice _____

    _____

    Mimicry Stage:

      1. Sentence Mimicry Drill - Part A_____

    _____

      2. Sentence Mimicry Drill - Part B_____

    _____

      3. Build-up Mimicry Drill (Not recorded today) _____

    _____

    Production Stage:

      1. Completion Production Drill (Not recorded today) _____

    _____

      2. Sentence Production Drill _____

    _____

      3. Simultaneous Production Drill _____

    Evaluation of Practice: _____

    _____

Evaluation Record – Continued

   C. **Communication**

      Types of People: _____

_____

_____

_____

      Responses: _____

_____

_____

_____

      An Experience: _____

_____

_____

_____

_____

_____

_____

      Evaluation of Communication: _____

_____

_____

_____

_____

II. Note and Classify Problems: _____

_____

_____

_____

_____

_____

III. Decide on the Next Step: _____

_____

_____

_____

_____

IV. Organize Material:

      3 x 5 card categories are prepared: _____

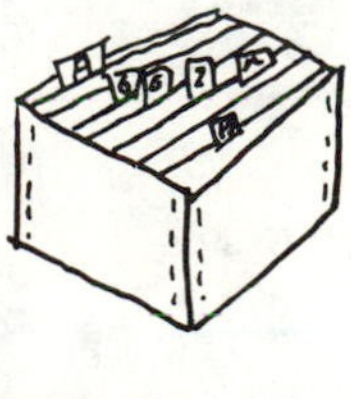

PREPARATION
STEPS
A. OBTAIN
B. CHECK
C. TRANSCRIBE
D. UNDERSTAND
E. NOTE PROBLEMS
F. RECORD

In the space under *Evaluation of Preparation,* write your observations relating to the preparation time spent with your helper. Think of your activities in each of the six preparation steps. Write your observations, problems, attitudes, and anything else that may help you complete preparation activities more smoothly. Were you careful in giving directions to your helper? Were you patient in helping him learn what you wanted to do?

B. **Practice.** Think about the time you spent drilling with your helper and with the tape recording. Write down, beside the name of the drill, any difficulties, problems, ideas, or comments relating to that drill. Be analytical and try to express your comments in ways that will be helpful to you in future practice drills. For example: *Sentence Drill B:* "Make pauses shorter after the sentences, so I don't get bored in the spaces."

Under *Evaluation of Practice,* write your comments about the following topics. Was the progression of difficulty through the practice steps organized into manageable units? If not, how could you make the steps more bite-sized? Think of your relationship with your helper during the practice activities — was your attitude consistently positive? How did you respond when he corrected you? Write down ways you can show your appreciation to him, and help him feel more at ease in correcting you. Were you patient with yourself? Were your self-expectations realistic?

Don't get angry
when corrected

C. **Communication.** Think of your experiences while you were using your speech in the community.

First, name some of the different *types* of people you met, and give the approximate percentages of each type. For example: children 15%, shopkeepers 30%, people in the park 20%, etc.

Describe briefly some of the different kinds of *responses* from different people.

Describe an *experience* that you had today which you would enjoy reading later — something you might want to include in a letter to a friend.

In the space under *Evaluation of Communication,* think of ways you can make your communication time more productive tomorrow. What types of people were most helpful and interested today? Name other types of places you might go tomorrow to find people to talk with.

What social mistakes did you make that you can avoid tomorrow? Were you disciplined enough in carrying out your

On the lookout
for places to go

schedule? How did you react to people's responses to your speech? What are your feelings as you assume the role of a learner? What did you learn about your adult inhibitions? What steps might you take to overcome your natural reticence to talk with strangers? What attitudes should you improve?

II. *Note and Classify Problems*

On the record sheet, describe a sound from today's text that was difficult to pronounce. Note the sound on a 3 x 5 card and list the word or words in which that sound occurs. Save this card and file it after Step IV of evaluation.

III. *Decide on the Next Steps*

Did you accomplish your objective today?

What is something you wanted to say today, but could not? This may provide the topic for one of your next cycles.

Don't forget to read *"Tuesday"* before tomorrow. Also read *Syllables* (pages 251-255).

IV. *Organize Material*

As you progress in your learning, you will want to use this time daily to organize your new materials. Today you don't have much data to organize, but it will be helpful to prepare categories for future material.

We recommend that you prepare a 3 x 5 card file with various sections. (Some people prefer to use 4 x 6 cards.) Sections of the card file can be as follows:

Pronunciation (File here the card that you just prepared)
Structure (Grammar)
Comprehension Activities
Methodology Ideas
"Things I'd Like to Say"
Daily Texts
Culture

Each day as you identify a problem or need, write it on a card, date it, and classify it in the appropriate section so that you can work on it later. Your response to the problem (a drill or activity) can be written on the other side of the card, and the card can be filed at the back of its section.

Date each card

Tomorrow you can have Kino write today's text on a 3 x 5 card, then date it and file it under: Daily Texts.

Postscript

On the next page is an outline of the procedures you have followed in today's activities. Seeing how all the activities fit together as a whole will help you understand the relationship of each to the others, and will help you internalize the methodology and budget your time more effectively.

In preparation for "Tuesday," carefully read the Syllables section of Chapter Four, pages 251-255. Especially note the way stress is marked (page 254) — on "Tuesday" you will be identifying syllables and marking stresses. Read *"Tuesday"* before your helper returns, and then play a game or do something else relaxing.

Congratulations! You have finished your first cycle.

The First Learning Cycle at a Glance

I. **Preparation**

    A. Obtain the Text:

       You described your objective to your helper, and he gave you a text in your new language.

    B. Check the Suitability:

       You had your helper shorten the text and check its naturalness and smoothness.

    C. Transcribe the Text:

       Your helper wrote it down today.

    D. Understand the Text:

       You understood the general meaning of the text.

    E. Note and Classify Problems:

       You identified a pronunciation difficulty.

    F. Record the Text for Practice:

       You recorded drills that progressed in difficulty.

II. **Practice** (for Fluency)

    A. Listen:

       Whole Text Drill (You were also listening during Preparation).

    B. Mimic:

       Sentence Drills,
       Build-up Drill.

    C. Produce:

       Completion Production Drill,
       Sentence Production Drill,
       Simultaneous Production Drill.

III. **Communication**

    You communicated your text to many people.

IV. **Evaluation**

    A. Evaluation of Methodology:

       You evaluated your activities in each of the four parts of the Cycle.

    B. You noted and classified problems.

    C. You decided on the next step.

    D. You prepared to organize material.

Communicating
to many people

"Tuesday"

Having followed the first day's procedures, you are beginning to develop a feel for the daily learning cycle. You are becoming familiar with the activities which make up the four major parts of the cycle. During Practice, you learned some techniques for gaining **fluency** with the text. Today, you will begin to learn various techniques for gaining **accuracy.**

By the end of this first week you will be well on your way to mastering the methodology of the entire learning cycle. You can then begin to become more flexible in response to your own needs and personality. The cycle is not intended to be a strait jacket; but rather, to be liberating by giving you wheels to roll on. With mastery in the use of the cycle, the chains of monolingualism and monoculturalism can be broken.

A main reason that native speakers of English often fail to learn a new language, even when they have the opportunity, is that they don't know *how* to proceed. The daily learning cycle is a programmed progression of techniques designed to meet this basic need.

As you become familiar with the parts of the cycle, you will be able to say to yourself — "Self, *what* do I do now?" And you will know how to respond. Then you can say — "Well, Self, *how* do I do it?" Again you will know the answer, and you will be able to proceed with the activity. Next, you might ask yourself — "When will I be finished with this part?" And you will have the criteria to determine the answer. As you finish each subpart, you will know what to do next. You will be able to proceed in the acquisition of your new language through manageable procedures.

"Self . . . ?"

Throughout your activities this week you will be following the same basic procedures which you have already completed. The mechanics and the sequence of the procedures will be the same, and you may want to refer back to *"Monday"* frequently. For *"Tuesday,"* the four major parts of the cycle will be somewhat amplified.

Objective: Your objective for *"Tuesday"* is to establish yourself in the role of a learner, and to continue communicating with people in your new language.

Prepare
What You Need

Each text must be expressed as the people of your new community would normally express it. It should "feel at home" — not foreign.

A sure way to have a text that seems foreign is to decide in advance what the wording of the message should be. This is often a subconscious "decision" based on the familiar word patterns of English and on our cultural habits. (This danger may be increased due to the English examples throughout LAMP.)

In order to elicit a text that "feels at home," you must describe a **setting** to your helper, and have *him* tell you the conversation that might take place in that setting. This week, during the Preparation part of your cycles, you will learn how to describe settings to your helper.

Today you will expand your greeting in order to more adequately initiate an informal conversation. You will also expand your text so that you can clearly establish your role as a learner; then learn a "thank-you" and maybe expand your leave-taking. You will also begin interacting with people, rather than just talking at them.

Obtain the Text

You can already say something like: "Hello. I'm learning _____. This is all I can say. Good-bye." Your text has a beginning, a middle, and an end. Today, obtain more material to flesh out this skeleton. Also find out what people might say back to you.

In the dialogues of this manual we will use the letter A to indicate what you, the *Alien,* says. The letter B will indicate the response or statement of the *Belonger.*

An English example of your text for today might go like this:

> A. "Hello."
> B. "Hello."
> A. "How are you?"
> B. "Fine, and you?"
> A. "Fine.
> This is my second day here.
> I want to learn to speak (language).
> This is all I can say."

B. "You are doing fine."
A. "Thank you.
   Well, I'm going now."
B. "OK."
A. "Good-bye."
B. "Good-bye."

Don't have Kino give you a literal translation from the English. This text is "right" for English, but other languages will do it in their own way. In English it has been arbitrarily "decided" that "How are you?" is *not* a diagnostic question — we don't really expect the question to be honestly answered. Instead, it means "I recognize you as a person, and I greet you." After this recognition, you can proceed with what you wanted to talk about. In other languages, this recognition would be done in different ways. For example, a greeting and leave-taking might go something like this:

"How am I? I'm, glad you asked! Well, my knees are giving me a bad time. I wonder if I need another operation. And my hands . . ."

A. "You're okay."
B. "You're okay."
A. "I'm okay."
B. "I'm okay."
A. "How's your body?"
B. "It's there, and yours?"
A. "It's there. How are your children?"
B. "They are there. And yours?"
A. "They are there. How's your wife?"
B. "She's there, and yours?"
A. "She's there. How are your cows?"
B. "They're there, and yours?"
A. "They are there. How are your ears?"
B. "They are there."
(Etc. — the longer the greeting, the warmer the recognition.)
— (Body of conversation) —
A. "I'm going."
B. "Go well."

Describe the setting. Ask your helper: "What does someone say when he greets another person on the street?" Find out if it would be appropriate for you to greet people that way. Then, have him tell you what the other person might say in response; then what the first says to be polite; the other's response; etc. Have Kino write down both parts A and B of the greeting.

Beginning   Body   End

For the body of your text, describe the situation for which you need language — the setting. You could ask Kino, "How can I explain to people that this is my second day here, or that I've just arrived?" After he says it, have him write down his answer. Then get something that will make your role as a learner more clear by expanding the phrase from yesterday: "I'm learning *(Swahili)*." Explain that you want to say something like "I want to learn to speak —————." Have Kino write the sentence in his language. Include the statement from yesterday's text — This is all I can say — then have Kino read the whole text aloud a few times to see if it flows smoothly together. Have him make any necessary changes. Also, get a way to thank the person you've been talking to.

Then ask Kino what someone says when he wants to leave after talking with another person. What might the other person then say? What else is said before leaving?

To help Kino understand that you want him to give you the conversation of *two* people, you might demonstrate in English by standing in one place and saying "Hello"; move to where the other person might stand, and respond "Hello"; then to the first place again, "How are you?"; and back to the second place "Fine"; etc. It would be helpful to have Kino actually go through the motions while giving you the local way of greeting and leave-taking, so you can clearly differentiate the two speaker's roles. (Having two helpers take these two parts would be another way of obtaining this text.)

Have Kino write the whole text including both parts A and B. Then have him make a tape recording of it. If you want to help keep the A and B parts separate, on the tape you can say "me" before the A parts and "him" before the B parts.

Check the Suitability

While obtaining the text you have already begun to check its suitability by encouraging Kino to express ideas in natural, rather than translated, ways.

In many languages, there are different greetings for different situations. You need to discover if there are situations in your new language for which it would not be suitable for you to use the greeting you just elicited. Here are some questions you can ask Kino in order to find out the range of suitability for the greeting.

Can this greeting be used any time of day?
Should women be greeted the same way as men?
Does a woman say the greeting in the same way a man does?

Is an older person greeted the same as a younger person?

Can you greet a more important person the same as you greet a peer?

Can this greeting be used with children?

Is this greeting appropriate for friends as well as for strangers?

Does the activity of the speaker or hearer influence the form of the greeting? (For example: "Greetings to you who are walking," or, "Greetings to you who are working.")

Are there any other common factors that should cause a change in the greeting?

The responses you received from these questions have probably shown you some of the limitations of your text. You may now be aware of some situations for which this greeting is not appropriate. Have Kino listen to the recording that was made as you were obtaining the text. Check with him to be sure that the greeting you practice is one that is suitable for you to use in the majority of situations you will encounter as you go out to communicate today. Have him make any changes that will make it more appropriate for you, and then record this new text.

NOTE: If the greeting ritual is quite complex, or if there is much variability from one situation to another, then you should plan to spend an additional cycle or two next week on this topic. This will give you opportunity to begin to sort out the greetings and to learn the ones most useful to you.

As you use today's text, you will be expecting a response from the people you greet. It is therefore important that your greeting be made up of sentences to which people will respond in a fairly standard way. By planning ahead, you should be able to stay in control of your conversations. The expanded greeting and leave-taking you learn today should not contain anything particularly original. It should be standard enough that the responses will be fairly predictable. Then you will be able to carry on the conversation even if you don't fully understand every response.

If the greeting is quite complex

Listen again with Kino to the recording you just made. This time, have him check to see if the text is standard enough so that most people will respond in essentially the same way. If it needs to be altered, have him do so, and record it again.

Transcribe the Text

Listen with Kino to the text you have now decided is suitable for you. Record your *Whole Text Listening Drill*, making certain that the sentences are spoken at a rapid, though normal, speed. Now, as a first transcription step, *hum* the melody and rhythm of each sentence (either with Kino or with your tape recorder). After humming a few times, *count* the number of syllables in each sentence. Represent each syllable of each sentence with a line, like this: ⸺ ⸺ ⸺ ⸺ ⸺ .

'Now indicate the "stressed 'syllables (see page 254) of 'each phrase. (This will 'also help you con'firm your "syllable 'counts.) It might now look like this: '⸺ ⸺ "⸺ ⸺ '⸺ . For today, try to transcribe the stressed syllables:
' bo ⸺ " tus ⸺ ' ak .

Also have Kino write the text. Indicate Parts A and B on the transcription, as on page 36.

Understand the Text

Listen again to the text Kino has just written down. This time, listen to it segment by segment. The first segment would include what is said by person A (the "Alien"), and the next segment would include the response of person B (the "Belonger"). At the end of each segment, stop the tape and have Kino tell you the gist of the meaning in English. Write down this general English meaning of each segment.

There will be words and phrases for which it would be difficult for Kino to give an explanation in English. Don't try to get a literal word-for-word translation. At this point, be content just to understand the gist of the meaning. (You will soon learn how to explore for more specific meaning of words.)

Note and Classify
Opportunities and Problems

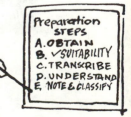

As you become more aware of a specific place in the text where you stumble, underline it in the transcription and identify the problem feature: Consonant? Vowel? Tone level? Or maybe it is the intonation pattern of a phrase? Maybe it is a difficult consonant cluster combination, or a tongue twister. Note also any difficulties in the transitions of sounds between words. Sometimes vowels (or consonants) may seem to drop out at the normal rate of speech flow but reappear when words are spoken separately — especially when one word ends in a vowel and the next word begins with one. What happens between words of this type?

Record for Practice

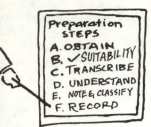

Preparation
STEPS
A. OBTAIN
B. ✓ SUITABILITY
C. TRANSCRIBE
D. UNDERSTAND
E. NOTE & CLASSIFY
F. RECORD

Briefly read through your evaluation of the first cycle's recording time on the Evaluation Record (page 28). As you record today, follow any of your suggestions that will help you improve your taping.

Yesterday you recorded a *Whole Text Listening Drill*, and two *Sentence Mimicry Drills*. In practice time, you also had Kino drill you with a *Build-up Mimicry Drill* and a *Completion Production Drill*. Today you will also record the *Build-up* and the *Completion Drills*.

Begin by recording a *Whole Text Listening Drill* following the instructions given yesterday on page 18. Note the footage on your tape as you begin each drill. Have Kino identify the roles by saying "A" or "B" before each segment. This listening practice gives a valuable opportunity to observe the melody and rhythm of the sentences.

Next, record a *Build-up Mimicry Drill* on the long sentences. Begin by recording the name of the drill.

Name: **"Build-up Mimicry Drill."**

Directions: "Mimic each unit in the pause."

A Build-up drill is recorded by having your helper combine the phrases into larger and larger units, with pauses after each unit, until the sentence is complete. Record a build-up drill for each long sentence in your text, following the pattern shown below. It is an example of the way this could be done with an English sentence. (Of course, your helper must determine what the proper phrase units are in your new language.)

"your language."
Pause
"your language."
Pause
"your language." — Pause
"to speak your language." — Pause
"to speak your language." — Pause
"to speak your language." — Pause
"to learn to speak your language." — Pause
"to learn to speak your language." — Pause
"to learn to speak your language." — Pause

"I want to learn to speak your language."
Pause
"I want to learn to speak your language."
Pause
"I want to learn to speak your language."
Pause

In Build-up drills, it is helpful to begin recording each sentence from the last phrase, as shown in the above example, in order to preserve a more normal intonation pattern. This may feel clumsy the first time Kino tries it, but it becomes easy and natural with practice.

Next, record a *Sentence Mimicry Drill*. If your tape recorder has a Cue/Review feature you may want to only record Sentence Drill B, then in fluency practice use the "Review" to practice as in Drill A. You will find the instructions for *Sentence Mimicry Drills* on pages 19 and 20.

In yesterday's practice you did a *Completion Production Drill* with Kino (page 23). He said the first part of the line and you completed the line. You may find it helpful to record Completion Production Drills three times. The first time Kino can record all but the last word of each sentence in the text as your cue. The second time through the text he would give about half of each sentence, and the third time he would only give the first word of each sentence. You can see the progression of difficulty — during the pauses of the first recording you mimic most of each sentence and only have to produce the final word; the second time you are mimicking about half and producing about half; and the third time you produce almost all of it. You might wish to call these Completion Production Drills "A," "B," and "C."

Name: **"Completion Production Drill A."**

Directions: "In the first pause repeat what was said and complete the sentence; in the second pause, repeat the corrected sentence."

Have Kino say most of the first sentence, omitting the last word or two. Leave a pause long enough for you to *repeat* what he said *and complete* the sentence. During practice, you will say a complete sentence in each pause. After the pause, Kino should say the complete sentence followed again by a pause long enough for you to say the complete sentence. This repetition will give you a model for the correction of any errors you made in the first trial. Repeat these steps as you record each of the other sentences in this same manner.

Here is an example of a taped Completion Drill:

> "I want to learn to . . ."
>
> Pause (In practice, your response would be: "I want to learn to speak your language," giving the complete sentence.)
>
> "I want to learn to speak your language."
>
> Pause (In practice, you would repeat this sentence correcting your first response, as needed.)
>
> "This is my first . . ."
>
> Pause (In practice, you would respond with the complete sentence.)
>
> "This is my first day here."
>
> Pause
>
> "This is all I . . ."
>
> Pause
>
> "This is all I can say."
>
> Pause   (This drill isn't as complicated as it looks!)

For **Completion Production Drill B,** follow the same procedures, but have Kino say about half of each sentence, pause, and then say the correct complete sentence, going sequentially through the sentences of the text.

For **Completion Production Drill C,** Kino can say just the first word or two of the sentence, pause, and then say the whole sentence, followed by a pause. Record each sentence of the text in this way.

Practice What You Prepared

The practice activities of your first cycle were designed to help you gain fluency with a text. With **Fluency Practice** alone, however, your growth is essentially growth by addition. Today you will be introduced to two kinds of practice which will turn simple additional growth into growth by multiplication. They are called **Comprehension Practice** (to stretch your understanding) and **Accuracy Practice** (to help you focus on both the structure and the pronunciation of your new language). First, however, you should practice the procedures you have already been introduced to, in order to gain fluency with today's text.

Fluency Practice With Your Helper

Reread the instructions for practicing fluency with the

helper — pages 21 to 23. Complete the portion of fluency practice which you can do with Kino. This will be primarily the listening and mimicry stages of practice. (Save Fluency Practice with the tape recorder until after you have completed Accuracy Practice with Kino.) Since Kino will be helping you with Fluency, Comprehension and Accuracy Practice, don't dismiss him until you are directed to work with the recording (page 50).

Greetings are often accompanied by some gesture or body language — a bow, curtsey, dip, hand-shake, embrace, smile, etc. Ask Kino to demonstrate the gestures that go with the greeting you are practicing. Are they optional or obligatory? Are they the same for women as for men? When one talks, should he look at the other person, or look away? What body language accompanies the leave-taking?

Greetings use
body language

As you practice your text with Kino, also practice the appropriate gestures that go along with the text.

When practicing, always be sure to *think* of the *meaning* of each sentence as you drill. Don't listen, mimic, or produce nonsense syllables — keep your mind in gear, not just your mouth. Please don't try to read the text as you do these drills — learn to trust your ears.

After you have finished the *Build-up* and *Sentence Mimicry Drills* and *Completion Drills A, B,* and *C,* you should be ready for a new drill called an **Alternation Production Drill.** For this, you simply role-play with your helper — you take Part A and he takes Part B (alternating back and forth). This is the same thing you will be doing with a score (or more) of different people later during your communication time. (Part B is fairly simple today, so you can probably change roles and do an *Alternation Drill* in which Kino takes Part A and you respond with Part B.) As you do the *Alternation Drill,* Kino should correct your errors. Role play until you can do Part A without stumbling.

Alternation

When you finish Fluency Practice with your helper, go on to Comprehension Practice.

Comprehension Practice

Don't miss out on this one. It's easy and fun for both you and Kino.

In Comprehension Practice, Kino instructs you to do something, and you do it. First, you observe him do it once, then you mimic by doing it with him, and very soon you respond to his words alone without visual reinforcement. It'll be easy to get the hang of this.

Have Kino write a series of instructions in his language, on a 3 X 5 card — instructions like:

Comprehension – Body movement   *February 17*

    Stand up.
    Sit down.
    Clap your hands.
    Squat down.
    Jump up.
    Run in place.
    Walk around.

To drill, have him give the first instruction while doing it himself: "Stand up!" You mimic by doing it too (just do it, don't say it). Then the second instruction is given — "Sit down" — and again Kino does it and you mimic *the action*. Then he alternates between these two instructions in rapid cadence and you respond by doing the correct activity. (He no longer does it unless you forget.) After alternating between these two instructions about half a dozen times, the next activity is introduced, and Kino does the action with you the first time — "Clap your hands." Now he gives any of the three instructions, returning to the new one frequently. Then the next activity is introduced in the same way. The most recently introduced activity should be returned to very frequently to *keep it in focus* while you associate the sounds of the instructions with the activity. It should be in focus at least 6 or 8 times before an additional activity is introduced. After the activity has been introduced, Kino should only give verbal instructions, but if you forget a response he should be quick to act it out again in order to refresh your memory.

No English is spoken during the entire drill, and it should move at a cadence of about one instruction every two seconds (or even faster). If you make a vigorous physical response, the meaning will make a deeper impression on your mind — do it with vigour! Four to eight minutes at a time is plenty for this drill.

After completing the Comprehension Drill, date the 3 x 5 card and file it under "Comprehension". You will review it tomorrow before doing another one.

Accuracy Practice

When an adult speaks a new language, he frequently has a "foreign accent." The reason for this accent is that he is using patterns from his original language while speaking his new language. This is called contamination. In Kenya, for example, there are sizable populations of Europeans and East Indians: KiSwahili as spoken by the Indians is called "KiHindi," and the European's contaminated form of KiSwahili is referred to as "KiSettler." Wherever the new language is different from the learner's native language in pronunciation, structure or vocabulary, the learner is likely to experience contamination. His old habits will interfere and cause him to speak the new language using the patterns he has practiced for so many years.

Of course, everyone feels most comfortable with old familiar ways. Each of us has been practicing our English ways for two or three decades, and therefore there is a strong tendency for us to feel that the English way of saying things is the only right way. Some may even have a mental block about adopting any other way. From force of habit, we try to use these "right" English ways when speaking our new language. But, for the new language they are wrong and foreign. Of course, our habits and notions about how to use a language are deeply ingrained. It will take a lot of practice to develop new habits and notions.

A mental block

As you begin to speak another language, a certain amount of contamination will be unavoidable, and there will also be times when you will confuse your listeners. Sometimes the difference between the *pronunciation* of two words will seem so minor that you will have trouble distinguishing them, and yet they have two different meanings, and confusion occurs if they are not pronounced accurately. Other times, your English habits will interfere and influence the word order you choose. The *sentence structure* will then, of course, be incorrect for your target language. In either case, whether you need to correct for pronunciation or structural interference, accuracy practice is helpful and important.

Accuracy *differential* drills help you learn to distinguish between two or more features which, at first, are difficult for you to differentiate. Accuracy *substitution* drills focus on one feature to help you learn to produce that feature correctly, with a minimum of contamination.

Today you will begin to learn how to prepare and practice an Accuracy Structure Substitution Drill. A substitution drill focuses on *one* feature. A Structure Substitution Drill focuses on one *sentence pattern*. By focusing on just one feature, you can work toward mastery of that feature.

Substitution Drill for Structure Practice. In a Substitution Drill for Structure practice, you will focus on one sentence pattern by using a variety of vocabulary substitutions. It is possible to produce hundreds of different messages, all based on the same sentence pattern, simply by controlled substitution.

The framework

During the first few days, you are learning only a small bit of the language each day; however, as you learn some of the basic framework of the language, you will be able to build on it. You will find that the pieces will start fitting together, and your rate of learning will accelerate. Your language facility will expand as you begin to learn new vocabulary which fits into the framework of the sentence structures you have practiced. In Structure Substitution Drills you learn how to produce new sentences using the patterns of sentences you have already learned. Once you have acquired a nucleus of sentence patterns and vocabulary, your language learning will snowball, and the amount you are able to say will increase rapidly.

Words in slots

In today's text you learned a sentence something like "This is my second day here." The same sentence pattern could be used to express: "This is my third day here", "This is my fourth day here". . . etc. Probably any number could be substituted in that *slot*.

The English sentence pattern — "This is my second day here" — has various potential slots.

Pattern: This is	my	second	day	here.
	your	first	hour	
	his	third	week	
	her	fourth	month	
	our	fifth	year	
	their	sixth		

Structure Substitution Drill   *Dec. 23*
Numbers & Time Units

This is
my first year here

One sentence pattern but with only these substitutions one could now say (6 x 6 x 5 =) 180 sentences!

Almost any complete sentence in any language can be used as a pattern sentence for a substitution drill. Slots can be identified in the sentence pattern, and different words can be substituted in those slots. However, do not expect the slots in your new language to correspond exactly with the slots in an equivalent English sentence.

If you were learning New Guinea Pidgin, you may have told your helper that you wanted to say something like "This is my second day here." The sentence he might have given you in Pidgin could be, "Nau tasol mi kamap long Nugini" (I just now came to New Guinea). This is essentially an equivalent sentence. In this sentence, however, it would be impossible to insist on a change so that you could say "This is my first day here." *Never try to make a sentence in your new language correspond with an English sentence pattern.* If a concept is stated in a different way, simply accept it.

This New Guinea Pidgin sentence — "Nau tasol mi kamap long Nugini" — could also be used as a pattern sentence. The following substitution table shows the *slots* and some examples of *fillers* for those slots. (The words that fit into a slot are called fillers.)

Structure Substitution Drill Pronouns and Places					Sept. 13
Pattern: Nau tasol	mi	kamap	long	Nugini.
tude (today)	yu yumi (us)	go		Canada Australia Madang

Choose a sentence from today's text, and work with Kino to find out where substitutions can be made in it. After you have identified the slots, choose two of them and make a substitution table, with three to five fillers in each of those two slots. Write this substitution table, with a heading, on a 3 x 5 card.

HOW TO PRACTICE A STRUCTURE SUBSTITUTION DRILL: Again, remember that there are three progressive stages of involvement in practice drills — listen, mimic, produce.

Make a substitution table

Listen: Have Kino say the pattern sentence, and pause briefly. Then have him say the first filler of the first slot, followed by another slight pause. Next, have him say the sentence, substituting the filler in its appropriate place. Have him continue in this manner, substituting each of the fillers into the pattern sentences. After Kino has substituted all the words individually he can substitute pairs of words into the sentence.

Here is an example of what the helper would say in the listening stage, for the following English substitution table.

This is my first
day here

Structure Substitution Drill *Numbers & Time Units*			*Aug. 12*
Pattern: This is my	first	day	here.
	second third	month year	

In the listening stage, the helper says:

"This is my first day here.(Slight pause)
   Second. (Slight pause)
This is my second day here. (Slight pause)
   Third. (Pause)
This is my third day here. (Pause)

This is my first day here. (Pause)
   Month. (Pause)
This is my first month here. (Pause)
   Year. (Pause)
This is my first year here. (Pause)

This is my first day here. (Pause)
   Second, month. (Pause)
This is my second month here. (Pause)
   Third, year. (Pause)
This is my third year here. (Pause)"

The brief pauses are important — they prevent the filler from becoming an abnormal part of the sentence intonation. Kino should say: "This is my first day here." (Pause) "Second." (Pause) "This is my second day here." (Pause). He should *not* say: "This is my first day here, second." — as if that were all one sentence. Nor should he say: "Second, this is my second day here."

Mimic: Have Kino follow the same order as above. This time, however, you mimic the pattern sentence. Have Kino repeat it as a correction. Then you say it a second time, making any improvements necessary. Then Kino says the first filler, you mimic, he corrects and you repeat correctly. Proceed through the substitution table as in the listening stage.

Produce: The fillers in each slot can be used as *trigger* words to guide you through the production stage. First, you produce the pattern sentence, then have Kino say the first filler (trigger). You respond to the trigger by producing the pat-

Pause

tern sentence with the word substituted in the appropriate place. Kino then says the sentence with the word substituted in the pattern. You repeat the sentence correctly. Kino then gives you the next trigger, and you produce the sentence with the trigger in its appropriate place. Again, Kino corrects and you repeat correctly.

After giving the triggers individually, two triggers can be given. Finally, the triggers can be given in random order.

Here is an English example showing the sequence of the production stage (using the table shown above):

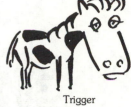
Trigger

Learner — This is my *first* day here.   (Pattern)
Helper — Second   (trigger)
Learner — This is my second day here.   (produces)
    Helper — This is my second day here. (corrects)
    Learner — This is my second day here. (repeats)
Helper — Third
Learner — This is my third day here.
    Helper — This is my third day here.
    Learner — This is my third day here.

(Return to the pattern sentence before going on to the second slot.)
Learner — This is my first *day* here.
Helper — Month
Learner — This is my first month here.
    Helper — This is my first month here.
    Learner — This is my first month here.
Helper — Year
Learner — This is my first year here.
Helper — This is my first year here.
Learner — This is my first year here.
(Return to the pattern sentence.) Two triggers:
Learner — This is my *first day* here.
Helper — Second, month
Learner — This is my second month here.
    Helper — This is my second month here.
    Learner — This is my second month here.
Helper — Third, year
Learner — This is my third year here.
    Helper — This is my third year here.
    Learner — This is my third year here.

Two Triggers

(Return to the pattern sentence.) Random order:
Learner — This is my first day here.
Helper — Year

OuTrigger

Learner — This is my first year here.
Helper — This is my first year here.
Learner — This is my first year here.
Helper — Second
Learner — This is my second year here.
Helper — This is my second year here.
Learner — This is my second year here.
Helper — Day
Learner — This is my second day here.
Helper — This is my second day here.
Learner — This is my second day here.
Helper — Fourth, year (two triggers)
Learner — This is my fourth year here.
Helper — This is my fourth year here.
Learner — This is my fourth year here.   etc.

Performance skills take practice

If this looks repetitious, it is! But you need plenty of repetition now since everything is new to you. *Think* as you practice. Keep your mind on the *meaning*. You should soon be able to develop a rhythm, or cadence, with your helper, which will allow you to accomplish a maximum amount of drill in your practice time. Drilling develops new habits. As in basketball, new habits are developed by practicing — not by discussion or horsing around. After completing the drill, file the card under "Structure."

You have now completed Accuracy Practice, Comprehension Practice, and Fluency Practice with your helper. You will not need the helper as you complete the rest of today's cycle.

Now you are ready to complete the Fluency Practice of today's text using the drills you recorded earlier.

Fluency Practice with the Tape

You need to practice today's text, to develop your confidence in saying it. You will want to be able to say the text with minimum stumbling.

Work through each of the drills you have recorded. You may want to repeat some of the drills three or four times (or more). Use the digital footage indicator for easy return to the beginning of the drill. The *Whole Text Drill* is a listening drill. The *Build-up* and *Sentence Drills* are mimicry drills. The *Completion Drills* are for production.

As a final fluency drill, play the *Whole Text Drill* and say the complete text *simultaneously* with the tape recording. Pay special attention to rhythm and intonation.

You are now ready to communicate what you know. This is the most important step of all.

Communicate What You Know

Read over the evaluation you wrote about yesterday's communication time (page 29). Take note of anything which you might want to keep in mind as you go out today.

Yesterday you were doing a monologue. Today you will be engaging in conversation with other people. They may not follow your script, so don't be flustered if they don't say what you expect them to, or if they say what you had planned to say. Be spontaneous. Carry on the best you can, including yesterday's modified text as the body of today's conversation.

Return to the places you found especially productive yesterday. You will want to try out new places, as well.

Before you go out, one last suggestion. It will probably surprise you to discover how well you can get around by using public transportation. Furthermore, it will give you many opportunities to converse with people. Westerners usually feel they "have to" have their own automobile. It is better, however, to avoid the use of the car if at all possible. A car is basically a capsule which isolates you from the language and culture. In it, you are packaged and insulated — you can't hear; you can't smell; you can't see anything that extends very far beyond the edges of the road. Your car is your environment. But, you don't need *isolation.* You need *involvement!* Don't short change yourself.

The car is
an isolating capsule

O.K., it's time to go. Enjoy making friends with many people in the community.

Evaluate What You've Done

Well, how did it go? Fine? OK, now for the formal evaluation . . .

Keeping on course

Don't underestimate the value of the evaluation part of the cycle. Soon you will be planning your learning activities based on your evaluation information. The evaluative questions "Self *what* do I do now?" and "Self, *how* do I do it?" should help keep you on course. To help you decide what to practice, you might make a habit of asking "What is my problem?" and "What kind of drill do I need to respond to this problem?" A related question that might be helpful is "On what page is that drill described?"

At this point, we want to help you evaluate your developing techniques. After you have mastered the methodology, however, your evaluation will focus more on your language learning progress and the problems or needs you are encountering.

The Evaluation Record Form for today is quite similar to the one you did for the First Cycle. In general, you can *follow the instructions on pages 27-31)* as you complete today's evaluation — but do pay special attention to evaluation of the new Fluency Drills you used today and to the procedures for the Comprehension and Accuracy Drills which you were introduced to. Write specific ideas that will help improve your procedures in future cycles. Future evaluation record forms will not list all of the Fluency Practice Drills, so be careful to include today any comments which will help these drills go more smoothly. After you finish, compare your evaluations of your first two days.

One thing more. Evaluate your working relationship with Kino during the different Preparation and Practice activities. Changes in tempo help avoid monotony for both you and him. Always remember that you are working with a person, not just an intricate machine.

After you complete your evaluation, you will have successfully completed today's cycle. Before Kino comes tomorrow, read ahead through *"Wednesday."*

Tomorrow, you will learn to do a Pronunciation Substitution Drill. In order for you to become more aware of the kinds of sounds your mouth can make, we recommend that you read the consonant and vowel parts of the Pronunciation chapter (Chapter Four, beginning on page 247). It will help you learn to accurately make your new language sounds. If your language is tonal, read the Tonal section as well.

Just think of all you know now that you didn't know two days ago!

Evaluation Record

Date:_____

Day 2 — Objective: To establish your role as a learner and to use appropriate greetings and leavetakings.

I. Procedures
  A. **Preparation**
     The Text:

_____
_____
_____
_____
_____

     Evaluation of Preparation: _____
_____
_____

  B. **Practice**
     1. Fluency Practice
        Whole Text Listening Drill: _____
_____
_____

        Build-up Mimicry Drill: _____
_____

        Sentence Mimicry Drill: _____
_____

        Completion Production Drill: _____
_____

        Alternation Production Drill (Not recorded): ___
_____

     2. Comprehension Practice: _____
_____

     3. Accuracy Practice (Structure Substitution Drill): __
_____

     General Evaluation of Practice: _____
_____
_____

C. **Communication**
   Number of people communicated with: _____.
   Types of People: _____
   _____
   _____
   _____

   Responses: _____
   _____
   _____
   _____
   _____
   _____
   _____

   An Experience: _____
   _____
   _____
   _____
   _____
   _____
   _____
   _____
   _____

   Evaluation of Communication: _____
   _____
   _____
   _____

II. Note and Classify Oppportunities and Problems: _____
   _____
   _____
   _____
   _____
   _____

III. Decide on the Next Step: _____
   _____
   _____
   _____
   _____

IV. Organize Materials:
   Are notes and records currently organized?_____

"Wednesday"

Now you know how to initiate and terminate conversations. In a sense, this is the major part of the battle. You can talk with anyone, and if he says something you don't understand, you can explain that you've just begun to learn his language. Then, you can terminate the conversation appropriately.

The opening and closing of conversations remains fairly constant. The options for the content of the body of the conversation are, of course, unlimited. Today you will use the beginning and ending which you practiced yesterday and, for the body of the conversation, you will learn to tell something about yourself.

Options for the content of the body

You will basically follow the procedures you have used before. Today, you will also learn a new type of drill for accuracy practice — a Pronunciation Substitution Drill.

Prepare
What You Need

As long as you can control conversations, you can speak and listen with adequate understanding. At the earlier stages you will of course be lost when you lose control of the conversation. For your first cycles, it is therefore important to learn to say things which will help you direct the course of your social interactions. A monologue is the most basic way to control a conversation. You are at a basic level, so a monologue is fine for you now.

Your first cycles

Obtain the Text

Today you will learn to tell a short story about yourself. It will be the body of a conversation, and can be inserted into your greeting and leave-taking.

Describe the setting to Kino. Your objective today is to tell people something about yourself. Mention to him various things you could say about yourself and be sensitive to his reaction to each. For example, you could mention the following items:

Where you are from.
Your marital status and number of children.
The area of town where you live now.
Your name.
Your age.
What you like about this country and its people.
How long you plan to stay in the country.

"I'm 39 years old."

Don't include anything which would be inconsistent with your role as a learner. Don't say, "I've come to be a teacher (or missionary)," or "I'm the new manager of X company."

Have Kino help you choose what is best for you to say, or suggest things you did not think of — he may know the questions that people are asking about you. He may suggest a preferable order for the topics of your story. He might also point out some topics which may not be appropriate in your new culture. Telling where you live, for example, might be inappropriate when speaking to a member of the opposite sex.

Your story might go something like this: "(Opening) This is my third day learning Kikamba. I am from Canada. My name is Mbethy Mblusta. I like your country very much. I want to learn your language well. I want to learn about your people. Can you understand me? Thank you for listening. (Closing)"

NOTE: Mbethy Mblusta is the way Betty Brewster came out in Kikamba. Get the local pronunciation for your own name.

After you have decided on the general content of your "autobiography," have Kino tell you what you could say for each item, while you record it. Remind him to give the text in the first, not the second, person — you want to say, for example, "*I* am from Canada," not "*You* are from Canada."

Play the recording for Kino. Be sure he understands that it should sound like a continuous story. Remind him to include the greeting and leave-taking which you used yesterday. Have him record it again, and also a third time. It may get smoother each time he tells it.

Check the Suitability

As you check the suitability of the text, you will decide if the length and difficulty are suitable for you. The sounds of the new language may seem strange to you, and as you listen to the text everything will probably sound like a series of nonsense syllables. Your reaction may be that it is too long and too difficult for you. If so, have your helper try to omit anything that is not necessary, in order to make the sentences shorter. If he is able to shorten it, have him record the shortened text and listen to it again to be sure it sounds natural to him. But don't shorten it too much until you have actually tried to learn it by following the Fluency Practice procedures. As you gain experience in using the cycle you will be able to more accurately gauge how much you can handle during the time you budget.

Check the suitability
of the length.

Transcribe the Text

When transcribing, learn to first pay attention to the longer units, and then work on refining the details as you go along.

Review *Transcribe the Text* (pages 38-39), and then transcribe the syllables of today's text. With practice you will be able to quickly estimate the number of syllables and the placement of the stresses. Now fill in the details. Have Kino repeat each word as needed while you refine your transcription. Note that the standard writing system of a language often represents slow, careful speech — but many sounds or even words can drop out in normal fast speech. Your transcription and your speaking should reflect the flow of normal, longer speech units — rather than individually segmented syllables or words.

If you stress the syllables correctly, and use good intonation, rhythm and speed when you speak, you will probably be fairly well understood even though all the details aren't right yet.

Understand the Text

You already have a general idea of the meaning of the sentences of your text. Today, however, try to learn something about how the language arranges the parts of its sentences. Accept the fact that some words may be impossible to translate and that Kino may be unable to explain the meaning of some words. (How would you explain the words "*do*" in "How *do* you *do*?") Don't expect to understand everything already. Don't ask *why* the sentence is arranged as it is. (Why does English arrange its sentences as it does?) Make some hypotheses about the relative order of the parts of speech in sentences.

Note and Classify Opportunities and Problems

The words of each sentence you use in your daily texts are organized according to a system. Many other sentences of the language will be organized in the same way. Capitalize on these opportunities by making a habit of developing a Structure Substitution drill for the new sentence patterns of your texts.

If you prepare some 3 x 5 cards you will always be ready to note and classify Structure Substitution drill opportunities. Your prepared cards might look like this:

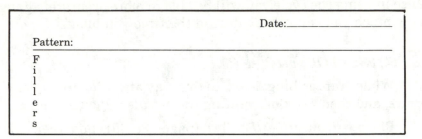

```
                                            Date:_____
          Pattern:_____
          F                                             ___
          i
          l
          l
          e
          r
          s
```

Opportunities
or problems?

During the first few months, each daily text will have some new or varied sentence patterns in it. When noting and classifying opportunities, write on the pattern line of a card any sentence which has a new pattern. In this way you can use the familiar sentences from your texts as the patterns for later drills. In an Accuracy Practice time, identify the slots you want to work with and have Kino help you with the fillers. You can then practice the Substitution drill from your card.

In transcription today you probably became more aware of the fact that it is difficult to represent the new language sounds with English symbols. Note the specific problems.

In Accuracy Practice today you will begin to learn to do a pronunciation exercise.

Record for Practice

Read quickly through your evaluation of yesterday's recording time (Evaluation Record, page 53), and make note of any suggestions which will help today's taping go more smoothly.

First, record a *Whole Text Listening Drill* (see page 18).

The Listening Drill gives you opportunity to observe the melody and rhythm of the text.

Now, here is a new one — *Phrase Mimicry Drill.* The technique differs very little from the *Sentence drills* — it just uses smaller bites. A phrase drill is particularly helpful for longer sentences and even for short ones which seem too long. (Maybe all of them seem too long at first!)

Observe the melody

Name: **"Phrase Mimicry Drill A."**

Directions: "Mimic each phrase during the pause."

Ask Kino to divide the sentences of your text into short phrases. Have him record the first phrase, and then pause long enough for you to be able to mimic the phrase when you drill it. Then, ask him to repeat the phrase, again followed by a pause. Proceed through the text in this manner phrase-by-phrase, recording each phrase three successive times with pauses.

For example, a drill of an English sentence could be done as follows. (Remember that the sentences in your new language will probably not be broken into phrases in exactly the same way that English sentences are.)

"I like"
Pause
"I like"
Pause
"I like"
Pause

I like Mexico

"your country" — pause
"your country" — pause
"your country" — pause
"very much" — pause
"very much" — pause
"very much" — pause

In order for the pauses to be of satisfactory duration, you need to *silently* mouth the phrase during the pause, and then point to the phrase with your pencil to indicate that you are ready for Kino to continue.

A slightly more difficult drill gives each phrase only once:

Name: **"Phrase Mimicry Drill B."**

Directions: "Mimic each phrase during the pause."

Ask Kino to go through the text phrase-by-phrase again. This time, however, record each phrase only once, rather than three times.

For example:
"I want"
Pause
"to learn"
Pause
"to speak your language."
Pause

Now record the other drills that you have previously used:

Build-up Mimicry Drill (page 40)
Sentence Mimicry Drill (page 19)
Completion Production Drill (page 41)

When you have recorded these drills, you are ready for the Practice part of the cycle.

Drills

Practice
What You Prepared

From now on, you should plan to spend part of your time on fluency drills, and part on drills for comprehension and accuracy. You need each type of practice to help you progress toward understanding and using the language accurately and naturally.

Fluency Practice With Your Helper

Do a Phrase Drill and also follow the instructions on pages 21-23 as you work through the mimicry and production stages of practice with Kino. Practice the text with the appropriate body language for the greeting and leave-taking.

Use appropriate
body language

Be sure to encourage Kino to correct your pronunciation and intonation. Show your appreciation when he does correct you. Don't let him feel he is doing you a favor by being "gentle" and not correcting you. The more you practice your mistakes, the harder it will be to correct them later. However, neither of you should expect that you will achieve instant perfection.

Work at correcting your errors, but don't get frustrated if there are some sounds you don't seem to get right. Jot down a note to remind yourself to work on an accuracy drill for pronunciation of the difficult sounds, and then go on.

Now that you have completed the listening and mimicry drills with your helper, practice a simple production drill with him. This drill is called the **Fill-in-the-Blanks** drill. Have Kino say the first sentence of today's text, leaving out some word. You say the word he left out, and then say the whole sentence, inserting that word in its proper place. Have him say the sentence again, leaving out a different word — then again if you like. Go through the whole text, sentence by sentence, having Kino leave out one word each time. You respond by saying the word and then saying the whole sentence (of course, do not follow the transcription as you drill). Go through the text again, following the same process, but this time encourage Kino to leave out the little "grammatical marker" words (prepositions, helping verbs, articles, conjunctions, etc.). This will help you focus your attention on these important little words.

Go through your text

Here is an example of how a *Fill-in-the-Blanks* drill could be done with an English text.

Helper — "I want to learn your (slight pause) well."
    Learner — "language" "I want to learn your language well."
Helper — "I want   learn your language well."
    Learner — "to" "I want to learn your language well."
Helper — "I want to learn   language well."
    Learner — "your" "I want to learn your language well."

See what this does? It makes you focus on those little words, and gives you a feel of the "rightness" of the sentence pattern.

If you need more reinforcement, you can have Kino correct you each time, and you repeat the correction.

NOTE: There are two potential problems that you should be aware of. One is that Kino may be unable to leave out the little function words when he says the sentences. If this happens, accept it and just have him leave out the major words. The second potential problem is that the focus on the function words may cause an unusual pronunciation. Function words are usually unstressed and somewhat slurred in natural speech. Be careful that you don't overstress or overenunciate these now that you are focusing on them. After this drill play the Whole Text Drill you taped earlier and listen carefully to the normal pronunciation of the function words.

Comprehension Practice

Review the directions for Comprehension Practice on page 43.

You will soon need to understand spoken numbers so that you can understand prices, etc. On a 3 x 5 card, have Kino write the following instructions in his language:

Comprehension Drill – Numbers   *June 1*

Clap your hands 1 time.
Clap your hands 2 times.
Clap your hands 3 times.
Clap your hands 4 times.
Clap your hands 5 times.

Give Kino the card from yesterday's drill, along with this one. Have him review the drill from yesterday first, then start today's — "Clap your hands one time," "Clap your hands two times," etc. Have him use full sentences and keep each new number in focus for a while by returning to it frequently. *Remember not to say what he says – just vigorously do what he instructs.*

Accuracy Practice

Today you will be practicing the use of substitution drills again. You remember that a substitution drill focuses on *one* feature. Yesterday you did a Structure Substitution Drill. Today you will also do a Pronunciation Substitution Drill. Let's do the pronunciation drill first.

Working on
a troublesome sound

Substitution Drill for Pronunciation Practice. Here's a drill that will help you work on a sound that has been troubling you. In a substitution drill for pronunciation, you will practice the sound in a variety of environments.

You have identified and listed one or more words which were difficult for you to pronounce and/or write. Write the word(s), using the spelling from Kino's transcription. (Chapter Four — Pronunciation — will provide helpful ideas for those of you whose new language is not written in Roman script.) Identify one pronunciation feature of this word to focus on today — is it a vowel, or a consonant? Ask Kino to give you other words which have this same sound, and write these down. After you have six or eight words, organize them in some way that focuses on this sound. For example, you could put all the words that have this sound at the beginning of the word, in one column. In another column you could write those words that have the sound in the middle of the word. In yet another column you could write the words that have the sound at the end. It is possible that the sound will not occur in all positions, or that Kino will be unable to think of words for one of the columns. If so, two columns will be satisfactory. Have Kino put the drill on a 3 x 5 card to practice with it, then to keep it on file.

An English substitution drill focusing on the "p" sound, might be organized like this:

Focus on the 'p' sound

Pronunciation Substitution Drill – "p"		*July 3*
Initial	*middle (after s)*	*final*
pill	spill	lip
pit	spit	tip
pat	spat	tap
(aspirated)	(unaspirated)	(unreleased)

If you were learning New Guinea Pidgin, you would soon discover that the "r" sound is pronounced differently than in English (it is a flapped "r" rather than a glided "r"). Since the "r" doesn't occur at the end of words in this language, you might organize the words for a pronunciation substitution drill in this manner:

Pronunciation Substitution Drill – "r"		*July 31*
Initial	*middle after vowel*	*middle after consonant*
rot	karim	tru
rait	orait	graun
	meri	pren
	glori	
(all "r's" are flapped)		

When you have organized your words for the pronunciation drill, have Kino write them on a 3 x 5 index card in parallel columns. Write an appropriate heading.

HOW TO PRACTICE PRONUNCIATION SUBSTITUTION DRILLS: Remember that there are three progressive stages of involvement in practice drills. First, listen. Then, mimic. Then, produce.

Listen: Have Kino repeat each word three times as he reads *down* the columns. Then, have him repeat each word three times as he reads *across* the rows. As you listen, concentrate on the way Kino pronounces the sound you are focusing on. Watch his mouth, lips and tongue, as you try to determine how the sound is made.

Go down the columns

Mimic: Have Kino follow the same procedure. This time, however, mimic each word after Kino says it. Go down the columns first, and then across the rows. In this way, you will mimic each word six times (more or less, depending on the amount of practice you need). Pay special attention to your pronunciation of the sound in focus.

Produce: Read aloud the first word of the first column and then have Kino say the word to correct your pronunciation. Say it again, correctly. Go down the columns producing each word and repeating Kino's correction. Now go across the rows in the same way.

As a final step of the Production stage, have Kino point to any word at random. Produce the word; have Kino correct any errors in your production; and then you say it again correctly. Continue the drill having Kino point to different words, in random order. In this way, he can keep coming back to any problem words.

Develop a rhythm

As you practice, develop a rhythm, or cadence, with your helper, which will allow you to accomplish a maximum amount of drill in your practice time.

TAPING THE PRONUNCIATION SUBSTITUTION DRILL:
If this is a sound you find particularly difficult, you can have Kino record the drill so that you can practice it again after he leaves. First, record the name of the drill (for example, *"Pronunciation Substitution Drill on 'p'"*). In taping, follow the same instructions as for practice, but have Kino leave pauses where your responses would be. One hint — At the Production stage, you may need to give yourself a cue and then a pause for you to say the word. For example:

"Production stage — read each word,
      going down the columns."
"Number 1."
      (Pause for production)
"pĭll" (Kino's reinforcement)
      (Pause for repetition)

"Number 2."
    (Pause for production)
"pit" (Kino's reinforcement)
    (Pause for repetition)
etc.
"Column two, Number 1"
    (Pause for production)
"spill"
    (Pause for repetition)
"Number 2."
    (Pause for production)
"spit"
    (Pause for repetition)
etc.
"Now, read across the rows —
First row, number 1."
    (pause)
"pill"
    (pause)
"Number 2."
    (pause)
"spill"
    (pause)
etc.

"Second row, number 1."
    (pause)
"pit"
    (pause)
"Number 2."
    (pause)
"spit"
    (pause)
etc.

Substitution Drill for Structure Practice. Choose a sentence from today's story about yourself. Preferably choose one of the longer sentences which has more parts and which may be a little harder for you to remember. As you prepare and practice the substitution drill, follow the instructions on pages 47-50. When preparing the drill, you should identify two or three slots, and have Kino help you find words that will work as fillers in those slots. Remember to put the drill on a 3 x 5 card for your practice and future reference.

TAPING THE STRUCTURE SUBSTITUTION DRILL: You may want to record the substitution drill so you can practice more after Kino leaves.

Say, for example, that you wrote the sentence "I live on South Road" as a frame sentence for a Substitution drill today. When you classified it as an opportunity for practice you only wrote the pattern sentence on your 3 x 5 card. After Kino helps you find fillers for the slots you want to work with, it might look like this on your file card:

"I stand on Queen Street"

Structure Substitution Drill				*June 1*
Place of origin				
Pattern: I	live	on	South	Road.
Fillers:	shop		North	Street
	work		East	Avenue
	walk		West	Boulevard

For the Mimicry stage, have Kino read the pattern sentence, leaving a pause for you to mimic. Then have him say the next trigger by itself with a short pause for mimicry. Have him say the sentence using the trigger, and pause for mimicry. Stay in the first slot until all its fillers are used, then go down the second slot in the same way. For example, Kino would say:

"I *live* on South Road."	— pause for mimicry	(Pattern)
"shop"	— pause for mimicry	(Trigger)
"I shop on South Road."	— pause for mimicry	(New sentence)
"work"	— pause for mimicry	
"I work on South Road."	— pause	
"walk"	— pause	
"I walk on South Road."	— pause	

****

"I live on *South* Road."	— pause	(Pattern)
"East"	— pause	(Trigger from 2nd slot)
"I live on East Road."	— pause	
etc.		

****

"I live on South *Road*."	— pause	(Pattern)
"Street"	— pause	(Trigger from 3rd slot)
"I live on South Street."	— pause	
etc.		

The taped drill for the Production stage will be similar, except that the pause after the trigger should be long enough for you to say the entire sentence inserting the trigger in its appropriate place.

"I *live* on South Road."	(Pattern)
"shop"	(Trigger)
(pause)	*(Production)*
"I shop on South Road."	(Correction)
(pause)	(Repetition)
"work"	(Trigger)
(pause)	*(Production)*
"I work on South Road."	(Correction)
(pause) etc.	(Repetition)

****

"I live on *South* Road."	(Pattern)
"North"	(Trigger)
(pause)	*(Production)*
"I live on North Road."	(Correction)
(pause) etc.	(Repetition)

****

"I live on South *Road.*"	(Pattern)
"Street"	(Trigger)
(pause)	*(Production)*
"I live on South Street."	(Correction)
(pause) etc.	(Repetition)

HE MARCHES ON ARMY ROW

You can work up to production with two triggers:

"I live on South Road."	(Pattern)
"shop, North"	(Triggers)
(pause)	*(Production)*
"I shop on North Road."	(Correction)
(pause) etc.	(Repetition)

Although it may look difficult, this drill is quite simple once you get the knack of it. If the sentence pattern is fairly easy for you, you can record just the Production Stage, and use that recording for both Mimicry and Production when practicing.

When you have finished Accuracy Practice, you can dismiss Kino for the day.

Fluency Practice With the Tape

Your objective is to be able to tell your story fluently. Work through the drills you have recorded, repeating them three or four times as needed.

One last exercise, difficult but always rewarding — the *Simultaneous Production Drill* (page 23).

When you can tell your story fluently without helps, and somewhat confidently (though not "perfectly"), you are ready for communication.

Communicate
What You Know

Now for the fun part.

As you communicate during this week, you will progressively demonstrate to those in the community that you are indeed learning to speak their language. This will reinforce the establishment of your learner role.

If you are making steady progress, most people will continue to be receptive to you, and will let you practice your new language with them. Some will even eagerly look forward to your daily visit. You should encourage them to help you correct your mistakes. Indeed, every native speaker of your new language may be able to give you some help in your language learning. You should try to cultivate as many of these helpful relationships as possible. Try to spend at least two hours out today communicating with a wide variety of people.

Every native speaker is
a potential language helper

We can assure you that it is impossible to talk with up to thirty people in communication time without returning with a tremendous sense of accomplishment. Go try it — you'll see.

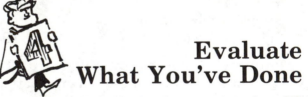

Evaluate
What You've Done

The evaluation record form for today has a somewhat different format, but the objectives are the same. Changes in format help avoid monotony. There is no one "best way" to do your daily cycle evaluation. After this first week is over you may wish to start a "language learner's diary" or keep notes in a daily schedule book or calendar. By the way, speaking of a daily schedule, *most successful learners do budget their time carefully.* A daily schedule really helps once you get the hang of how to keep track of your time. For *"Thursday"* and *"Friday"* we are going to include a simple schedule form in the evaluation record so you can experiment and learn the value of keep-

ing track of your time. Plan on it for tomorrow. It is a good idea to plan a schedule for your time, even though you may occasionally need to be flexible. A plan will help you avoid indecision and procrastination.

When Preparation skills are mastered, you can easily finish the six Preparation steps in an hour. Two and a half hours may be about right for the various Practice activities; however, it may take longer while you are gaining skill with the techniques. In two hours of serious Communication time it is easy to talk with up to thirty people — especially in the earlier stages when your conversations aren't very extensive. That, plus half an hour for Evaluation comes to about six hours a day.

Much of what you did today reviewed the procedures you were introduced to in your first two days. The new techniques today were the *Pronunciation Substitution Drill,* and the *Fill-in-the-Blanks Drill.*

Developing drills

You will want to focus on developing correct pronunciation habits in the next few weeks, by developing specific drills that respond to your pronunciation needs. If you fail to pay adequate attention to proper pronunciation, you could develop some long-standing bad habits.

The *Fill-in-the-Blanks* Drill is, in a sense, both a fluency drill and an accuracy drill (though in this manual it is classified as a fluency drill). *Fill-in-the-Blanks* is a fluency drill because it helps you practice saying the full sentences of your text. It is an accuracy drill because it helps focus your attention on accurately using words — especially the little "grammatical marker" words.

Even with the different format, your evaluation should continue to focus on four areas as before: the cycle procedures and content along with your working relationship with your helper; noting and classifying problems; planning and preparing for tomorrow; and keeping your material organized and up to date.

Again look at pages 27-31 from *"Monday's Evaluation"* for ideas to guide in this self-evaluation. Write ideas to help you improve your procedures with the new drills.

Organizing taped material. Part of "organizing data in your file system" includes keeping taped material manageable and accessible. We suggest that you keep one tape just for your daily texts. Each day have Kino put the new text on this tape just as in the *Whole Text* drill. This should be enough for your permanent record of texts, and will give you material for passive listening. The working tape you are using for Fluency practice will soon fill up but you can probably erase it after a week or so if you keep a permanent record tape of your texts.

You may find it helpful to have various working tapes and corresponding permanent record tapes. For example, you may want a set for Comprehension activities, one for Pronunciation exercises, and one for Structure practice. You may also need a tape for miscellaneous use. The miscellaneous tape can be cleared when it is full if you first classify what is on it and transfer onto your record tapes anything you want to save.

Mark each tape clearly with a number or code.

> Tape F 04 (Fluency tape, #4)
> Tape P 01 (Pronunciation tape, #1)
> Tape S 02 (Structure tape, #2)
> Tape T 03 (Text tape, #3)

Keep with each tape a running list of what is recorded on it. For example:

Tape T 01

001 Whole Text Drill. Greetings and learner's role, Sept. 2
021 Whole Text Drill. Expansion of greeting and role, Sept. 3
040 WTD. Story about myself. Sept. 4
060 WTD. *What* questions. 9/5
082 WTD. Getting help in the language. 9/6.

In addition, on each text and drill file card you will want to write the tape number and footage where the drill can be found.

> Text — Story about myself. Sept. 4
> "This is my third day learning Kikamba.
> I am from Canada.
> My name is MBethy MBlusta.
> I like your country very much.
> I want to learn your language well.
> I want to learn about your people.
> Thank you for listening.
> (leavetaking)"
>
> On Tape T 01, at 040.

Relax!

Be sure to read *"Thursday"* before Kino comes tomorrow. And that's it. Relax! And have a good evening!

"Wednesday" **Evaluation Record**

Date: _____

Today's New Text Material

_____
_____
_____
_____
_____

General Meaning

_____
_____
_____
_____
_____

Fluency Drills: _____
_____
_____
_____

Comprehension Activities
Review: _____
_____

New: _____
_____

Pronunciation Substitution
Write the Drill data

_____
_____
_____
_____

Structure Substitution
Write the Drill data

_____
_____
_____
_____

Feature in Focus: _____

Feature in Focus: _____

Total number communicated with _____. Number you shared all
of today's text with _____.Number you elicited and practiced
new material with _____.
An Experience in Communication: _____
_____
_____

Impressions, questions, cultural observations, and observations
about self: _____
_____
_____
_____

Note and Classify Opportunities and Problems, and Decide on
Next Steps: _____
_____
_____
_____
_____

Is all data currently organized in file system: _____

"Thursday"

Rudyard Kipling immortalized the helpers — *"who, what, when, where, how,* and *why."* They will be especially helpful to you as a language learner. One, however — the "why" question — must be used with caution. "Why" questions about language don't lead to practicing the language, they only lead to talking *about* language. (Talking about the language will be OK when you can do it *in* the language, rather than in English.) Furthermore, "why-questions" usually would need a grammarian to answer them, and Kino probably isn't a grammarian. Besides, even if they could be answered, you might not understand anyway. Few people really understand statements of grammatical relationships. Most "why" problems will resolve themselves as you get the *feel* of the language. Even "why" questions related to culture are often best resolved as you get a feel for the culture.

Preparation

Today you will begin to use some of these helping questions. Yesterday you told people about yourself. Today you will continue to do the same, but you will also begin to ask others for some information about themselves.

Today's evaluation sheet includes a time schedule so you can keep track of how your time is invested. It is listed in half-hour units — 8 hours worth in case you include lunch and breaks. Write your starting time now (page 99) and put a bookmark there so you can make notes regularly.

Obtain the Text

As you describe the setting to Kino, explain that your objective is to learn to ask some simple questions. You want some of the questions to be related to things you can already talk about. For example, find out how to ask what someone's name is.

Also, learn to ask the equivalent of "What is this?" Find out what body language goes with this question. In some cultures, pointing is considered indecent. They might point with the lips or chin rather than with the index finger. Maybe you can indicate the object you are asking about by touching it. In many cultures, however, you must be careful to touch with the right hand. Have Kino show you what is best.

A question like "What is he?" can be helpful when you are looking at a person who is in uniform or doing some kind of work.

A question like "What is he doing?" will open up much information to you. From one culture to another, people do different things, and do familiar things in different ways.

A sample text might be as follows:
A. (Greeting)
B. (Response)
A. "This is my first week here.
   I'm from England.
   My name is Paul. } from yesterday
   What is your name?"
B. "My name is Akeal."
A. "What is this?"
B. "That is a banana."
A. "Banana?" (You need to repeat the new word and write it down.)
B. "Yes, it's a banana."
A. "Banana.
   What is he?"
B. "He is a vendor."
A. "What is he doing?"
B. "He is selling beans."
A. "Thank you."
B. "You're welcome."
A. (Leave-taking)

How do I say
"What is this?"

When you have decided on the text, have Kino record it. Let Kino listen to it and then have him record it again. Encourage him to record it at normal conversational speed. It may be helpful for you to review the section concerning the recording of a dialogue, on page 37.

Uh . . . One more suggestion. "Uh" is what we say in English when we are thinking between phrases and we aren't ready to give up the floor yet. Do you say "uh"? Even in your new language? Chances are that they have their own marker for this kind of conversation filler. In Spanish they say "este-e-e-e . . ." The Yorubas say "eme-e-e . . ." In other places it might be "ahhh" or "mmm." Learn to do this "right" for your new language and you will overcome a significant part of your foreign accent.

Check the Suitability

Build on what you have

You will notice how you can build on what you have previously used. When checking suitability, make a point to ask yourself if this is a text you could build on in later learning. You are able to manage a longer text as you incorporate phrases which you've used before.

Ask Kino about the cultural appropriateness of your questions. Is it okay to ask someone what his name is? (In a few places you shouldn't ask a person his name since it is taboo or embarrassing for a person to say his own name. Be sensitive to this possibility as you check the suitability of today's text. In these situations it is usually acceptable to ask someone what another person's name is.)

Transcribe the Text

Review Tuesday and Wednesday's *Transcription* sections (pages 39 and 57), and transcribe today's text. You shouldn't spend more than 10 or 15 minutes doing a transcription — it's only a *representation* of the real thing (spoken speech), anyway. Learn to trust your ears and your mimicry, rather than your writing and reading.

Chapter Four will help you become aware of sounds that are not familiar English sounds. Learning the relevant symbols will help improve your transcriptions.

Understand the Text

You may already understand the gist of each phrase, but you should check to be sure.

Today is probably the first day you have asked questions in the text. Get a translation of the words in the questions, as you did for sentences yesterday (page 57). Make a hypothesis about the word order for questions. In your evaluation time, compare this with the hypotheses you made yesterday.

Note and Classify Opportunities and Problems

Make careful notes of problems you encounter in this new text. They will constitute an important agenda for your practice period.

Do you remember to pronounce vowels clearly — especially at the ends of words? English sometimes turns vowels into "uh." How about the transitions between words? Where non-English clusters occur, do you stumble?

The "h" sound like in "hop" never occurs at the ends of English words or syllables. Say "poh." Some dialects of Spanish (Argentinian for example) often replace the "s" at the end of words with an "h" sound. They call it "swallowing" the s. Some West African languages also use a syllable-final "h" sound. Have you been hearing this sound?

hop

poh

Record for Practice

First, review your evaluation of previous recording times (pages 28, 53 and 71) to refresh your memory of ideas which may make today's taping more effective.

Record today's text by selecting some of the following drill techniques:

> *Whole Text Listening Drill*   (page 18)
> *Phrase Mimicry Drills*   (pages 59 and 60)
> *Build-up Mimicry Drill*   (page 40)
> *Sentence Mimicry Drill*   (page 19)
> *Completion Production Drills* (page 41)

(The page numbers for the instructions on taping these drills are given in parentheses, but you may already be sufficiently familiar with some of these techniques so you don't have to look up the instructions.)

When a text has two people speaking (i.e., parts A and B), then an *Alternation Production Drill* can really help. Here's how to record it.

Name: **"Alternation Production Drill - With Correction."**
Directions for Practice: "In the space provided, *produce* the A part; in the second pause *repeat* the correction of the A part."

After recording the name of the drill and directions for practice, say "Start" on the tape, then pause long enough for the first A part. Have Kino give the opening statement of person A and then pause long enough for you to repeat it when practicing. After the pause, have him give the response of Person B and then pause long enough for you to silently mouth the next A part. (During practice you will listen to B's part and then give A's next response; then the tape will correct your A response and in the second pause you can repeat this correction.) Repeat these recording steps as you record the other segments of the text in this same manner.

Here is an example of a recorded Alternation Drill With Correction for the text on page 73. (The learner's A parts are in italics.)

"Hi. How are you? This is my first week here. This is a recording."

> "Start"　Pause (During practice you will Produce A's first statement)
>
> *"Hello"*　(A1)
> Pause (During practice you will repeat A1)
> "Hi"　(B1)
> Pause (In practice you will produce A's second part)
> *"This is my first week here. I am from England. My name is Paul.*
> *What is your name?"*　(A2)
> Pause (Repeat the correction of A2)
> "My name is Akeal."　(B2)
> Pause (Produce A3)
> *"What is this?"*　(A3)
> Pause (Repeat the correction of A3)
> "That is a banana."　(B3)
> Pause (Produce A4)
> *"Banana?"*　(A4)
> Pause (Repeat A4)
> "Yes, it's a banana."　(B4)
> etc.

Notice that on the tape Kino goes straight through the text saying A1, B1; A2, B2; A3, B3; etc., with pauses. During practice you will say *only* Part A, but you say each response of A *two* times: once to produce it, and once to repeat the correction. (If you produced it correctly the first time, you will simply be repeating it the same way the second time.) The recorded B parts will cue your A responses.

Here is a summary statement of the taping sequence for the *Alternation Drill With Correction.*

> "Start" Pause for A1
> Kino says A1
> Pause for A1 repetition
> 　Kino says B1
> Pause for A2
> Kino says A2
> Pause for A2 repetition
> 　Kino says B2
> Pause for A3　　　　etc.

After you have practiced an Alternation Drill With Correction, you will be ready to practice an Alternation Drill Without Correction. First, record the name of the drill and directions for practice.

Alternation

Name: **"Alternation Production Drill-Without Correction."**

Directions: "Produce the A part in the pause, B responds on the tape."

Say "Start" on the tape, and then pause long enough for the first A part. This time Kino will only say the B parts on the tape. After each B part have him pause long enough for you to say the next A part when practicing with the tape. The recorded drill for the text on page 73 could go like this:

". . . Start"	
— Pause (during this pause, silently mouth A's part when recording)	(A1)
"Greeting"	(B1)
— Pause (This will be a long pause for, "This is my first week here . . . What is your name?" — mouth this A part in the pause when recording.)	(A2)
"My name is Kino."	(B2)
— Pause (Mouth the next A part.)	(A3)
"That is a banana."	(B3)
— Pause	(A4)
"Yes, it's a banana."	(B4)
— Pause	(A5)
"He is a vendor."	(B5)
— Pause	(A6)
"He is selling beans."	(B6)
— Pause	(A7)
"You are welcome."	(B7)
— Pause etc.	(A8)

He is a vendor

Notice that this time Kino only says the B parts on the tape, and *you* say the A parts when you practice with the tape. In this way, you can "converse" with your tape recorder. It will work best if the pauses are short enough to keep you moving at a good clip.

Practice

The text which you have obtained is the focal point of your practice. Do not practice things at random. Draw your problems right out of your text. If you are faithfully making a habit of talking to new people about new things every day, you will almost always have enough real problems to practice and work on for any given day.

Mechanical repetition

As you drill, be careful not merely to repeat mechanically — keep your mind actively focused on the meaning as well as on the language feature you are practicing.

Fluency Practice With Your Helper

Have Kino help you with the mimicry stage of fluency practice. Do the *Phrase Drills, Build-up Drill,* and *Sentence Drill.*

Comprehension Practice

Review the comprehension exercises in your file, and for today have Kino make a new card with the following instructions. Drill it as before (pages 43 and 44).

Comprehension Practice   *Jan 17*
Arm positions

        Stretch your arms, and yawn.
        Reach your arms up.
        Reach your arms down.
        Put your arms in front of you.
        Put your arms in back of you.
        Put your arms down at your sides.
        Put your arms out to the sides.

Enjoy this one! Keep it going fast. If you want to do another one later today, pick an idea from Chapter Three.

Accuracy Practice

Accuracy practice helps develop the new habits you need and it helps overcome the problems of your English contamination of the new language.

"Tuesday" you learned to do a Structure Substitution Drill, and on *"Wednesday"* you were introduced to the procedures for Pronunciation Substitution Drills. *Substitution* is one basic kind of accuracy drill. The other kind is called *Differential,* and it too applies to both pronunciation and grammatical structure.

This matrix shows the *purpose* of each of the four types of accuracy drills.

	Pronunciation	Structure
Substitution	To practice **one** sound by substituting it in different "environments."	To practice **one** grammatical structure (one sentence pattern) by substituting various words in the "slots" of the sentence.
Differential	To practice distinguishing **two** sounds which are similar (and may not sound different to you at first) by differentiating them in the same or similar environments.	To practice distinguishing **two** or more similar sentence patterns which differ in only one feature, by contrasting the sentences.

In a Pronunciation Substitution Drill, *one* vowel or consonant sound is in focus and is drilled in the environments which may slightly alter it.

In a Pronunciation Differential Drill the *difference* between *two* similar sounds is in focus.

In a Structure Substitution Drill *one* particular *sentence structure* — the pattern — is in focus.

In a Structure Differential Drill the language feature which indicates a *change* is in focus.

Accuracy *Differential* Drills help you learn to distinguish between two or more features which, at first, are difficult for you to differentiate. Accuracy *Substitution* Drills focus on one feature to help you learn to produce that feature correctly, with a minimum of contamination.

Substitution

These drills are needed because your new language uses vowels and consonants which English does not have — your English habits won't let you pronounce accurately. Also, your new language has unfamiliar grammatical features and word orders. Fortunately, any language has a limited number of consonant and vowel sounds, and a limited number of basic sentence structures. Accuracy drills give a systematic way to master the new sounds and structures.

Differential

Sometimes contamination is relatively mild, and even though the foreigner has an accent or uses a slightly foreign word order, he can still be understood. If, however, the interference is greater, it often becomes more than a matter of simple accent — the listener will not understand; instead, he will be confused.

On a sheep?

For example, a foreigner might say, "I sailed across the ocean on a sheep." The context would help you realize that he really meant "ship", and you would probably not be confused. On the other hand, if he were to say, "Today I saw a sheep," you would be confused if he actually meant "ship." His native language probably does not make a distinction between the vowel sounds of "ship" and "sheep." His language may only have one vowel where the English has two. To him, this vowel difference would seem minor or non-existent.

As you begin to speak another language, a certain amount of contamination will be unavoidable. Whether you need to correct for pronunciation or structural interference, accuracy practice is helpful and important.

All that's left now is to do it. So let's start.

Pronunciation Differential Drill. When learning another language, you will often find pairs of sounds which are difficult for you to tell apart or to pronounce correctly. You have the same kind of problem as the man who said that he "sailed across the ocean on a sheep."

The first step is to collect pairs of words that are very much alike, except for the sounds you are focusing on. For example, the foreigner who had trouble distinguishing between the vowel sounds in the words "ship" and "sheep," could collect and practice pairs of words like the following (align the words so that the sound in focus is in a vertical line):

Pronunciation Differential Drill – ĭ, e̅e̅ *August 12*	
Column 1	Column 2
1. ship	sheep
2. hip	heap
3. pick	peak
4. tip	steep
5. winking	weakling
6. pictures	peaches

Of course, *you* don't have trouble distinguishing between the above two vowels since you already speak English. But there will be other sounds in your new language that you will have trouble differentiating. For example, if you were learning Korean, you would need a drill to´ help you hear and produce the difference between the three kinds of "t" sounds. If you were learning French, you might need to practice hearing and saying the difference between the nasalized vowels and the non-nasalized vowels. If you were learning Arabic, you might need to hear and pronounce fronted "k" and backed "k", etc.

Six Tease

Have Kino help you collect pairs of words which focus on the difference between two sounds you are having trouble differentiating. Ideally, it would be nice to have pairs of words which were identical except for the difference in focus. The sounds would then be contrasted in identical *environments*. In the first three pairs of the above English example, the vowels were in identical environments: ship-sheep; hip-heap; pick-peak. That is, the sounds around the vowels are the same for each pair.

Identical environments are not always possible or easy to find. The last three pairs of the above drill are not in identical, but rather in similar, environments. In the pairs of words you get today try to find environments that are as similar as possible. When you have prepared the drill, write it on an index card with the appropriate heading.

HOW TO PRACTICE PRONUNCIATION DIFFERENTIAL DRILLS:

Remember the progressive stages of involvement in practice — listening, mimicry, production.

Listening: Have Kino repeat each *word* three times as he reads down the columns. Then, have him repeat each *pair* three times. As a check on your ability to hear the sounds, have Kino read any two words; you listen carefully to the sounds in focus and say whether the words are both from the same column or from different columns; Kino should confirm or correct each response. For example, Kino might say "hip, pick" and your response should be "Same column" (the sound in focus — the vowel — is the same). If Kino said "tip, heap" your response would be "Different columns" (the vowels in the two words are different). Finally, as he reads single words in random order, you say whether the word is from Column 1 or Column 2, and have him confirm or correct your response.

Column I or Column II?

Mimicry: Have Kino follow the same procedure, as you mimic. First, mimic each word, and then mimic the pairs of words. Kino should confirm or correct each response.

Production: Read aloud the first word of the first column, and then have Kino say it to correct your pronunciation. Say it again, correctly. Go down the columns, saying each word and repeating Kino's correction. Then, read the first *pair* of words and have Kino correct you. Say each pair, and repeat Kino's correction. Next, have Kino point to a pair at random (or say the number — in the language), and you say the pair; have Kino correct your pronunciation when needed, repeat the correction.

As a final production step, say the words at random, and have Kino indicate whether it is from Column 1 or Column 2. This is *not* to test Kino, it is to check your pronunciation — if Kino indicates the wrong column, you know your pronunciation needs improvement.

Differential Drill for Structure Practice. This is a drill to help you begin to compare and contrast grammatical structures. A Structure Differential drill focuses on two, or more, related sentence patterns to help you see the relationships between them.

"Is this not a butterfly?"

In today's Structure Differential drill you can contrast the positive statement pattern ("This is a ____.") with the related negative statement pattern ("This is not a ____."). (If needed, you could first do a Substitution drill on the two individual sentences.) A Differential drill helps you accomplish two things: to be able to take a sentence of either pattern and quickly produce a related sentence of the other pattern; and to be able to verbalize a "rule" about the relationship between the patterns.

Use a list of near-by objects and prepare a Differential drill based on the following pattern. Write it on a 3 x 5 file card as a guide for Kino. Do not read the card yourself as you practice.

"Don't look"

Structure Differential Drill: *April 2*
Positive vs. Negative Statements

Positive	*Negative*
This is a pencil.	This is not a pencil.
This is a book.	This is not a book.
This is a table.	This is not a table.
This is a chair.	This is not a chair.

Do not read the card yourself as you practice.

HOW TO PRACTICE A STRUCTURE DIFFERENTIAL DRILL:

Listening Stage: Listen as Kino repeats each of the positive sentences two or three times. Then have him repeat each of the negative sentences two or three times. Next, have him read the pairs of sentences. Listen as he reads the positive sentence followed by the negative sentence, and repeats each pair three times. Then have him reverse the order and put the negative sentence before the positive one, and repeat the pair. (You decide how many times you want the sentences repeated in the listening stage, depending on how complex or difficult the sentences are.)

If the patterns are so similar that it is difficult to hear the difference, have Kino say the sentences at random and you say whether they are positive or negative. (This is related to what you did in the Pronunciation Differential Drill, page 81.)

As you listen, form mental "rules" about the relationships between these two patterns. For example, a couple of rules about these English sentence patterns could be:

> To make a negative sentence out of a positive one, add the word "not " after the verb.

> To make a positive sentence out of a negative one, just omit the word "not."

Mimicry Stage: Mimic, while Kino follows the same procedures as for the listening stage.

Production Stage: You will produce a sentence of one of the patterns, in response to a sentence of the other pattern. This can be done in various ways.

a. Have Kino say each negative sentence ("This is not a pencil.") and you respond with the positive sentence ("This is a pencil.") as you touch the correct object.

b. Have Kino say each positive sentence while touching the named object, and you respond by saying the related negative sentence while touching any other object.

c. Kino can say either a negative or a positive sentence at random, and you respond with the sentence of the other pattern.

Which pattern shall I use?

If you wish, you can record the Differential drill for extra practice. (See pages 96 and 97 for recording directions.)

Get a handle
on the meaning

There is another pattern which is closely related to these two — it is the question pattern, "Is this a pencil?" Since you have already practiced the other two patterns, it won't take long to add this to today's drill.

Listening Stage: Listen as Kino says this type of question ("Is this a ____?"), touching each of the objects you have just been using. (Be sure to act this type of drill out with objects whenever possible because it really helps you get a handle on the meaning.) He should repeat each question two or three times. Next, have Kino say the question followed by the positive answer — repeat this two times. Then, he can say the same question followed by the negative answer — repeat two times. Go through the other questions and answers this same way. For example:

Is this a pencil?	This is a pencil.
Is this a pencil?	This is a pencil.
Is this a pencil?	This is not a pencil.
Is this a pencil?	This is not a pencil.
Is this a book? repeat	This is a book.
Is this a book? repeat	This is not a book.
etc.	

While you listen, formulate mental "rules" about the relationships between the question pattern and the two types of answers.

Mimicry Stage: Mimic while Kino follows the procedures of the listening stage.

Production Stage: Again, there are various activities you can do at the production stage.

a. Kino can ask the question ("Is this a pencil?") while touching any object, and you respond correctly, whether positively or negatively.

b. Kino says either a positive or a negative statement about any object, and you respond by asking the related question while touching another object.

For example: Kino can say, "This is a pencil" while touching a pencil, and you can then ask "Is this a pencil?" while touching a book. Or — Kino can say, "This is not a pencil" while touching a book, and you can say "Is this a pencil?" while touching the pencil.

c. This last activity involves all three sentence patterns. Kino asks the question ("Is this a pencil?") while touching the wrong object. You respond by saying both statements — "This is not a pencil. This is a table." Continue this practice until you can respond easily and quickly.

NOTE: By using these sentence patterns you can get extra drill on new vocabulary while talking with people. You can touch an object and ask "What is this?" They may answer, "This is a Kefala." You can then touch a similar object and ask "Is this a Kefala?" and they will answer positively or negatively.

If you are talking with children, this can become quite a game and give you lots of practice with new words. Children will often catch on, and participate with you in the game. First, you can ask the questions while they answer. Then you can trade roles and let them ask the questions while you try to answer. If you enter into the spirit of the game, everybody can have fun while you practice vocabulary.

The spirit of the game

When you have completed accuracy practice, you won't need Kino any more for today. Thank him for all his work. Remember to note your time in the schedule on the Evaluation Form.

Fluency Practice with the tape

Follow the instructions on page 50.

Communication

Carry your data book and pencil as you go into the community. You will have opportunity to hear the names of many different objects. As you learn what they are called, write them down — especially ones which would be helpful for you to learn and remember. You might also want to write down the names of a few people whom you expect to meet with again. To really learn these new terms, you might need more drill, but you will become aware of much new vocabulary today, and awareness is the first step toward learning.

Remember that communication is the heart of the Daily Learning Cycle. Keep the heart beating. Also remember that *Communication time is talking time – not walking time!* Be where the people are (parks, markets, buses, stores) and spend your time *talking.* Learn to fully enjoy these many opportunities to talk with people. Today's communication time can be especially fun and rewarding, so go ahead and begin.

The heart of the cycle

Evaluation

We hope your communication time was especially enjoyable today.

Keeping track of where your time goes takes some discipline, but it can help you stay better organized. With the introduction of the Differential technique your practice time was full today!

You have now used all the techniques you need in order to learn a language. You will learn to modify and adapt them as you go along. Be experimentive. As you become skillful with the procedures you can adapt them as needed and use them spontaneously to respond to any of your needs.

You have noticed that we redesigned the evaluation form for *"Thursday."* It is two pages again, with the language content on the second side. We will use this one tomorrow also. We want you to have a variety of format ideas for evaluation because after tomorrow you will be on your own.

Turn to the back side of the Evaluation form, and write today's text with its general meaning.

Which Fluency drills did you choose to tape? Did you choose enough for easy mastery of the text? Was there an adequate progression of difficulty between the drills?

Are you beginning to feel the way Comprehension Drills stretch your ability to understand? Which drills did you do today?

Today especially note the Differential Pronunciation and Structure drills, and write any ideas which will make them go more smoothly next time.

What experiences did you have in communication time today? Did you have any unusual ones you will want to write down for future reference?

Now, back to side one — what about cultural observations?

Observe people

Learn to be a careful observer of the actions and conversations of the people. When people are just passing, do they say the greeting or do they say what your thought was "good-bye"? After they shake hands, do they move the right hand toward the chest? When people talk with you do you think they stand too close or talk too loud? After you observe behavior, find out from someone what is appropriate for you.

Daily Evaluation Record

Time Schedule
½ hour frames

1 _____
2 _____
3 _____
4 _____
5 _____
6 _____
7 _____
8 _____
9 _____
10 _____
11 _____
12 _____
13 _____
14 _____
15 _____
16 _____

Impressions, Questions, Cultural Observations, and Observations about Self: _____
_____
_____

Note and Classify Problems and Opportunities. State Hypotheses. _____
_____
_____

Next Step: _____
_____

Ideas for New Texts: _____
_____

Is all data currently organized in file system: _____

Today's New Text Material   General Meaning
(Compare your transcription with Kino's transcription — any
differences may indicate a potential need for pronunciation drill.)

_____   _____
_____   _____
_____   _____
_____   _____
_____   _____
_____   _____
_____   _____
_____   _____

Fluency Drills: _____
_____
_____
_____
_____
_____
_____

Comprehension Activities
Review: _____
_____

New: _____
_____

Pronunciation Drills   Structure Drills
Substitution/Differential   Substitution/Differential
Write the Drill data   Write out the Drill data

_____   _____
_____   _____
_____   _____
_____   _____
_____   _____
_____   _____
_____   _____
_____   _____

Feature in Focus: _____   Feature in Focus: _____

Total number communicated with _____
Number you shared all of today's text with _____
Number you elicited and practiced new material with _____
An experience in communication: _____
_____
_____
_____

Write the preliminary "rules" you made about the relationships between positive statements, negative statements, and questions. These are, of course, just preliminary hypotheses. As you learn more, you may have to add to or revise these rules. (For example, a person learning English may have stated the rule: To form a negative sentence, add the word "not" after the verb. However, he might later learn the sentences — "He is coming soon/He is not coming soon." He would then need to revise the rule to account for the insertion of "not" in the middle of the verb phrase. He might then find other sentences — The car runs/The car does not run — for which he might need to form different rules.) Much of language learning is a matter of formulating hypotheses, and then checking them out and forming improved hypotheses.

Hypotheses

What new words did you learn in your communication today?

What sounds are you having difficulty with? Are you having trouble pronouncing them, or hearing the difference between them?

Are there some sentence patterns that are difficult for you? Are there some new sentence patterns you would like to learn? Write them down.

Next step: Briefly describe what type of drills you could use to help you master the sounds and sentence structures you described above.

What cultural situations have you encountered that you did not know how to respond to? These situations may offer topics for future texts. Which of the topics would you like to work on first?

"Thursday's" Summary

Today you began to learn how to use the Differential drill technique. Soon you will have the characteristics of differential drills and substitution drills firmly in your mind. You will then be able to say to yourself, "Self, what is the nature of my problem?" And you can answer the question. You can then say "What is the drill which will help me overcome the problem?" You will then be able to answer the question, set up the drill, and proceed with the practice.

The Differential structure technique which you began to use in your practice time today will be helpful as you work out relationships, comparisons, and "rules" for the grammatical structure of the language. In this way you will begin to discover for yourself some of the "whys" of the language.

NOTE: If you become overly frustrated with a pronunciation or structure feature, let it go for a while. When you are up-tight your efficiency drops off, and it can even affect the rest of your cycle activities. Learn how to sleep on a problem and let your subconscious work on it. A good night's sleep will often resolve a problem.

In your conversations and practice you are *actively* listening to each thing that is said. Active listening requires concentration and creative energy. It is also helpful to listen *passively*. Of course, you won't learn to speak your target language by osmosis, but you can begin to become aware of words as you hear them repeatedly. Passive listening also helps you feel at home with sentence melodies (intonation) and rhythm (timing). While you relax or do other kinds of work, you might be able to listen passively. Maybe you can be someplace where people are talking. A tape recording of conversation can provide materials which can be listened to repeatedly. Radio can be helpful if you can find a talk, rather than music, oriented station. Television usually has more talking than radio, but television viewing could waste your valuable time. Maybe you could turn the picture toward the wall! Anyway, the point is: listen passively during your spare time. Never substitute passive listening, however, for active communication — you need both.

Read through *"Friday."*

Now, do something relaxing for a while — like coloring the flowers.

"Friday"

Thank goodness it's *"Friday"*!

From time to time, you will feel the need to review previous material so that you can assimilate and consolidate it. Plan material so that it builds on and incorporates what you have previously learned. Try not to let structures you have once used fall into disuse. You may never again use some of the sentences you learned for the first cycle, but you should use the structures frequently. For example, you might not say "I want to learn to speak your language," but part of that structure is included in "I want to learn to buy soap," or "I want to buy soap." Notice that a differential drill could help you modify the pattern "I want to learn to speak your language," into something like "I am learning to speak your language."

So, your cycles which help you review previously learned material should also help you gain flexibility with that material, so that you can use it in a broader range of situations.

Today you will pull together some of the week's text materials for review. Also you will learn how to ask people to speak so that you can understand them better, as well as get something that will encourage people on the street to correct you.

The language materials you elicit each day should be useful to you at your level of learning. Topics for your texts this week have been chosen with the needs of the new communicator in mind. In Chapter Two you will find a wide variety of suggestions for future texts. In general, they are progressively arranged according to the needs of a typical language learner. After today you will be choosing useful and relevant topics yourself, based on the ideas from Chapter Two and on your own felt needs which you identify during your daily evaluation time. You can keep track of your time again today on the time-schedule (page 99).

Pull together
your materials

Have a coffee break

Preparation

Greet Kino today in his own language. Try to make his time as enjoyable and rewarding as possible. Have a soda or coffee break (what is the local drink?) with Kino at least once a day, and plan to spend other social times with him as well.

Obtain

Review the texts you have used this past week, and the structure drills (Substitution and Differential) which you have practiced. Note the sentences which you seem to be able to say fairly fluently. Have Kino help you build a text (hopefully one which hangs together) which will help you revive some of the structures which still seem to be somewhat difficult.

For a bit of new material today, explain to Kino that you need to be able to ask people to speak in a way that you can better understand. In an English-speaking culture it might go like this:

> "Say it again please."
> "Excuse me, I didn't understand you."
> "Could you say it more slowly please?"
> > more clearly
> > more loudly
> > more quickly

You also need to encourage the people on the street to correct you — you need all the help you can get! It would be good to start the body of your conversations with a request for correction.

> "Please correct me if I say this wrong." or,
> "Please correct me when I make a mistake."

A closing question could be,

> "Did I say that correctly?"

Then maybe a more profuse thanks like,

> "Thank you very much for your help."

Again let us caution you about the possibility of just getting translations of English sentences in your texts. We have encouraged you to establish a setting for the conversations, and then elicit appropriate sentences for the setting. If you give an example of the way it might be expressed in English, then talk to Kino about the setting again. This way the setting can be more prominent in his mind than the English example.

Check, Transcribe, Understand, And Note Opportunities and Problems

For these steps today you will be on your own. But how? Well, recognize that the boundaries between these steps hardly need to be exact, and they don't have to be done in this order. The important thing is that each step be included and that it receive its share of attention.

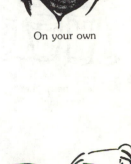

On your own

As needed, review the previous description of activities for these steps. You are probably beginning to discover that you can do some of these activities while you are obtaining the text. This will be increasingly true as you gain more skill with the procedures.

NOTE: You may have noticed that we have not recommended writing the text repeatedly as a means of learning it. Our reason is that language is primarily a speaking skill, rather than a writing skill. It is likely that most of the multilinguals of the world neither read nor write. Writing is apparently helpful, however, for many Westerners as an aid in remembering. (Does this come from the old school-house formula? — "Jason! You will stay after class and write 100 times 'I will not dunk Anabell's pigtails in the inkwell'!") If writing helps you remember the text, or the relationships within it, you can feel free to write it. But remember, your objective is not just to learn to write the language. You learn what you practice, and so it is important that you practice hearing and speaking the language. One way to reinforce your memory through writing, and at the same time practice hearing, is to write while listening to taped fluency drills. For example, using *Phrase Drill A* (or the *Build-up Drill*) you could write a phrase from memory and then hear the phrase a couple times to check your transcription while simultaneously mimicking.

"Jason!"

Record for Practice

The longer and more complex a text, the more fluency drills you need in order to master it. Record the fluency drills which you feel will be most helpful in learning today's text. The fluency drills you have previously recorded are:

Listening Drill — *Whole Text* (page 18)

Mimicry Drill — *Phrase Drills* (pages 59 and 60)
Build-up Drill (page 40)
Sentence Drills (pages 19 and 20)

Production Drills — *Completion Drills* (pages 41 and 42)
Alternation Drills (pages 75 and 76).

Practice

The following suggestions will help you use your practice time to the fullest:

Keep the rhythm of the drills fairly rapid. This will help prevent monotony and boredom. It will also force you to respond faster. Soon, basic phrases will begin to come almost automatically — this will free you to think of the meaning, with less concentration on the pronunciation and sentence structure.

Keep the rhythm
fairly rapid

Concentrate your creative energy on the material you are drilling. Don't let your mind wander. It is possible to drill with your mouth, without mentally grappling with the material. Then, when the real test of conversation comes, you might find that you haven't internalized the pattern even though you have drilled it.

Don't waste drill time talking about language — you can do that during your free time. There is nothing harmful in talking about language, but talking about it is no substitute for practicing it.

Fluency Practice With Your Helper

Have Kino help you with listening and mimicry Fluency drills. You can also practice the *Fill-in-the-Blanks Drill* (page 61) with him.

The review of previous material can be done fairly rapidly. Much of your fluency time can be spent on the new material which asks people to say things again in different ways and asks for correction.

You are now beginning to learn expressions that you can use with Kino in your practice time — "Say it again." "Say it more quickly." "Did I say it correctly?" **Make a commitment to yourself to use the language with Kino whenever you can.** Over the next few weeks you shall be using consistently less and less English in your work with Kino. Whenever you notice that you keep saying the same thing in English to Kino, learn how to give that instruction in the language. Soon you can discipline yourself to use English only in those situations where it is really necessary. Encourage Kino to talk to you in the language. By consistently using the language with Kino and having him use it with you, you will increase your skill in the language and your ability to think in the language.

Comprehension Practice

Let's do two kinds of Comprehension exercises today.

Start off with a regular *physical response* drill using instructions to touch your eyes, nose, shoulder, and other body parts.

Story Comprehension. Here is another way to get materials which will stretch your understanding. Have Kino record a series of very short stories about you and your communication activity. Your understanding will be facilitated if the taped stories include things you can already say, though it might be somewhat altered (to the past tense, or third person, for example).

Have Kino pretend that he was a clerk in a shop where you came in to give your text. What short story might he tell to his wife about your visit? He might tell how you approached him, and what you said in your text, then his reaction to it or the reaction of other people in the store. It might go like this:

> You know what happened today, wife? This American came in the shop and said that this is his first week here, but he wants to learn to speak Yoruba. He said his name, and then asked what various things were. He would repeat, "This is corn." "This is bread," and so on. Then he would write it down. One woman wanted to help him spell it right. Then he said, "That's all I can say," and everybody laughed. He said he'd be back tomorrow — I hope he does come back.

Now have Kino record a second but similar story about one of your other experiences. Maybe pretend he is a bus driver and you rode his bus today. He tells the story of how you got on the bus and were talking to various people in the bus. He also tells how he felt about it and how someone on the bus responded.

On the bus

Note the tape footage of these stories and listen to them repeatedly in the next few days. Try to understand a little more each time you hear them. After a couple days or so have Kino help write them down. Work on the tape a little each day until you can understand it all.

We suggest you tape a short comprehension drill like this once or twice a week. More ideas are included toward the end of Chapter Three.

Accuracy Practice

Yesterday you did Differential pronunciation and structure drills with Kino. Today let's record one of each so you will have experience with the procedures. Sometimes, rather than preparing accuracy drills on the current day's text, you may want to build them on material you have previously encountered, and on needs you have noted during evaluation.

Pronunciation Differential Drill. Choose a pair of closely related sounds (not the pair you practiced yesterday) and prepare data for a differential drill (see pages 80 to 82). A recording of the drill will help you get extra practice in distinguishing these sounds.

Here's how the taping might go:

First, record: **"Pronunciation Differential Drill.** *Listening stage."* For this stage, have Kino read the words two or three times each, going down the first column. Then down the second column. Then reading pairs of words, repeating each pair three times. To check your discrimination, have Kino record words at random, pause, and then name the column the word belongs in. (When practicing you will name the column in that pause.)

Next, record: *"Mimicry stage."* Repeat the above procedures, but leave pauses for mimicry.

Finally record: *"Production stage."* The drill proceeds in the same order as before — down the first column. Down the second column. Then the pairs. To cue your production, say on the tape "Column one, number one," and leave a pause for you to say the first word. Then Kino says the word and leaves a pause for repetition. Then say "Number two". Go through all the words of the first column in this fashion. Next, say "Column two, number one." After going through the second column, say "pair number one," pause, then have Kino say the first pair and pause again. Cue, pause, correction, pause.

Don't try to tape the final production stage in which you say a word and Kino identifies the column — do this live with him tomorrow. After practicing you can demonstrate your ability to distinguish between these similar but different sounds. To do this, read any word from the drill at random, and have Kino tell you if the sound fits the first column or the second. For example, let's say you are contrasting nasal and oral vowels, and your words for the drill are set up like this:

Pronunciation Differential Drill   October 9
Oral vs. nasal vowels

Oral	Nasal
bo	bǫ
sot	sǫt
kapal	kapạl
bukop	bukǫs

Your production of the difference should enable Kino to identify the correct column every time.

Structure Differential Drill. As an example for the recording technique of a Structure Differential drill, let's use the following question-answer frame.

Structure Differential Drill   *November 10*
Question & Answer

Column 1	Column 2
Did I say it correctly?	Yes, you did say it correctly.
Did I tell it accurately?	Yes, you did tell it accurately.
Did I pronounce it clearly?	Yes, you did pronounce it clearly.

Your objective is to produce one of the pair when the other is given as a stimulus. First, record the *listening* stage by having Kino read the sentences of the first column, then those of the second column, then the pairs. Keep your recording cadence moving fast.

For the *mimicry* stage, record as above, but leave pauses. For the *production* stage, Kino records a sentence from Column 1, then a pause (in practice you will say the corresponding sentence from Column 2). Then Kino gives the Column 2 sentence as correction, with a pause. Then on to the next pair.

Try reversing them now. Kino gives a Column 2 stimulus and in the pause you respond with the Column 1 counterpart.

Now random order: Kino gives a sentence from either column and in the pause you give its mate.

So there you are.

Thank Kino for his help this week and wish him a happy weekend.

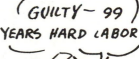

Giving a sentence
from a column

Fluency Practice With the Tape

Review your text in preparation for communication time. Practice the fluency drills which you have taped. Top it off with a *Simultaneous Production Drill* before going out to communicate.

Communication

To learn another language when one's own works so well, requires a deep commitment to the people of the new language. Do you feel a desire to isolate yourself from the people of your new community? Be aware of any rationalization that you may be using as an excuse to keep from being involved. (Here are some examples of rationalizations we've heard: "I don't know today's text well enough to go out." "I learn easier from books." "I'll do it tomorrow." "I'm too busy." "I'm too tired.")

Steps in communication

Actual use in conversation is the best way to review and consolidate what you are learning. Of course it takes a generous amount of courage to go out and communicate what you know. But once the text is practiced, you are ready. The steps of the Communication part of the cycle are those taken by your own two feet. Get up. Go out. Get started! Find the first likely prospect and tell him what you know.

Evaluation

This week we have primarily guided you to focus your evaluation on your learning of the methodology of the cycle. You will need to use each procedure a number of times so that you thoroughly know the advantages and disadvantages of each, and so that you can draw on the best one to respond to your particular need at any given time. Evaluate methodology as needed to refine and sharpen your tools. You should keep an evaluative eye on the procedures for at least a month or so.

Learning about yourself: How are you reacting to correction? Are you careful to express your appreciation for correction given? Do you take correction seriously?

How's your sense of humor?

How do you react to people in the community? Have you learned to respond graciously when you do not know what people are saying to you, or when it is obvious that they do not know what you are saying? Have you gotten used to having children follow you around because you are a foreigner? Are you exercising your sense of humor?

Read pages 86-89 again as you fill in today's Evaluation Record. This one has the same format as *"Thursday's."*

Daily Evaluation Record

Time Schedule
½ hour frames

Date _____

1 _____
2 _____
3 _____
4 _____
5 _____
6 _____
7 _____
8 _____
9 _____
10 _____
11 _____
12 _____
13 _____
14 _____
15 _____
16 _____

Impressions, Questions, Cultural Observations, and Observations about Self: _____
_____
_____
_____

Note and Classify Problems and Opportunities. State Hypotheses. _____
_____
_____
_____

Next Step: _____
_____
_____

Ideas for New Texts: _____
_____
_____
_____

Is all data currently organized in file system: _____

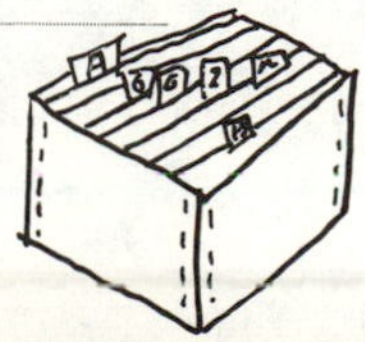

Today's New Text Material   General Meaning

_____   _____
_____   _____
_____   _____
_____   _____
_____   _____
_____   _____
_____   _____

Fluency Drills: _____
_____
_____
_____
_____
_____

Comprehension Activities
Review: _____
_____

New: _____
_____
_____

Pronunciation Drills   Structure Drills
Substitution/Differential   Substitution/Differential

_____   _____
_____   _____
_____   _____
_____   _____
_____   _____
_____   _____
_____   _____

Feature in Focus: _____   Feature in Focus: _____

Total number communicated with _____
Number you shared all of today's text with _____
Number you elicited and practiced new material with _____
An experience in Communication: _____
_____
_____
_____
_____

The evaluation each day has included a space for noting and classifying problems. As you become increasingly aware of your needs you may find that your card file is more convenient.

Here are some ideas for organizing your material in the future. Your primary focus for evaluation in the future will be on your actual language learning needs and progress, rather than on the methodology.

We have recommended that you keep a card file with various sections. As you identify an opportunity, problem or need, write it on a card and classify it in the appropriate section so that you can work on it later. Sections of the card file might be as follows:

Pronunciation: In this category identify the vowels, consonants, intonations, tone levels, rhythms, etc. which you have problems with.

Structure: Note the new sentence patterns you have encountered, and put each on a card as the pattern sentence. Also identify the sentences for which you tend to interchange the word order (probably due to your English habits), the structures which have grammatical-marker words which you tend to omit, verb forms which give you problems, etc.

Vocabulary: List the topics for which you lack vocabulary, vocabulary you would like to explore, and any sets of words you tend to confuse with each other. Can you design a Comprehension drill on the topic?

Comprehension Activities: Keep all your Comprehension drill cards in this category. Review them and add to them regularly.

Methodology: Write down any ideas you have on new procedures or new ways to use old procedures.

Things I'd like to say: This unsophisticated section can provide ideas for the content of a large percentage of your cycles. Carry file cards with you during communication time. Whenever you encounter situations for which you would like to say something in the language, but are unable to, describe the situation on a card along with the type of thing you wish you could have said. In future cycles, you can explore with Kino the appropriate things to say in such a situation, maybe build it into a text, and practice it.

Texts: Record each text you develop on a card or in a notebook and review the texts from time to time.

Comments on Cultural Situations and Behavioral Differences:
Note any things about people's behavior, or the culture in general, that puzzle or interest you. Talk about these with Kino or with the other people you develop as your cultural advisors.

During evaluation times, decide on the content of some of the steps for the next cycle. You may choose a topic for the next cycle from the *Things I'd like to say* category (other ideas are given in Chapter Two). You can pick out an opportunity or problem from the Structure and the Pronunciation categories, and identify the types of drills to respond to those needs.

Pick an opportunity
from the cards

When Kino helps you develop a drill to meet a specific need, write the drill on the back of the card on which you wrote the problem. After it is practiced, you can file the card at the back of its section.

Date each card when you note the opportunity or problem. When you have worked on the feature, write the response — whether it is a drill or a short description — on the back of the card, with the date. These cards become your *progress record* — your record of language needs met. At one time you couldn't pronounce that sound, or didn't know the meaning of that word, or couldn't use that sentence structure, or didn't know what to say in that situation — but now you do. Progress!

Learning the language is your goal, but at times it may seem that you have hit a plateau and are getting no closer to your goal. To avoid frustration, keep daily goals manageable. Your daily goal can be to develop fluency in some small area of the language and move toward accurately pronouncing and using some new structure. If you meet your daily goals, your "solution" cards will be a record of your progress toward that ultimate goal, and should keep you from getting discouraged at what seems to be a series of endless plateaus. Keep the plateaus short. A consistent realization of manageable daily goals will lead you to the realization of your language learning objective.

M	T	W	Th	F
	2	3	4	5

The first week

Looking Back at the First Week

Just think how much you have learned in five days!

During this week you have prepared texts which enable you to politely greet people, tell a short story about yourself, ask a couple of basic questions, and get correction — all in your new language. You are beginning to become bilingual.

Our objective this week has been to present an integrated body of practical activities which, when used, will lead to bilingualism. We are trying to show you *how to learn* a language, rather than teaching you some particular language. The person who knows how to learn can continue growing and learning throughout his future. In contrast, many who study in a language course do not know how to continue after the instruction of the course is ended. The learner who has carefully worked through these five learning cycles will have a good basis for continued learning and, as a fringe benefit, will have already enjoyed considerable experience actually conversing in the new language.

An integrated body

You have now practiced with all of the basic procedures which will enable you to become bilingual. As you continue to use these procedures, you should review this *"week"* from time to time, until you are thoroughly competent with all the activities — especially practice procedures for accuracy.

With more practice in using the cycle you will always be able to determine what you can do next. You will know where you are in the cycle, and how to adapt the schedule to your own needs. You should be able to proceed with a sense of accomplishment, for each day you will tackle something you know you are unable to say, yet by the end of the day you will have said it many times. If you are bored you can cover more material or go faster; if you are frustrated you can back up some or go more slowly. Your rate of learning, then, can be *self-programmed*. Of course, this does require self-discipline. Keeping a regular schedule will help. If a group of two or more are serious about learning the language, it could be possible for them to provide mutual encouragement and discipline. This does assume that each one is committed to the same objective, both short-term and long-term (many who say they want to learn a language lose interest after they find it takes some effort).

The basic presentation of the content of the learning cycle is now complete. The next chapters will help you refine it and fill it in. The **KEY** on the following pages might be your guide for at least the next few weeks as you become familiar with the remainder of **LAMP**.

"It's surprising what you see when you are cycling that don't even notice when you are in a car."

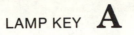

LAMP KEY **A**

The Daily Learning Cycle *Methodology*

"A disease of the tongue that affects the vision."
— Don Larson

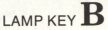 

Content for The Daily Learning Cycle

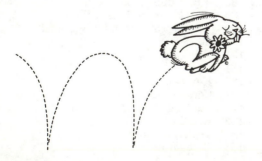

PART TWO

GOING ON!

PART TWO

GOING ON!

Y ou have now been exposed to the daily learning cycle. By consistently using the cycle over the next few weeks, you will develop skill and spontaneity in its use. Sure, you may want to go through Chapter One another time or two with new content. That's fine. The **LAMP KEY** can then guide your continued procedural refinement, by providing an index to both methodology and content.

Be creative and imaginative in your use of the cycle. Please don't think of the cycle as a set of procedures that you are locked into every day. Some times the boundary lines between procedures may be fuzzy and, with practice, you may learn that you can sometimes do two or three activities simultaneously. The more you experiment the more you will find good ways to mold these basic fundamentals into your own personalized, natural style.

Imaginative, flexible cycle

The major goals of this manual are to help you become involved and independent. Involved, because that is where communication is at. And independent, because each person learns at his own rate — self-programmed learning is only possible when one knows what to do, and how to do it.

Part One intended to explain the *how-to,* and get you involved. Part Two is intended as a resource of ideas so you will know *what* to do. Each chapter of Part Two corresponds to a Learning Cycle activity. Chapter Two gives ideas for the Preparation of texts which you will practice for Fluency. Look to Chapter Three for Comprehension Practice ideas. Accuracy Practice includes both pronunciation and structure. Chapter Four covers the first, and Chapter Five the other. The Appendix will help in periodic Evaluation. As a self-programmed learner, you can pick something each day from each of the following chapters and work them together into your own individualized daily cycle.

You will probably need everything that follows, but you need it all at once about like a canary needs to be watered with a fire hose. We recommend that you read the initial part of each of the following chapters for starters, so that you will know what to expect. Over the next couple weeks, make a point to read ahead through everything to become familiar with what is there

watering

Chapter Two gives topic ideas for your future texts. The topics are arranged in an order which we feel will approximate your needs. Refer to this chapter when obtaining a text at the Preparation stage.

Chapter Three gives ideas for Comprehension Practice drills, so you can push ahead with your understanding skills.

Chapter Four gives the background you need to become flexible with your mouth and skillful in the identification and pronunciation of new sounds. A technique is presented to help you determine the limited number of sounds of your language. Refer to this chapter for ideas in Pronunciation Accuracy Practice.

Flexible mouth

Chapter Five gives ideas for exploring and mastering grammatical structure features. By using the language and by formulating and checking hypotheses, you will internalize the "rules" of the structure of the language, enabling you to speak accurately and confidently. Refer to this chapter for ideas in Structure Accuracy Practice.

The **Appendix** is different. It provides a means for you to monitor your learning progress. Read it today and set goals for your own achievement. Then, each month, do a self-evaluation of your speaking proficiency. The Appendix also contains a suggested Monthly Report Form that agencies may want their new field personnel to use; and a suggested Language Learning Progression Schedule that can help you set and reach intermediate goals.

¿Questions? and ¡Answers!

Before going on to Chapter Two, let's try to anticipate and respond to some of the questions you might have.

Which is
The Most Difficult Language?

Children the world over

This is a very common question. Some speculate that the hardest language is English, or Chinese, or Navaho. Language learners are often convinced that the most difficult one is the one they face! The fact is that all languages, in the spoken form, are equally easy. Regardless of the language, children the world over begin to speak at about the same age. For an adult learner, however, it is generally easier to learn a language which is closely related to his first one. The reason is that in a closely related language there are more similarities which the learner can build on. But there is a danger that because of the many similarities the learner may tend to ignore the important differences.

By using the Daily Learning Cycle method to communicate regularly you can make consistent progress regardless of the language. Any language is manageable. Since your focus is on using what you know instead of on learning grammar rules you may not even be aware that it is supposed to be a difficult language. ✑

What is the real value
Of the Learning Cycle?

The Learning Cycle can prevent you from floundering or from going off on a tangent. Many people, for example, try to master features sequentially, rather than simultaneously. They start by learning conjugations or compiling vocabulary. Or try to master the pronunciation, or learn all the grammar rules.

Unfortunately, that effort seldom results in communication. The secret of success is to develop all of the necessary skills simultaneously and to use what you know every day. The Learning Cycle has a place for everything, and provides an efficient, step-by-step method of handling all of the dimensions of language each day.

Other advantages stem from the fact that the learner is self-programmed with the Learning Cycle. With it you can tackle any language anywhere since formal materials, experienced teachers, and school programs are unnecessary. Furthermore, when a learner is directly involved in the community while independently learning, he is usually more motivated. He himself is responsible and can't unwittingly shift responsibility over to a teacher.

Then what should my Learning priorities be?

Glad you asked. Clearly you can't emphasize everything at once, even though some attention is given daily to each dimension of the language. The priority focus of the first week was learning the *methodology*, but the methodology will diminish from focus as it becomes second nature to you.

Next to come into focus should probably be accuracy of *pronunciation*. Failure to master accurate pronunciation in early weeks could be a tragic mistake. It's just like the tennis player who wants to improve but is hampered by an old bad habit. Unlearning the bad one and relearning another is much more difficult than it would have been to learn to do it right the first time.

It would be best if your pronunciation remained in primary focus for about a month or so if you are devoting full time to language learning. All of Chapter Four should be completed by then. After that, pronunciation drills should continue, but move to the background.

Next, *grammatical structure* should move into center stage. Of course you will be using grammatical structures from your first day, and by the time your month of focus on pronunciation is completed you probably will have used about 95 percent of the simple sentence structures. While the spotlight is on grammar, you should analyze the organization of each sentence structure you have encountered. Not only do you want to use each structure spontaneously and know where you can substitute what, but you should formulate and check out hypotheses and arrive at "rules" about the structures and their variants. Chapter Five (beginning on page 313) can serve as your guide.

Spotlight on grammar

After about four months turn your focus to *reading*. Start by reading children's readers. This will allow you to read with high comprehension. Note and learn the vocabulary you don't know. Move on

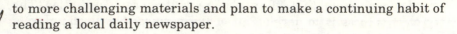

to more challenging materials and plan to make a continuing habit of reading a local daily newspaper.

"What? Me a writer?" Sure. Start with *writing* simple children's stories about your own experiences. Then personal letters to friends. Then more formal business letters.

Learning *vocabulary* and *culture* is the ongoing process of "getting inside people's minds" so we can know what they know. Even in English we are continuing to learn more vocabulary with each new area of interest. Just this past week you have learned meanings for words such as "slot," "filler," "differential," "trigger," "LAMP," "text." So it should be in your language from now on. Keep stretching yourself through reading and involvement. Make a point to talk to new people about new things every day.

The following time chart illustrates the way each of these dimensions is used simultaneously with the others, with the primary focus moving from one to another as the priorities shift.

Keep stretching

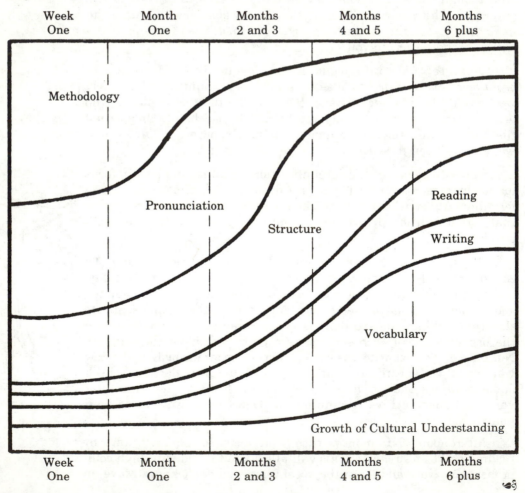

Week One	Month One	Months 2 and 3	Months 4 and 5	Months 6 plus

Methodology

Pronunciation

Structure

Reading

Writing

Vocabulary

Growth of Cultural Understanding

Week One	Month One	Months 2 and 3	Months 4 and 5	Months 6 plus

How do I learn Vocabulary?

We don't recommend flash cards or lists to memorize. As a general rule, you should only learn a word which you can use correctly in a sentence. So, sentence substitution and differential drills are the best place to start learning vocabulary.

All words have a *range of meaning* which permits them to be used in various sentences in a variety of ways. Many words have primary meanings, and secondary or tertiary meanings. The primary meaning is usually the first one given in a comprehensive dictionary. The primary, and all of the secondary meanings of a word are included in the word's range of meaning. For example, the word "table" has the primary meaning of a flat-topped piece of furniture. A multiplication table is different, and it is also different to table a motion. The meanings of a table mountain and a record player's turn-table borrow from the primary idea of flatness. Even within the primary meaning of *table* there are many varieties like coffee table, end table, and pool table. Most are made of wood, but metal and plastic are also common. The secondary meaning of multiplication *table* is similar to a variety of statistical tables and even accuracy substitution tables. You can see that the range of meaning of *table* is fairly extensive. Now, here comes the important point — you can be assured that the word that means "flat-topped dining furniture" won't work for all these other meanings in your new language.

Turn table

The range of meaning of words is never the same from one language to another. Sometimes when people learn vocabulary with flash cards or lists, they assume that the word they learn will work for the same things covered by the range of meaning of that word in English. In fact, each has its own spectrum of usage (its own different range of meaning) within the language. You can now see why it is always best to learn the meaning of words within the normal context of sentences.

NOTE:You have probably noticed that many of the cartoons in this book have capitalized on the difference between primary and secondary meanings of words. Hopefully the text makes it clear when we are using a secondary meaning of a word, but the primary meaning provides the basis for an illustration. This lack of equivalence between the secondary meaning in the text and the word's primary meaning allows for a kind of pun. Examples include "Go down the columns," "Make a substitution table," "The spirit of the game," etc. Of course, if the primary meaning is taken when the context calls for a secondary meaning, then confusion results.

All languages have at least four different kinds of words. (When you encounter a new word, first determine what kind it is.) Some

Encountering a new word

words are names of *things* — we call them object words or nouns. Some words are names of *actions* — we call them event words, activity words, or verbs. Other words are *description* words — sometimes called modifiers or qualities. English adverbs and adjectives are description words. The fourth kind, or classification, are words that show *relationships* between other words. These are prepositions and conjunctions, and they give orientation within time and space — when and where.

Most of the topics from pages 141 to 159 help you talk about words. Those topics will enable you not only to get a meaning of a word, but also to understand its range of meaning and its relationship to other words.

Another way you will stretch your vocabulary is through *Comprehension exercises.*

We don't recommend vocabulary learning activities which involve translation from English. English words don't really describe other languages' meanings. *Instead of translating, associate the new word with the thing, action, quality or relationship that it stands for.* You will thus learn the meaning more accurately and, besides, you will find yourself thinking in the language much quicker.

Associate the word
with the thing

Will my daily procedures
Always remain the same?

In the early weeks of language learning, everything is new and it is necessary to memorize everything. During practice much mimicry is needed and your communication is, by and large, "recitation." You are quite dependent on Kino for your language learning.

In contrast, once you have a good start in the language, much is familiar, and therefore less must be memorized. Words and structures which you have already drilled are "old friends" so learning your text comes more easily and quickly. For example, Phrase and Build-up drills won't be needed after full sentences come easily. With reduced need for mimicry, your focus will then be on production. While early communication is basically recitation, later communication involves *discussion on a theme* – having gained flexibility with the basic patterns, you can now generate new sentences based on these patterns to use new vocabulary.

Cultivating
community relationships

At first, you are dependent on Kino, but you increasingly become more dependent on the community. You are cultivating community relationships and learning to more effectively get needed help from a variety of informal helpers in the community. Kino's role will continue to be important, for you can work with him efficiently in getting new texts and in drilling them. He also should take the initiative in correcting your mistakes and helping you understand the culture.

Should Preparation
Always be my first step each day?

The time which is devoted to language learning should be the hours that your creative energy is at its highest. This may vary from person to person. Actually, some learners have found that it works best for their schedule to do the Preparation part in the evening. They start their day by practicing what was prepared the evening before. A difficulty might be that the helper is needed both in the evening for Preparation and in the morning for Practice; however, some learners might overcome this problem by arranging to have two helpers — one for evening and the other for the mornings. Other learners may find it more convenient to have Preparation and Practice time in the afternoons, and start each day with Communication time using material prepared and practiced the previous afternoon. Evaluation would then be completed just before the helper comes to help you prepare material for the next cycle.

NOTE: Subconscious learning often takes place during sleep. Many times we find that when we "sleep on it" our subconscious mind begins to come up with solutions to the day's situations, and the text seems to have opportunity to "gel" in our minds. Some people therefore find it best to have Preparation and Practice in the afternoon or evening. In the morning, a review of Practice with the tape recorder is just what they need before going out for Communication.

Theoretically, the cycle could end and begin just about anyplace. The important thing is that all four parts be completed each day — whether the order is Preparation, Practice, Communication, Evaluation; or Communication, Evaluation, Preparation, Practice. We do not recommend that you spread the four parts out over two or more successive days. The lack of continuity would waste too much time, and much would be forgotten due to lack of reinforcement. Do a whole cycle each day. Short cycles are better than partial cycles.

Short cycles?! Some may feel that all the activities are difficult to crowd into six hours. We acknowledge that the first cycles may seem heavy. The reason is that you are not only learning a language, you are also learning a methodology — you are learning *how* to learn a language. After the methodology is second nature to you, you can selectively choose activities from each part of the learning cycle. Thus, when necessary, you will be able to finish a complete, though shortened, cycle.

Short cycle

Do I have to spend a third (or more)
Of my time communicating?

It is not uncommon for a language learner to be tempted to slight communication time — *don't* fall into that trap!

He only makes progress
when sticks his neck out

By communicating with people in the community you face your shortcomings as a communicator and become aware of your language needs. And you realize that there are things you want to say, people you want to understand, and a whole different cultural perspective which you want to begin to learn. By developing texts that respond to these needs you will keep your learning meaningful, interesting, and rewarding. Remember the turtle — he only makes progress when he sticks his neck out.

Every day in your communication time you will make mistakes. Sometimes you will make mistakes in grammar, other times in pronunciation. Sometimes you just won't have the vocabulary to converse in a situation — you want to say something but you can't. (Keep your data book, or 3 x 5 cards, with you all the time to record these mistakes and needs.) These experiences will bring your practice needs into focus, thus providing you with valuable feedback. Your positive response to this feedback, by means of drills and practice, will ensure that your accuracy continues to improve.

In your communication time it is a good idea to talk with new people as well as with old friends. By talking to new people you will be exposed to a variety of new ideas and interests. By talking regularly with old friends you will be forced to talk about things on an increasingly deeper level, and your old friends can better note your progress.

Go out into the community

If I hit a plateau, What do I do?

Plateaus often result from rationalization. A learner finds he can "get by" at an elementary level. Then he convinces himself that getting by is all he really needs to do (besides, he found it's hard work to learn a language.) As part of the rationalization, he modifies his objectives and expectations, and a plateau results. This kind of plateau can be remedied by re-evaluating one's original purpose: "I am not here to play a mediocre role. To fulfill my calling I am determined to become an effective communicator."

NOTE: You will probably have people occasionally compliment you on your language ability. You will want to respond politely. But when compliments come don't jump to the conclusion that you are doing a super good job. If you believe what you hear, you might conclude that you no longer need to press on in the language. Compliments may often be an expression of appreciation for your language learning effort and an encouragement to keep at it. Often the person who uses the language skillfully doesn't get compliments — his speaking no longer calls attention to his use of the language. By the way, if people give up on you and think you will never get any better, then you will also stop getting compliments.

Sometimes progress seems quite slow due to a specific difficulty with a pronunciation or structure feature. You may need to focus your time, for example, on the tone system for a week or so to get over an obstacle. Or, where possible, you may profit by consulting with someone about your specific difficulty.

It is common for learners to feel that their learning seems to pass from stage to stage. A period of advancement may be followed by a period of consolidation. Such periods of consolidation are a normal part of growth and provide a foundation for the next advancement. Sometimes a change of intensity or pace might get the advancement going again.

Expect some plateaus from time to time. They are probably normal. Make a point, however, to try to keep each plateau short. Plateaus that are too long can, in fact, lead to a slump or retrogression. The recovery of this lost ground then requires extra effort.

Remember that conscientious work will be rewarded with steady improvement. This improvement or growth should be a continuing encouragement to you. Make a habit of comparing yourself with where you used to be. Don't be discouraged because your ability is less than you would like it to be. You proficiency will come with consistent work.

The best way to avoid discouraging plateaus is to make a practice of setting manageable short-term goals. A major goal such as "I am aiming at the Four Level of speaking proficiency" is too vague and will seem too distant — discouragement could result. We feel it is best to set weekly and daily goals. Each day set a goal to tackle something that is new to you, practice it as needed, and go communicate exercising your new skill. Short-term, manageable goals can be a consistent source of encouragement and can help keep plateaus very short. ✍

A discouragingly distant goal

What should I do About my inhibitions?

Recognize that feelings of inhibition are normal. It *does* take courage to communicate. It is certainly easier to remain with people who are like us, and it takes a conscious determination to decide to become deeply involved with those who are different from ourselves. But we assume you wouldn't be reading this if you weren't determined to learn a new language and culture. So you must decide to be master of your inhibitions, rather than let them master you. ✍

"It's my inhibitions, Doc."

What is culture?

There have been many definitions of culture. One that seems to be most helpful for language learners defines culture in terms of knowledge. When a group of people belong to the same culture they share the same body of knowledge. In other words, the people of a culture have a *shared cognitive orientation* (SCO). North Americans "know" to look first to the left before crossing a busy street. In Britain, people "know" to look to the right. We "know" that it is all right to give and receive things with the left hand, but others "know" that the left hand is never used for this.

Our cognitive orientation consists of all we know — our knowledge. When people *share* knowledge, then a culture or subculture exists. Chemists share a cognitive orientation, and a chemists' subculture results.

The people of your new language have a shared body of knowledge. Learning their culture is the process of finding out what they know. Acculturation is this process of coming to share the cognitive orientation of people in a second culture.

What's so funny About that?

What's so funny?

You will, no doubt, provide many laughs for the people, and you should learn to laugh along with them. But the jokes you *try* to make may fall completely flat. Puns, plays on words, and language-related jokes require a pretty comprehensive understanding of the culture (as well as the language).

Humor often plays on some aspect of general knowledge which can be quite subtle. Often the language learner doesn't yet have the broad knowledge that enables him to understand the joke. When you encounter a joke which you don't understand, it probably indicates that there is cultural knowledge you might want to acquire. You can use it as a basis for further cultural exploration.

We have an Indonesian friend who speaks English very well. (He holds a doctorate from the University of Texas.) One day he asked us about a *Dennis the Menace* cartoon he had seen which he didn't understand. It was a two-frame cartoon. In the first frame Dennis came running into the house. In the second frame he had gone to stand in the corner and was saying, "Look in the driveway." This is a good example of the broad knowledge base that humor utilizes. North Americans know that standing in the corner is a form of punishment (we've never heard of any other culture that disciplines children this way — even in our culture it is perhaps more idiomatic than real). By going into the corner on his own initiative, Dennis illustrates his own guiltiness about something — he did something that deserves punishment. His statement, "Look in the driveway", gives us a pretty good idea of what he did — he probably left his bike there and Dad backed the car over it. By questioning us, our friend used this as an opportunity to learn more about American cultural patterns of discipline, guilt and child-rearing.

When you don't get the point, ask someone about it. Take advantage of the opportunity to explore another facet of the insider's knowledge.

Should I work on the cycle Together with someone else?

Working on the cycle together

This question always arises when a married couple is learning a language. And friends or associates wonder about working together, too. This is fine provided each one masters the procedures for himself and does his own communicating. It is hard to learn by proxy.

The authors work together a lot in language learning. (And Betty Sue gets it faster than I — *Tom*.) We generally like to get separate material on the same topic. In communication we can both talk to people and both say different things that (kind of) fit together. Another advantage for us is that when one is conversing with someone the other can write in his data book the new words or questions we are asked. (Sometimes your helper might go with you and help make notes this way.)

A potential problem with working together is that individuals learn at different rates, and language needs are not always the same. We suggest that you try it both ways. You may find some things that you can do together, while other things may need to be drilled individually. We know couples who find it best to use two tape recorders so one can practice while the other records the material he needs.

NOTE: By the way, *mothers* **shouldn't give up hope about learning the language themselves. They may need to recognize that their husbands have more available time for language learning. The responsible mother should be sure to compete with herself, not with her husband. It is interesting that wives frequently learn more easily than their husbands. Maybe they are more relaxed, or maybe communication just comes more easily for most gals. A mother may have another advantage — with the children she may be welcomed into homes for conversation with local mothers.**

A small group of two or three might provide some mutual motivation to maintain a disciplined schedule. This requires, however, that each group member is truly committed to the mastery of the language.

If you are learning together it is probably best not to compete with each other. Rather, mutually encourage each other. Children learn language at varying rates and so do adults. No one should feel inferior to another because of a slower rate of learning. Compare yourself with where you have been rather than with where someone else is.

For some people the tensions of language learning get very close to their central nervous system. Unnecessary competition with someone else can lead to the creation of a psychological block, and withdrawal from language learning and involvement altogether. Mutual support and encouragement is best.

If you are working with a partner, you might encourage each other to use just the new language when the people are around. Soon you might also agree to use only the new language with each other for a specified period of time each day.

Should I use
Two helpers?

This can be a big advantage for it can help ensure that your texts are more natural and suitable. One helper might give you a way of saying something and the other realizes "That's not the way we would usually say it." Two helpers can role-play in order to better illustrate the settings. And they can confer to determine a better way of saying things.

A disadvantage is the increased cost.

If two people are learning together, then having two helpers could be ideal. Get them together for role-playing while eliciting the text material and then separate for practice.

In some cases the two helpers might have different dialects. This could be a disadvantage if disagreements result. But to be exposed to two dialects might prove, in the long run, to be quite advantageous indeed.

Should I work with a helper
Of my own sex?

If you are single or doing language learning individually, this is probably best. Men and women have their own ways of talking and they sometimes talk about their own topics — i.e., mechanics and babies. So every learner should work at least some of the time with a helper of the same sex.

Studying grammar

Should I buy a grammar book
About the language?

Sure. (You are going to anyway, so we might as well condone it.)

A grammar book is a book of answers about the characteristics of the language. The problem is that you don't know the questions yet! Even if you understood an answer you wouldn't know its significance. Thus the book may give you an answer, but it may go in one ear and out the other. But, when you *discover* something for yourself then it is really yours. So, we recommend that you probe in the language, making your own hypotheses and asking your own questions. *Then* the answer book can help you with an insight and you will have internalized a much more complete understanding.

Be cautious of grammar books which describe the language in terms of English, or Latin, rules and parts of speech. Often older books of this type even suggest that a language is "deficient" if it doesn't have certain structures, or "abnormal" if it has structures which don't occur in a European language. This attitude is one you should be particularly wary of.

NOTE: There is one kind of word we've always wanted to end a sentence with. A word like of. Or with. Or at. Or on. English composition teachers say that one can successfully violate the rules when he becomes an "accomplished" author — that's what we are now counting on. Grammar books and teachers have tried to convince us that it isn't grammatical to end a sentence with a preposition because in Latin it was looked down upon. Yet, English is a language it can be done in. There is a lesson here that you should think about. It is that languages have their own patterns which they adhere to; and their own rules which they should be described by. Well, let's not rub it in.

It is not a disaster to be learning a language which has no grammar books. Through careful listening and a consistent evaluation and response to your mistakes, you will become aware of all of the structures and grammatical relationships in the language, and through practice you will master them. (Based on your experience, you might even be able to write a grammar book, if you like.) ❧

How does the Learning Cycle compare With the way a child learns?

Virtually all children learn a language. In Africa, Asia and Europe many, if not most, people learn a second or third language. The Learning Cycle concept has grown out of an analysis of both child learning and adult learning. What do they know that makes language learning manageable? Are there universal principles that can apply to the English speaker as he learns a second language? We think so.

Foundational to success seems to be the fact that language must never be an end in itself. Rather, the goal of language learning is communication with people. Baby wants to communicate with Mommy. An African adult wants to communicate with people of another tribe, so he listens and then uses the verbal symbols needed to get messages across. He wouldn't think of himself as a language student — he just wants to communicate. In contrast, students in structured foreign language programs often fail to see how study activities directly relate to communication goals. The student may feel he *has* to learn the language. That attitude can be counterproductive. What you *have* to do is learn to communicate.

In the Learning Cycle the communication objective is the foundation. Each activity leads directly to sending or receiving verbal messages, and communication skills grow with each day's involvement in the community. Everything is geared to "street work", not homework.

Another parallel builds on the fact that successful learners (children or adults) know how to be *involved* and *independent*. Children and multilingual adults don't isolate themselves from true-life communication situations; nor are they dependent on a "teacher" or "language curriculum" or a "spoon-feeding" program. The Learning Cycle seeks to counter the tendencies that English speakers have toward isolation and dependence, by maximizing the learner's interaction with people and by giving him tools to help him become a self-programmed learner.

Children and multilingual adults know how to do Fluency, Comprehension, and Accuracy drills. Of course they do them informally and spontaneously. (Once you really learn the procedures you will be more spontaneous and informal in your drills, too.)

Fluency drills, whether formal or informal, proceed through an initial stage of observation by listening, then a mimicry stage since plenty of repetition is needed both for children and adults. Then, independent production skills follow.

"Where is Daddy's watch?"

Comprehension "drill" is a technique used by every mother. "Where is Anna's ear?" "Where is Mommy's mouth?" "Where is Daddy's watch?" Correct physical response triggers an enthusiastic show of approval from Mother, and Anna may even clap for herself. All the physical activity helps reinforce the learning. Soon, the comprehension leads to production. Mommy asks "What is this?" If Anna responds with anything resembling "mouth", Mother will take Anna into her arms and give her a big congratulatory celebration. All the to-do gives a strong motivation for Anna's continued language learning.

Accuracy drills are also a natural part of the less formal learning of children and multilingual adults. Both structure and pronunciation are commonly practiced, by differentiating one pattern from another, and by substituting within the various possible patterns.

The child concentrates attention on that which is important in meeting his own felt needs. He observes the behavior of others and imitates it, and learns how to simplify the patterns that adults use. He begins by talking to people about a few very useful topics. When he is corrected he takes it seriously. Everyone is his coach. A child works at a pace that is comfortable — no one pushes him faster than he wants to go, and nothing restrains him when he wants to forge ahead.

See, being child-like isn't a bad idea after all.

Can I do some
Of my practice informally?

While it is important to get plenty of formal Accuracy Practice, you can also gain much valuable help by informal practice on Sounds, Comprehension, and Structure. You can probably get neighborhood children and young people to give you lots of informal practice if you make games of language learning. Keep the spirit light and lively. It's not so much what you do that will make your informal practice fun — it's how you do it. Exercise your creativity, humor, enthusiasm, and imagination.

Sounds. There may be various language games focusing on sounds, which local people can teach you — tongue twisters, word rhythm games, and rhyming games.

Tongue twisters

If there are two sounds which you have difficulty distinguishing, try some *informal pronunciation Differential* practice. Collect a few pairs of words whose major difference is the pair of sounds in focus (for example: ship/sheep, lick/leak, hill/heel). Have a friend say the words and you respond by pointing to the correct object or drawing. Encourage him to say the words quickly and with normal enunciation. Once you are responding correctly, change roles and see if you can say the words clearly enough for him to hear the difference and point correctly.

Miss Smith
dismisseth
us.

If there is one troublesome sound, try *informal pronunciation Substitution* practice. Have friends see how many words they can collect which have that sound. Keep a running list of the words and review them often with friends until you master them.

Comprehension. Teach your friends to direct you in *informal Comprehension Exercises*. You could have a group game in which each person directs the group to repeatedly perform three or four activities. Encourage them to keep it repetitious enough for you to learn to respond correctly.

Structure. When you are learning a new sentence pattern, you can do some *informal structure Substitution* practice. Have a friend, or group of friends, act out activities to substitute in the event slot, and point to objects or people to substitute in the other slots. You say the sentence, substituting the name of the action or object.

With a bit of imagination you can find a variety of ways to have fun in *structure Differential* practice with a friend. For example, you might be learning the difference between positive and negative sentences. As you went for a walk with a friend, he could describe various things along the way and you could turn the sentence into a negative description of a different object — B. "This man is tall." A. "This girl isn't tall."

Once you have begun learning *structure Expansions,* you can play a game like "In My Grandmother's Trunk," in which each participant expands on what the previous person said:

A. In my Grandmother's trunk is a hat.
B. In my Grandmother's trunk is a white hat.
C. In my Grandmother's trunk is a small white hat.
D. In my Grandmother's trunk is a small white hat and a coat.
    Etc.

Take advantage of any local language games to increase your mastery of the language in fun and natural ways.

(P.S. You may have to relax your dignity a bit and learn to laugh with others at your own mistakes in order to let these be games rather than formal exercises. Make a point of seeing the humor in the situation.)

What about Language schools?

A dillar a dollar,
an Eight AM scholar

Language schools have one major advantage — if classes start at 8:00 AM then the student is there on time and ready to go. Without a school, the same discipline must come from within oneself, rather than from an externally imposed schedule.

Language schools almost never have all four parts of the learning cycle in their curriculum. Materials are prepared and practice is common, though often practice is insufficient to enable the student to use what he is exposed to. Sentence forms that may be more difficult (which you therefore need more practice on) are often saved to the very end of the course, when little practice time remains. The most important step, communicating daily what you know, is almost never part of the curriculum. Nor is self-evaluation. Curricular materials are seldom prepared with the immediate communication needs of the new learner in mind. It is interesting to note that some schools even prohibit the students from talking with average people on the street. The classical "proper" form of the language is taught, though people speak the vernacular form rather than the classical. The teachers even speak the vernacular to each other!

Another common problem is that language schools usually approach language and culture as bodies of knowledge to be memorized rather than as sets of skills to be acquired.

We should make it clear that we are not saying that you should avoid attending a language school. But while in school, always ask yourself, "Are my communication needs being met?" Then creatively use the learning cycle, or the appropriate parts of it, to supplement what you are getting in the school.

What about living
In the home of a local family?

Excellent! Obviously this maximizes involvement. Even families with children can usually manage this if they decide they want to.

Usually the first order of business when moving to a new locality is to get settled. But we recommend that you delay the process of getting settled for a month or more. Why? Because you only know how to settle in a Western way, and you have no idea of what that itself might communicate to those you want to be involved with. For starters, it is good to live in a local (not tourist) hotel. Then try to establish relationships in the community so that you might soon be invited to live in a local home. After a month or so you would know an alternative way to settle-in, and you would have a much better idea of what is communicated by your life-style.

Settling in a Western way

When arranging to live with a family, it is best to make a short-term commitment of a month or two. You might later decide to stay longer, or to live with various different families at different times.

Will living in another culture
Cause emotional disturbances
In our children?

Your children are much more flexible than you are. They don't like to be different from their playmates, so identification and language learning are usually second nature to them.

We feel that the *attitude* of the parents toward both English and the new language and culture is the critical factor contributing to the emotional health of children who are growing up in a second culture. If parents, for example, have the attitude that English is somehow superior to the new language, then children will have conflicts when their friends don't speak English. Recognize that any language is just a set of verbal symbols used to communicate. Nothing more, nothing less. Any language works fine for its communicative purpose, and none can be ranked as better or superior to another. If parents demonstrate that they believe this, their children can learn one language and then the other, or both simultaneously as opportunity permits. To be raised in an environment where one can be bilingual and bicultural from his youth is hardly a liability, rather it is an *asset* of a very high order.

How about a technique
For cultural exploration?

Field observation

There is a simple four-step field observation procedure which you can use to stretch your understanding of the local culture. If you put it into practice you will be distinctly set apart from the typical superficial tourist. You may want to devote a few minutes of your daily Communication time to these procedures. The four steps are:

1. Make observations.
2. Make assumptions about your observations.
3. Attempt to validate your assumptions.
4. Classify and apply your new information.

This method of inquiry will enable you to gain a relatively broad understanding of the local culture in just a few weeks. Let's amplify the procedures.

Make observations. Visit homes, schools, businesses, factories, police stations, clubs, churches, recreational areas, and hospitals. Observe everything you can. Observation is more than just seeing. It is perceiving the environment with *all* of your senses. The observant person notices the *texture* of a fabric, the *sounds* of a factory, the *smells* of a market, the *methods* of construction, and the use of *colors*. Observe not only material things, but also the *behavior* of people and their *attitudes*. If you concentrate, you will see much more. We recommend that you write your observations on a page that is divided into three columns. Maybe your observations would include statements like this:

Observations	Assumptions	Validations
Women wear long dresses in public.		
Clothing is neat and colorful.		
Many buses		
Buses are usually full.		
Etc.		

Make assumptions about observations. The next step is to jump to one or more tentative conclusions concerning the meaning of your observations. Of course, many times the assumptions you make will be in error. You should make hypotheses anyway, and write your assumptions in the column beside the observation. Try to answer the questions: "What does this mean to them?" "Why do they do this?" "What does this show about their culture?"

Observations	Assumptions	Validations
Women wear long dresses in public.	High value on modesty.	
Clothing is neat and colorful.	Value placed on personal appearance.	
Many buses	Buses go almost everywhere.	
Buses are usually full.	People can go where they need to by bus.	
	Bus travel is inexpensive	

Validate your assumptions. Are your assumptions accurate, or have you perceived things incorrectly? You should expect many or even most of your assumptions to be incorrect, since you are looking at their world through your own foreign background. One way to validate your assumptions is to *get more observations* and see if these substantiate your original assumptions. The most valuable means of validation is through *interviews with people.* Talk regularly with Kino and others about your assumptions. Often you can validate assumptions by *experimenting or participating in activities with people.* Some validations might be made through *library research.* Of course, inaccurate assumptions should be discarded for more valid ones.

Observations	Assumptions	Validations
Women wear long dresses in public.	High value on modesty.	Multiple observations. Talked with Kino's sister.
Clothing is neat and colorful.	Value placed on personal appearance.	Talked with people — Most women don't own many dresses but try to keep them clean and neat.
Many buses	Buses go almost everywhere.	Got a bus route map — extensive routes.
Buses are ususally full.	People can go where they need to by bus.	Experiemented and found I could get all over town by bus.
	Bus travel is inexpensive.	Experience — cheap! I could ride buses every day for less than car *insurance!*

Validation:
"It is cold — and wet!"

Classify and apply information. Most observations can be classified according to one of the following sociological categories. You will have a good cultural foundation when you understand the working of each of these categories or systems in your new culture.

The Kinship system. The family provides a means for adding new members to the society. It also provides an environment for the training and socialization of children. The kinship system relates to all aspects of the family or extended family including elements such as descent, family authority, area of residence, inheritance, moral values and marriage.

The Education system. All societies provide a means of transmitting information to its young members. This prepares the individual to live and function within the society in an acceptable way and to do so with some degree of independence. Elements of the educational system include schools, teachers, family members, books, and materials.

The Economic system. Each society has a means of acquiring and distributing goods and services which sustain the lives of its members. Many roles and institutions are in operation to meet these needs. They include the population of working people, the different types of enterprises, means of payment or exchange, and ecology.

The Political system. All societies regulate themselves and their relations with others. This regulation provides protection for the whole group. The political system controls the competition for power within the society. Elements of the political system include public services and utilities, government institutions such as courts, police, and legislative bodies.

The Religious system. Every culture is built around basic beliefs and values which provide an understanding of man's existence and his place in the universe. These beliefs are often manifested in the form of rituals and organizations.

The Recreation system. All societies provide a means for recreation and relaxation. This includes games, dancing, singing, sports, story-telling, artistic pursuits, drinking parties, and pastimes.

The Associational system. In every culture, people who have similar interests tend to group themselves together. These associations may be for recreational, political, economic, or other reasons. For what purposes are groups formed? How many people belong to the different groups? Do they use symbols or slogans to identify themselves?

The Health system. All societies are concerned about the survival of their members. Elements of the health system include nutrition, mother and child care, control of diseases, hospitals, medical personnel, and beliefs about health and its relation to medicine or the spirit world.

The Transportation and Communication system. Every culture provides a means for people and goods to get from one place to another, and for information to be disseminated throughout the community. This includes postal service, bus system, roads, telephones, mass media and language.

NOTE: We are indebted to John D. Donoghue, whose Community Development Research led to the development of these systems of classification.

After you make observations, assumptions and validations, you should classify the information according to one (or more) of the above systems. You might want to keep a separate page for entries relevant to each category. Recognize that these systems are closely *interrelated,* and that an entry in one system may have ramifications for other systems.

Analysis and classification should not be an end in itself. You also need to *apply* the research data to your own situation. Ask yourself: "What does this mean to me?" "How should this affect my living in this culture?" "How will this affect my communication?" Questions like this can turn your assumptions into information that will aid you as you develop a strategy for effective involvement in the new culture. Keep a summary of these applications.

Personally apply
the data

Classification	*Application*
Kinship (moral values)	Since modesty is valued, if I want to be respected, I will probably need to avoid wearing jeans, shorts, and short skirts when in public.
Economics	It might be best to wear a limited wardrobe since most people don't have many clothes. I will need to keep my clothes always clean and neat.
Transportation and Economics	By riding public transportation, I can be with lots of people, and save money, too.

A word of caution is in order. You must recognize that your observations, assumptions, and validations are being perceived and interpreted through your own foreign patterns of organizing knowledge. Even information from "validated" assumptions must be considered to be tentative as long as you are an outsider. More definite confirmation of hypotheses will come as you learn to share the knowledge and cognitive orientation of local people. The deeper level of understanding can only come after you know the language well and are an active participant in the culture.

What books
Might be helpful?

Here is a list of a few books that some of you might want to read.

William Carey Library (1705 North Sierra Bonita Ave., Pasadena, CA 91104) offers a variety of useful books on language and culture learning.

Among them are:

Becoming Bilingual. Donald Larson and William Smalley. 1972.

Manual of Articulatory Phonetics. William Smalley. 1964.

Readings in Missionary Anthropology. William Smalley. 1967.

Culture and Human Values. Jacob Loewen. 1975.

Translator's Field Guide. Alan Healey, editor, 1970. (This book has hints on learning a language where it is difficult to get a helper who speaks English or any other intermediate language.)

Other helpful books on language learning:

Learning A Foreign Language. Eugene Nida. Friendship Press (New York). 1957.

Customs & Cultures. Eugene Nida. Harper & Row (New York). 1954.

Self-Guide to Linguistic Fieldwork (with tape). Paul Turner. Impresora Sahuaro (7575 Sendero de Juana, Tucson, Arizona 85718), 1972. (Focuses on phonetics and phonemics.)

Field Linguistics. William Samarin. Holt, Rinehart and Winston (London and New York), 1967.

How to Learn an Unwritten Language. Sarah Gudchinsky. Holt, Rinehart and Winston (London and New York), 1967.

A couple of books on culture learning:

The Silent Language. Edward Hall, Fawcett Publications (Greenwich, Connecticut), 1959.

The Cultural Experience. James Spradley and David McCurdy. Science Research Associates (Chicago and Toronto), 1972.

Books can be a source of ideas and they can sometimes unlock a mystery. But a word of caution — don't get sidetracked into reading about language learning or culture learning. Doing it beats reading about it.

CHAPTER **2**

Things To Talk About In Texts

"**W**here do I go from here?" This chapter will help answer this question by describing a variety of language and culture situations which can serve as topics of the texts in your future cycles.

Your objective each day should be to learn to communicate something you haven't been able to say before — something useful, relevant to your needs, appropriate for your level of learning, and something which will provide ample opportunity for communication and involvement with the people of the community.

The text ideas of this chapter are arranged in **four sets of topics.** The *first set* includes early texts which should probably be worked on in your first 4 to 7 weeks of full-time study. The *second set* of texts relates to further exploration in vocabulary, language styles, and current needs. This second set can be completed in about 4 to 7 additional weeks. The *third set* of texts relates to exploration of simple cultural themes. They may take 9 to 15 weeks to complete. The *fourth set* of topics explores deeper cultural values.

We feel that the topics described in the first two sets are presented in an order which will probably correlate fairly highly with your actual needs. The suggestions are based on an assessment of the learner's immediate needs in his host country, and are designed to allow you to learn from the people in the community.

The arrangement of text ideas within sets three and four is somewhat arbitrary. You could easily choose to work on the texts within a set in a different order from that which is given here. But you probably would be wise to work on the majority of text topics within a set before going on to the topics of the next set.

During your first week you may have been following our topic suggestions fairly carefully. But from now on, additional options are open to you — you can alter the content of one of the topic ideas, omit ideas which are irrelevant in your situation, or make up your own ideas based on the needs and mistakes which you identify in your communication time. It is important for you to be meeting your *own* felt needs as you continue learning. You are not just "learning a language" — you are learning to *communicate* by using a new language in a new culture.

If you find that a suggestion results in a text that is too long for you at your stage of learning, you may want to split the text into two parts and spend two cycles on it. On the other hand, other texts may prove to be too short or too simple — feel free to combine two similar text ideas or expand one idea into a longer text. Tailor the ideas to fit your own needs.

You may want
to split a long text

Beside the name of each of the following text ideas is a blank line on which you can write the date when you used it in a cycle. This date will help you find the text in your card file, and also let you tell at a glance which topics have been previously explored. You may feel you have only scratched the surface on a topic. If so, you can remind yourself to come back to it by drawing a second dateline in the margin or on the other side of the title. Indicate in the paragraph the idea or ideas which you want to focus on later. When you return to the topic, write the date on the line you drew.

Date

NOTE: It is a good idea to plan your text topics a few days ahead of time, so that you can do Comprehension Drills on the topic in advance.

As you use these text ideas be careful to clearly establish the settings with Kino. Don't let him just translate the ideas given here. Think them through with him in relation to the culture and language, and let him develop a text which fits the culture and sounds natural in the language.

Set 1 — **Topics**
For the Beginning Learner

The topics in this set can be completed in about 4 to 7 weeks if you are devoting full time to language learning.

Finding a Place to Live _____
<small>Date</small>

Most North Americans overseas adopt a foreign, American life-style. But if you want to be an effective communicator in your new community, you may want to carefully weigh the communication implications of the way you live. The best way is to live and eat with a family for your first few months. You will learn how to adopt a meaningful life-style and you will **maximize your opportunities to use your new language.**

For a text, tell people that you are learning the language and you hope to find a family you can live with for a few months. Then ask the question, "Do you know of a family I might be able to live with?"

For communication time, ride a bus and say your text to all the passengers. Then get off and board another. Also, talk with people in neighborhood stores. Keep talking with people, and someone is almost sure to invite you in. In our experience, couples and even families with children have been warmly welcomed. Persistence pays off. Of course, you will want to arrange to pay the family for your accommodations and food. ✌ঁ

Using Public Transportation _____
<small>Date</small>

Language is learned by being involved, but to be involved you may need to be able to get around. Besides, your curiosity will compel you to want to explore the nearby territory. Good. But make a point of sight-seeing and **exploring by means of local public transportation.** You will do yourself and your language learning a big favor if you avoid the use of any private car in which an isolated English-speaking environment occurs.

Public transportation may be via bus or rickshaw; but the people who know get around fine within the system. What do you need to know to make the system useful to you?

For your text you may want to learn to ask — "What bus goes to El Wadi?" "Where does the bus stop?" "Where is the _____ (post office, monument, store, etc.)?" Find out what Kino knows about the public transportation. Role-playing with him might elicit helpful language.

Get a map of the area. Develop a comprehension drill on the names of special places.

For communication time, take your map with you and explore the entire area by public transportation. See how many buses you can ride and how many times you can say your text. While you are riding, talk with fellow passengers using previous texts.   ◦§

Developing a Route of Listeners

Date

Advantages of a route
People will "show you off" to friends — for more speaking practice, plus new friends

You can develop long texts "serially" — "That's all I know how to say, I'll tell you more tomorrow"

You need people to regularly talk with each day, so you can use your communication time efficiently. (Remember, this time is talking time, not just walking time.) Here's an idea that has been an important **key for developing relationships.**

Learn to tell people that you learn something new every day and need to say it to people so you can practice the language. Then ask, "May I come by each day and say to you the new things I learn?" With this text, you can easily develop a route of sixteen to thirty people in the neighborhood who will look forward to your daily visit (and miss you if you don't come). They will know you are a learner and will correct your mistakes in language and cultural behavior and rejoice with you in your progress.

By the way, **your positive response to your mistakes** can be your greatest stepping stone to learning. Make careful note of mistakes and corrections. Learn to say, "Yesterday I made a mistake when I wanted to say '. . . . . . .' Am I saying it correctly now?" In this way people will see that you are serious about responding to correction. This will help them feel comfortable about giving you the correction you need.   ◦§

Greetings, Leave-takings
And Expressions of Appreciation

Leavetakings

You have learned at least one way to open and close conversations, but you will need to know other **appropriate greetings and leave-takings.** Learn the difference between the way friends greet each other, the way strangers greet, and the way casual acquaintances greet. The questions on page 37 will help you discover different greeting settings. Ask similar questions concerning leave-takings. Greetings and leave-takings often vary depending on how long since you last saw one another and how long before you expect to see one another again. They probably vary from formal to informal in relation to the setting. Maybe it would be OK for you to use an idiomatic informal closing with certain friends, something like "So long," "See you later," "I'll be seeing you," or "God bless you."

Since people are indispensable to your learning, you will want them to understand that **you sincerely appreciate the help they give you.**

Your statement of appreciation should **help people feel good about spending time with you.** Ideally, they will want to chat with you for a few minutes every day. Having a few people take you under their wing in this way will be immensely valuable to your language learning — so let them know you appreciate their time and help.

Develop a text with Kino that will show a variety of ways to express your appreciation to people. The following ideas would be helpful for someone learning English.

"Thanks, you've been a big help to me. I hope we'll soon meet again."

"Thank you so much for all your help. I really appreciate your taking time to listen to me."

"Thank you for correcting me."

"You have helped me a lot. Can I come and talk with you again sometime? Thank you."

Your Role as a Learner

You have learned a lot in a few days. Here is a fun cycle theme which can bolster your ego and confidence while continuing to **reinforce** you in your **learner's role.** Develop a text with Kino in which you explain that you have only been in the country a few days, and you are here to learn the language. Explain that you are not just a tourist.

Ask to be corrected if you say something incorrectly. You could tell the person what you have learned by saying something like: "So far I have learned to tell a little about myself . . . (say it). Stop me if I say something incorrectly. Also, I can ask some questions like . . . (ask them). So far this is all I can say. Each day I'm learning a little bit."

In addition to your text, learn the **simple things** that people say in conversation **to affirm what the speaker is saying** and allow the conversation to be extended. For example, in English a listener can say things like: "Yes." "Aha." "True." "It is?" "Oh." "Is it really?" "I see." He can also repeat what the speaker has just said: "Oh, you just came from Mombasa." Watch for the little phrases that other people say as they are listening.

Personal Questions

You may find that people tend to ask you a variety of questions about yourself. Questions like: Where do you live? What country did you come from? In what part of that country did you live? Where were you born? How long have you been in this country/town? What are you doing here? Are you married? Do you have children? What do you want? Where is your family? What is your name?

If you don't know what questions people are asking you, talk to Kino about it. He probably knows what kinds of questions people have been asking him about you, and what kinds of **questions people generally ask strangers.** (In your Communication time a day before working on this text, you might want to make a point of having people write down any question they ask which you don't understand, or of writing it down phonetically yourself.)

Develop a text in which you learn to ask and answer the questions which people most frequently ask.

Polite Phrases

You may find conversations with strangers less abrupt if you can open by **explaining that you are practicing the language.** For example: "Hello. Are you free? (Or — Do you have a few minutes to talk?) I'm learning to speak Kikamba. I'd like to practice talking Kikamba with you."

Describe various common settings to Kino and have him tell you the appropriate **polite expressions** which you should use in these settings. For example, how do you announce your presence if a door is open — Do you call? Knock? Cough? What should you say if you commit some social blunder? How do you politely excuse yourself after having talked with someone for a while?

You may need a few more polite **ways to talk about language.** "Please say it again and then I'll repeat it after you." "How do you pronounce _____?" "I didn't understand what you just said because I only know a little _____. Maybe in a few days I will understand you better." (People often assume that you know more than you do, so you need to remind them of your limitations.)

Transitional phrases help you gracefully steer the conversation around so that you can **discuss the topics you are learning.** Some English examples of this type of phrases are: "By the way, today I learned . . ." "Say, did you know that . . .?"

Steer it around

Role-play these settings with Kino when eliciting the text, so that he will more easily think of the natural expressions.

Responding to a Welcome _____

If you have occasion to be welcomed by a church or other group, you will want to work with Kino on developing a short text which would **appropriately respond to the welcome.** You might want to include a brief expression of appreciation for the welcome, as well as a brief statement about the fact that you are learning the language but don't know very much yet. You might be able to make some simple changes in the text which you told about yourself ("*Wednesday*" page 56) in order to make it fit a public speech.

Classification, Affirmation, and Denial _____

In English, parts of speech fall into categories like noun, verb, adjective, adverb, etc. These parts of speech don't necessarily work in other languages. It is more helpful to think in terms of the following *classes of words: objects* (basically nouns in English), *people* (nouns), *activities* (usually verbs in English), *qualities* (usually adverbs and adjectives in English), *time words, space words,* and "*other*" (generally words showing relationships, and grammatical markers). When exploring the meaning of a new word it is helpful to **first determine which of these classes the word belongs to.**

Work with Kino in developing questions like the following to help you begin to classify new words you hear in communication.

"Is X (the new word) a thing?"
"Is X an animal?"
"Is X a kind of person?"
"Is X something that people do?"
"Is X a place?"
"Is X a time word?"
"Does X describe something?"

"Is X a kind of person?"

Today you can also learn the **little "tag" questions for simple yes/no answers about statements.** This type of question can give you a lot of practice in the language. When someone makes a positive or negative statement about one object you can use one of these tag questions to talk about another object.

He: These are beans.
You: These are beans, too, aren't they?

_____

He: This is not a banana.
You: This is not a banana,is it? (Indicating a different object)

_____

He: That man is a policeman.
You: That man is not a policeman, is he?
        (Indicating a different man)

Exploring Objects

What kind of thing
is an X

Once you have found out that an unknown word is the name of an object, there are some other kinds of questions you can ask to understand the meaning more fully.

The first set of questions help you **further classify the object** and **find the names of other similar objects.**

A. What kind of thing is X?
    (Example: What kind of thing is an apple?)
B. It is a fruit.
A. What other kinds of fruits are there? (Or: What are the names of some other kinds of fruits?)
    B. There are pears, oranges, grapefruits,. . .
A. What kinds of apples are there?
    B. There are Golden delicious, Roman beauty, and others.

Another pair of questions can help you **find out about part/ whole relationships**.

A. X is part of what? (Or: What kind of thing does X belong to?)
    (Example: What kind of thing does a "ceiling" belong to?)
    B. It is part of a building.
A. What are some other parts of a building?
    B. Floor, walls, windows, doors, . . .

The third type of question relates to **ownership**.

A. Whose book is it?
B. It is John's book.

The fourth type of question gets the name for a **group** of objects when they are lumped together.

A. What is a group of _____ called?

English examples:

Fish	School
Lions	Pride
People	Crowd
Angry People	Mob
Cows	Herd
Sheep	Flock
Trees	Forest

(In English, group-names apply mostly to living things)

NOTE: Often a word is paired with another in people's minds. Fill in the following English pairs yourself: shoes & _____
paper   & _____   **knife   &** _____   **love   &** _____
cup   & _____   **bread   &** _____   **horse   &** _____
Maybe you can make a game with Kino or another friend to find pairs of words in your new language.

Descriptions ———

You can begin asking questions which will help you learn to **describe objects and events in terms of qualities and quantities.** Some of the **quantity questions** that might be relevant to learn to ask **about objects** relate to number, cost and age.

> How many puppies do you have?
> How old is this puppy?
> How much does this puppy cost?

"How much is that doggie in the window?"

NOTE: English has what are called "count" nouns (bananas, cars, dogs) and "mass" nouns (milk, bread, money). So in English we have two kinds of quantity questions — How much? How many? For example: "How much bread do you have?" but "How many loaves of bread do you have?" If you were learning English, as you learned a new object word you might want to learn to ask whether "much" or "many" goes with it — "Should I say, 'How much bread' or 'How many breads'?" "Should I say, 'How much dog' or 'How many dogs'?"

As you learn the language you may not find a difference between "mass" nouns and "count" nouns, but you probably will find that certain object words have to be treated differently from other object words. Accept that fact, and learn how to use the words correctly.

You can learn to ask questions to help you **describe objects in terms of qualities** such as color, size, and other qualities Kino feels are important.

> What color is your puppy?
> How big is the puppy?
> What sound does it make?
> What sex it it?

> What does an apple smell like?
> What does an apple taste like?
> What is its shape?
> What does it feel like? (Rough, smooth, sticky?)

You can learn to ask for a description of an **event** in terms of its **quantity:**

> "How many times did you go to the city?"
> "How often do you go to the city?"

You can also ask for a description of an **event** in terms of a **quality:**

> "How is John walking?" (Answer — "John is walking very slowly.")

Shopping ———

Explain to Kino that you want to be able to **buy things.** Work

with him in developing an appropriate text for greeting a seller, discussing price, purchasing the item, and taking your leave. You may need to be specific about whether you are buying food in an open market, or clothing in a store, as there may be different shopping methods. Find out from Kino whether there are some places where **bargaining** is expected and other places where it is not done. Are there some types of objects for which you should bargain and others which have fixed prices? If bargaining is expected, how do you go about it? It is appropriate to handle objects before you purchase them? How about food items?

For communication, plan to buy a small quantity of items repeatedly for extra practice. As a matter of fact, it is a good idea from now on to buy in small quantities — Why buy a dozen bars of soap at one time when you can get much more practice and involvement by buying the bars of soap one at a time? *Be creative* in finding ways to stretch your involvement.

Restaurant

A simple meal

Get a text which will let you **order a simple meal in a restaurant** or other eating place. How do you get the attention of the waiter or person selling the food? How do you greet him? Is there a polite request form to use when ordering the meal? If various people are together, does one person order for all, or does each person order his own meal? Do you leave a tip? How much? Do you thank the waiter after the meal if you enjoyed the food? How do you ask for the bill? If you are with a group of people, does each person pay his own bill; does one person pay and then all settle with him; or does one person usually pay for everyone?

Arithmetic

Your text can include practice in the **basic math functions** — addition, subtraction, multiplication, division. You need practice in doing mental arithmetic without resorting to English.

There are various ways to use this text:

Shopping.

Maybe you could get a shopkeeper friend to let you add up and announce prices to the customers for a few minutes. (Be careful to be accurate, and don't overstay your welcome.)

You could engage some school-age children in numbers games, or in practicing the times-tables.

Questions about People ――――――
And Introductions

Develop a text in which you can ask appropriate **questions about people.** Questions like:

Who is he?
What is his name?
What does he do?
What kind of _____ (doctor, farmer, seller) is he?
What is he like?
How old is he?
Whose son is he?

What does he do?

Since most of these questions will probably be similar to other questions you already know, today you may also want to learn **how to introduce people** to each other. Have Kino help you develop a text which you can use to introduce one friend to another. When you check the suitability, find out if you would say it differently if you were introducing your friend to a small group of friends in an informal setting. There may also be different styles of introduction depending on the relative age, sex or status of the people involved.

In a later cycle you may want to learn the proper form for a formal introduction of a speaker or other participant at a meeting. ◆ら

Exploring Space and Time ――――――
By Getting Directions

Have you wished you could ask for directions? Being able to **find your way around** is essential, especially with the emphasis we place on involvement. Elicit and practice a text which will help you get directions.

Describe your objective to Kino, and have him help you develop a text which is expressed in a way that is natural in your new language. Place the setting somewhere downtown and choose a destination which would require a couple changes of direction. A sample text might go as follows:

A. (Greeting) — "Excuse me."
　B. (Response)
A. "Where is the Post Office?"
　B. "Go to the next corner and turn right."
A. "How far is it?"
　B. "After you go three blocks, the post office will be on your left, just after the bridge."
A. "When does it close?"
　B. "It closes at four o'clock."
A. "What time is it now?"
　B. "It is now 3:45."

When does
the wrist watch strap shop
shut?

A. "How long does it take to walk there?"
B. "It takes about five minutes."
A. "Thank you very much. Good-bye."

NOTE: Here are some Comprehension exercises to help you practice materials relating to this topic, and to reinforce it kinesically.

On a map of the community, identify some of the major places, such as: city hall, post office, cathedral, central mosque, plaza, cemetery, clinic, etc. Have Kino direct you from one spot on the map to any other spot. As he gives the directions in his language, you trace the route on the map with your finger. Continue doing this until you easily respond to directions like "Turn left," "Turn right," "Walk straight ahead for five blocks," etc. (You may not be able to respond yet to the finer points like, "Turn through the first alley on the other side of the cemetery," etc.) (See also the Comprehension Drills on page 230.)

If you find that the map is too abstract for your helper, you can set up a miniature village in your living room or yard, using chairs and other furniture as the main points of the town. Have Kino give directions for you to follow as you walk around this "village."

Another option would be to take time out and have Kino direct you on a short walk to the corner store or restaurant (where you can reward your hard labors by buying cokes or coffee for both of you). This exercise is similar to what you will be doing in Communication, except that now Kino is with you to direct you and give immediate reinforcement.

An abstract map

In Communication, go out and ask people for directions. Of course, you know where the Post Office is — *ask people anyway!* When you ask a passerby for directions, try to understand his response. Then move in the indicated direction until he is out of earshot, and ask someone else. Later, go to another location so the response will be varied. But ask as many people as possible in each general location. Today's text is a natural for initiating conversations with strangers. You should be able to talk with more people today than previously.

You may find that some people will take you where you want to go, instead of just directing you. That's OK; chat with them on the way, using your previous texts. If you ask people to give directions for places that are in the opposite direction from the way they are going, then they are less apt to walk with you. Either way is OK — you are *involved* and *communicating in the language.*

Exploring Space and Time
With Public Transportation

You have already learned how to use public transportation. Expand that text with questions like the following:

A. "Where is this bus going?"
B. "It is going to Ngong Road."

A. "Where does the Wabera Street bus stop?"
B. "It stops here, too."
A. "Did the Wabera Street bus leave yet?"
B. "No, it hasn't."
A. "When does the bus leave?"
B. "It should leave soon."
A. "How often does a bus go to Wabera Street?"
B. "About every twenty minutes."
A. "How much does it cost to go to Wabera Street?"
B. "It costs ten pesewas."
A. "Is this the Wabera Street bus now?"
B. "Yes, it is."

(Although this text is fairly long, various of the question patterns are closely related to those of the previous text, so you shouldn't have trouble learning them all.)

After you practice the text, go out and do it!

Exploring Activities ———

There are many questions you should learn to ask about **activities.** Learn to ask for general information (What is he doing?), as well as asking for more specific information such as — **who benefits** from the activity, **with what instrument** the activity is performed, **where** is the activity done, **who** receives the item, what the **goal** of the activity is, and who are the **co-actors.** Here are some examples of how these questions could be asked in English.

Activity performed
with an instrument

NOTE: Certain words are in italics in the examples on this page and on the following pages to make clear to you the kind of information that is being sought. Do *not* expect that this kind of information will result from translations of these words or from the use of equivalent sentence patterns in the language. Be careful to elicit a natural local expression for seeking this information by carefully establishing the settings with Kino. We cannot emphasize this too strongly.

A. *"What* is he doing?"   (General Information)
B. "John is cutting down bananas."
A. *"Who* is he cutting the bananas *for*?"   (Beneficiary)
B. "He is cutting the bananas for his children."
A. *"What* is he cutting them *with*?"   (Instrument)
B. "He is cutting them with a knife."
A. *"Where* is he cutting the bananas?"   (Location)
B. "He is cutting them in the back yard."
A. *"What* did he give *to* the girl?"   (Object Transferred)
B. "John gave her a banana."
A. *"Who* did John give the knife *to*?"   (Recipient)
B. "He gave it to Jim."

A. *"What* did you see Susan doing?" (General Information)

   B. "I saw her walking."

A. *"Where* was Susan walking *to*?"   (Goal)

   B. "She was walking to the store."

A. *"Who* was she walking *with*?"   (Co-actor)

   B. "She was walking with Mary."

For part of your Communication time you might want to take a walk with Kino or another friend from the community and use the questions you learned today to ask about every activity you see happening.   ◦§

Co-actors

Exploring Activities
In Space and Time

Here are some questions you can learn to ask as you explore the **relationship between activities and their setting** in *space* and *time*.

A. "Did you go to the store *yet*?"

   B. "Yes, I did."

A. "Did you go very *long ago*?"

   B. "No, I just went a little while ago."

A. *"When* are you going *again*?"

   B. "I'll be going later this evening."

A. *"Where* is Mary?"

   B. "I think she is at her mother's house."

A. *"When did* Mary leave?"

   B. "She left the 23rd."

A. "Oh, *what date* is today?"

   B. Today is the 30th."

A. "She has been gone nearly a week. *When will* she return?"

   B. "She plans to return the 3rd of next month."   ◦§

Exploring the Circumstances
Of Activities

Learn to ask questions about the circumstances relating to activities — **When** they happened, **why,** for what **purpose, how,** etc. In English, these questions could be expressed in the following ways.

A. *"When* is Bill coming?"   (Time)

   B. "He is coming tomorrow morning."

A. *"Why* is he coming?"   (Reason)

   B. "He's coming because his boss sent him."

A. *"Why isn't* James coming with him?"   (Negative

   B. "Because James has too much work to do." Reason)

Exploring
the circumstances

A. *"What* is Bill coming *for?"*   (Purpose)
   B. "He's coming to buy some equipment."
A. *"How* is he coming?"   (Means)
   B. "He is coming by train."
A. "Will Bill come *even if* it is snowing?"   (Concession)
   B. "Yes, he has to come even if it snows."   ◄§

Descriptions and Expansions _____

Develop a text with Kino in which you ask people to **describe objects and people.** From their answers you can learn much about the categories of descriptions which are relevant to them.

Also work with Kino to learn how to **repeat** what people have said **by slightly expanding** it. You can probably do this by adding emphasis words or descriptive words.

So, if someone makes a simple statement about an object or an activity, you can expand the sentence by repeating with an added **descriptive** word:

   B. "That is a Volkswagen."
A. "That is a new Volkswagen."
   B. "The baby is walking."
A. "The baby is walking cautiously."

If someone makes a descriptive statement, you can expand the sentence by repeating it with an added **emphasis** word:

   B. "That's a nice car."
A. "Yes, that's a very nice car."
   B. "That man is walking slowly."
A. "That man is walking quite slowly."   ◄§

Telephones _____

If there is telephone service in your area, develop a text to help you use the telephone. When obtaining the text and checking its suitability, you might ask Kino some of these questions. What do you say when you answer the phone? How do you speak when you are calling someone else? How do you identify yourself? How do you ask a person to give a message to someone else? How are the greetings of business calls different from those of social calls? How can you ask the operator for information or for help in making a call? Are there times when it is not proper to call? How do you use a public telephone?

Your communication time today can be done by telephone. Practice by making a variety of calls — social calls, business calls, calls for information. You can even ask some friends to call you back to give you practice in receiving calls. This is *a good rainy day text.* ◄§

Set 2 – Topics

For Further Exploration
In the Language

The topics of Set 2 will give you the means of broadening your vocabulary, and learning to alter your language styles and to express your emotions. These topics can be completed in about 4 to 7 weeks of full-time language learning.

Get and Give Instructions

Date

The setting: You want to be able to **ask someone to give you instructions** on how to do something — make a dress, fix a car, cook a local dish, etc. Your request could be something like: "Please show me how to do that." You also want to know how to **give instructions** if someone else asks you.

Requests

Work out with Kino a text that includes patterns for a polite **request for positive action** and its corresponding polite positive response (B1), and polite refusal (B2). Also get a polite **request to not act,** along with a polite agreement not to act (B1), and a polite disagreement (B2). For example:

A. "Please pass the bread."
   B1. "Gladly. Here it is."
           or
   B2. "I'm sorry, the bread is all gone."

A. "Please don't open the window. I'm chilly."
   B1. "OK. I won't open it."

           or
   B2. "I'm sorry, but I must. Mother told me to air out the room."

The comparative status, age, sex, or acquaintance between speaker and listener is often very important. In many languages the request form will vary with certain of these relationships. You may want to spend a couple of cycles on variations of request — housewife to help, adult to child, buyer to shopkeeper, stranger to stranger, friend to friend, male to female, etc.

Another variation of style occurs when one person talks to a **group,** either formally or informally.

Formal: A. "Let us sing."
       B1. "Yes, let us sing."
           or
       B2. "Excuse me sir, but we don't have any song books."

Let us sing

Informal: A. "Let's go buy a coke."
       B1. "Yes, let's!"
           or
       B2. "Sorry, I can't. I don't have any money."

       A. "Let's not eat spaghetti today."
       B1. "OK. Let's eat pizza instead."
           or
       B2. "I think we should eat spaghetti. It's cheap."

Comprehension Instructions _____

Develop a text in which you **give instructions to people so they can direct you in brief comprehension drills.** Explain to them that you need much repetition in order to learn their language correctly. Tell them you only want to learn to respond to the sentences today and that later you will learn to say them.

Children, especially, will enjoy directing you in comprehension activities. They can make it a group activity in which each one takes turns telling the group (and you) what to do. Encourage them to keep it repetitious enough for you.

Vocabulary Building _____

This vocabulary building section consists of topics designed to help you explore the meanings of words by means of questions which you can ask people in the community. A week or two of cycles will help you master these questions. They will add an entirely new dimension to your vocabulary acquisition.

When exploring the meaning of words, the first step is to determine what type of word it is. You have already learned questions that help you classify words (page 141). Four major classifications of words are the names of *Objects, People, Activities,* and *Qualities.* Within each of these classifications your understanding of the meaning of a word can advance on three different fronts: (a) it can be *Described;* (b) *Differentiated;* and (c) *Expanded.* You need *questions* to help you probe on each of the fronts within each of the four classifications. The following matrix illustrates the relationships.

Fronts of Meaning Exploration:

Classes of words:	a. *Describe*	b. *Differentiate*	c. *Expand*
1. *Objects*	1a	1b	1c
2. *People*	2a	2b	2c
3. *Activities*	3a	3b	3c
4. *Qualities*	4a	4b	4c

The questions presented in the following topics can be used to help you understand almost any kind of word throughout your language learning, regardless of where you encounter it.

1. Objects and Animals

Date

Work with Kino in developing questions like the following to begin exploring vocabulary about objects (things). Once you have learned today's questions, go out into the community and begin using them to explore words for objects — words like rug, lantern, folder, apple, soil, lake, jug, zebra, aardvark, etc.

1a. DESCRIBING AND DEFINING. Here are some questions to help you **describe and define objects.** (Put the object word in place of X in each of the questions.)

What other objects is X like?
What objects is X opposite to?
What does X look like?
What are some other characteristics of X?
What do people do with X?
What is the purpose of X?
Who uses X?
When is X used?
Are there different kinds of X?
What is X made of?
Who makes X?

Exploring objects

(All of the above questions, except the last two can be used to ask about animals. In addition you can ask: What does X do?)

1b. DIFFERENTIATING. Learn questions to help you **differentiate** two similar object or animal words. Base your questions on some of the descriptions you have just learned.

> An X is similar to a Y, isn't it?
> Does an X have _____? Does a Y also have _____?
> Is an X made of _____? Is a Y also made of _____?
> Does an X do _____? Does a Y also do _____?
> Where do you see X? Where do you see Y?

An example of the differentiation questions in English might be:

> A tiger is similar to a lion, isn't it?
> Does a tiger have stripes? Does a lion also have stripes?
> Does a tiger hunt at night? Does a lion also hunt at night?
> Where do you see tigers? Where do you see lions?

1c. EXPANDING. Here are some questions to help you **expand** your understanding of the word:

> Can you tell me more about X?
> When you hear the word "X", what other words do you think of?

You now have a battery of questions to ask in exploring the meaning of words for objects. The questions do not necessarily need to be used in this order. Rather, you have a repertoire from which to draw the questions that would be most relevant in any given situation. At the end of this section on vocabulary (page 156) are some examples of vocabulary exploration using these kinds of questions.

A totem pole is similar to a telephone pole, isn't it?

2. People _____
Date

Have Kino help you develop questions you can use in **exploring names for categories of people** — names like senator, housewife, man, sister, blue-collar worker, Indian, blond, gentleman, teen-ager, friend.

2a. QUESTIONS TO DESCRIBE AND DEFINE:
> What kind of work does X do?
> What is X's position in the group?
> What is X's relationship to the others?
> What are X's responsibilities?
> What is X like?
> What other types of people is X like?
> What are some of the characteristics of X?
> Are there different kinds of X?

What kind of work does he do?

2b. QUESTIONS TO DIFFERENTIATE:

Does X do _____? Does Y also do _____?

Does X have _____? Does Y also have _____?

Is X _____? Is Y also _____?

(Example: Is a "teen-ager" young? Is a "guy" also young?)

Where does X work? Where does Y work?

2c. QUESTIONS TO EXPAND YOUR UNDERSTANDING:

What more can you tell me about X?

When you hear the word "X", what other words do you think of?

NOTE: Among labels for categories of people you might find sets of words which relate to men and women in general — words like: woman, lady, gal, girl, female, doll, ma'am, miss, Mrs., Ms., chick; and man, gentleman, guy, sir, boy, male, youth, Mr., buddy. Explore these carefully. When is each one used? When is it inappropriate to use certain of these? What are the connotations of each? Are some more casual or slangy? Are some technical, or formal? Which ones can be used when talking *to* the person? Which ones should be used when talking *about* the person? Which ones can be used with friends? Which ones with strangers? Maybe you can role-play various settings with Kino to get a feel for the appropriate use of the words.

---

3. Events and activities

_____
Date

Have Kino help you develop and learn **questions to explore activity words** such as: eat, smile, crow, climb, surface, walk, sleep, cry, view, smell, hit, make, shoot, give, kiss, repel.

3a. DEFINING AND DESCRIBING:

Who Xs? What Xs?

To whom (what) is X done?

For whom is X done?

Where do people X?

When do people (things)X?

Why do people X?

How do people X?

How often do people X?

How long do people X?

What do people X with?

Who do people X with?

A. "What do people travel with?"

B. "Too much!"

3b. DIFFERENTIATING:

Where can you X? Where can you Y?

Where can you X but not Y?

Who Xs but does not Y?

When do people X but not Y?

3c. EXPANDING YOUR UNDERSTANDING:

Who else does X?
Where else is X done?
When else is X done?
Tell me more about X-ing.
When you hear the word "X", what else do you think of ?
(You may sometimes find it helpful to ask this last question
earlier, before you clutter up his mind with your ideas of X.)

Here are some additional questions you should learn to ask
which can expand your understanding of event words:

What causes X to happen?
What else is done at the same time as X?
What happens after you X?
What happens if you don't X?
What is another way to talk about X-ing?
What is the opposite of X-ing?

4. Descriptions and Qualities _____
Date

Some qualities relate to objects: red, old, sweet, smooth, sharp,
big, conscientious, colorful, repetitious, electric. Others relate more to
events: quickly, sadly, crazily, smoothly, crookedly, passionately,
clumsily, expertly. Adapt your questions to objects or events. (Replace
X with the *quality* word in each of these questions.)

4a. DEFINING AND DESCRIBING:

What things are X?
What are some other things that have X quality?
When are things X?
How do things (people) become X?
What is the opposite of X?
What events can be done X-ly?
How do people act when they are X?
Describe to me what a person does when he _____s X-ly.
   (Example: Describe to me what a person does when
   he runs crazily.)
How long can you _____ X-ly?
   (Example: How long can you run quickly?)

4b. DIFFERENTIATING:

What is X but not Y?
   (Example: What is "sharp" but not "dangerous?" — "Ched-
   dar cheese.")
What is Y but not X?
   (Example: What is "dangerous" but not "sharp?" — "A
   tank.")
When can you be X but not Y?
What can you do X-ly but not Y-ly?
   (Example: What can you do "softly" but not "quietly?")

Sharp and dangerous!

4c. EXPANDING YOUR UNDERSTANDING:

What else is X?

What else is Y?

Tell me more about an X thing.

Tell me more about doing something X-ly.

When you hear the word "X", what else do you think about?

Following are some examples of vocabulary exploration using this type of question.

If you were learning English and wanted to learn about apples, here is how an interchange might proceed.

What kind of thing is an *"apple"*?

It is a fruit.

What does an *apple* look like?

Oh, it's round, and about this size and usually red when it is ripe.

What are *apples* used for?

For food.

Who eats *apples*?"

Anybody, even horses like apples.

How do you eat *apples*?"

You can eat them raw, or you can make them into apple pie or applesauce.

I like sliced apples

What is your favorite way to eat *apples*?

Apple pie with cheese.

When do you eat *apples*?

Whenever you want — for snacks or salad or dessert. We even have a saying — an apple a day keeps the doctor away.

Are there different kinds of *apples*?

Yes.

What are some of the kinds?

Oh, there are Delicious, and Rome, and others — there are also crab apples.

How do you tell the kinds apart?

Mostly by color and shape I guess, also by their size and texture.

Can you tell the difference by the taste of the *apples*?

Some people can.

What are some of the characteristics to look for when buying *apples*?

Depends on whether you want to eat them raw or use them for cooking. The main thing is to be sure they don't have bad spots.

What are some other common fruits besides *apples*?

Pears, peaches, oranges, cherries.

Here is another sample interchange referring to an object you are probably not familiar with:

What is this?
>It is a tinaja (pronounced tee-ná-ha).

What kind of thing is a *tinaja*?
>It is a water carrier.

What is a *tinaja* used for?
>Women use it to carry water on their heads from the spring, and also to store water in the house.

Are *tinajas* used only by women?
>Yes.

How often do they have to carry water in a *tinaja*?
>Whenever they run out. Usually a couple times a day.

What is a *tinaja* made of?
>Baked clay.

How is a *tinaja* made?
>Some people on the other side of the village make them. They shape the clay by hand and then bake it in a special oven.

Are there different kinds of *tinajas*?
>Not really — just different sizes. The smaller ones are for carrying water and the larger ones are for storing water.

What are some things to look for when buying a *tinaja*?
>If you are going to use it for carrying water, get one that is small enough for you to carry when it is full of water.

What are some other kinds of water carriers besides a *tinaja*?
>The other kind is used by men. These are large square cans tied to a rope at each end of a long pole. The man balances the pole across his shoulders.

Do women ever use these cans to carry water?
>No!

Tinaja

A male water carrier

Notice how the name of the object is repeated in the questions. This gives you practice in saying the word, and helps impress it on your mind.

In a small Middle East village, the authors established a friendship with an Arabic-speaking shopkeeper. One day we asked him some questions about an object in his shop. The following are some notes we made from that conversation.

What is that?
>It is a khorj.

What kind of thing is a *khorj*?
>It is something people use to put things in when they ride on a camel. If you were going to take a camel trip of about seven days, you could put a *gerba* (camel-skin water jug),

A camel trip

some food, and some tea in it for your journey. You only have to take along enough water for yourself because the camel can go seven days without water. We call him the "desert ship."

How would you describe a *khorj*?

It is two bags connected to each other by a wide band or strap (like large saddlebags).

What is a *khorj* made out of?

It is made out of sheep's wool, which they paint (dye) and the Bedouin women then make it by hand. This one has a cross-strap made of camel's hair with bands of goat's hair on each side, and the bags are made of sheep's wool.

How can you tell the difference between a wool *khorj* and a camel's hair *khorj*?

The camel's hair is the strongest and softest. Camel's hair is more expensive. You can only clip a camel about once every five years and you only get a little bit of wool from it — a few handfuls. Also, we don't dye the camel's wool, because of religious reasons, so the camel's hair cloth is usually brown or black or tan. Camel's hair cloth lasts a longer time and is much warmer than sheep's wool. It's more expensive, too. For example, that Bedouin wool cloak you saw the other day — if it were made of camel's hair it would cost three times more.

When is the *khorj* used?

Whenever you want to carry something when you ride on your camel. Let me tell you a story about how it used to be in the old days. Let's say that you, Tomas, liked Betty, and let's say that I am her father. You come to me and ask me for her, but I say, "No." You like her, so you go to her and say "Meet me on that hill tonight." At night you go with your camel and put her behind you on the camel and take her to another Bedouin sheik. If you are a good man and really love her, you don't touch her or kiss her on the trip. You tell the sheik what has happened and then he would come to see me. He would tell me, her father, that you had brought Betty unharmed to his place, and that if I didn't accept you as my daughter's husband, there would be trouble between his tribe and mine. If I am rich and he is important I won't even ask you to pay any money — I just agree to let you come back and apologize. That is how it used to be.

"He would come to see me."

How is the *khorj* used?

It is put on the camel over the *shdad*. The *shdad* is the wooden saddle frame. Under the *shdad* they tie two pieces of cloth full of cotton.

Are there different kinds of *khorj*?

There are big ones like this for camels, and smaller ones for horses.

How is the *khorj* made?

The Bedouin women do the weaving. They put two long poles in the ground and tie a stick across the bottom. They measure how long it needs to be and then tie a stick across the other end. This becomes the loom. The women work together. Different friends might come each day and compete to do more than the others. Unmarried girls work especially hard, to develop a good reputation as workers. When there are other women helping in the tent, the husband doesn't come in; he goes to eat with other men. When the women are weaving the strips of *beyt* for a tent, they weave goat hair very tightly. It is so tight that water can't go through. On a new one, a little water might go through the first time it rains, but none after that. Because it is woven so tightly, it is too hot to use in the summertime so they roll it up and use cotton for the summer tent. The *beyt* strips last at least seven years, but each year the wife makes a new strip about a couple meters wide, to replace the oldest strip. By replacing one strip a year, she doesn't have to weave a complete tent every seventh year. If a man has many sons, the tent must be very big, since his married sons often live with him. In this case the mother has help with the housework and weaving. She assigns specific tasks to each of the daughters-in-law.

How long would it take to make a *khorj* — a day or so?

You must be thinking of machines — it takes more than one month to make one! First, she has to take two boards with nails in them and do like this to card the wool. Then she has to take it and leave it at the place where they dye the wool — it may take about a week. She spins the thread from wool and then puts it into water to soak for seven days. She washes it well so it smells nice. After it has soaked she spins the thread again to make a tighter twist. Then she can begin to weave the cloth. There is good help between the Bedouin women, and they often make things at the same time. If Betty is making a *khorj,* Miriam might ask her how much wool for each color she is using, and make a *khorj* at the same time.

What characteristics do you look for when you buy a *khorj*?

Make sure there is no cotton in it. Cotton only lasts two or three years. Goat or sheep wool will last ten years.

It is interesting to note:

— His use of stories and personalized forms — for example, naming the fictitious neighbor woman, Miriam.

— His spontaneous remarks touched on various themes. These yield topics which could be noted for further exploration — reconciliation through mediators, family relationships, relationships with neighbors, roles of men and women, use of domestic animals, standards of morality, etc.

— Questions did not always yield the information which the questioner had in mind. Nevertheless, much useful information was gained.

—New vocabulary items were used which could be explored — words such as *shdad* and *gerba*.   ◄§

Queueing up

Small Talk
<u>   </u>
_{Date}

The setting could be riding on a bus, sitting in an office waiting room, standing around waiting for the plane to come, or standing in line at the Post Office. Find out what **topics** are **appropriate for strangers to talk about** when making small-talk. Can you talk about the weather, family, sports, recent news, politics . . .? When is it appropriate to talk? When is it best not to talk?

Learn a small-talk text which would be appropriate for a common situation you experience.   ◄§

Appointments

Learn how to **make business appointments.** How do you ask for an appointment? At what time should you arrive? Where are business appointments usually kept — at home, office, cafe? If you can't keep the appointment, how do you change it?

How are friendly appointments made? Do friends ask each other over for dinner at specific times? At what time should you arrive? Should you bring a gift for the hostess? If you are the hostess, when should you expect your guests? Are friendly appointments often made to meet somewhere other than the home — in a cafe or restaurant? What formalities are involved?

In Communication time, you might want to make one or two appointments, as well as talk with people about their experiences in making, keeping, and breaking appointments.   ◄§

Giving Directions

You have learned to follow directions. If you have not already done so, learn the **appropriate way to give directions.** Since people may think you are a stranger, few people may ask you for directions. If so, you will have to be creative in introducing this text to people. Maybe you could use it as if you were looking for confirmation:

"I'm going to the Post Office. To get there you have to go down this street and turn left. Is that right? The Post Office will be on the right just after turning the corner. Right?"

Or you could use it as though reporting on what you've done:
"Say, you know what? I've just learned how to go to the Post Office. You go down this street and turn left. The Post Office is on the right just after you turn the corner." 🖐

"The PO is on the right."

Personal Interchanges _____

The setting and the relationships between the participants will affect what is said and the way it is expressed.

Settings can vary from informal (a chat on the street) **to very formal** (a speech at a large gathering). Slang and chatter that are appropriate in the first setting may be quite inappropriate in the more formal setting. And, conversely, the formal tone of voice, the technical vocabulary, and the more stylized mannerisms that are appropriate in the formal setting may be out of place or even offensive if used with close friends in a casual setting.

The **relationship between the people speaking** is also important. Learn what the appropriate differences are — age? sex? social standing? education? occupation? family ties? economic standing? degree of acquaintanceship? For example, in Javanese, relationships are based on age, social standing, and family ties. There, a different style of language and different vocabulary are used depending on whether you are talking to your peer, to someone of a higher social standing, or to someone of a lower social standing.

Look back over your previous texts which involve interchanges, and find out what changes you should make depending on the setting and your relationship to the other person.

If the changes are very complex you may wish to spend more than one cycle on this topic. You might spend one cycle looking at the changes that depend on the setting, and another cycle or two working on the changes that depend on the relationship between the participants. 🖐

Your Host Country _____

Have Kino help you develop a short text in which you **talk about your host country.** Tell people that you have found life pleasant in their country and have made friendships. Tell them what you like best about their country.

Learn to use this both as a conversational text and as a more formal short speech you could give to a group of people at a meeting. 🖐

I found life pleasant here.

Advice

Getting informal advice from friends ("Ingrid, which color tie goes best with this suit?") is probably different from getting advice from professionals ("Dr. Gomez, my child has a stomach ache, what should I do?"); it may also be different from getting advice from strangers ("Excuse me, sir, which train should I take in order to arrive in Paris before 3 p.m.?"). Base a couple cycles on **how to get (and give) advice from different categories of people.**   ✍

Sharing Interesting Experiences

Develop a text in which you **tell a short story about an interesting experience** which has happened to you since you arrived in the country. Use it in conversing with a number of people. Learn to modify it so that it can serve as a short speech before a group of people.

Also, **ask other people to tell an interesting event from their own life.** The event they choose to tell will give you valuable information about their interests. Since this is an open-ended question, the response will be a challenge to your comprehension. Try to tape some of the experiences. Transcribe them and study story-telling techniques. Learn how to adopt some of these techniques.   ✍

Telling Stories About Others

Develop texts in which you tell short stories about others. Learn to take a story that someone has told you about his own experiences, and you retell it to others as a story about a friend (a third person account). (Ask Kino if you should get the person's permission before telling the story to others.)

You should also learn to correctly restate a story to someone after he has told it to you. In retelling the story to the original teller, you will be using second person forms.

NOTE: When telling a story about yourself, the first person form is used: "*I* went to town." A story about a friend is said in a third person form: "*He* went to town." The second person form, "*You* went to town," is used in talking about the person to whom you are speaking.   ✍

A high-status picture of yourself

Telling about Your Plans and Goals

Develop a text in which you **describe your goals and plans** for being in their country. Use it conversationally and also learn how to modify it for use in a public speech. (Don't jeopardize your role as a learner by painting too "high status" a picture of yourself.)   ✍

Your Neighborhood ———

Spend a couple days with Kino discussing (in the language) your immediate neighborhood, and visiting some of your neighbors with him to get to know them better. (If Kino does not live in the neighborhood, perhaps a friend from the neighborhood can help you with this.)

As you learn about your neighbors, *develop a map* of the neighborhood on which you record the name of the family, the names of the members, and their relationship to one another (mother, aunt, friend). Jot down on the map any things of interest about the family or their house (for example: "This family recently moved here from the southern part of the country." "Kino says that the house is considered a landmark — it was built by one of the early city fathers." "The man of the house is the mayor's brother.").

#27 RAMÍREZ	#31 Ramírez	#39 Our house	#43 Ochoa	#55 Empty
José - father (shoemaker) Maria - Mother (Takes in laundry) Sra. Juana - maria's mother Josefina - daughter, 16 Carlos - Son, 10 Francisco - son, 8 (called "Panchito")	Joseito - Husband (shoemaker) (Son of family in #27) Celina - Wife (Expecting baby in October)		Ramón - Father (butcher) Angélica - Mother (sister of Luisa in #36) Amélia - Daughter, 6 Ramonsito - son, 4	

Texts during this time can be expansions of your texts from the past few days, or can build on topics you need to know in order to discuss the neighborhood more intelligently.

As you visit in the neighborhood, you may wish to *take snapshots* of the family groups. Plan to give a copy to the family, and to keep a copy for yourself on which to write the names of the people in order to learn their names better. ✍

Talking about a picture ———

Sometimes you can get a lot of information by having people talk about a photograph. It may not always be convenient to talk about activities while they are in progress, but a newspaper photo or one you take yourself might stimulate people to talk at length about some activity or current event.

Develop a text to ask people to tell you about a picture. Who is involved? What is the activity? What is the importance of the activity? How often is it done? Why are they doing it? ✍

Expressing Your Emotions

The following four text ideas relate to the expression of emotions. Emotions are expressed by words, rhythm, melodies, and volume of speech, as well as by non-verbal cues such as facial expressions, gestures, and posture. These verbal and non-verbal expressions differ from culture to culture.

1. Telling someone you feel good or happy _____
_{Date}

Learn the appropriate **ways to express your joy** to other people, and to communicate to them your good feelings. Learn also what kinds of responses to expect from people. How will some people express their sharing in your joy? How will some people show indifference? How will these expressions vary depending on their relationship to you in terms of age, sex, status, and familiarity?

2. Telling someone that you recognize he is happy _____
_{Date}

Happy

Learn how to recognize the signals that other people are happy or in a good mood — Do they smile a lot? Laugh? Whistle? Joke? Look solemn? When you recognize that someone is happy, how can you **express that you recognize his happiness**? How will he respond? Will some people pass it off — how?

3. Telling someone you feel sad or unwell _____
_{Date}

Learn the appropriate **ways to express your sadness** to other people — because you feel ill, or are tired, or lonely, or had a sad experience, etc. What kind of responses can you expect? How will some people express their sympathy? How will some people express their indifference? How will these expressions vary depending on their relationship to you in terms of age, sex, status, familiarity?

4. Telling someone he seems sad or unwell _____
_{Date}

Sad

Learn how to **recognize the signals** that other people are sad or unwell — Are they extra quiet? Do they sigh? Groan? Look sad? Frown? Shout? When you recognize that they are unhappy, how can you **express your sympathy**? How will he respond? Will he accept your sympathy? Will he pass it off — say he is OK?

Set 3 – Topics
For Exploring Cultural Themes

The people of your new language *know* a lot about many things. What information and what skills are common? The topics of Set 3 help you explore the culture of your new language. These topics will probably provide the full-time learner with 9 to 15 weeks of text material.

In Nigeria the anthropologist, Charles Kraft, was once walking down a forest trail with some friends when they heard a snake. Of course they jumped aside, and Kraft followed suit. A couple days later Kraft complimented them on what they knew. He mentioned that one member of that group hadn't heard that snake. "In fact," he confessed, "I *can't* hear snakes." "What!" they all exclaimed. "You can't hear a snake?!" Then the truth came out that all of his years of education didn't really help him know any of the real important things of jungle survival.

"I can't hear this snake!"

Average people in your new language also have significant information about a great variety of topics. Some of this important information is in areas for which you may not even have categories. Like the snake-hearing category, for example. To get at the vast store-house of cultural information, you must conscientiously continue to engage in conversation with new people about new things every day. Remember, too, that a most important part of conversation is listening. You will come to understand what people know by listening to them.

The topics of Set 3 cover categories familiar to you. Through discussion, find out what people know in these categories. (Each of the questions in Set 3 may represent areas of knowledge which you need to learn to share.) You will also discover other categories that you can pursue. Begin each learning cycle by learning from Kino the relevant questions and vocabulary for the day's theme. Then, in communication time, talk with many people on the topic. Be sure to establish friendly relationships with the people you talk with, and make certain your learner's role is evident. Don't

An uncomfortable spot

put people in uncomfortable spots, and don't become an impersonal interrogator.

Some cultures are quite complex while others are not as complex. The complex societies have a great deal of specialization and specialized knowledge, and they have a variety of subcultures which do not fully share each others' knowledge. The less complex societies are generally smaller, face-to-face societies where most people share the same activities, knowledge, and culture. In a complex society you will get a wider range of answers to your cultural questions than in a less complex society.

For comprehension practice, make tape recordings of Kino and others talking together on these topics. Record a variety of speakers and speaking styles — old people, children, men, women, laborers, professional people, educated, illiterate, country people, city people, people who speak distinctly, people who mumble, people whose dialect is different from the one you are learning. Get all the practice you can in hearing and understanding all types of speech. Listen repeatedly to the tapes and analyze them until you understand each one. You may want to transcribe some of these in order to compare the use of vocabulary, transitions, grammatical markers, and sentence styles in these different types of speech.

By the way, a bit of variety in your daily procedures can provide a refreshing and practical change. Maybe occasionally you can arrange to spend a complete day with someone in his normal daily activities. Try to arrange a day with a farmer and another with a store-keeper, for example.

Make a habit of relaxing with the people. Play marbles, or hike with the kids. Fish or chop firewood with the men. Gals could sew or make baskets with the ladies.

Most of the following text ideas are written in the form of questions which you can discuss with Kino as you prepare the text. Sometimes you may wish to prepare questions in your text, to ask people in the community. Other times you may wish to prepare a brief monologue or speech on the topic to use when talking with people in the community. Or you may wish to tell it as a short story. Occasionally you can talk about a topic as a comparison between this country and any other country you know of (beware of negative comparisons). In short, be creative. *Vary the style of your texts.*

The topics have, in general, been arranged with similar themes together. However, there is no need for you to learn them in the order they are given. Read all of Set 3, including the section at the end on *Categories,* then work on the topics as they meet needs you feel and interests you have at the time. With some topics, you may wish to follow the model given in the Category section to help you keep records of what you learn as you work with Kino and as you talk with people in the community.

Follow the model

Family Life

_____
Date

Is it polite to ask a person how many children he has? Or to ask a child how many brothers or sisters he has? What is the usual **family unit** — parents and children only, or does it include grandparents, uncles and aunts? What are the lines of authority? Do relatives usually try to live in the same neighborhood, or is there much mobility?

Who disciplines the children? What kind of **discipline** is common in the homes? What are the norms of discipline? Who takes care of the children most of the time?

By the way, who names a child? How are names chosen? What special meanings do names have? Are nicknames used? Which ones? How are they acquired?

Develop a text that will enable you to ask questions and discuss the topic of family life.

Homes

_____

Have Kino help you develop a text in which you discuss homes. Include the following topics: Use of space in the home. Different kinds of rooms. What changes in heating, ventilation, or covering are made to adapt to changes in temperature? Do homes have yards around them? How are they tended?

Homes

Who owns a home? How many people generally live in a home and what is their relationship to one another (i.e., parents, grandparents, etc.)?

Who is invited to the home? How often are people invited? At what times? Which rooms do guests enter?

You may want to describe a friend's home (one who is a member of the culture) and then **encourage people to describe their homes** if they would like.

NOTE: To close each of these topics with a repeated suggestion for you to develop a text would soon become redundant. It is, however, expected that each topic would serve as the theme for at least one Daily Learning Cycle text.

Meals

What meals are usually **eaten with the family**? How many times a day do people usually eat? What are common foods? How is the food served? What is the usual seating arrangement? Do people talk at meal times? What are expected table manners?

Who prepares the family meals? What foods are considered especially nutritious or healthy? What foods are less nutritious?What foods are essential for a good meal? Is variety a good thing? What foods are prepared for special occasions? What are your favorite foods?

What are some common beverages? How are they prepared? Are alcoholic beverages commonly consumed? Who drinks them? How often?

What do people **eat between meals**? Are there special times for between meal teas or snacks?

Do people often **eat away from home**? What is a favorite restaurant meal? Are there different kinds of public eating places? Are some of these used more at one time of day and others at other times? Which is your favorite restaurant or cafe?

Snack time

Sex-Related Roles

What **kinds of work** do males do in and around the house? What are considered women's duties? When there are things to be carried, who is expected to carry them? What work is considered improper for a woman? For a man?

What **courtesies** should men show to women? Women to men? Who opens the door? Who stands to let the other sit?

How does relative **age** affect the relationship between men and women? Would a man act the same toward an older woman as he would toward a woman much younger than he? How would a woman treat a man much older than she?

What **activities** do men engage in with other men? What do women do with other women? Do unrelated men and women ever spend time together as friends or in discussions? What recreation do men and boys participate in? What about women and girls?

What does it mean to be a man in the society? What does it mean to be a woman in this society? Who has more **influence** in the home? In commerce? In the community? What do women own? What things do men own?

How are dress, decoration, ornaments, and cosmetics used to differentiate the sexes?

A woman's role

Qualities _____

What are some of the qualities of a good person?

What qualities are **desirable** in a man? In a woman? In a community leader? In a friend? In a religious leader? In a teacher?

What qualities are **undesirable**?

Friends _____

How are friendships formed? Are there clubs or other group organizations to foster friendships? Does a person usually have lots of friends, or only a few select people whom he counts among his friends? What kinds of things do friends do together? If a person moves to another area, does he still maintain close ties with his previous friends? What are some qualities of a good friend? What are the **duties** or **obligations** of friends toward each other? What **privileges** do friends have with each other?

In addition you could ask: Who is one of your close friends? How did you meet? What things do you do together? How often are you together?

Friends

Courtship and Marriage _____

How do young people get to know each other? Is there a counterpart to the Western custom of "dating"? Do young people spend much time together before they are married? Are they always chaperoned?

What are considered good qualities to look for in choosing a wife? What are good qualities to look for in a husband?

Does a young person **choose** his own **mate**, or do the families choose the mates? Has this pattern changed much in recent years? Does a young man propose directly to the girl, or is the proposal made through a friend or other mediator? Is a dowry expected? How much?

At what age do people marry? Are there wedding ceremonies, feasts, or other formalities? Who pays the expenses of these?

Does the young couple usually plan to live near his relatives, her relatives, or neither? What are their **financial responsibilities** to their parents? What are the financial responsibilities of the parents to the couple? Do the young people now make their own independent **decisions**, or do they look to their parents? Are they expected to continue obeying their parents and elders?

Here comes the bride

Different standards
of dress

—————— Appearance and Dress

Is it important to always look nice? How do you keep looking nice? What standards of personal cleanliness are important? How do **standards of dress and appearance** differ on different occasions? What are some things one should avoid wearing on specific occasions? Are some **colors** more appropriate than others for certain occasions or certain types of people? Are there different standards of dress for young people than for adults? Have dress standards or habits changed much in recent years? What were they like before?

What kinds of clothing are considered immodest? What is considered to be in poor taste? Are there different standards for different types of people?

Who uses makeup or **cosmetics**? Under what conditions and in what circumstances is it used? Are there any age distinctions in the use of cosmetics?

Adult education

—————— School

What is the **school system** like? How many years do people usually go to school? Is school compulsory? Is it free? How much homework is given? Is it appropriate to ask a young person what year of school he is in? Are there classes to learn specific trades? Are there any classes for adults?

What **basic education** is essential for everyone to have? How are learners rewarded? How is **discipline** carried out? What misbehaviors are disciplined?

Tell me about a teacher who greatly influenced your life.

What about **informal education** — What things are learned at home? At church? From friends?

You might learn a text in which you describe the school system in your own country and then ask questions about the school experiences of the person you are conversing with.

—————— Health

How can one stay healthy and **prevent illnesses**? What are some common **health problems**? What are the different **kinds of diseases**? Are there different kinds of pain?

If you get sick, how should you care for yourself? Are there good home **remedies** for some minor ailments? Are there stores that specialize in selling medicines? How does one go about getting the services of a **medical practitioner**? What kinds of practitioners are there?

What is the relationship between **health** and personal **cleanliness**? What standards of hygiene and public sanitation are observed?

What illnesses do people **fear** most? Ask Kino: What sicknesses have you experienced? What happened? What did you do to get better? What did you avoid doing during that time?

Who smokes? What is smoked? Is snuff used? How? What attitudes do people hold toward smoking or snuff? Where are tobacco products sold? Are there occasions when it is considered improper to smoke? Does smoking come under the realm of health? ✍

Remedies

Safety _____

Is safety an important thing? How can one keep safe? What things are unsafe to do? What places are unsafe? How can one prevent accidents? What causes accidents? ✍

Birthplace _____

Tell me something about your birthplace and where you have lived. Are relatives still living there? In the same house? What is the **importance** of your **birthplace**? Is there any special way that you show this? How about your present home? Is its location important? Why? ✍

Important People _____

Who are some of the important people in your town or in other places where you have lived? What have they done? How does your town show honor or respect to them? ✍

Personal Possessions _____

What things do you own? How did you come to own them: Through inheritance? Through purchase? What are your most important possessions? What possession would you find hardest to give up? What possession are you most pleased to own? Do any of your possessions have a particular sentimental value for you? What do you not own that you would very much like to have?

If appropriate, share these questions with people of varying socio-economic positions, and with people of a variety of occupations, to learn what things are considered **basic**, and which ones are nice extras or **luxuries**. ✍

Basic possessions

Machines

Who uses machines? What kinds of machines and appliances do most people own? Car? Refrigerator? Stove? Freezer? TV? Radio? Air conditioner? Hot water heater? Washing machine? Dryer? Electric iron? Sewing machine? Lawn mower? How do people without these appliances get these jobs done?

What is the role of the car? What percentage of people own cars? How do people go about getting a license to drive?

NOTE: As a means of achieving material comfort, Americans have developed machinery for efficiency and convenience in daily life. We take our love for machines with us when we go overseas — cars, air conditioners, central heating, and hot water heaters are seldom optional for us. The American overseas usually feels that some machinery is necessary in order for him to successfully complete his task. What do those without machines do to get the same jobs done? If you did that would your communication opportunities be increased?

Repair

Develop a text to use as you visit repair shops for various types of machinery and appliances. What types of machines can be repaired locally? How are maintence personnel trained? What parts are available? What are the options when parts are not available? Handmade parts? How expensive are repairs?

Work and Occupations

"Are you copperbottoming um, my man?"
"No, I am aluminuming um, mum."

Is it polite to ask a person what his occupation is? Does a person choose his own occupation, or is it usually decided by the family? What occupations are considered especially **appealing**? What occupations are considered **less desirable**? Does a person usually keep the same job for his lifetime, or is job changing common? How many **hours a day** do people usually work? On the average, how much money do people earn each week? What is the **minimum wage** allowed by the government? What kinds of jobs are paid at this minimal level? What jobs are higher paying?

Ask: What occupations have you had? If you had a choice would you prefer some other job than your present one? Which one? Why?

Do children or young people work after school hours? What kinds of chores, errands, or odd jobs do they do? Do they get an allowance when they work for the family? How much do they get paid when they work for other people? When they work outside the home are they expected to give some of their earnings to their family to help with family expenses? Are they expected to save their earnings to help pay for school expenses?

When money is saved, is it deposited in a bank? Are savings accounts common? Is thrift considered a virtue? ✒

Public Servants _____

What services does the community offer — fire protection, police protection, mail delivery, garbage collection? Try to spend an afternoon with some public servants to learn about their **roles** and learn some of their **vocabulary**. Are they paid, or are they volunteers? What is their training? What are their responsibilities? What is their status? ✒

Male man

Your Trade _____

Spend a day (or more) with local people who are involved in your trade, whether you are a doctor, teacher, businessman, agriculturalist, housewife, preacher, coach, or druggist. Learn a little about the way this trade is carried out by the local people. Begin learning some of the **specialized vocabulary** that is used. How are people trained for these positions? How much are they paid? What are their special **responsibilities**? What are the **particular problems** they face? ✒

Country-wide Transportation _____

Are there buses or trains or other means to get to other parts of the country? How often do they run? How much does it cost? Do people travel much? Should you take food along, or is food served, or do you stop at restaurants along the way to eat? Do you make reservations ahead of time, or do you just go and buy a ticket when you want to leave? ✒

Canal transportation

Variations of Life-Style _____

Is life quite different from one area of the country to another? Are there different dialects of the language spoken in different places?

What are some of the **differences** between life in the city and life in the rural areas? Are there differences in housing, economic status, occupations, or customs between the country and the city?

Are the cities pretty much alike? What are the differences between them?

In your text, you could ask people what part of the country they are from. If they are from another area, you can ask them to tell you about the differences between that area and this. You could also ask questions like: What do you miss most now that you are living here? Do you still have relatives there? How often do you see them? What made you decide to move? What do you like best about living here? What has been the most difficult thing to adjust to? Are you glad you came? Do you plan to stay here?

If they are from this area, you could ask them to describe the differences between here and any other part of the country they have visited, or differences they have heard from friends or acquaintances who have been in other areas.

Ask: If you had a choice of living anywhere in the world, where would it be? Why?

Special Places

Are there resort areas in the country that are especially popular for vacations? Do people like to go to their family home for vacations, or into other areas of the country? What areas of the country are especially scenic? What areas are of particular historical interest or cultural interest? Are there favorite camping areas?

In your text you could learn to **ask people about their favorite place** — where it is, why they like that place, how often they go, what they do there, etc. You could also describe to them the places you have been and **ask them to recommend other places of interest** for you to visit.

Special Days

Which day of the week (if any) is designated as a *day of rest*? What do people do on this day? What is not done? Is the observance of the day a matter of law, or of custom? Does everyone have the day off from work, or just certain types of workers?

Develop a calendar with Kino of the **holidays** or **special days** of the next few months. Have Kino help you with a text which will let you discuss an upcoming special day with some understanding. Learn what the **central theme** of the celebration is. Learn some questions which let you *explore* what other people *know and feel* about the day. You can also learn about other related holidays and how they are celebrated.

Free Time Activities

Develop with Kino a text which will give you a basic vocabulary for understanding some favorite pastime of the people, some pastime which you can join in. It could be volleyball, chess, hiking, cycling, parlor games, or any other pastime which would *involve you* with people who have *time to relax and talk* with you.

Learn what days or times of day are most appropriate for the activity. Learn the basic rules of the game and the basic "sportsmanship" principles which you should follow.

You might want to learn **various types of pastimes** — active, passive; indoor, outdoor; those most liked by children, or young people, or older people; those that involve skills and those which involve chance; etc.

NOTE: A fun way to work on vocabulary is to *play word games in the language* **with Kino and other friends. Ask Kino about any language games that are common in the culture, and learn to play these. You may also find that your friends would enjoy learning to play games like Password or 20 Questions. Once they have learned the games, you can learn a lot about the language by watching them play with each other, as well as by playing with them.**

20 Questions **is a game for 2 people. One person has a word in mind and the other person tries to identify the word by asking questions that can be answered by "yes" or "no." Questions like: Is it an activity? Is it a quality? Is it a thing? Is it alive? Is it something used for work? As you play or as you watch two of your friends play the game, observe carefully the questions they ask. You can learn a lot about the characteristics that are important to them in identifying objects, activities, and qualities.**

Password **is a game for 4 people. Two people alternate in giving one-word clues to the other two who are trying to guess the word. When you play, or when you watch your friends play this, take notes of clues which don't seem to make sense to you. Write them down and afterward discuss them with your friends or with Kino. The clue may be part of an idiom you don't know, or of a cultural situation you are unaware of.**

Be sure to play these games in the language, rather than in English (even if your vocabulary is still relatively limited), because the cultural and language cues will come through much more strongly.

Sports

If organized sports are popular, learn to talk about them intelligently. Are the teams professional or amateur? Which are the popular teams or players? When are the games played? What are the basic rules and objectives of the game? Do the spectators cheer, chant, clap, sing? Are the games free to the public? Learn to ask people about their favorite sports and players.

Hobbies and Crafts

What hobbies or crafts are common? Are they mainly done for fun or for profit? Are the skills handed down from parent to child as a *family tradition*? Do most people have a hobby or do a craft? Is it appropriate to ask a person about his hobby or craft? Can you ask to see something he has made? Would it be polite to ask someone to teach you how to do that craft?

Your text could include phrases like: "I have a friend who enjoys _____(carving, for example). Do many people _____? What do you enjoy doing? Is it difficult to do? May I watch you?"

NOTE: You can have a lot of fun in language learning through active use of a hobby. You might collect and/or sketch local plants or insects. Children would be happy to help you collect specimens and talk with you about the activity. If you have a skill with some craft you might form a little club and help others learn the skill.

Some of you who have athletic skills might join a local basketball of soccer team. Social time with team members could be good conversation time in the language.

Entertainment

What do families usually do for relaxation and entertainment? Are there popular parks and playgrounds? What equipment or services do the parks have? Are there cultural things like museums, historical places, exhibitions, etc? What about musical programs, drama, and poetry readings? Are there zoos? Movies or theatres? How do you get tickets for these? What about circuses, rodeos, races, bullfights, animal shows, cockfights, fairs?

Besides learning to discuss entertainment, make plans with Kino or other friends from the community to *attend some local entertainment together* in the evening or over the weekend. (Set yourself a ground-rule of not talking English — make a habit of relaxing in the language.)

Music

What are some of the popular **musical instruments**? Where are they made? Do most people learn to play some musical instrument?

Is vocal music popular? Are there work songs? Are there game songs? Who are some of the well-known composers of past or present? Who are some of the well-known singers and musicians of past or present? What opportunities exist to learn and practice instrumental or vocal music?

Try to learn a few of the best known folk songs.

Art

What kinds of local art are common? Are there *characteristic styles* of local art? Who are the better known artists of past or present? Are there different folk art styles in different areas of the country? Is there a traditional art form? ✑

Color Perception

Develop a text to help you explore the color spectrum in your new language. People everywhere physically perceive the entire visible range of the color spectrum, but the colors are *categorized* and named differently from one culture to another. For example, compare English color category names with those of Shona and Bassa:

Shona:	... *cipswuka* (colored)		*citena* (blackish)		*cicena* (whitish)		*cipswuka* ... (colored)	
English:	*purple*	*blue*	*green*		*yellow*	*orange*	*red*	
Bassa:	*hui* (cool?)				*ziza* (warm?)			

(It might be easier to illustrate the Shona color names on a cylinder, as the word "cipswuka" includes both ends of the English color spectrum.)

Learn to use the color names appropriately in your new language. Find out the **principal names** for colors (their "primary colors"). Then ask people to name **different shades** and distinguish between them. Colors are everywhere — open your eyes and you will see literally thousands which you can talk about. ✑

Geography

Develop a text in which you briefly describe and compare the geography of your home country with that of your host country. Learn the names of the **landmarks** of the country — rivers, mountains, lakes, deserts, valleys, geological oddities. ✑

Natural Resources

Tell me something about the value of your country's land and natural resources. Should they be developed more? By whom? How? In what order? To what extent? Who should decide? ✑

Plants

What **kinds of plants** are there? What plants are good for your health (medicinal)? What plants are most nutritious? Are there any poisonous plants around here? How do you recognize them?

Do you have any **legends** about how certain plants came into being or about their use?

What are some common **decorative plants**? Do people have gardens for both flowers and vegetables? What kinds of flowers are used in home decoration or flower arrangements? Do people often have cut flowers in their homes? What is your favorite flower?

Do homes have lawns around them? How are they tended?

Do many people grow their own vegetables? Who tends the gardens? What **kinds of vegetables or fruits** are commonly grown in this area? What is your favorite fruit or vegetable? Who grows the vegetables and fruits we buy in the market?

If there is a fruit tree beside the road, who can pick the fruit? If people rent property with trees, whose is the fruit — the landlord's or the renter's?

What are some good ways to eat _____(a fruit or vegetable you are not familiar with)?

Is it appropriate to ask people about their **gardens**? How do you compliment a person's garden? Is it appropriate to ask people for a slip or cutting of a plant to start one of your own?

(If you are a gardener, you can learn how to ask people's advice on growing particular plants — soil, watering, fertilizer, pruning, sunshine needed, etc.)

_____ Insects

What are some of the common insects in the area? Which ones are **helpful**? What do they do? Which ones are **harmful**? What do they do? How can you protect yourself or your crops from the harmful ones? Do you have any legends about insects?

_____ Animals

Various texts can probably be built around animal topics.

Do people have **pets**? What kinds of animals are normally kept as pets? How are they cared for? Are they usually the pet of an individual or of a family? Do the pets also have a useful function?

You can learn about other **domestic animals**. What are they kept for? Who tends them? Where are they kept? Which ones are considered most valuable? Are they owned by individuals, families, clans?

A wild animal

What **wild animals** are in the area? Are they considered helpful, harmful, or neutral? How can you protect yourself from the harmful or dangerous ones? Where do they live? Do people hunt any of the wild animals? Which ones are good to eat?

Are there **legends** or folk-tales in which an animal is the main character?

Idioms and Figurative Language

As you learn to use idioms and exclamations appropriately you will surprise and delight your hearers. Your speech will begin to sound more natural, interesting and colorful.

Whenever you learn an idiom or figure of speech be sure to note its *connotation* — is it used for comic effect? Is it complimentary? Is it sarcastic? Is it derogatory? Is it inappropriate for certain occasions?

There are various ways to elicit this type of language.

1. Many languages **equate people with animals**, based on certain **characteristics**. For example, we can speak of a person as being "foxy," or "a bear," or "a skunk." Check to see what animals in your language are used to describe people.

2. **Body parts** are often associated with expressions for emotions, and with other idioms. Some examples from English are: "It did my heart good." "It's a pain in the neck." "He wouldn't lift a hand for her." "It cost me an arm and a leg." "My eye!" "She's my heart throb."

In another language they might say: "It sits well with my liver." "He is a fishbone in the throat." "I have a heavy stomach" (sorrow). "My stomach is hot" (anger). "I love you with all my stomach" or "I love you with my whole shoulder." "He has bowels of compassion."

If you keep an eye open (and if you have a nose for news and your ear to the ground) you may find a variety of idioms in your new language which relate to body parts.

3. The **extremes of common adjectives** will often yield figurative language — "as slow as molasses," "as quick as a wink," "as hungry as a bear," etc. Using the adjectives you know, find out what figures of speech are used to describe their extremes.

4. Give your helper **examples** of idioms and figures of speech from English, to get him thinking along these lines. Often one idiom will trigger a whole series of idioms in his mind. (Emphasize that you don't want translations of American idioms; you want examples of common idioms in his language.)

5. **Colors** often have an idiomatic meaning, and are frequently used in figures of speech — "as white as a sheet"; "green with envy"; "true blue"; "blue streak"; "Blue Monday" (in German, "Blue Monday"

Date

"Squirrely"

Brave as a lion

means a long weekend). We say that a person in debt is "in the red" — the Italians say he is "in the green." While you are exploring the figurative use of color words, you may also wish to explore the connotative meanings of colors. For example, to us the color white often signifies purity and so is the appropriate color for a bride or for certain religious orders. But in Korea, white signifies mourning and is appropriate for funerals.

Date

6. Most languages have **euphemisms** — ways to talk about delicate subjects (such as death, sex, elimination) indirectly. For example, in English we can talk about death with a variety of expressions such as — he went to his reward, he went to the happy hunting grounds, he passed on, he kicked the bucket, etc. While you are on the topic of euphemisms, you will want to learn what words are *taboo* — words not used in polite speech or used only under certain circumstances.

7. You will also want to learn the appropriate **exclamatory words**. We use exclamations like, "Oh-oh!" "Ow!" "Ouch!" "Wow!" "Hey!" etc. What expressions do they use in similar situations?

8. Another picturesque kind of words are those which very closely **resemble** the **sounds** they represent — ding-dong, tinkle, gurgle, meow, moo, whoosh, bang, knock-knock, rat-a-tat-tat. For us, a rooster crows "cock-a-doodle-doo"; for the Spanish it crows "ki-ki-ri-kí"; how does it crow in your new language? Find out what various animals "say" in your new language. Also, elicit words for the sounds that make a story expressive — sounds for falling, splashing, bells, drums, wind, water, fire, etc. Listen as people tell stories and relate experiences, and make note of these expressive sounding words which they use.

You might not want to devote seven cycles entirely to idioms and figures of speech, but you could invest a few minutes a day for various days to begin learning picturesque speech in your new language.   ◦§

Stories

Learn how to ask people to tell you a story. Older people might especially enjoy telling you stories. If you want, you can specify the type of story — folk tale, legend, history, story about their childhood, children's story, a recent experience, etc. You may ask some people for permission to record a story which you could use as a basis for some future text of your own.   ◦§

Folklore _____

You will learn a lot about cultural values, *and* endear yourself to people (especially older people) if you show an interest in their folktales.

Have Kino teach you a short, well-known folktale. Tell people you have learned it and ask if you can practice telling it to them. Try telling it the next time you are chatting with a group of children or old folks.

Legends, folk tales, folk songs, myths and traditions often illustrate *themes which are important to the culture,* and often they have an implicit or explicit moral attached. Learn new ones regularly.

In some languages, folklore and songs use an archaic or stylized form of the language. You will want to check on this.

The Past _____

Learn to talk about the country's history intelligently. You could learn about topics such as:

What are some of your country's greatest accomplishments of the past?

What are some of the key events in your country's past?

Who are some of the famous people in your country's past? What did they do?

Key People _____

Develop one or more texts in which you ask others to tell you about people who have influenced them in their life — people such as relatives, neighbors, peers, fellow workers, teachers, community leaders, religious leaders, and others. As you listen to them tell you about the important people in their life, you can begin to understand the **patterns of influence** in the culture. Do younger people ever influence their elders? What roles are the most influential? Do women ever influence men? Do lower status people have much influence on higher status people?

A famous leader

Community Aspirations _____

What are the goals and aspirations of your community? What are the major concerns of your leaders? What are the most important **problems** in the community, and what are the basic causes? What **issues** do you feel are important? Why? What advice would you give to a leader if you were asked? What can the *average person* do to help the community meet its goal or solve its problems?

_____ Sharing Personal Ambitions and Hopes

Develop a text in which you share your personal dreams and hopes. Ask others about their hopes and aspirations.

Listen to a variety of people talk about their hopes. Are there certain ambitions which seem to be community-wide? Are there some aspirations which are common to just certain segments of society? ◄§

_____ Sharing Important Experiences

Develop a text in which you share with people an important, key experience in your life, and then ask them to tell you about a key experience in their life.

As you listen to other people, note what **types of experiences** are most commonly shared. Are key experiences most often in the area of religion? Education? Family life? Community life?   ◄§

_____ Reading Matter

What do most people read — books, newspapers, comic books, novels? Do people generally have much reading matter in their homes? Do people enjoy reading as a pastime? Who are some of the more popular authors? What books/stories/poetry are considered the "classics" in the language? Who are the current popular authors? Where do people get their reading matter?

In addition to communicating about this topic, get a good simple book (perhaps a children's book) and begin reading.   ◄§

_____ Letter Writing

When you are writing in the language, what is the appropriate way to begin and end a **personal letter**? A **business letter**? What margins are used? Where does the date go? How is the date written? Do people usually have special signatures? What styles of handwriting are used? What kind of writing instruments do people use? Do people have special stationery? How do you address the envelope?

How often do friends write to each other when they are separated? Do people generally consider it a pleasure or a chore to write friendly letters?

Related to this, learn about the **postal service** — How is it organized? How does it serve the people?

If your language uses a Roman script (or if you have learned to write in a non-Roman script), you may wish to take this opportunity to write a friendly letter in the language. Have Kino look at it to correct the style. (Don't use this as an excuse to neglect your communication time today. Go out and talk to people about letters.) ◄§

Categories

Let us include in Set 3 a discussion of the concept of categories and categorization. This elaborates on the ideas of *classification* which you used when exploring vocabulary in Set 1 (pages 141-142) and in Set 2 (pages 151-159). It may provide you with the means of organizing the new information you now have access to.

You see, the *knowledge* you have is *organized* in categories in your mind. (This organized knowledge will be discussed more in Set 4.) It is as though your brain were made up of *cubby-holes*, and each new bit of information you receive is processed and then filed in one of the cubby-holes. Even the categories themselves are organized and classified. Some categories will be included within other categories. In other words, knowledge is structured.

NOTE: All knowledge must be categorized, in order for us to be able to respond to the millions of stimuli that reach us daily. The complexities of the real world are reduced by categorization. Let's consider color, for example. Psychologists tell us that the human eye can distinguish 7,000,000 colors along the entire color spectrum — the reality of the sensory world is overwhelmingly complex. So, how do we handle it? We reduce the complexity by drawing boundaries and making categories; and these boundaries are arbitrary. This is illustrated by the fact that some people in our culture believe that indigo is a color, while others don't see it that way.

Imagine what it would be like if categories didn't exist. Every time we saw a tree or chair or book we would have to respond to it as though it were a completely different item from other items we have responded to in the past. Every individual item or activity would have to have its unique name. Even the same item when seen at different periods under different conditions would have to be responded to in a unique way. If today you see John and he is happy (a category, by the way), and tomorrow you see him dressed differently, slightly older, and in a different mood, he no longer is exactly the same person and so he might be perceived as a totally new item in your inventory of things. As a matter of fact, even to discuss the possibility of non-categorized thinking, we must use category names — happy, dressed, mood, item, activity, respond, name. Otherwise we would have to invent totally new words every time we talked, because the message would have to be unique to fit all the unique situations — and you would have no way of knowing what we were talking about. There could be no communication without shared categorizations and category names.

If you have no cubby-hole for a phenomenon, then it may not become part of your knowledge, or it may not even be perceived. To use computer language, it is just data and doesn't become information until it is organized. We've all had the experience of becoming aware of some new word that we think we've *never* seen before. Yet, shortly after we have a category for it the word seems to pop up in quite a variety of places, causing us to suspect that we may have previously encountered it without it registering. Much of what goes on in your new culture is just data to you since you may not have the cubby-holes to organize and understand it.

Another factor is that even when you "understand", you may understand wrong. This happens because your cubby-holes are not the same as those of the people of the new culture. Categorization is arbitrary within any culture. It is the on-going process of classification by grouping similar things while keeping separate the things that are considered to be different. It is important to note that what is similar and what is different is arbitrarily defined by convention within each culture and is not governed by some external logic. The result is that people of one culture have different cubby-holes than people of another culture.

Different cubbyholes

In New Delhi the authors saw a highly ornate set which for Indians fits into one category, but it will take a number of English categories for us to describe. Each item of the set was carefully hand-crafted and ornately decorated with the same intricate, colorful pattern. The set included six stools with the pattern engraved on the seat, and a round table surfaced with the same pattern. On the table were serving dishes and a punch bowl of the same material and pattern. There were also drinking vessels, plates, and full settings of table-ware even down to small tea-stirring spoons — all with the same ornate engravings and color pattern. This set intersects the English sets of furniture, serving ware, dishes, silverware, and even art.

Another example: We would put cow dung in the *category* of "fertilizer" or "refuse." But some African cultures use it as an antiseptic to freshen the walls of a room; others use it as a material to harden a dirt floor; and in parts of Asia it is used as a decoration on the outside of a house; or as fuel. In parts of Latin America it is used as a building material — houses are framed with cross-hatched sticks which are then filled in and surfaced with a mixture of clay, straw and dung. (As a matter of fact, some of our forefathers in their trek to the West used dried dung as a dentifrice.)

A meal of grasshoppers, caterpillars, ants

All people have a *category* of food — things that are appropriate to eat. But not all cultures include the same items in this category. For example, some people include things we would call "insects" (definitely not "food" for us) — like ants, grasshoppers, locusts, caterpillars. We include some animal meats in this category of "food", while categorizing other meats as "non-food". But other cultures may put some of the "non-food" meats into the "food" category — horse, lizard, dog, small rodents, grubs. Some Orientals eat "bird's nest soup" — bird's nests for us fall into a category which is not at all related to food.

A major error of most language courses, when language is taught in isolation from culture, is that the student learns a lot of foreign words, but he only understands them from the framework provided by his own cubby-holes. He never has opportunity to learn to really understand the people, because their knowledge doesn't fit his foreign classification system.

Learning a culture is the process of learning what its people know. In a sense, learning a language, learning a culture and learning the way people think are one and the same thing in the final analysis. What is involved is "getting inside" people's heads in order to understand how they preceive the world. To understand their knowledge, you must understand their organization of knowledge — their categorization system.

"OK," you ask, "How do I learn their classification system — their cubby-holes?"

To find categories, look for a *common name* or *response* to an array of different objects or events. Many, though not all, categories in a culture have a category name.

Often you can ask a general question that will elicit different category names. For example, you can get an inside perspective on carpenters' categories by asking a carpenter a general question like, "What do you do in a typical day?" In his description of the day he may name categories of objects — tools, furniture, soft wood, hard wood. He may mention categories of events — choosing the wood, deciding on the basic designs, and measurements. He may mention categories of people — fellow carpenters, apprentices, relatives, buyers. He might mention categories of places — his shop, buyers' homes, wholesale merchants, furniture stores. Categories imply both similarity and contrast. If a person is classified as a "buyer", he is in some ways similar to other buyers, and he is also in some ways different from people classified as "carpenters" or "apprentices".

"I pound nails
on a typical day"

Date

You can then begin to ask questions to explore these categories. What are the different kinds of furniture you make? What are the different ways to prepare the wood? What are the different kinds of buyers?

Explore one of the categories you find, by probing with questions. The sample questions below explore the concept "chair."

Definition and *description:*
(See page 152)

What is a chair?
How would you describe a chair?
What are some of the characteristics of a chair?

General name of the *larger category* that includes this one:
(See page 142)

Is a chair a kind of something?
What kind of thing is a chair?

Names of *related categories* included in the larger category:
(Page 142)

What other kinds of furniture are there for people to sit on?

Benches

Names of *included sub-categories:*
(Page 142)

Distinguishing characteristics:
(Page 153)

Expanding your understanding:
(Page 153)

Are there different kinds of chairs?

What kinds of stools are there?

What are the main differences between chairs, stools, and benches?

In what ways are chairs and stools like benches? In what ways are they different?

Is a chair more like a stool or like a bench? Why?

Tell me more about a chair.

When you hear the word "chair," what other words do you think of?

A king's stool

NOTE: Not only do cultures have different categories, but the distinguishing characteristics will also be different. We have the categories *chair* and *stool,* and the main characteristics that differentiate between these are generally size, shape, number of legs, and perhaps function. You may work in another culture which seems to have categories similar to *chair* and *stool,* but the differentiating characteristic might be quite different — it might be construction material, prestige value, religious value, cost, or color. Exercise caution when assuming that they have the same categories or that they associate the same attributes with your categories. Be alert to the fact that even the questions you ask may be asked from the framework of your cultural categories and perspective, and thus bias your co-speaker's response as well as your own understanding.

Sometimes you may wish to develop a "tree" with Kino to help you see the relationships and levels within a hierarchy (see the sample tree on the next page). Having Kino do this with you will help you see how his knowledge is organized and categorized. You could add to this tree and to the resulting descriptions, as you talk with people in the community. (Some of your data may not fit a tree diagram, but much probably will.) On the tree the most generic is at the base, and the more specific items are in the higher levels.

Stools

Distinguishing characteristics:

Chairs have four legs and a back. They may be padded. One person sits on a chair.

Stools have one, three or four legs. They usually don't have a back. They may be extra tall or extra short. One person sits on a stool.

Benches have four or more legs. They may have a back. They are not padded. Usually they are big enough for more than one person.

Expansion:

Other words thought of were — hair, sitting, relaxation, upholstery, wheel chair.

Sample of Category Exploration

Topic: CHAIR

Description and definition: A chair is a piece of furniture. It has four legs. One person can sit on it.

Categories:

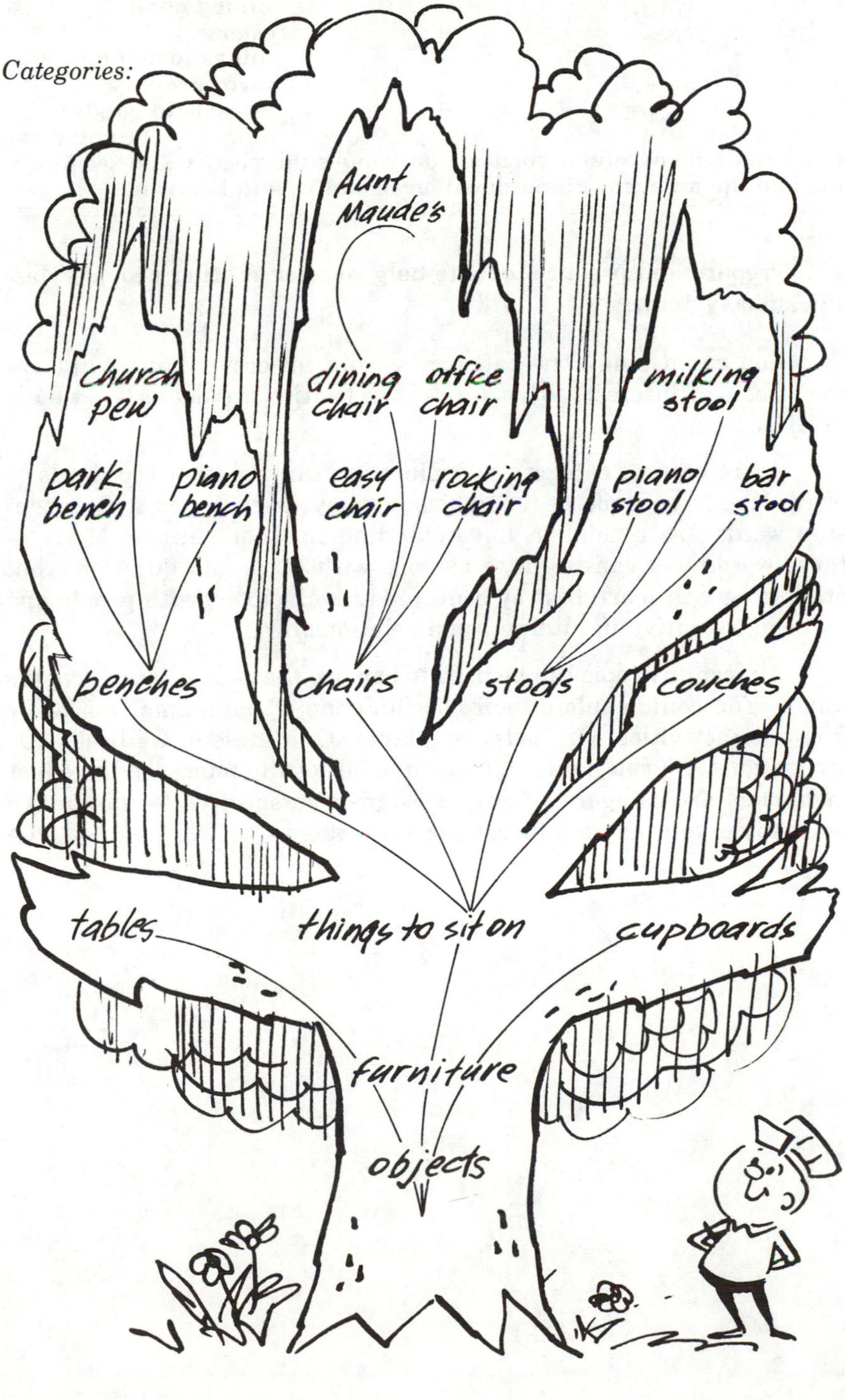

NOTE: Classification trees can be very complex, so making a tree could get out of hand. Notice that the chair that the carpenter made might fit into a hierarchy like the following: **Aunt Maude's chair**
maple
Ethan Allen
colonial
dining chair
chair
things to sit on
furniture
household goods
object.   In any given day's study be careful to focus on only one subcategory and see how it fits into the adjacent hierarchical levels above and below it.

Prepare and practice texts to help you get at other people's classification systems.

Date

You could study one category within an occupation. What are the objects of interest? What kinds of activities are done? Or, who is involved?

An important category to explore is social relationship words — words like friend, mother, neighbor, enemy, partner, boss. Relationship words are crucial in understanding another culture. Many of these words you can begin to explore with texts and questions, but others you will learn best by continued involvement with people and by being sensitive in interpersonal relationships.

Almost any topic can be used to explore the categories of people's minds. You could explore their classification of the animal world. Or free-time activities. Or foods. Or plants. Or illnesses. Or books. Or occupations. Or you name it. Of course, all of the topics we have just mentioned are categories from an English perspective — they make sense to us, but may not be categories to them.

Set 4 – Topics
For Drawing on
The Local Knowledge Bank

The topics of Set 4 are designed to help you become a successful participant and an effective communicator in your new culture. These topics are best suited to the learner who has acquired at least two plus level of speaking proficiency (see the Self-Rating Proficiency Scale in the Appendix).

Make a commitment to *join* your new community. To be *a successful participant* in your new culture, there is a great deal that you need to "know". We use quotes here, because in addition to knowledge as information, people have knowledge in the form of beliefs, assumptions and values. To each person his own beliefs and perceptions of reality are both "true" and "right". They are part of what he knows. We, for example, make the assumption that democracy is best and right. This is something we "know" (though America is really a republic rather than a democracy). Also, we put a value on privacy, and we "know" it is right. But the things we "know" to be true may be different from the things that others, with other assumptions and values, "know" to be true. We may know that the universe is governed by physical laws, while they may know that the universe is controlled by spiritual forces.

People from different cultures have different experiences on which they base their assumptions about the world. As a result, people from different cultures have different ideas about what is "true".

To be a successful participant in a new culture, you must be willing to accept the validity of differing realities, assumptions, and values. Ethnocentricity causes a person to feel that his own assumptions are "right" and all others are "wrong" or inferior. Being bicultural implies the ability to accept both

I know you believe
you understand what
you think I said,
but I am not sure
that you realize
that what you heard
is not what I meant.

189

systems of perception as valid, or "right" for the respective cultures. Becoming bicultural is a process of "blowing one's mind" for it implies the understanding and appreciation of the new system and the adoption of parts of it. (Rejection of the old, and total acceptance of the new is probably impossible and would never be a wise goal.)

Culture is not what people *do*, but rather, what they *think*. *Belief systems and values are the essence of any culture* or civilization. Since culture primarily exists in people's minds, the behaviour that is different in your new culture is probably the result of something different that the people "know." Their belief system obliges them to follow a distinct way of life as they meet their reciprocal responsibilities. In learning your new culture you will need to begin to get inside people's minds so that you can know what they know and develop an appreciation for it. You can ask the question, "What does he know that enables him or causes him to do that?"

One of your goals in acquiring new cultural knowledge is to use this knowledge in order to appropriately anticipate the settings and activities of the society — given certain circumstances you will know what is likely to occur. Each culture provides a system of "rules" to organize life so that people know what to expect in each given situation. Things are predictable — for the insider. The outsider finds things to be unpredictable. He finds that it takes a lot of energy and time to carry out his activities of daily living. Accomplishing even small things becomes a big ordeal. In India, Betty Sue wanted to find out what time there was to be a church service at the hotel. She called the desk and this conversation resulted:

Betty: "Good morning. What time is the church service held here in the hotel?"
Desk: "You want room service? Just a minute."
B: "No, I want —" (desk hung up)
Room Service: "What is it you want ma'am?"
B: "I'd like to know what time the church service is."
RS: "You say you'd like an orange juice — large or small?"
B: (Very slowly) "No, I'd like to know what time —"
RS: (Interrupting) "What time is it? — It is 7:00 a.m."
B: (Slower and louder) "No, I want to know what time the church service is held in the basement of this hotel."
RS: "I didn't understand, could you repeat that please."

Outsider

Insiders

Betty Sue gave up in exasperation. A minute later the room service bell boy knocked at the door, wanting to know if we had just called down to order morning tea. Betty Sue told him we already had our morning tea; we just wanted to know what time the church service started. (She didn't get through to him, either.)

If things continue to be unpredictable, the stresses of the new culture add up, and the outsider may want to go home. Don't give up! There is hope, if you are willing to cultivate a sense of humor about yourself and an objectivity about your frustrations while you are internalizing the cultural knowledge of the local people. Write down your frustrations and then talk about each one with different people, for a variety of daily texts. As you do so, you will discover their "rules", and people will begin to "child-train" you and help you make the necessary adjustments. People who guide you in this way are helping you learn to feel at home in their country. Thus, you will begin to recover from the cultural stresses as you learn what to expect in each situation. You will be learning the "rules" of the new culture. As things become predictable you will become a successful participant in the culture.

To become *an effective communicator* in a new language it is necessary to tap the knowledge bank of the people. Let's illustrate with a simple diagram of a cross-cultural communication model. In this model, the Sender and Receiver come from different cultures. One is a square (you) from the square culture — the other is a round in roundsville. Both sender and receiver have a knowledge bank: each has knowledge and the knowledge is classified and organized systematically. *When a person speaks he reflects* the organization of his knowledge, and *when he listens he interprets* what he hears according to the previously organized categories of his mind. In cross-cultural communication, the knowledge bank of one person is organized in a square way, while the other's knowledge is organized roundly.

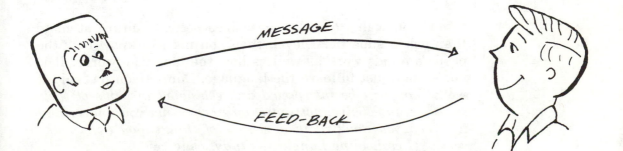

Integrating
new information into
previous categories

We have included *feedback* in this communication model, and feel we should emphasize its importance. Feedback comes in the form of questions, restatements, facial expressions, etc. Too often people think they have communicated when they have only sent a message. But communication is never complete unless the receiver has *understood* and *integrated* the new information into the organization of his own knowledge bank. As he integrates this new information into his categories, he often alters or reshapes the message. Feedback reflects the receiver's understanding and organization. Even when sender and receiver share the same culture this confirming feedback is indispensible to the individual who has a responsibility to be understood when he communicates.

Do you listen to feedback? If you think much of what you know and little of what your listener knows, then you will talk more and listen less. This is risky because you don't then know what your listener is doing with what you say.

Sometimes people learn to give speeches in a language and therefore assume they have a satisfactory proficiency. But they have little idea what their listeners actually understand. And if someone later asks an important question, they may be at a loss to give a meaningful response. Performance in two-way communication with individuals is a much better indicator of speaking proficiency than the ability to deliver a memorized speech at a group.

NOTE: The authors have occasionally encountered individuals and organizations who had communication objectives in a second culture, but were unfortunately unaware of the fact that people have different ways of understanding things. They blindly assumed that everyone must be the same as themselves. The need for initial listening did not occur to them. And they didn't know the second language well enough to get much feedback. It is ironic, for they felt they needed to make haste to do their communication thing yet they had no idea what their receptors actually understood by their message.

If you want to make sense in a second culture at more than just a superficial level, then you need to know how the people's minds work as well as how the language works. It is not enough just to learn the language. Don Larson has said it well: *"You will be interpreted and evaluated in terms of their system of knowledge, not yours, whether or not you understand it! When you don't fit their scheme of things, you don't make sense." (Deschooling Language Study,* page 162)

A *good* communicator is not just concerned about what he says, but rather, he is primarily concerned about what his hearers *understand*.

People who are to be change agents in a second culture (teachers, missionaries, business men, advisors, etc.) should be particularly concerned about communicating in ways that will be easily understood within the framework of the local knowledge bank. Innovations brought by the foreign change agent may, after he leaves, quickly die away or become unrecognizably changed if they are not presented in a way which makes sense in the local culture. If an idea is not understood it cannot be successfully integrated into the life-style.

A problem in cross-cultural communication

NOTE: Hopefully, change agents will carry out the responsibilities of their assignment without naively assuming that it has to be done in their Western way. For Christian missionaries there should be an understanding that will help them separate what they are because of their culture from what they are because of their Christian faith. They might then be able to present the Gospel without automatically integrating it with incomprehensible Western cultural baggage. Being an American of course is not bad, but it is irrelevant outside of the United States.

To participate and communicate effectively, your *cultural awareness should proceed on two fronts:* (1) You need to understand your second culture; (2) You also need an insightful awareness of your first one. You see, our first culture has influenced every area of our life — our attitudes, values, behaviour, beliefs, and the organization of our knowledge bank. But much of what we are culturally is at a subconscious level. In learning a new culture it is helpful to bring to awareness this subconscious cultural knowledge. If you are aware of the way your culture has shaped you, and if you understand some potential alternative ways of being shaped, then you will be better equipped to explore the cultural characteristics of the people who speak your new language.

Perceptions of the world

Orientation in a new culture is *more* than learning a language. It is also learning how people perceive the world — How do they think? What is the frame of reference through which they will interpret the message symbols they receive?

The following suggestions for cycles proceed on each of the two fronts simultaneously. Topics are designed to help you become more aware of yourself while you come to understand the content of the local knowledge bank. We will present some cultural characteristics that are typical of most speakers of English, particularly North Americans. We don't want to oversimplify your culture or your new culture, for they are both very complex. Within each culture most different perspectives might be represented, and contradictions will occur (for example, the American value of equality is sometimes incompatible with the value of achievement), nevertheless it will be helpful to discuss cultural differences by means of some generalizations. If a generality doesn't apply to you, then you can modify it as needed.

know
where you are

NOTE: In general, Americans hold to three broad belief systems. Americans feel that these are "right," just as people of other cultures feel that their beliefs are right. Many of our American values, assumptions, and world-views can be traced to one or more of these belief systems.

They are: The democratic belief system
The work belief system
And the free-enterprise belief system.

Each of these belief systems has various components.

The **democratic system** includes:

The belief that all men are equal in dignity and worth. The belief that no wise or good person is wise or good enough to have arbitrary power over any other person. And the belief that each person is entitled to have his "say" concerning how he is governed.

Our **work belief system** includes the following beliefs or "Knowledge":

We believe that striving for excellence in employment is the proper way to earn self-respect and the esteem of others.

We believe that any type of honest employment offers an equal opportunity for a person to prove his worth.

We believe that the person who is a creative innovator deserves more respect and esteem.

We believe that society:
A.   Should provide equal opportunity for individuals to develop their potential.
B.   Should offer a wide range of work opportunities so that each individual's productive abilities are utilized effectively.
C.   Should enable each individual to earn a fair wage for his contribution.

We also believe that through productive work, individuals, groups, and even nations can realize their dreams.

Our **free-enterprise belief** system includes:

The belief that successful capital, and land accumulation is the measure of true distinction.

And the belief that people who don't value the work ethic may not provide for themselves and they are therefore undeserving of social acceptance.

Some of the above beliefs are of course in the process of change.

Go back and ponder each of the above beliefs and ask yourself what life might be like if people didn't hold to them or value them in the same way that Americans do. This contemplation might help you to be more open to the beliefs and values of your new culture.

The topics of Set 4 are arranged in three broad categories. The first few topics deal with values related to the *physical world*. The middle group of topics (the majority of Set 4) explores the values and assumptions related to the *personal world*. The last topics explore people's understanding of the *supernatural world*.

You should continue to use the general procedures of the Daily Learning Cycle. In the Preparation stage, elicit a text that deals with the topic by exploring Kino's knowledge. Also, be on the lookout for paragraphs in books or periodicals written about any of these topics. Work current events into your texts from time to time — you should now be regularly reading the local daily newspaper and keeping up with current events through the various forms of mass media. Another Preparation alternative would be to elicit material from community members who seem to be particularly knowledgeable on the subject in focus.

Get topics
from the media

You will probably want to spend at least one day on each topic. Draw an additional *dateline* beside the topics which yield information you would like to pursue. The dateline will serve as a reminder to yourself to return to the topic.

Practice your texts as usual, and be sure to develop a way to introduce the topic to people during your communication time. The assumptions and value systems of a culture are seldom surface characteristics. Rather, they are usually at the very core of a person's being. They are characteristics which may seldom be talked about, for they are largely integrated into the local knowledge at a sub-conscious level. Be sensitive when probing. Learn ways to creatively introduce these topics into conversations in sensitive, non-threatening ways. Also, develop an alertness so that when the topics are introduced by others you can discreetly ask further questions along these same lines.

Your task while talking with people is to systematically discover the knowledge which they have learned and are using. Ask "What do people see themselves as doing?" Try to learn the criteria that *they* use as they observe, interpret, and describe their own experiences. Of course a good deal of your communication time must be spent *listening*. Try to listen to a wide variety of viewpoints on each theme. Evaluation time should include analysis and comparison of the various perspectives.

Listen to a wide
variety of viewpoints

Remember that your initial objective is not to change the way people think so that it conforms to your own. To be an effective communicator, your first objective must be to observe and learn their perspective.

The Physical World

Date

English speakers usually "know" (assume) that the earth is material and that it doesn't have a soul or spirit. People from the non-Western world often "know" that things around them are naturally existing forms of life. These different assumptions about reality lead Western man to exploit the physical environment for his own purposes, while leading others to preserve a "naturally existing" integrated relationship with nature.

For us, the physical world is real, and is sharply distinct from the supernatural world. The physical world is governed by predictable laws which we can discover and use. We can exploit and control it by scientific study and technology. To others, the physical world may be controlled by spiritual forces. In order to have any influence on nature, man must appease these spirits. The operations of the physical world are arbitrary and unpredictable.

Develop a text with your helper to **explore the assumptions about the external world.** What is considered to be animate? What role do spirits play? What is the perceived hierarchy of living things? What is exploitable? In man's relationship with the world around him, are there certain taboos — things it is not proper to do? How did the world come into being? What can man do to prevent or control disasters such as floods, drought, and lightening?

Disease

Specialists

We "know" that disease comes from germs. Others may "know" that disease is a result of some evil done by the individual, a relative, or an ancestor; or it may be the result of a hex put on by an enemy; or maybe some taboo was violated. Doctors tell us that maybe 90% of the illnesses of Americans may be psychosomatic. In other cultures the same may be true. Healing for most of these illnesses often comes after proper treatment by a "specialist." The specialist may be a medical doctor, psychiatrist, acupuncturist or medicine man. They each have their own rituals or "hocus-pocus" and if the patient believes, healing results. It is often kind of a placebo effect. (Dr. Livingstone referred to African medicine men as his "professional colleagues".)

NOTE: Bruce Olson, a young missionary among the Motilone people of Colombia, describes a thoughtful and wise way of treating non-psychosomatic disease. An outbreak of pink-eye had spread through the village and the tribal "medicine person" had unsuccessfully tried her potions and incantations. Olson had a tetra-myecin ointment and offered it to her. She refused it, saying she had tried potions and they didn't work. Olson then went out and touched the eye of a villager and infected his own eye with the pus. In a few days his eyes were as bad as the rest. He then took the ointment (his potion) to the health specialist inviting her to use it while performing the proper incantations. She did so, and within a few days his eyes were better. He gave

her the rest of the ointment and she used it to treat each of the villagers. By introducing medicine in a way that did not compete with the local medical specialist, the stature of the specialist was enhanced. By serving as a catalyst, Olson earned a welcome for himself among the people, and established a basis which permitted him to have a hearing for other innovations and for the introduction of the Gospel. *(For This Cross I'll Kill You,* **Creation House, Wheaton, Illinois)**

Ask people about the causes of various kinds of ailments. How are illnesses treated? What precautions can be taken to avoid various illnesses? What should be done if sickness strikes? What skills does a local medical specialist have? How did he get these skills? Is **illness and health** a common discussion topic? How much value or importance is attached to good health?

The *Personal World* topics which follow cover general areas of life-style, motivational rationale, reasoning, and interpersonal relationships.

Life Style

All peoples have their own ideas about what "ought to be" — these represent the *values* to which they hold. Most Americans cling to the values of being physically comfortable and possessing material things. To attain these values Americans spend most of their time, effort, and money on big houses, comfortable automobiles, labor-saving devices, nice clothes, etc. On the other hand, people of India have different assumptions and values, and as a result they might give away their possessions, deny themselves material comforts, dress in rags, and spend years wandering in pursuit of spiritual grace.

Develop a text to examine what people think "ought" to be — their **values concerning physical comfort and material possessions.** Ideally, what do people think is the wisest way to spend time, effort and money? What things are of permanent and lasting value? What is most important in human life? What does a person want most of all? After ones essential needs have been met, what other things are worth striving for?

The answers to these may help you understand what you are communicating by your own personal life style.

Economics

Money factory

Some people of the Pacific Islands think that America is a land of money factories. The Americans they see don't work, but spend enormous amounts of money — sometimes they spend more in a week than local people might earn in six months or more.

The American overseas usually takes his **standards of health, physical comfort, and materialism** with him. He may have less than he had at home, but local people compare his possessions with theirs. Often, the overseas American spends most of his time in activities of daily living. It simply takes more time to maintain a U.S. living standard where such a standard is uncommon.

Americans often think that if other people had the chance, they would be just like Americans. It is difficult for us to comprehend the rejection of American values by those who value the aesthetic or the spiritual over the economic and material.

Spend a day talking with people about the physical comforts they enjoy. What material possessions are essential in life? What can one not do without? Why is it needed? Try to determine what assumptions people may have made about you based on your standard of living.   ◦§

Private Property

"It is mine!" "This is our property — you kids should go away." Americans draw a clear line between private and public property. A man has almost absolute **jurisdiction over** his own **property.** It is not uncommon for others, however, to live on communal or public land. If something is taken from our yard, we view it as "stolen", but others might view it as "borrowed". If it was left unwatched, some might consider it public property and available to the first person who would value it enough to watch it.

Talk about property today. Who has "borrowing rights?" Can some things be borrowed without asking permission? Do houses and property belong to individuals? or families?   ◦§

Watched property

Motivation

We usually do things because we are motivated; because we want to make some progress, or to make an improvement. We often need to prove ourselves in order to establish our identity and be successful in our achievements. **Success** is a value for us. We especially like our accomplishments to be visible and measurable. We develop our **identity** based on what we accomplish. Other people of the world often have their identy based on what they are, not on what they do. They fall someplace into a social structure; they are born into a family that carries out a particular occupation, etc. In order to behave according to the obligations of the social group, the expected duties are performed — their work preserves or enhances their position in the social structure.

Begin to find out **why people do what they do.** Develop a text and talk with people about reasons for their activity. Will they work toward meeting an objective through the kind of motivation you are familiar with, or through the expectations of the social group they are a part of, or. . .? You might choose to ask questions like: If you had a chance to change jobs, would you primarily look for one with a higher salary, or one which would be more enjoyable? Why are some people successful when others are not? Does luck or good fortune play a part? How? Is it good to have ambitions? Is it better to always try to avoid failure, or to always try to work toward success? If you are not successful what should you do? What can cause lack of success? Is it good to be more successful in any way than your neighbors?

Visible Achievement _____

Perhaps you have heard of someone who had become "Americanized". This term is usually used in a derogatory way to describe citizens of the third world who don't feel "at home" among their own people. National representatives of American organizations are often Americanized. This characteristic is, unfortunately, considered a value by many organizations because cross-cultural communications is then a diminished problem for them. But the Americanized person is often looked at with suspicion by his fellow countrymen.

What is the strangeness that is noticed? (You may have the same kind of strangeness.) There are no doubt many factors, but a major one seems to fall into the concept of "measurable achievement". For Americans, achievements need to be *visible* and *quantifiable*.

Learning to be visible

The Americanized person has learned to be visible, and to give statistics. With these characteristics he can fit in with an American organization. The Americanizing of people might not be necessary if Americans overseas would become bilingual and bicultural. Then, communication could take place where the people are, instead of where the (short-sighted? mono-lingual?) Americans are.

Sometimes knowing more about ourselves helps in our relationship with others. What are your own objectives? If they are measured in statistical terms of quantity rather than quality, then your behavior may be misunderstood in the new culture. Talk with people about the meaning of their lives. What do they want out of life? What is the purpose of life as they see it? What are the needs they feel? Can your communication objective be fullfilled in a way that improves the quality of their life from their own perspective, rather than in a way that just gives you another statistical accomplishment?

Time scurrying

Change and Progress

We "know" that the present can be improved on, and that to do so is right. We know this because we value action and we are future oriented. (For us, time hardly stops at the present, while it scurries from the past racing into the future.) But, for the Latin American, life is being lived for the present. For the Chinese, the **traditions** of the past are a value. The result is that **change** and **progress** may be neutral or negative, rather than positive, good and right. We have heard a present-oriented person exclaim, "You Americans, you always want to change things"; and a past-oriented person sagely observed, "Cancer, too, is progressive you know".

How do people feel about traditions and change? Do people feel they would like to return to the "good old days"? What changes have been good or helpful? What changes would they like to see? What do they wish had not been changed? Do they define "progress" in the way you would? Spend a day listening to, and discussing people's opinions on change and progress. This will be valuable feedback (feedforward?) which will enable you to be a better communicator in the future.   ∼§

Action!

"Oh, dear! Oh, dear! I shall be too late!" *(Alice in Wonderland's* White Rabbit).

"I shall be too late!"

We are always busy, in a hurry, and doing something. We like to think of ourselves as people of action. What a person does is more important than what he is. We are future-oriented, and we want to be accomplishing something — we expect to be able to see results. **Time, efficiency,** and **activity** are very closely related in our minds. We don't like to waste time, for "time is money." (A Latin American once expressed: "The trouble with you Americans is you don't want things done today, you want them done yesterday!")

In your new culture, when people consider an activity, the *being* of those involved may be given more importance than their *doing*. They may feel that a time of meditation should preceed action. Perhaps for them, time should be man's servant, not his master.

Talk with people today about their attitudes toward time. It is good to always be busy or in a hurry? How should one spend his time? Do people sometimes just "do nothing"? Is that OK? What does a person do during a typical day?

For your continued learning, maintain an attitude of *being* involved — don't be just *doing* involvement activities. Make involvement a way of life.

NOTE: Americans overseas are often expected to train some of the local people. However, if they are unable to effectively communicate, they often find it easier to do the task themselves, rather than train others. We like to be "doing," and we have a way of thinking up solutions and courses of action for just about any situation. If it becomes customary for the foreigner to make all the decisions about what to do, then local people may never gain a comprehensive understanding of what is being done. They may even be alienated by the innovations that are being pushed through. If this happens, then the innovative accomplishments won't "take". As soon as the foreigner's influence diminishes, the innovation may be unrecognizably changed or else terminated. Westerners on short-term assignments should be especially aware of this likelihood for some of their projects which are supposed to have quick impact. To avoid this problem, innovations must be integrated into the social structure. This happens as innovations are implemented via established cultural and traditional patterns. The innovator thus needs to have liberal access to the local knowledge bank.

Work and play

Work and Play

For us, a person is either working, or else he is playing, relaxing, etc. These form a *dichotomy* which are not supposed to be mixed for us. But a Latin American businessman may conduct his work as a continuing social event. Private meetings or concise brief discussions may seldom occur.

Develop a text so that you can find out what people know (their assumptions and values) about work and play.

Reasoning Patterns

You have no doubt occasionally said or thought something about the "disorganization," "poor planning," and other characteristics of people around you — something like "these people... (some less than complimentary remark)." What you mean is that you don't understand the way the people think. North Americans generally value analytical **inductive** logic which organizes evidence, and, through steps of linear logic, arrives at conclusions. Others, however, may be accustomed to **deductive** reasoning. Conclusions are drawn by looking at the "whole" and anything relevant to it, without any ordering of the steps in a linear way. This pattern of thinking is often called *contextual*.

Often we seek to identify the cause of some effect so that we can plan another course of action for the future. Others, however, may feel that we over-simplify the task, and that it is important to consider a multiplicity of causes. The wisdom of the ancients may also be carefully weighed before planning any course of action.

Court session

Attend tribal meetings or court sessions and learn what general line of reasoning is observed in approaching and deciding a case.

When people around you do something in a way different from what you would do, it may mean that you don't understand the way people think regarding the activity. Maintain an attitude which lets you accept the validity of their way. Keep notes about these differences, for they will provide you with many topics for texts. For your text today, isolate a behavior which you don't understand. Talk about it with many people and try to gain a sympathetic, insiders' perspective.

NOTE: The acceptance of the validity of other people's values is not easy for an outsider to communicate. Due to the English speaker's subconscious tendency to dichotomize (*good-bad, right-wrong, work-play,* etc.) **a simple discussion of previous experiences or American life-style could communicate an attitude of superiority. The mere presence of an outsider in a technical role almost automatically suggests superiority to the local people. Any comparison with things at home implies that American standards are better. Be careful to describe things as "different," not as "wrong," "bad," or "inefficient."**

—— Decision Making

From childhood, an American is taught to decide for himself and develop his own opinions. We learn to put ourselves and our desires at the center of our world, and consider ourselves to be quite independent and self-reliant. Even when we are faced with the necessity of making a decision for which we need expert counsel, the expert is treated as a resource person to help us make up our own minds — we seldom ask him to decide for us.

In many other cultures, children are taught to become group members. The group is the focal point and **individual decisions** are secondary. Decisions which we would consider personal might be made by the group (the family or the community): who to marry, where to live, what religious faith to follow, what kind of work to do, etc.

The English-speaker participates in making **group decisions,** but he expects a "fair opportunity" to express his views, and equality for all group members. He likes an agenda and may expect to follow *Robert's Rules of Order.* Other cultures do not necessarily hold to similar **values of fairness or equality.** In such a group, the outsider may be seriously misunderstood if he operates on his own cultural assumptions.

Western man talks about **democracy** — government by the people — yet he may allow a 51% majority to rule. In many non-western cultures the rights of the minority are respected, and the majority will compromise until a *consensus* of some kind is reached. To defeat someone would cause him to "lose face," and "saving face" is a more important value than majority rule.

Americans expect to be involved in making a decision if they are affected by it. We enjoy being *proponents of action* which we recommend that the group follow. In the Orient, however, for an individual to urge the acceptance of his opinion as the course of group action might be offensive. For us, the individual suggests the action, and he is largely held accountable for its success or failure — we like to have a person to blame. The Oriental would probably offer his opinions by means of circumlocution so that it might become the group's opinion — and the group's responsibility.

Develop a text so that you can talk about the way individuals make decisions. What are the factors which have to be considered? Questions: When you have to make an important decision, who do you consult? Do you occasionally make such decisions without consulting anyone? What important decisions have you had to make recently? How did you go about making up your mind? What factors did you take into account? What types of people did you consult? Did you ask them to advise you, or to make the decision for you?

Making a decision

Develop another text to talk about group-decision attitudes and procedures. Are there leaders within the group who shape opinions and influence decisions? What has caused them to have this responsibility?

Of course, a day or two of language learning devoted to decision making will not be sufficient for you to learn all the relevant values and assumptions. But your expectations will begin to be adjusted, and your awareness increased.

Authority

In all societies, people are subject to those who are over them, and many times they themselves are in authority over others.

In America, the **authority-subordinate relationship** is confined to specific settings — primarily school and work. The person in authority is responsible for the well-being of his subordinates only while they are on the job or at school.

In some other places, the authority figure is seen more as a benevolent benefactor or "patrón" who is responsible for the all-around well-being of his subordinates. providing housing, recreation, and social security for them.

Authority figures

Find out who people take orders from. Do they also give orders to anyone? Talk with people about the relationship between those who give orders and those who take them. How do people feel about those who are in authority? What happens if a subordinate does not carry out an order? Should a person carry out an order which he feels to be unethical or against his conscience? What about an order which is distasteful or very difficult? If he shouldn't carry it out, what should he do? What responsibilities and obligations do those in authority have toward their subordinates? What rights?   ◄§

——— Social Interaction

As Americans we hold the assumption of equality of all men; we believe that all men are created equal (though sometimes we violate this assumption through prejudice). Our interpersonal relationships are horizontal, and the participants are presumed to be equals — even if one happens to be the manager. We like to demonstrate equality by calling everyone by his first name. (In many cultures this is improper.) We are often confused in cultures where social hierarchy is the norm. It is hard for us to appreciate the fact that people often prefer to be in a **social hierarchy** with its predictable forms of interaction with people both above and below the individual's own social status.

Develop a text to help you explore the social structure of your new culture. What is the hierarchy? What factors determine a person's place within the hierarchy? Who has power? How did he get it? What are the symbols of power? Does status relate to finances? Family ties? Occupation? Education? Does a person's social status ever change? How? Are there *visible signs* of status in the way people dress or live? Is special status or respect given to people who are very old or wise?

Old and wise

How do people treat those of a higher rank? What obligations do they have? How do they show their respect?

How do people relate to those of a lower status? What obligations do they have? Do they treat their subordinates with respect, familiarity, aloofness?

How do peers interact? Do peers have obligations to one another? Is there an extra degree of familiarity or informality between peers?

Where do you fit in this social structure? How can you know? What should be your proper behavior toward people above your status level? Below your status level? When you meet someone new, how can you tell what his comparative status is? If you are unsure, is it better for you to treat him as a peer or as a person of higher status?   ◄§

Direct vs. Indirect Relationships _____

The directness and aggressiveness which comes easily to us may be viewed as briskness, or aggression by others. In some cultures, interpersonal relations are very indirect — maybe even done through an intermediary. An African chief is usually addressed formally and **through an intermediary.** In many countries, disagreements are settled by a mediator. Marriages may also be arranged by a mediator. This procedure allows both sides to agree or disagree without losing face. English speakers are notoriously insensitive about this matter of "saving face." Open **confrontation** is the American way.

You can explore these relationships by asking questions like the following. If you wanted to invite your superior to a special occasion (wedding, birth ceremony, etc.) would you do it in person, by mail, or through a friend? How would you go about asking a favor from a friend? Would this be done differently if the person were only a passing acquaintance? If you wanted to come to an agreement with someone else on the price of a large purchase, such as a house, how would you go about it?

How would you handle a conflict with your boss or a superior? If a person under you failed to carry out your orders, what would you do? Would you reprove him? Speak to someone else about it? Ignore it? What should you do if two of your friends or co-workers are having a dispute — should you get involved, or is it better to let them settle it on their own? Is it important for both of them to save face? How can this be done? What should you do if someone continually tries to annoy you or is just hard to get along with? Would you talk to him directly? Talk to friends about it? Avoid him?

Ask friends to tell you if you are perceived as being too aggressive or abrupt.   ✍

Friendship _____

The American's informality allows him to initiate friendships easily. A friend to an American can be a casual passing acquaintance or a life-time intimate. We have different friends for different activities — church friends, work friends, social friends, neighborhood friends, etc. For others, friendships may mean a deep bond with an obligation of almost constant companionship — and no secrets. For Americans, competition between friends is common, but it is sometimes hard for others to comprehend — friends are for cooperation, not competition. In some places, friends do not include members of the opposite sex. For some, true friends are not common and not shared, and as a result friendship may be jealously guarded.

Friends are
to share with

Americans like to be popular — they like other people to like them. This can be a problem for the person who has services to render in a situation where being liked or disliked is completely irrelevant. In some cultures, friendship is the condition for establishing warm personal relationships, while for us friendship is often a superficial measure of social success.

Today, talk about friends. Learn who has friends with whom. How many people do individuals count among their friends? What is the nature of their relationship? What are the obligations or responsibilities involved? What do friends know about each other? What do friends do together?

Other questions to ask Kino and people in the community might be: If one of your friends were upset with you for some reason, how would you handle it? Is it important to try to settle differences between friends, or is it better to just hope things will improve with the passing of time? What would you do if your best friend abandoned you? Should you forget about him? If not, how would you go about restoring your friendship?

Kinship

Your knowledge gives you an understanding of the way the kinship system is organized in your own culture. You not only know about kinship relationships, but you also know about the obligations and privileges which are associated with these relationships. You cannot assume that your knowledge of your own kinship system can be superimposed to describe the family relationships or the obligation patterns of your new culture.

Kinfolk

Develop a text that will help you discuss and learn about the kinship system of the people. Our kinship system includes terms like: mother, grandfather, uncle, sister, cousin, second cousin, daughter, nephew, grandson, and daughter-in-law. The new system you are learning will no doubt have different **relationships of importance.** Perhaps relative age is important, and so there may be different terms for older sister, younger sister; older brother, younger brother; father's older sister (aunt), father's younger sister. Perhaps relationship to your mother or to your father is important, so there may be a different word for father's brother than for mother's brother, or a different term for a cousin related to your father than for one related to your mother. Perhaps comparative sex is important — there may be a name meaning "sibling of the same sex", and a different term for "sibling of the opposite sex". So, two brothers might call each other "om" and two sisters could also call each other "om", while a brother and a sister might call each other "oy".

Whatever the kinship system is, it will fit and reflect the cultural patterns, so learn to use it, and learn how it operates in terms of daily life — rights, courtesies, obligations, etc. If the system is fairly complex, you may want to spend a number of cycles on it — a cycle or two to learn the basic vocabulary, and some cycles to learn what the social relationships are between the various categories of kinship relationships.

To begin probing *relationships* and *obligations,* you might ask questions like the following.

Who are the people who really need you? What do they depend on you for? What would happen if you couldn't meet this obligation? Which of your other relatives would you feel most obliged to help if they had a specific financial need? Who do you depend on? For what? When a man becomes ill or dies, which of his relatives (if any) is expected to care for his family?

Which relatives have the right to ask others to do things for them? Are there sets of relationships in which one member typically is indulgent toward the other (for example, grandparent to grandchild in our society)? Which relatives must a person not marry? Are there advantages in marrying a distant relative? Which relatives have the right to discipline or reprove? In what form is this discipline given? For what kinds of wrong-doings? Is this discipline given only to children, or to adults also? What relative usually has the most influence on the family group? Does a parent or grandparent often make decisions for the whole family group? Are family decisions sometimes made by group consent?

Indulgent grandparent

Are step-children or adopted children full family members? What terms are used to identify them? What relationships are important from an inheritance standpoint? What clan relationships exist, and what is their importance? If polygamy is practiced, what terms are used for co-wives? In such cases a child may, or may not, refer to all of his father's wives as "mother." What other complexities does polygamy introduce into the kinship system?

The kinship chart can be useful in visualizing kinship relationships. We have filled in the English terms to help you see how our kinship system works. Make your own chart of the kinship terms in your language. (Don't expect the kinship system of your new language to be equivalent in its use of terminology — some areas will be more complex and others less complex. For example, there may be various words for the people we would call "cousin", whereas there may only be one word for all relatives before your parent's generation.) All the items on one level of the chart are in the same generation; the ones at the top are the earliest generation, and those at the bottom are the most recent generation. A line going down indicates descent. Reading from left to right within each set, those on the left are older than those on the right. The symbols are: = for marriage, Δ for male, and ○ for female. The chart is set up so that *all* the names show the relationship of everyone to one individual in the center, called "**ego**." (Some of the kinship terminology may be different for a female ego than for a male ego. If so, you may need to indicate these differences on your chart in some way.) Write in parentheses any names that *can* be used, but are not necessarily always used. For example, in English we can say "older brother", "younger brother" to distinguish between them, but commonly we just say "brother." So on the chart, the words "older" and "younger" could be in parentheses — (older) brother.

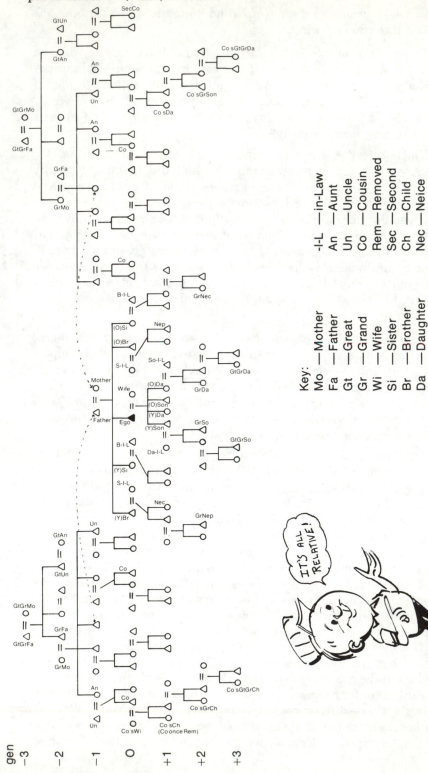

Key:
Mo — Mother
Fa — Father
Gt — Great
Gr — Grand
Wi — Wife
Si — Sister
Br — Brother
Da — Daughter
O — Older
Y — Younger

-I-L — in-Law
An — Aunt
Un — Uncle
Co — Cousin
Rem — Removed
Sec — Second
Ch — Child
Nec — Neice
Nep — Nephew
gen — Generation

IT'S ALL RELATIVE!

gen
-3
-2
-1
0
+1
+2
+3

Gift Giving

Date

We give gifts on birthdays and Christmas, or we may invite people to share a social time. If we respond by thanking the giver then our social obligation is probably satisfied. There is usually no obligation to reciprocate. In other cultures, social acts are often a means of fulfilling an obligation or a duty. A reciprocal act may be expected. Failure to respond might depreciate the meaning of the previous overture.

To whom do people feel they should give gifts — to family members, friends, employees, boss, or public servants like the postman or trash man? On what occasions? What is the proper way to respond when you receive a gift? What responsibilities do you incur — should you give a gift in return? What is then the limit of your obligation or indebtedness? Is it ever improper to give or receive a gift? Might it be interpreted as a bribe or as blackmail? How does one refuse a gift?

Talk with different people about gift giving and invitations to social events. What social act is appropriate in each of various situations? What is the proper response? What do people think if the proper response isn't given? What complications arise if the participants are not of the same sex?

Gift giving

We believe in charitable giving through institutions and other impersonal means, and we look down on giving to beggars which demands a more personal involvement. For others, however, the more personal involvement might be valued. What do people think of beggars? Do people feel obligated to give to beggars? What is given? Under what circumstances? How much is given? Are there times when it is considered inappropriate to give?

Individuality vs. Uniformity

All cultures have situations for which uniformity is expected, and they also have ways of permitting individuality. These situations, however, are not the same from culture to culture. Problems can occur because North Americans value individuality where **many others value uniformity.** We as Americans are influenced by the work ethic: hard work will be rewarded with success. "Where there is a will there is a way." We seldom feel that what we get is at the expense of others, for we feel we live in a world of abundance. Exploitation is a way of life and **individual achievement** which sets us off from the crowd is the way we establish our *status*. In many other cultures, however, people know what their social status is. Good relations are maintained with the group by looking and acting like everyone else. People dress alike, eat alike, live in similar houses, etc. To do otherwise would make them stand out from the other members of the community and would be viewed with suspicion. They work, of course, but maybe to survive and meet their needs, rather than amass wealth.

Date

Sometimes the lottery provides a culturally acceptable way of trying to gain individual prestige. Winning in the lottery is intervention by an outside agent. It is non-threatening to others and therefore acceptable.

In many societies the person who has more economically has more obligations as well — friends and relatives expect a share. Sometimes a poor person prefers his status and feels he is better off for he doesn't have all the extra responsibilities.

Develop a text to talk with people about the way individuality is perceived. In what areas of life is it best to be uniformly like others? When is individuality accepted? When encouraged? Is it ever good for a person to earn more money than his friends or neighbors? When working on a job should one try to become the best workman there? Are there times when it is bad or harmful for a man to be different?

Competition

Do people in your new culture play volleyball or some other kind of game without keeping score?! Many people are not as competitive as Americans. They participate for the intrinsic satisfaction of it, and do not need to be able to say they won or they beat someone else. People of many other cultures are dependent on other group members to a greater extent than we are and cooperation is essential. Competing against others and causing them to lose face is therefore not desirable. Competition is a primary method of motivation for Americans, but this approach is *not* effective in many other cultures and it may even result in undesirable consequences. You might tend to be competitive when others wouldn't.

Find out what people think about individuals who are very competitive. Is competition used to motivate people to study harder or work more? Do people prefer to play games that involve competition with others, or those which require group cooperation? Do people perceive you as being overly competitive? If so, maybe someone could be encouraged to give you reminders when needed so that you can modify your behaviour.

Being Sick

When we are sick, all of our obligations and responsibilities cease. If we stay at home we go to bed and expect to be left in *privacy*. If our case is bad enough we become a patient in a hospital. There we submit ourselves to a mechanical routine. We expect to receive visits from minister, relatives and special friends — during visiting hours. Similarly, our elderly are put in an institution, and later transferred to a hospital to die — often away from family and loved ones.

In other cultures, however, sickness often provides reason for a *social get-together* of loved ones. Sick ones and the elderly are treated at home where family and friends may congregate. For them, sterilized treatment is less of a value than being among loved ones during times of trial.

Spend a day learning how sick people are treated. What does a sick person do? What should he avoid doing? Where does he stay? What social interaction is expected of relatives? Of friends? What are the attitudes toward the elderly? What are the relationships between the very old and others? If someone is about to die, what do others do?

Crises

Crises

Crises are never easy in any culture. There are, of course, culturally appropriate and inappropriate **ways to respond during times of stress.** Your own knowledge bank already includes information that helps you respond to crises in a Western way. But how do people respond to crises in your new culture?

This topic may not be easy for people to talk about. It might be best to develop a short story about some crisis you have had and your response to it. Also, any daily newspaper has accounts of different kinds of crises happening to various people — you could build texts on these stories. When you use your own personal stories, or public news items, you may help people to feel more free to discuss this topic and perhaps even share an account of one of their own crises. You might then be able to ask questions like the following.

How should you handle yourself in times of crisis — accident, injury, financial trouble, death of a friend, marital problems? How should you respond to them? Should you remain calm? Worry? Try to escape from the situation? What about suicide? Is there anything you should specifically avoid doing during times of crisis? What causes such crises? To whom do you go for assistance?

What are you most afraid of? Why? How can you avoid these things?

Have you ever had a terrifying experience? What happened? Why? When did it happen? Who else was involved? What caused it? Are there any continuing effects? How can you prevent it from happening again?

What causes arguments between members of the society? Quarrels between husband and wife? Troubles between members of a family? How can these be avoided? What happens when one person is abusive to another? Is it ever right to take vengeance? Is violence ever the answer?

What are the causes of crises in society? What are some of the targets of the society's hate or condemnation? What things have caused war in the past? What could cause fighting today? What prevents fighting?

Emotions

Emotions are the external *expression* of your deep **inward feelings.** Some emotions are joy, love, sadness, anger, excitement, fear, annoyance, hatred, contentment. You can think of others. A text on each emotion would provide you with valuable information for your knowledge bank. Here are some questions for starters.

What would you do if someone were angry or annoyed with you? Why would he act this way? When is anger justified or excused? How should it be expressed? When should it not be expressed?

Do husbands and wives (or fiancees) ever express their love in public? Is it common for a husband to tell his wife that he loves her? How does a wife respond to this? How do parents express their affection toward their children? Are there times when it is inappropriate to express affection? How can love be most appropriately expressed?

Modify questions to talk about other emotions. Again, it might be helpful to prime the pump by talking about your own expressions of emotions, or by telling a short story on the topic.

Happy, angry,
contented, scared

Religion and the Supernatural

Try to tap people's understanding and knowledge of supernatural things by exploring what they believe about God, spirits, religious duties and rites, religious ceremonies, places, people, objects, and concepts. This will take various texts.

Some of our readers are Christian missionaries whose objective is to communicate the Gospel. To communicate a new message effectively it is first necessary to understand the organized knowledge which people already have about supernatural matters. As you become aware of the categories that people already have, you can better communicate your message in clear understandable ways. When communicating, you should be careful to continue to get the feedback that will reveal the actual understanding of your hearers.

Even if you are not a missionary, don't neglect these topics — the supernatural is a basic part of any people's knowledge bank. The paragraphs that follow are made up of questions on various topics relating to the supernatural. We suggest that you build each paragraph into at least one Daily Learning Cycle. Discuss each topic with various types of people in the community each day, to get a variety of points of view.

Date

What is **God** like? How many gods are there? How did God come into being? Did God create man? How does He act toward men? What are His attitudes toward men? As far as God is concerned, are there different kinds of people — good and bad, religious and irreligious, etc.? Is God concerned about man's relationship to his fellow man? Has God ever spoken to men? How? What are man's duties toward God? How can a man please God? How can a man communicate with God?

Date

How is **supernatural guidance** gained? Is supernatural insight about future or past events ever possible? How? Is it possible through religious means to learn the truth about a crime, or the cause of an illness? What are the procedures which should be followed? What is the significance of dreams?

What kinds of **spirits** are there? What do they do? Why? Should any of them be honored? Should any of them be feared? What is man's relationship to them? Do spirits ever possess human beings? Is this desirable? How does someone become spirit-possessed?

What is the **soul**? Does everyone have a soul? Do any animals or things have souls? Can the soul ever leave a living person? What does it do then? What happens to the soul when a person dies? What should a person do to prepare for death and for his soul's welfare? Is there a special reward in the afterlife for good people after they die? What is it like? Is there future punishment for the souls of evil people? Can living relatives do anything to help improve the lot of those who have died? What activities do the departed ones engage in? Is reincarnation ever possible? Under what circumstances? Do people believe in resurrection?

How does your religion affect your **daily life**? What does it teach you about daily ethics, virtues, attitudes, morality? Tell me about a religious belief, practice, or experience that has been important in your life.

How should religious values be **taught**? To whom? Who should teach them? Which ones should primarily be taught? When? How have you come to your present religious understanding? Who influenced you most in your religious development? Tell me about your religious **literature** — poems, essays, songs, dramas, etc.

Who are your **religious leaders** or **prophets**? Are there different kinds of religious leaders? What are their responsibilities? How are they supported? What do they wear? Are they more holy than others because of their position or because of rituals they follow? What is their basic message or doctrine? How did they become religious leaders? What has been their training?

Are there **special days** set apart for specific religious celebrations or activities? What do you do on those days? What do you avoid doing on those days? Are there special **times** for worship or religious duties during ordinary days?

Are there **special places** set aside for worship or other religious activities? Why were these places chosen? What is their significance? What legends are there about these places? What do you do there? How often do you go? How do you dress? Are there any special **objects** for use in worship? Who performs ceremonies at the sacred places?

Are there **ceremonies** that mark transition points in life — conception, birth, puberty, initiation, marriage, sickness, menopause, death, anniversary of death? Are these ceremonies essentially religious in nature? How are they observed? What do these ceremonies mean? Why are they carried out? What would happen if they weren't done properly?

What **worship activities** are commonly performed? How do people pray? When do they pray? Where? What do they pray for? To whom do they pray? Are offerings made? To whom? What kinds of offerings are there? Why are they offered? How often? How are they given? Is prayer or a ritual commonly made when eating? Are there any ceremonial meals, feasts, or special foods that have religious significance? Are there any foods or activities which should be avoided for religious reasons? Is magic a part of religious activities? What taboos and fears are associated with religion? Are special music forms or musical instruments important at religious activities? Is there a special religious type of language? Is there a stylized intonation or vocabulary that is used in ceremonies, prayer, songs, or sermons?

What actions are considered **sinful** or especially **bad**? What are the results of such bad deeds? When a person does wrong, who is he sinning against? Is God offended? Is a relationship broken or hindered? How can a person atone for what he has done? How can a relationship between God and sinful man be reestablished? Should sacrifices or offerings be made? What is the cause (origin) of evil in the world?

Christian missionaries may also wish to probe areas of **spiritual need** with questions like these. Do you feel that God is concerned about our peace of mind and happiness? If you could be God's friend would that be a good thing? Do you ever wish you could know God more personally? Do you sometimes feel that God is angry with you? What important spiritual questions are unanswered in your mind? Are you afraid of death or of what will happen to you after death? What are man's deepest spiritual needs? Do you have spiritual needs that aren't being met?

A Theory of Culture

Some of you who have reached this point of involvement in your new culture may recognize the value of pursuing an even deeper cultural understanding. If you have responsibilities as a change agent in the culture, it behooves you to seek to understand the implications and ramifications of the social, spiritual or technological changes which you propose to introduce. And, on the positive side, you may discover cultural "vehicles" that will lead to the acceleration of the fulfillment of your objectives. Cultural beliefs do change and sometimes it is an outside cultural force which influences the change. This should provide a basis of optimism for the cultural change agent, but he should be prepared to be patient.

Throughout this book we have attempted to be completely practical, rather than theoretical. To discuss a theory of culture may seem to violate our purpose. But we feel that for some, theory can be the means to a very practical application. We will be careful, and will try not to lose you in the next few pages.

NOTE: This section is based on the work of Dr. John Monroe Brewster (Tom's uncle). After receiving his doctorate from Columbia in 1936, Brewster worked as a leader in the Department of Agriculture until his death in 1965. He was an economist in a change-agent role. The development of government agricultural policies was his responsibility, but he was equally concerned about the farmer's acceptance of federal agricultural policies. His research led him to develop a comprehensive theory of culture and to analyze the American cultural system. The Department of Agriculture recognized that farm innovation needed to be based on thorough cultural understanding. A theory of culture was the basis for practical results in the farms of America.

Brewster's paper "The Cultural Crisis of our Time" presented the theory, and was the first chapter in a memorial book published by his colleagues and the Farm Foundation. The book, *A Philosopher Among Economists – Selected Works of John M. Brewster*, was published in 1970.

This section, and the note on page 193 are based on Brewster's work, and almost everything in it should be in quotes except that we have rewritten it with the language learner and overseas change agent in mind.

Brewster defines culture as: *the Belief Systems People use in Guiding Their Striving for Significance*. The theory has six basic concepts.

1. **Striving for Significance.** The essence of any specific culture is its belief systems. This is currently expressed in the phrase "culture is knowledge". The belief systems of a culture guide its members in their striving for significance. This striving for significance is the *one underlying universal* to all cultures. People the world over strive to act in ways that merit an increasingly favorable image or evaluation of themselves. Regardless of the culture, *everyone* wants to feel good about himself, and wants others to value him as a person. The striving for significance is never fully gratified until one finds a course of action which fulfills his need for being the person he wants to be, both in his own eyes and in the judgment of others. The assurance of significance is our most highly valued treasure. It can't be photographed or weighed or saved, yet we seek it above all else, both individually and collectively. To be completely undeserving of a favorable evaluation by anyone, including oneself, would result in terrifying anxiety. In 1890, William James observed:

> No more fiendish punishment could be devised ... than that one should be turned loose in society and remain absolutely unnoticed by all members thereof. If no one turned around when we entered, answered when we spoke, or minded what we did, but if every person we met 'cut us dead', and acted as if we were non-existing things, a kind of rage and impotent despair would ere long well up in us, from which the cruelest bodily tortures would be a relief; for these would make us feel that, however bad our plight, we had not sunk to such a depth as to be unworthy of attention at all.

The need for assurance of significance is evident on every hand. From the *individual* standpoint, it has led soldiers to certain death and saints to martyrdom. It moves families from slums to suburbs. It shapes the style of the whole man, influencing the kind of clothing he wears, the car he drives, the home he seeks, and the career, friends, and associates he chooses. It influences the way he works and plays. And the courage he displays under stress and strain. Virtually everything a natural man does is done with a view to enhancing the prestige of his person, and above all to avoid damage to the treasured image that he and others have of himself.

From a *collective* standpoint, the striving for significance is the need that each person has to be a valued part of a group like the family, the business, the office, the nation, the world, and even the generations to come. The personal approval of an individual in his own eyes is not enough. Far greater fulfillment is achieved through identification with a group, especially with a group which one views as superior to other groups. (All peoples everywhere are ethnocentric.) Being first on one's team is gratifying, but this is nothing when compared to being valued on a team which excels all others. The collective aspect of the need for significance reaches its zenith in the life of nations. Churchill braced his countrymen for the Battle of Britain with a challenge so to bear themselves that "if the British Empire and its commonwealth last for a thousand years, men will still say: 'This was their finest hour.' " The need to be accepted and prized as equals has also provided the dynamics for the African and Asian drive for nationalism.

Each culture has its own different beliefs and characteristics, yet universally, people of all cultures are motivated by the striving for individual and collective significance.

2. **Beliefs.** In each culture, people are guided by beliefs. *Beliefs are the cultural variables of societies*. The striving for significance is the one cultural universal, but there are almost unlimited varieties of beliefs and belief systems.

The local knowledge bank consists of these beliefs and the values, or weights, assigned to the beliefs, plus the information common to people of the culture. Beliefs guide people to organize their ways of life and work so that individuals can be the type of person that the society values. In other words, beliefs are concepts of ways of

Recognition
of
Significance

life and work which people *feel obliged to follow* for the sake of proving their worth.

NOTE: There are no beliefs without mental concepts, but mere concepts are not beliefs. We can have a concept of head-hunting as a way of life, just by thinking about it. This concept would be a belief only if we were convinced that proficiency in head-hunting would be the *proper* way to gain personal esteem and the respect of others.

The Yir Yoront group of Australian aboriginals believed that the significance of a man was directly related to the ownership of a stone axe. By a complex set of ideas, the stone axe was an important symbol of masculinity — only older men were permitted to make or own an axe. The stability of kinship roles and society relationships was reflected in the owning and borrowing of the axe, and everyone in the society accepted these beliefs. The axe therefore stood for two important beliefs of the culture. The first was the superiority and rightful dominance of the male (chauvanists?). Women were expected to cut large quantities of firewood, so they needed to borrow an axe frequently each day. They could only borrow from certain people and had to return it promptly. The axe also represented the value and prestige of age, as symbolized by the younger people's need to borrow it. Near the turn of the century, traders and missionaries introduced steel hatchets. By winning favor at the mission, a woman might be given a steel axe which she alone possessed. She would no longer need to borrow an axe from a male relative. Young men and boys also obtained steel axes from the mission. The introduction of steel axes indiscriminately and in large numbers led to a revolutionary confusion of age, sex, and kinship roles. Those who now owned steel axes became independent and less subordinate. With the collapse of the stone-axe belief system, which was closely related to many other aspects of the culture, there followed a sudden and complete cultural disintegration which may even foreshadow the extinction of the group.

We can have a *concept* of a society with an important role for the hatchet, just by thinking about it. For them, however, it was more than just a concept. It was in fact a *belief system* which guided people in their striving for significance — a hatchet belief system.

On page 193 the American belief systems were described. Imagine the crisis that would result if the democratic belief system, the work belief system, or the free-enterprise belief system were suddenly inoperative in the United States. People would similarly be without a means of establishing worth and of being significant.

Beliefs then, are the concepts of ways of life and work that people feel obliged to follow as they relate to each other in society and fulfill their reciprocal rights and duties.

3. **Values.** When people of a culture are committed to a belief, that belief makes certain *action demands* on individuals. These action demands are reflected in what people feel obliged to do as they strive for significance. *Values* are the *relative weights* that people attach to their various beliefs, and the related action demands — i.e., *how much* do the people feel obliged to act in a prescribed way? For example, most everyone believes in telling the truth, but not everyone attaches the same significance to truth-telling. Some take it lightly, while others would scarcely tell even a "white lie." Often people share the same beliefs and yet have different values, because they attach different weights to their beliefs. Along with a commitment to telling the truth, most people also feel a commitment to protect sick people from anxiety over a fatal illness, but they may attach different degrees of importance to the action demands of these commitments. Some may therefore feel obliged to tell the patient the full truth, while others might feel obliged to forgo truth-telling for the sake of protecting the patient from worry over his condition.

4. **Interdependence of Beliefs and Values.** Since values are the relative weights which people assign to the action demands of their various beliefs, it follows that belief and value are as interdependent as the two sides of a coin. You can't have one without the other. Beliefs have *related* activities or practices which are valued to some degree. If the activity and practice is highly valued then the related personal or social qualities are also perceived to be highly significant. For example, the practice of truth-telling is valued and so the quality of honesty is esteemed; or where the practice of head-hunting is valued, the quality of courage is esteemed.

Though beliefs and values are interdependent, it should be obvious that beliefs must precede values. Trying to identify a

people's values without first identifying their beliefs is fruitless. There is nothing to measure, no point of reference, nothing to sink one's teeth into and no significant hypothesis to guide investigations.

5. **Policy Problems and Crisis Problems.** Changing conditions generate two different kinds of conflict among groups. One kind of conflict constitutes *policy* problems, and the other kind constitutes *crisis* problems.

Policy problems

Changing conditions may cause different groups to change the degree of *value*, or weighting, which was previously assigned to a belief. The change of value is reflected in changes of behavior. A cultural conflict of this kind, when beliefs are constant but the values are changed, presents a *policy* problem. In such conflicts, the bonds of common beliefs are strong enough to withstand the differences in values and behavior.

In sharp contrast, *crisis* problems arise when changing conditions lead a sizeable group to alienate themselves from *beliefs* which bind them to the existing social order. The alienation comes as they identify themselves with new beliefs that turn them against their social order.

Crisis problems

Crisis problems are thus disagreements in which each group increasingly tends to equate its own beliefs and behavior with moralistic absolutes of natural or divine law. In such cases, the alienated group often feels obliged to use whatever means it can (including violence) to overpower opposing groups. This is a process through which one civilization rises and another passes away.

6. **Inner Beliefs are Reflected in Outer Institutions.** In societies, people interact with each other and have reciprocal rights and responsibilities. *Institutions* provide the environment for these social interactions. Institutions are the external manifestation of the concepts of ways of living and making a living that people feel obliged to follow. Social institutions include the family, free elections, private ownership of property, polygamy, labor unions, congress, the army, schools, etc. Each culture has its own unique ways of *reflecting its beliefs* in

its behavior, and this social behavior is through culturally approved institutions. As overt ways of life, cultural institutions are outside of people, but they reflect the inner beliefs of people. These culturally approved institutions provide the means for individuals to become worthwhile citizens by satisfying the striving of each member for his own significance.

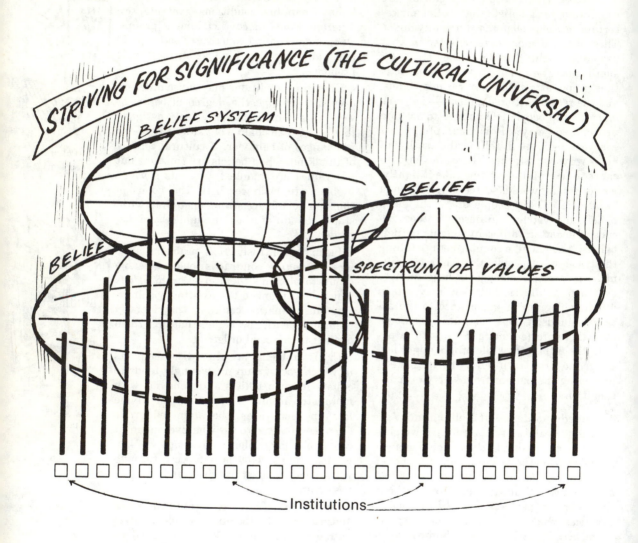

STRIVING FOR SIGNIFICANCE (THE CULTURAL UNIVERSAL)

BELIEF SYSTEM

BELIEF

BELIEF

SPECTRUM OF VALUES

Institutions

In summary:

1. The cultural universal is the *striving for significance*.
2. The cultural variables are *belief systems*.
3. The relative weights attached to beliefs are *values*.
4. Beliefs are *inseparable* from their related values.

5. Cultural conflicts are of two types:
   a. Value changes produce *policy* problems.
   b. Belief changes produce *crisis* problems.
6. Social organizations and institutions provide a means for the outward expression of cultural beliefs (knowledge).

Going On and On

Learning what people know is an ongoing process. By now we would expect you to be at a Level Three or maybe even Level Three Plus of speaking proficiency. Here are some ideas to help you continue going on. The best way to ensure continued progress is to *make a daily practice of gaining some new knowledge by talking with new people about new things.* Retrace your steps through the topics of this chapter but focus on some aspect which is not yet part of your knowledge. Read a lot in the language and talk with people about what you read.

Another technique that can help you continue probing people's value system involves the use of **completion projective statements.** You can do this with Kino and others who catch on to the technique. You may want to develop a questionnaire and keep a record of people's responses. Tell people, "I will read the beginning part of several sentences. You listen and then complete the sentence in whatever way you think is best." Your questionnaire could include starters like:

The most important thing in life is. . .
The things I am most interested in are. . .
What I really want to do is. . .
The thing I worry about most is. . .
Death is. . .
Those who have died. . .
The ideal woman would. . .
The most desirable quality of a husband is. . .
If I quarrel with someone. . .
When we do not have rain. . .
The way to be happy after death is. . .
When I am sick it is because. . .
The ancestors. . .

The ideal woman

You can make projective statements to probe any area you need more information about.

Some people finish a language school or language course and then perch themselves on a perpetual plateau. In one's first culture he keeps learning new vocabulary, figurative language, and new information throughout his life. Don't ever adopt the attitude that your new language and culture learning is a thing of the past — i.e., something you did when you were "studying the language." Now that you have a solid foundation, this is not the end but *the beginning.*

Going on!

CHAPTER 3

Things To Do In Comprehension Drills

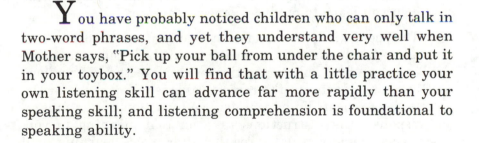

You have probably noticed children who can only talk in two-word phrases, and yet they understand very well when Mother says, "Pick up your ball from under the chair and put it in your toybox." You will find that with a little practice your own listening skill can advance far more rapidly than your speaking skill; and listening comprehension is foundational to speaking ability.

Why Stress Listening Comprehension?

The verbal sounds of your new language are only a series of nonsense syllables until meaning is attached to the symbols. Comprehension drills are an effective way to begin to rapidly attach meaning to a large number of verbal symbols.

What you practice doing is what you develop skill at doing. If you want to be able to comprehend, spend time listening and relistening. Listening skill develops more quickly than speaking skill, and resists forgetting more than the speaking skill. You get more progress per drop of sweat invested.

Listening comprehension proficiency has several practical benefits. Any true conversation requires receiving as well as sending. You can learn a lot from listening to others. Being able to listen with comprehension unlocks vast treasure-houses of information about, and insight into, the culture and the people. You can gain from lectures, radio programs, sermons, conferences, songs, etc. You can accompany people and participate. You can understand the answers to the questions you learn to ask.

A greater ability to understand what people are saying will increase your motivation and enthusiasm for being involved with people. Often a learner's reluctance to be involved in the community comes from a fear of not understanding what people are saying. As your comprehension increases, involvement will become easier and more rewarding.

When you are trying to respond in the language, your ability to listen with comprehension is often reduced. If you feel any anxiety about your ability to speak accurately, your comprehension tends to be inhibited. This suggests that you should devote specific time to comprehension practice in which you don't have to speak. If you take a little time to improve your listening comprehension, it will pay dividends in your speaking ability also. Your ability to correctly interpret what you hear will help you learn to produce correct sentences.

The more kinds of association that you make to an item, the better you learn and remember it. In these comprehension drills you are first able to see the meaning of the instructions as Kino himself acts out the correct response. You can hear the instructions repeatedly as you drill. As you supply the muscular response, the instructions take on real meaning to you. Long-term memory usually results after a few learning drill exercises in which you physically respond to the commands.

In Comprehension practice you can use much larger chunks of the language than in speaking practice. Comprehension drills allow you to internalize chunks of speech rather than just words.

Comprehension Drill Procedure

Comprehension drills will train you so that you can move forward rapidly in your understanding of the language. The procedure follows the observation, mimicry, and production stages. You move to the production stage almost immediately — however, your production is not in terms of speech, but in terms of physical response to Kino's speech.

Comprehension drill activities can be quite vigorous — Kino can instruct you to do actual calisthenics such as bending, stretching, jumping, doing deep knee bends, or even pushups and situps. On the other hand, they can be relatively mild drills in which two objects are moved about in relation to each other.

To prepare for a Comprehension drill, you need to plan a list of related activities and have Kino make up a 3 x 5 card with the activities written in his language. The activities for the first day might include sit, stand, squat down, clap your hands, scratch your leg, stretch your arms. In the drill, Kino will instruct you *in his language* to do an activity; for example, "stand up." He will stand up and you observe and then mimic the action by standing yourself. Do not say what he says. Kino then introduces the second item, performing the activity while giving the verbal instructions. You mimic the activity — for example, "sit down." Kino then again gives the first instruction, "stand up", and you respond by standing. Then Kino can give the instructions without acting them out himself — "sit down," "stand up," "sit down," "stand up," "sit down" while you respond to his verbal directions. When doing comprehension drills, respond rapidly without hesitation and make a distinct robust response with your body. If you respond with gusto, the meaning of the instruction will be reinforced all the more securely in your mind.

Kino then introduces the next activity — "clap your hands." When he first tells you to do it, he will also do it himself, and you will mimic the activity. Kino should then back up and give the previously drilled instructions and *return to the new activity frequently to keep it in focus* — "Stand up," "Clap your hands," "Sit down," "Clap your hands," "Clap your hands," "Stand up," "Sit down," "Clap your hands," "Stand up," "Clap your hands," "Sit down," "Stand up," "Clap your hands." When you are consistently responding correctly to the three instructions, the fourth activity is introduced. Then, it is in focus while the previous activities are reviewed. Each new activity should have a period of time when it is in focus while the previous activities are reviewed. Then the focus changes to a new activity. If you forget the activity for an instruction, Kino should remind you by spontaneously doing the activity himself and then review by bringing that activity into focus again for awhile. If you find that you don't remember how to respond to two or three activities, it is an indication that the items were given in a way that did not permit each one to remain in focus for a long enough period of time.

A rapid cadence

You will find that you are able to rapidly respond to quite a few new instructions. Kino may, however, get the impression that you really know all you are responding to, and he may be inclined to give you a greater variety of new instructions than you can adequately internalize in a short amount of time. When this happens, you may be able to respond to an item when it is first given to you, but you will soon forget it since there are too many things to remember simultaneously. There are **two ways** to overcome this difficulty. The first is to have *plenty of drill* with each new item to keep it in focus. The second is *plenty of review*. (One advantage of the Comprehension Drill is that Kino can immediately tell when you haven't remembered a command — either you do nothing, or you do the wrong thing.)

Train Kino to go through Comprehension drills with a rapid cadence, changing activities about every two seconds. At the beginning stages you might think of your responses as a form of calisthenics in the language. The Comprehension drill itself might only last four to eight minutes at a time. You may find that you will want to do two or three comprehension exercises a day if you are studying full time. During each succeeding drill time you will want to have a brief warm-up time in which you review the preceding activities and then have Kino introduce five to seven new activities. Occasionally remove a card at random from your file, for review.

Seem to be in a rut

Whenever you are doing any of the Daily Learning Cycle activities but seem to be in a rut or in need of variation in the routine, have Kino spontaneously liven up the session by making up some kind of Comprehension drill that requires your physical activity. Comprehension drills are natural exercises for the beginning or end of a break time.

Keep on file the cards of the Comprehension drills you have done, and have Kino review them with you periodically. The cards don't need English translations on them since they are just used to remind Kino of the activities you are to do. If you were working in Spanish, a card like the following would help Kino give you instructions to touch various indoor objects: table, book, chair, etc.

If you are doing two or three successive drills with the same basic focus, the added material can be written on the same card.

Comprehension Drill –	*Jan. 5*
Focus: Indoor objects	
Toque la mesa.	Toque la ventana.
Toque el libro.	Toque el cuchillo.
Toque la silla.	Toque el tenedor.
Toque la camisa.	Toque la pared.
Toque la pluma.	Toque el lápiz.
Toque el plato.	Toque el vaso.

In a Comprehension drill, the objective is to correctly respond to instructions, rather than to speak. Many of the themes, however, represent topics you will want to learn to talk about in a few days — after you practice them for comprehension. (In the following pages, drills in which you give instructions are called "production" drills.)

After you have become thoroughly familiar with certain instructions, you might exchange roles with Kino and begin producing the same instructions. This time you tell him to perform the activities and he responds by doing them. A word of *caution* is in order, however. Be careful not to use the command form (giving instructions) to people in the community. The material you drill in Comprehension drills helps you become exposed to a great deal of the language rapidly and helps you to comprehend many things in the language. However, you should probably not use the command sentence structures in the community unless you find children or others who are willing to follow your instructions in a "game" — a language learning game in which they are helping you.

Preview

The rest of this chapter is divided into three parts. The *first part* lists some general categories of instructions for physical response comprehension drills.

The *second part* gives examples of many different physical response comprehension drills which you can do. You may not want to do the drills in the order they are given. When you do one of these drills, you can write the date that you practiced it on the line beside the name of the exercise. This way you can see at a glance which drills you have practiced, and you can periodically review previous drills.

The *last part* gives some brief ideas about other methods of practicing listening comprehension.

Preview of Categories
For Physical-Response
Comprehension Drills

Body movements — Sit, Stand, Walk, Jump, Turn left, Turn right

Moving part of your body — Stretch, Reach out, Touch your nose, Clap your hands, Close your eyes

Focus on numbers — Clap three times, Indicate "two" on your fingers, Point to 32, Write 512, "Pay" me a quarter, Two plus two

Direction — Turn left, Walk four steps north, Go to the first corner

Showing emotions — Smile, Sneer, Giggle, Wink, Laugh, Cry, Look angry

Focus on objects — Indoors: Pencil, Pen, Book, Paper, Comb, Brush

— Outdoors: Tree, Leaf, Puddle, Dirt, Flower

Focus on activities — Smell, Take, Stroke, Point to, Give, Shake, Examine

Focus on qualities — Colors: Red, Yellow, Blue, Green

— Size: Big, Small

— Comparatives: Big/bigger, Small/smaller, Nice/nicer

Focus on space relationships — Above, Under, Between, Next to, In, On

Focus on time relationships — Clock time
Calendar and dates
Tenses
Before, After, While

Series of instructions — Take the notebook. Open it. Take out a blank sheet of paper. Fold it. Unfold it. Wad it up. Throw it in the trash.

Ideas
For Physical-Response
Comprehension Drills

Moving part of your body _____

Kino can give you directions to move specific parts of your body: "Reach your arms out." "Reach your arms up." "Touch your nose." "Touch your foot." "Shake your arms." "Raise your eyebrows." "Touch your lips." "Pucker your lips." "Close your eyes." "Open your eyes." "Open your mouth." "Close your mouth."

Numbers 1 to 5 _____

Have Kino give you instructions to "Indicate 'one' with your fingers," "Indicate 'two' with your fingers." He should do it with you until you connect the meaning with the activity. He should alternate between these two activities, then add "Indicate 'three' on your fingers", and gradually work up to five. Responding with your fingers to the numbers 1 to 5 should be enough for one drill.

NOTE: When we count on our fingers in English we usually start with our index finger, then put up our other fingers in succession, and number 5 is the thumb. Don't expect people in your new culture to follow this same system. Be sure to do it the way Kino shows you. For example, in Swahili the numbers 1, 2, 3 are represented by holding up the index, middle and ring fingers as in English, but 4 is represented by all fingers up (including the thumb) and forming a "v" between the ring and middle fingers. Five is shown by the closed fist. Numbers 6 - 9 are shown by touching the tips of the fingers of the right hand to the fingers of the left hand starting with the little finger. Ten is represented by both closed fists.

Numbers 6 to 10 _____

Learn to respond to the numbers 6 to 10 by clapping, and by indicating numbers with your fingers. Kino will say "Clap your hands six times," and he will do it. He says it again and you do it. "Clap your hands seven times" — he will do it and you do it. Have Kino alternate between these two instructions repeatedly as you respond, then add "Clap your hands eight times." After 8 has been in focus, then add 9, and later 10. Then Kino can say, "Indicate the number 'six' on your fingers", and do it to show you how. Work up to 10 and then alternate between clapping and indicating, with any numbers 1 to 10 in random order. ◈

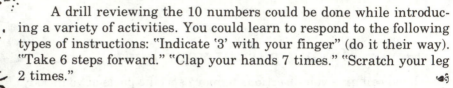

_____ Review of Numbers 1 to 10

A drill reviewing the 10 numbers could be done while introducing a variety of activities. You could learn to respond to the following types of instructions: "Indicate '3' with your finger" (do it their way). "Take 6 steps forward." "Clap your hands 7 times." "Scratch your leg 2 times." ◈

_____ Numbers 11 to 20

To drill the numbers 11 - 20, both you and Kino could have pencil and paper. Kino says a number and writes it down and you also write it. Then he says the numbers as you write them down. The instructions should be given in the form of short sentences: "Write the number 'eleven'." Have Kino alternate between 11 and 12, and then gradually work up to 20. Then Kino could name any number between 1 and 20 in random order and you write it down. ◈

_____ Numbers 1 to 30

Using a big calendar page, drill the numbers 1 to 30 by having Kino direct you to point to the numbers on the page. Since the numbers 20 to 30 are new, you will want more practice on them at first. ◈

_____ 10's and Repeated Numbers

The same kind of drill as above can be done with the following chart:

10	20	30	40	50
11	22	33	44	55
60	70	80	90	100
66	77	88	99	111

Prepare the chart on a sheet of paper, and have Kino direct you to point to the various numbers. ◈

_____ Numbers 1 to 100

Have Kino direct you in writing the numbers 1 to 100 in random order. The instructions should be in the form of short sentences like: "Write the number 'fifty-two'." ◈

Numbers 100 to 1,000 _____

Drill the numbers 100 to 1,000 as in the previous drills. First learn the numbers for the hundreds (100, 300, 500, etc.), then learn how to recognize combinations in order to write numbers like 432, 554, 627, etc. Kino may want to use the numbers from the following table of random numbers.

132	168	741	920	246	365	770	227	841	650
212	990	199	615	902	974	352	389	107	362
370	478	509	648	183	242	385	466	527	270
304	810	986	287	174	120	344	117	387	739
388	649	384	378	192	596	724	119	873	206
946	662	801	397	181	322	605	467	589	373
894	804	976	987	692	904	592	278	537	638
415	657	697	985	312	332	124	779	892	1979
240	524	196	783	240	587	493	804	750	432
347	709	878	900	832	314	229	463	1000	745
151	429	856	603	733	441	632	989	757	764

Strange strategic statistics

Production of Numbers _____

After hearing the numbers repeatedly in these types of drills, you will find that you will soon be able to orally produce them as well. You could reverse the roles and have Kino write the numbers as you give the instructions: "Write the number 'four hundred seventy two'." If he responds by writing 472, then you know that you have communicated adequately. (You may want to use the table of random numbers.)

Numbers and Money _____

If money units have names which do not indicate the specific number unit, then you can develop a Comprehension drill that helps you focus on the values of each. (For example, in the U.S.A., coins representing 1 cent, 5 cents, 10 cents, 25 cents, 50 cents, and 100 cents all have other names — and it would be necessary to learn the values represented by the names "dime," "penny," "quarter," "nickle," "half.") To prepare for this drill, gather various coins of each denomination and perhaps also some bills. Kino can give you instructions to "pay" him 2 dimes, 1 quarter, 4 pennies, etc., or to make change for a quarter. (Have him show you the appropriate local way to count out change.)

Production: Numbers and Money _____

Have a number of items to "sell." Kino could ask you the price of each and you could respond in a full sentence — "It costs twelve shillings." Kino could "pay" you, and thus you could see if you correctly communicated with him.

"It costs five cents."

Time

Do people tell time with clocks? Make a simple "clock" by drawing a circle with numbers. Attach two cardboard hands with a pin (or a brad, or thumbtack). Have Kino, in quick succession, name random times. For example: 4:20, 5:55, 10 past 6, quarter to 11, half past 2, 4:05, etc. You respond by indicating the stated time with the hands of the clock. ◄§

Numbers: Addition & Subtraction

Have Kino direct you to perform arithmetic functions by verbally instructing you in the accepted local way (for example: "7 minus 4", or "4 from 7", or "7 take away 4"). You write the complete frame including the answer: 7 − 4 = 3. Work on both addition and subtraction. ◄§

Production: Addition & Subtraction

Kino can point at random to any two numbers on a calendar and tell you to add or subtract. You respond by saying the formula and the answer: "Fifteen and three are eighteen." ◄§

Left and Right

When learning *left* and *right* it is a good idea if you and Kino stand side-by-side facing in the same direction. Kino can instruct you to :

Touch your left leg.   Touch your right arm.
Scratch your right elbow.   Scratch your left eyebrow.
Rub your right ear.   Rub your left shoulder.
Shake your left arm.   Shake your right leg.
etc. ◄§

Directions

An early Comprehension drill should help you begin to understand directions. Kino's instructions might be: "Face me." "Turn left." "Turn right." "Turn right again." "Turn right once more." "Walk straight three steps." "Face the door." "Face the wall." "Face the window." (You could alternatively work on North, South, East, and West if these are commonly used in giving directions.) ◄§

Turn right!

Map

Get a local map of the city (with streets and principal landmarks), and a map of the country.

City drill: Left, Right, Go straight,. Number of blocks, Landmarks.

Country drill: Roads, Cities, Rivers, Mountains, Surrounding countries, Lakes, Islands, North, South, East, West. ᵔᵌ

Emotions _____

Have Kino instruct you to give an indication of emotional feeling: Sigh, snear, giggle, shrug, wink, smile, laugh, cry with tears, frown, look angry, yell, etc. ᵔᵌ

Indoor Objects _____

Comprehension drills can be used to help you learn the names of almost any objects. Prepare for the drill by setting up various items in front of you and your helper — items like pen, pencil, book, paper, comb, brush, shirt, plate, glass, spoon, etc. Instructions could include: "Touch the pen." "Touch the chair." "Touch the table." "Touch the spoon." "Touch the plate." "Touch the pencil." "Touch the glass." "Touch the paper." "Touch the comb." "Touch the shirt." "Touch the paper." "Touch the book." "Touch the brush." (Remember that the drill progresses by first alternating between two, then adding one at a time, and keeping each new one in focus for a period of time before adding another one.) ᵔᵌ

Outdoor Objects _____

Go outdoors with Kino and have him direct you in touching, or pointing to various items like: stone, seed, leaf, twig, flower, tree, grass, dirt, puddle, sky, cloud, etc. ᵔᵌ

Activities and Objects _____

Another comprehension drill might use some of the same objects with other directions. The objects could be in a pile and Kino might say: "*Take* the pen." "*Take* the leaf." "*Give* me the leaf." "*Touch* the leaf." "*Smell* the leaf." "*Stroke* the leaf." "*Point* to the book." "*Give* me the leaf and the stone." "*Shake* the shirt." "*Examine* the pen and the pencil." "*Open* the book." ᵔᵌ

Pronouns _____

Have places at the table for two imaginary participants — a man and a woman. Give each of these "participants" local names, and make name tags for them. The instructions could be: "Take the leaf and give it to Lolo." "Take the stone and give it to Nina." "Give the comb to *me*." "Give the leaf to *him*." "Take the brush and keep it *yourself*." "Give the pen to *her*." ᵔᵌ

———— **Plural Objects and Pronouns**

For this drill you need at least two of each of the objects. Instructions could be: "Take a comb and give it to them." "Take two stones and give them to him." "Take a pencil and book and give them to me." "Take the paper clips and keep them yourself." "Take two leaves; give one to me and the other to Nina." "Take a comb and a brush; give the comb to her and the brush to Lolo."   ❧

———— **This & That, Here & There**

Kino could say, "Take the pen and give it to her." "Give the leaf to him." "Take the book and put it here." "Put this pencil over there." "Take a comb and a pencil and put them here." "Take the two paper clips and put one here and one there." To begin with, Kino can direct you with his eyes or chin to indicate the intended object and place. But soon you should respond to only verbal stimuli without the visual reinforcement.   ❧

———— **Possessives**

A further modification of the drill can be used to introduce possessives. For this you need four sets of objects. (The sets do not have to contain the same items.) Place one set in front of Kino, one in front of yourself, and sets in front of Nina and Lolo. For the purpose of the drill, the items in front of each person "belong" to that person. Instruction could then proceed as follows: "Take *my* comb and give it to her." "Take *his* leaf and give it to yourself." "Take *your* comb and give it to him." "Take *Lolo's* pen and leaf and give them to Nina." "Take *Nina's* comb and give it to him."   ❧

———— **Color**

Adjectives relating to color can be drilled. For this drill, collect a number of similar items with a variety of colors — colored pencils, strips of colored paper, colored socks, ribbons, etc. You can include various activities you have already drilled. "Hold the red pencil." "Take my blue book and give it to Nina." "Put the green sock here." "Put the red ribbon over there." "Touch the pink paper." "Point to Nina's yellow ribbon." "Shake Lolo's green pencil."   ❧

———— **Size**

A similar drill can focus on adjectives of size. "Take the small stone." "Take the large leaf and put it here." Commands can include: "move," "touch," "Exchange the large one with the small one," "Exchange the small green leaf with the small yellow book."   ❧

Production: Singular & Plural objects _____

You respond in singular to a plural stimulus, and with plural to a singular stimulus. For example:

Kino: "These strips of paper are blue."
You: "This strip of paper is blue."
Kino: "This leaf is large."
You: "These leaves are large." Etc.

Space Relations — I _____

Vocabulary related to space relationships can be introduced with the same objects. "Hold the pen above the book." "Hold the pen under the book." "Hold the pen between the two books." "Hold the pen next to the small book." "Hold the pen above you." "Hold the pen in front of you." "Hold the book behind you." "Hold the book at your left side." "Hold the leaf in your right hand," etc.

Hold it above you

Space Relations — II _____

Preparation: Gather seeds or pebbles and a small box. Directions: "Put one in the box." "Take one out of the box." "Put some in the box." "Take some out of the box." "Put two to the left of the box." "Put one on top of the box." "Put three in front of the box." "Put one behind the box." "Put one far from the box." "Put two to the left of the box." "Put three close to the box." (*For production:* Kino does an activity and you describe the resulting relationships — for example, "Two seeds are at the left of the box." "One seed is in front of the box," etc.)

Variation in Instructions _____

Today, have Kino use a variety of request forms like: "I would like you to put the pebble in the box." "I want you to take one pebble out of the box." "I am asking you to put two pebbles beside the box." "Please put a pebble in the box." "Would you please put three pebbles near the box." "Kindly put all the pebbles in the box."

Opposites _____

To prepare, you might have a good tomato and a bad one, a large rock and a small one, a narrow strip and a wide one, a cold cup of tea and a hot one, etc. Kino can direct you to perform various activities: "Pick up the large rock." "Touch the narrow paper." "Look at the hot tea." "Drink the cold tea."

Opposites

Comparatives

Have Kino collect pairs of items according to the characteristics he feels are relevant. Each set can have two items with similar qualities; for example: a small pebble and a smaller one, a good and a better pen, a narrow and a narrower strip of paper, a pretty and a prettier picture, a big and a bigger comb. Other comparatives might include fatter, nicer, colder, hotter, longer, shorter, taller, thinner, thicker, brighter, redder, etc.

NOTE: In comparative drills you should always be careful to avoid forcing English categories onto your new language. Be careful to drill the comparisons which are relevant to Kino.

After Kino has classified the objects into categories, discuss them with him to be sure you understand the way he has classified the objects by their respective characteristics. Instructions: "Place the good pen by the better pen." "Put the small paper clip by the smaller clip." "Hold the prettier picture in your left hand." "Put the good pen in your right pocket and the better pen in your left pocket." "Place the smaller leaf next to the big comb." ᵉ§

Comparatives and Superlatives

It may be possible to have a similar drill using three objects — small, smaller, and smallest pebbles; narrow, narrower, and narrowest leaves; good, better, and best pens, etc. Instructions: "Put the smallest paper near the biggest stone." "Give me the prettiest picture." "Put the narrower paper on top of the narrowest one." ᵉ§

The farthest stone

Comparatives and Distance

Have Kino set up two stones (or any two items) near each other; one stone larger than the other. A third stone smaller than the other two can be placed at a distance from both of those. Kino could direct you: "Place a paper clip near the smallest stone." "Put two paper clips near the farthest stone." "Move the two stones together and place a clip near them." "Place a clip far from the stones." "Place another farther." "Touch the nearest clip." "Move the farthest one nearer." (Later you could give the directions and have Kino follow them.) ᵉ§

If — Then

You can drill the "if . . . then . . ." construction while reviewing comparatives and superlatives. Kino: "If the pen is longer than the comb, put the pen here." "If the leaf is greener than the stone, put it here." "If this picture is prettier than that one, give it to me." "If this leaf is older than that one, throw it in the wastebasket," etc. ✍

Production of Modifiers _____

Kino says a sentence with modifiers. You repeat the basic sentence without modifiers.

Kino: "The blue jug with the pretty flowers is on the high wooden shelf."
You: "The jug is on the shelf."
Then reverse roles — he says a simple sentence and you embellish it.
Kino: "This is a book."
You: "This is a good book about the people of this country."
Kino: "This is a candle."
You: "This is a red candle."
Look around you. You can talk about virtually any object, then re-state it with modifiers. ✍

Pictures _____

Take a large photograph from a calendar, or a painting by a local artist. First, Kino can name the objects in the picture as he points to them, in a frame like "This is a tree," and you point too. Then he can direct you to point to the various objects. Later you can use the same picture to drill relationships. Kino can direct you: "Point to the two men who are standing together." "Point to the dog under the tree." "Point to the woman walking on the path." "Point to the man who is holding the spear." You can use a different picture to drill other objects and relationships.

Pictures that can be discussed should include a wide range of local life. Maybe even snapshots you took when you first arrived. Pictures of a local village, pictures in a home, of a family, in a food market, pictures of a monument or a bridge, newspaper stand, airport, busy intersection, traffic jam, local transportation, a farm with animals. ✍

"Point to
the mischievous mouse"

Days and Dates _____

Using a calendar of the current month, have Kino direct you around the calendar by first teaching you the names for "day," "week," "month," then by indicating the names of each of the days of the week. Instructions: "Point to the column of Sundays." "Point to the column of Mondays." "Point to the column of Tuesdays," etc. "Point to the date of the third Tuesday." "Point to the second Monday." "Point to the 23rd of the month." "Point to the 14th." "Point to today." "Point to yesterday." "Point to the day after tomorrow." ✍

Year Calendar

Using a calendar which represents the whole year on one page, have Kino teach you to respond to the names for the months, and then direct you to indicate specific dates (January 23rd, December 1st). Also, learn the names for years: 1950, 1783, etc.   ◦ᗋ

NOTE: Don't assume that their concept of day, week, month, or year will be just the same as yours. By Jewish reckoning, the day begins and ends at sundown. The Nsoq people of Cameroon have an eight-day week, with 45½ weeks in a year. Oriental reckoning of years is according to a cycle in which animals are used to represent the recurring years. Learn to comprehend and use calendar time the way they see it.

_____ Production: Days and Dates

    Kino: "Today is Tuesday."
You: "Yes, today is Tuesday."
    Kino: "Was yesterday Sunday?"
You: "No, yesterday was not Sunday, it was Monday."
    Kino: "Will tomorrow be Thursday?"
You: "No, tomorrow will not be Thursday, tomorrow will be Wednesday."
    Kino: "Will tomorrow be Thursday?"
You: "No, tomorrow won't be Thursday, the day after tomorrow will be Thursday."
    Kino: "Was yesterday Sunday?"
You: No, yesterday wasn't Sunday, the day before yesterday was Sunday."

    You could hypothetically change "today" by putting a marker on a different day of the week.

    Kino: "Will tomorrow be the 23rd?"
You: "No, the day after tomorrow will be the 23rd."
    Kino: "Was yesterday the 21st?"
You: "No, yesterday was not the 21st, today is the 21st."   ◦ᗋ

NOVEMBER						
SUN	MON	TUE	WED	THU	FRI	SAT
«»	«»	«»	1	2	3	4
5	6	7	8	9	10	11
12	13	14	15	16	17	18
19	20	21	22	23	24	25
26	27	28	29	30	«»	«»

_____ While, Before, After

    Follow Kino's directions: "While I am clapping, you clap." "You clap after I clap." "After I clap, you clap." "Clap before I clap."   ◦ᗋ

_____ Temporal Relationships

Drill relationships like: before, after, successively, slowly, quickly, first, second, then, with, at the same time as, while, simultaneously, sequentially. Follow Kino's directions: "Stretch both arms." "Stretch your right arm after your left." "Stretch your right arm before your left arm." "Stretch slowly." "Stretch quickly." "First stretch your right arm, next stretch your left arm, then touch your toes." "Stretch with me." "Walk with me." "Stretch your arms simultaneously." "Stretch while I walk."

Tenses ─────────

The future tense can be imbedded into a command. "When I walk to the window, you will write my name on the blackboard." The past tense can also be incorporated into the command structure. "Josephine, if I already walked to the window, you stand up."

Production: Tenses ─────────

Kino could give instructions, for example: "Put a pebble in the shoe box." You could respond with a *series* of sentences: "I will put a pebble in the shoe box." "I am now putting a pebble in the box (while doing it)." "I have put the pebble in the shoe box." Other verbs that could be drilled in past, present, and future in this way could be: "take from (the box)," "give," "go (to the window)," "come," "go out," "go and return," "stand up," "sit down." *Kino:* "Please stand up." *Response:* "I will stand up." "I am standing up." "I have stood up." Or: "You asked me to stand." "I will stand." "I am now standing." "I stood."

"I am putting pebbles in the shoe."

Abstract Vocabulary ─────────

One way to drill abstract words is by writing words like love, faith, hope, honor, government, justice, belief, etc., on strips of paper, and then manipulating the strips of paper like any other object. Rather than calling it a strip of paper, it is called by the name that is written on it. (This procedure, however, is *only* valid for learning the vocabulary words themselves. It is not valid as a means of understanding the range of meaning of the words or how the words are used in the cultural setting. To drill these meanings, take a topic — for example, love — and have Kino give about a one-minute talk on love, which you record. Listen to the tape repeatedly for understanding. Transcribe the whole story to get a feel for how transitions are used and note any particular usages related to the theme of love. Have Kino tell a short story on any abstract theme which you do not understand. You would, of course, not need to transcribe many of them, but you would want to listen repeatedly to them.)

Project Instructions

Follow Kino as he gives you a *series of instructions* on a topic and demonstrates the activities. For example: "Put the onion on the board. Open the drawer, and take out a knife. Slice the onion. Your eyes are watering; dry them with your handkerchief. Put the onion slices on a plate. Wash the knife and board." Mimic his motions a couple times and then do it once or twice obeying the instructions without having him do the actions. Then have Kino give the instructions in random order to see if you can comprehend them individually. (This procedure can be followed for sequential instructions on a wide variety of topics . . . . gardening, cooking, handcraft, mechanics, woodwork, etc.)

Gardening

You may find it helpful to have your tape recorder running during this type of Comprehension drill. Physically respond to the instructions as they are being recorded. At a later time you could listen to the tape and follow those instructions; this way you would get to review the activities of the drill without taking any more of Kino's time. The repetition you need could be insured this way without boring your helper.

Here is a different series of instructions which Kino could tape: "Take a pencil and a piece of paper. Draw an outline map of Africa. Hold it up and look at it. Make some improvement over on the western side of the continent near Liberia. Draw in the Nile River. Put Lake Victoria toward the eastern side of the continent. Look at the map again at arm's length. Make a frown of dissatisfaction with its quality. Crumple up the map and throw it in the wastebasket."

Here is another series of instructions — how to build a fire. Instructions might go as follows: "Gather some paper. Gather some small twigs. Gather some logs for burning. Take each piece of paper and wad it up. Put the paper in the area of the campfire. Put the twigs on top of the paper. Be sure to stack them so the fire can get plenty of fresh air. Take a box of matches from your pocket. Strike the match and light the paper in two or three places. As the fire gets larger, put other sticks and finally logs on it. As it starts to get warmer, hold your hands out to warm them beside the fire. The warmth feels good — you relax by the fire. Smoke blows in your eyes and your eyes begin to water. Wipe your eyes. The breeze is blowing the smoke your way. Go to the other side of the fire."

As you listen to the tape, act out the response to each of the commands. You could do it with actual objects or pantomime. By listening to the tape repeatedly, you can increase your comprehension of vocabulary and instructions. A series of instructions could be recorded for Comprehension drills on a multitude of topics: preparing a meal, working in the garden, butchering an animal, etc. The first time you hear the series of instructions, have Kino act out the drill by responding to each of the commands himself. The second time you listen to it, have Kino act it out while you simultaneously act it out. From that point on you should be able to respond to the instructions on the tape independently — either in pantomime or with the real objects. After you are confident that you can perform each of the activities in a given drill, have Kino give you the instructions outside of the context of the total drill. In other words, have him give you the same instructions but in random order. You respond by acting out the response in pantomime or by manipulating the objects of the drill.

Be sure that instructions for drills fit the local cultural context. This is a good way to begin to learn to act in culturally appropriate ways. For example, have a drill that focuses on preparation of a local food. Another one might be on the eating of the meal. Instructions could be: "Ask your wife to bring a pan of water to wash your hands. Dry them on the towel she provides. Reach the fingers of your right hand into the ughali and tear away a small handful. Work it until it has a smooth texture. Poke your thumb into the end of it and make a dipper of it. Dip it into your stew. Bite off the end of it. Chew it. Swallow it. You complete your meal. Ask your wife to bring you water in a pan for you to wash your hands again. Wash them. Dry them on the towel."

Date
_____
_____
_____
_____

_____
_____

Various Methods For Improving Ability In Listening Comprehension

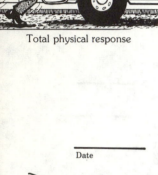

Total physical response

Most of the examples given in this chapter relate to physical responses — Kino gives a command and you physically respond to the command. This type of listening comprehension drill called *Total Physical Response* is especially valuable for the early stages of language learning.

Following are some other kinds of listening comprehension activities.

1. *Expanded Repetitions*

Date

The whole thing went over his head

In rapid speech, sounds blend together or are dropped. For example, in English, when speaking to a friend you might say, "Skweet" — in slower speech you would probably say, "Let's go eat," or, "Let us go eat."

Get your helper and a friend to carry on a casual conversation for you to tape. When you play it back, Kino repeats more slowly and deliberately the sentences that you couldn't figure out — or just selected sentences if the whole thing went over your head. Try to see how sounds blend together and which sounds get dropped altogether in more rapid speech.

2. *Various Versions of a Story or Text*

Give Kino a topic. Ask him to talk on that topic for a given length of time. Warning: 30 seconds is a lot of material! In the beginning weeks you may only want 10 seconds, and gradually work up to 30 or 45 seconds. At the end of the stated period of time, interrupt with a "Thank you!" Then ask Kino to repeat the information, adding no new content, and leaving out no content. He can restate the content any way he likes. Tape three to five versions in this manner. You can learn much from comparing the different versions. Next, you and your helper can transcribe from the tape (use double spacing). Try to see to it that everything is transcribed — even the false starts and midsentence changes. (Don't insist if your helper seems to be defensive or uneasy about it.) Avoid writing translations in English on the text transcript — make any necessary notes or translations on a matching page. Number, identify, and date each sheet.

When Kino is giving a story on tape, encourage him to talk at normal speed or even slightly above normal speed. At the beginning stages, when you would like him to talk slower, *a better alternative to talking slowly is to have him talk at normal speed but give slightly lengthened pauses at the end of phrases.*

Choose topics according to your interests. In the initial weeks and months, keep the content of the narratives really close to yourself, your surroundings, and your activities. You might ask your helper to pretend he's introducing you to someone. Ask him to describe you, your daily routine, your activities, your language learning efforts, how you and he work together, the work you've come to do, your food preferences. Later you can extend your vocabulary into any area you wish.

Date

Many things you have already learned to say can elicit a variety of responses from the people you are talking with. You could have Kino record one of your recent dialogues, with your part (Part A) and a variety of possible responses for Part B. Use this for listening comprehension so that you can learn to recognize these responses. Your tape could go like this:

A. "Hello, How are you?"
B. *Possible responses:* "I'm fine thanks, and yourself?"
　　　　　　　　　　or, "Fine thank you, and you?"
　　　　　　　　　　or, "Pretty good, how are you?"
A. "Fine thank you. Could you tell me the way to the bank?"
B. *Possible responses:* "Yes. Go to the corner and turn right; it'll be on your right about a block down."
　　　　　　　　　　or, "Turn right at the next corner and then walk about a block. It will be on your right."
　　　　　　　　　　or, "Turn right at the light. The bank will be on the right hand side, right after the big shoestore."
A. "Thank you very much."
B. *Possible responses:* "You're welcome."
　　　　　　　　　　or, "Glad to be of service."
　　　　　　　　　　or, "Don't mention it."
　　　　　　　　　　or, "That's OK."
A. "Good-bye."

The more limited your ability, the more *immediate* should be the content. "Immediate" means what you can see, touch, do, or easily visualize.

Whenever you and your helper do something or go somewhere together, ask him afterward to describe the activities on tape. Keep it brief. He can take various points of view, resulting in one monolog told as "we," another as "they" (as though he were a bystander talking to a fourth party), another as "you," etc.

Have Kino pretend he was one of the people you visited in the village as you were giving your text in your communication time today. Have him tell the story of his encounter with you. Let him pretend he is telling it to a friend.

Have Kino tell about what you are going to do today as you are involved in the community. This might be a somewhat detailed account of the places you will go, or the people you will see, or hypothetical reactions of people toward your involvement with them.

Kino could tell any story, then paraphrase it and tell it from a different perspective. He might tell about a traffic accident. First he could tell the story from the policeman's perspective. Then he might tell it again from the perspective of a person who was not at fault in the accident. He could tell it from the perspective of the person who was at fault and then maybe a fourth time from the perspective of a person who just happened to see it.

All of these stories should be done entirely in your new language and should be recorded. You can listen to the recording repeatedly for comprehension practice. There may be parts of the story that you do not understand. In order to help you understand, have Kino act out the various roles or explain in other ways without using English. He could act out the story using various gestures, or paraphrase by telling the story in different ways.

First-hand account

Keep this in mind: your goal is immediate comprehension, without translation. Any writing, analysis, study, memorizing that you do **must** be made to serve this one goal: immediate comprehension. Start with listening to the text. End with listening to the text.

As you listen to the stories for Comprehension Practice, it is often a good idea to listen with your eyes closed. Having your eyes closed helps eliminate distractions and increases listening concentration.

Listen
with your eyes closed

After you understand a story fairly well, have Kino tell it again, this time have him speak faster than normal. Record it and listen to it until you are able to comprehend it completely. Again, practice comprehension with your eyes closed.

It is a good idea to plan the topic of your texts approximately three days in advance, when possible. This way you can practice some comprehension drills on the topic before you actually learn to speak about it. You might plan, for example, to develop a text that would help you make purchases in a clothing store. Kino could tell a short story which you would record about what might go on in a clothing store and what would happen in the transaction of actually purchasing something. By listening to this text repeatedly in Comprehension Practice, you become aware of vocabulary, as well as culturally appropriate ways of acting and speaking in the situation. After you have listened to the material repeatedly, it would not be difficult to learn a text on the topic.

3. *Repeated Listening to Other taped Materials*

A. Conversations. It is an excellent idea to get two people to converse together for you. Be sure to get the microphone close to both. Be alert for people who would enjoy doing this and could do it naturally, using the kind of slang you need to be able to understand. Emphasize very high frequency vocabulary in the beginning. When two people begin to talk, what they say in the first ten seconds will probably be very high frequency vocabulary. The next twenty seconds will usually yield high frequency vocabulary. After that, much of their vocabulary will be of lower frequency. So it is especially productive to be able to capture on tape the first ten seconds of a dialog or monolog. You can get a lot of repeated listening with a tape loop. *

B. Radio — especially news and weather, where certain vocabulary items are likely to recur frequently.

C. Popular songs.

D. Recordings of poems, drama, famous speeches. (Keep in mind that when an average person reads aloud, his style is often somewhat different from his usual speaking style. It is a person's normal, casual, unguarded speaking style that you must focus on learning to comprehend.)

A tape loop
for repeated listening

*By the way, TDK makes cassette tape loops in 20, 30, 60, and 180 second lengths.

4. *Selective Listening*

As you listen to one of your tapes, focus on *one* feature at a time. One time it can be the ups and downs of pitch. Next it's the rhythm and placement of stresses. Next it's certain vowels. Then focus on selected consonants. This exercise will help you tune your ears to the *sounds* of your new language.

If you are listening to a record or tape, listen for particular words. You can ask Kino to help you pick out *theme words* that are used several times in the text.

An excellent exercise is to get a list of the grammatical or "function" words — the pronouns (he, she, it), conjunctions (and, but, or), question words (who, what, where), prepositions (in, on, beside), verb auxiliaries (do, was, have), articles (a, an, the), demonstratives (this, those), modals (can, may, might, should, could, must, would, have to). These are just examples of some of the kinds of *function* words in English — other languages will have different types of grammatical function words. These words, though few in number, make up a great percentage of any text. Practice listening for them — not all of them

Date

at one time, but one by one. This exercise helps you to begin to tune in on the *grammatical structure* of the language. You may have to have your helper help you identify these words in speech. They may not sound like they are spelled.

Then you could study each sentence in the story to see how it fits with the rest. Find the markers that make it "belong" — relationals, connectives, pronouns and their antecedents, use of definite and indefinite articles, etc.

Date

Passive listening

5. *Passive Listening*

There is much value in immersing yourself in the sounds of the language — by having it in your environment whether you can be paying attention to it or not. Passive listening helps you "tune in" to the language.

Listen to songs, radio, T. V., spoken records, your own tapes. You may want to make a 60-minute tape of several people in succession telling about their early childhood years, telling about an important experience in their life, or talking about anything that will produce a lot of casual, colloquial speech.

Expose yourself to the language with passive listening whenever you are doing things that don't require intense concentration.

By the way, you should be aware of the possibility that people (even your helper) may be talking to you in an oversimplified form. To compensate for this, and to advance your general comprehension ability, you should spend much time listening to native speakers talking to each other.

6. *Taking Dictation*

As you are learning the writing system (or, in the case of non-Roman script, you can write phonetically), you can practice by dictation. Kino can read a passage twice while you listen. Then he should read it phrase by phrase without repeating, as you write. Then he reads sentence by sentence, giving you a couple of seconds to make additions and corrections. After he finishes reading, he should show you your comprehension errors (not necessarily spelling errors) and you write in the corrections.

Step two: Follow the above procedures with the same passage the next day. This time, after your errors have been corrected, study the passage, and read it aloud. Your goal on the third day is to write it from dictation without a single error. Distinguish between spelling errors and errors of comprehension — it's the latter you should zero in on.

Materials can be found everywhere — particularly if there are books for children in the language. Don't take really hard stuff in the beginning. In fact, a dialog you've learned can be changed just a little and turned into a good dictation exercise. Remember that you are focusing on *comprehension,* not writing.

Pressing On
In the Language

The beauty of listening and re-listening lies in the way you can continue to use it to your advantage until you achieve truly bilingual and bicultural knowledge and ability. You don't need to stop growing in ability at that point where you begin to be able to understand most of what is said directly to you on familiar or professional topics. Continue growing in proficiency until you can understand two native speakers talking to each other about any topic. Tape a conversation, and take it to your helper — check your comprehension by trying to rephrase what you hear. Don't be satisfied with a vague, general "ballpark" comprehension. Aim for proficiency with accuracy.

Books for children

From Comprehension
To Active Use

"Use a word three times and it's yours." Your tapes and transcriptions can be a valuable source of new vocabulary. To be able to use the words and idioms in your speech, however, you must make a point to work them into your vocabulary. Use new words and idioms in other contexts from the one you found them in. Try these out on your helper before you use them with others, just to be sure you've understood correctly. Use the new word or idiom (or grammatical feature) at every opportunity until it's solidly *yours.* Actively listen whenever other people are talking, and try to use what you hear.

Listen!

Listen!

Listen!

CHAPTER 4

How to Master
The Sounds
Of Your Language

Good pronunciation is crucial, for it is through sounds that knowledge moves from one person to another. Every language consists of sounds that are produced by the human vocal organs and received by the human ear. Who knows how many different speech sounds occur throughout the world? Your vocal organs can produce hundreds or maybe even thousands of distinct speech sounds. But take heart, for each language utilizes only a few of these many possibilities. Some languages may use as many as sixty sounds, while others may use as few as twenty. The average is in the middle somewhere. You are already accustomed to hearing and producing the set of English sounds. These ingrained English habits will get in the way as you learn your new language which has its own set of sounds. The two sets will probably overlap some, but you need to develop new habits for those sounds which don't overlap.

Take heart

It is important to develop good pronunciation habits at an *early* stage of your language learning. Otherwise, poor pronunciation could become habitual and unconscious in a short period of time — you could practice poor habits and soon your helper, and a few others, might learn to understand your "dialect"; and you might become satisfied with this incorrect pronunciation. A large percentage of your Accuracy Practice time during the first few weeks should be spent in Pronunciation practice. This will enable you to bring your pronunciation habits up to a level of awareness and help you make steady progress.

By identifying and working on one pronunciation problem each day or two, you can systematically refine your pronunciation skills. The last pages of this chapter give suggestions that will help you identify your needs and develop pronunciation practice exercises.

Sometimes English speakers feel that English pronunciation is the "right" pronunciation. It is right for English, but it is not right for another language. The right way for any language is the way the native speakers pronounce it. Our way is the right way for English, but then we are native speakers of English.

In order for you to learn to pronounce your new language correctly, you should become *aware* of your English pronunciation habits. Then you can learn to produce different sounds by varying some of these familiar sounds and learning how new ones can be made. As you identify the different pronunciation patterns of your new language, you will need to develop and practice pronunciation drills to increase your pronunciation accuracy.

Hebrew

Our alphabet is a system of *written symbols* which presumably represent the sounds of English. When something is written with a separate symbol for each different sound, then we say it is written "phonetically." In this chapter we will represent each different sound by a different phonetic symbol. The sounds of any language can be written with phonetic symbols. If your new language is written with Roman letters (like our alphabet), then many of the symbols we use may stand for the same sound in your new language. (But there are various writing systems, and each language has its own unique features. As a result, your new language will use alphabet symbols in its own way to represent its own sounds.)

ภาคผนวก

Thai

NOTE: The earliest writing of man was probably picture writing. Some early cave paintings are kind of like comic strips, relating an event with a series of pictures. The next step seems to have been the symbolic representation of ideas in forms like the ancient Babylonian cuneiform clay tablets, the Egyptian hieroglyphics and the Chinese characters. But then, in the ancient city of Byblos (which still thrives on the Mediterranean coast of Lebanon) a dramatic innovation occurred. Those Phoenecians decided to let their written symbols stand for spoken language sounds, rather than for ideas. The alphabet was born! (Our words for Bible, book and bibliography come from the name of that city — Byblos.)

You should be able to quickly learn to use symbols as they are used in your new language if the written symbols correspond closely to the spoken sounds. Some languages, like English and French, use various spellings for the same sound. (Andrew Jackson apparently once quipped that it was a mighty poor mind that couldn't think of more than one way to spell a word!) If the written symbols of your new language do not closely correspond to its sounds, then you may find it helpful to write your study materials for a while with the symbols given in this chapter. Those who are learning a language with a different set of symbols for its writing system (like Arabic, Hebrew, Hindi, Korean, or Thai) will need to use a phonetic writing system for a longer period of time. In this case, don't try to learn the writing system until you have used the Learning Cycle four to six weeks or longer. By then, you will be comfortable with the different sounds, and it will not be difficult to learn the symbols as they are used.

기쁜 성탄과 희망의
새해를 경축하나이다
Korean

NOTE: Non-Roman writing systems like Hebrew or Korean can be easily learned with drill. Have your helper write the alphabet in his script, then make a list of short words for each sound.

In English the lists might look like this:

a	a	b	c	c	d	e
able	act	book	cook	celt	dog	(etc.)
acre	after	boy	cope	cinch	dip	
ape	atlas	bang	crate	cycle	drag	

(Occasionally an alphabet symbol may have two or more sounds. The English "a" can be pronounced as in "able" or as in "act"; the "c" can sound like "k" as in "cook," or like "s" as in "celt." In such cases, it is best to have separate columns like above.)

In Greek the lists might look like this:

ʼα	ʽα	β	γ	δ	ʼε	ʽε	ζ
ʼάγω	ʽάγια	βάλλω	γάλα	δέ	ʼεγώ	ʽελκόω	(etc.)
ʼαλλά	ʽάλας	βλεπω	γάρ	δέκα	ʼέξω	ʽέξω	
ʼαμήν	ʽαλίζω	βοάω	γέρων	διά	ʼεκ	ʽεκών	
ʼανά	ʽάπαξ	βόσκω	γῆ	δόξα	ʼεν		

Have Kino read a column a couple of times, then you mimic him while associating his alphabet symbol with the sound. Do a Comprehension drill with Kino saying the sound, or one of the words that begins with the sound, and you point to the symbol at the top of the column. (Only try to learn a few symbols each day.) In the next step, Kino could say the name of the letter (or a word beginning with the sound) and you could respond by writing the letter (in the same way that Comprehension drills on numbers are done, see page 228).

今後の
ビジョン

IT'S ALL GREEK TO ME!

If you are learning a Chinese language where the writing system represents ideas rather than sounds, then you will need to use a phonetic system of spelling for a much longer period of time. (The Chinese system can be mastered by learning to recognize and make five or six symbols daily, and spending half an hour each day searching a daily newspaper for the day's symbols and those previously learned. For adults, this might be expected to take up to five years.)

Cree

Amharic, Cree, and some languages of India represent syllables rather than individual sounds with the symbols of their writing systems. In such cases, more symbols are usually necessary. Amharic has about 250 symbols. The Cree language basically has syllables made up of one consonant followed by one of four vowels. The writing system has a symbol to represent each consonant. Each of these symbols can be pointed up, down, left or right depending on the vowel — a very effective system. If your language uses syllabic writing, you can learn the written system as you practice associating symbols with the sounds they represent. You could start by using drills similar to the Number Comprehension Drills on page 228.

In this chapter we will help you become aware of the way you produce English consonants, vowels, rhythm, and tone. As we go along, we will describe how these can be varied. By watching your helper and listening carefully, you should be able to determine with him the consonants, vowels, rhythm and tones of your new language. We will give additional examples of Pronunciation Differential and Substitution drills, as illustrations of the kinds of drills you can develop during your Accuracy Practice time.

If you have previously studied phonetics, much of this chapter will be review for you. If you have never studied phonetics before, be sure to read carefully and *practice* making all of the sounds so you can become aware of your own pronunciation habits and learn how to alter these habits in order to pronounce your new language correctly.

Babies
play with sounds

Pronunciation is a performance skill. You don't learn to pronounce accurately simply by reading this chapter or thinking about sounds. Babies learn to pronounce by babbling and playing with sounds. Lay aside your own inhibitions and play with sounds again. To do so is child-like — but it is not childish. Practice saying each of the sounds *out loud,* so you can learn to produce them. OK?   OK.

Syllables

Syllables are made up of sounds we call **consonants** and **vowels**. Vowels are usually the nucleus — the high point — of the syllable. Consonants are like the bread in a sandwich — they fit around the main part.

English syllables have a variety of shapes. Here are some:

Consonants are like
the bread of a sandwich

(Consonant + Vowel)	C V	pa
(Vowel + Consonant)	V C	an
	V CC	ant
	V CCC	ants
	C V C	pan
(Glided Vowel)	C V gC	pain
	CC V	spa
	CC V C	span
(Glided Vowel)	CC V gC	Spain
	C V CC	pans
	C V CCC	pants
	CC V CC	plant
	CC V CCC	plants
	CCC V CC	splint
	CCC V CCC	splints
	CC V CCCC	glimpsed

(Don't be misled by the spelling of this last one, concentrate on the sounds — we don't say "glimps-ed".)

What is the shape of the following syllables:

hm _____

sprig _____

rents _____

Each language has its own set of syllable patterns. Pick out a few sentences from one of your texts and make some guesses about the shapes of syllables in your new language.

Occasionally there are syllables with no vowel sounds. The expression "hm" is an example. The shape of this syllable is CC̣ — the consonant ṃ is taking the place of the vowel in the syllable. The little line under the letter indicates that this is a consonant that is taking the place of a vowel in the syllable.

Say "turtle"

When a consonant takes the place of the vowel in a syllable, it is called a **syllabic consonant**. Another example is found in the word "turtle." Say "turtle." Ignore the spelling and concentrate on the sounds. It sounds like "tṛtḷ" or even "tṛdḷ." (Note that we do not say "toor-del.") The consonants ṛ and ḷ are syllabic consonants in this word. Both syllables have the shape: CÇ. The following phrases have some syllabic consonants. Pronounce them exactly as they are spelled, being careful not to add any extra vowels between the consonants:

"ɑ lɑ tṛ vɑ tḷ rɑ pṇ ɑ"

"kḷ kṃ kṇ kf kṣ kṛ".

Look at what you wrote above for the syllable shapes of "sprig" and "rents" (CCCVC, and CVCCC). Both of these words have a group of consonants together — that is called a **consonant cluster**. English has many consonant clusters. You can think of words that have the following clusters: *sp-, spl-, spr-, pl-, bl-, gl-, str-, br-, -mp, -ts, -ks, -nt, -mpst.* Some of these clusters do not normally occur at the beginning of words in English — for example: *-mpst,* glimpsed; *-mp,* hemp; *-nt,* tent; *-ts,* bats; *-ks,* box (focus on the sounds, not on the spellings).

You will probably find that your language has different clusters than English. If the clusters occur in initial or final position where they do not occur in English, you may tend to mispronounce the cluster. For example, "Tsɑvo" might be pronounced as if it were "sɑvo." "Tlɑk" might be mispronounced as "tɑlɑk".

It is a universal tendency for a language learner to substitute close sounds from his native tongue for the unfamiliar sounds of the new language. This accounts for the distinctive accents of foreigners.

NOTE: Much of the material in this chapter is based on Dr. William A. Smalley's work. For a more detailed treatment with drills read: *Manual of Articulatory Phonetics,* **by W. A. Smalley, 1962, published by William Carey Library (1705 N. Sierra Bonita Ave, Pasadena, CA 91104). Accompanying recorded drill tapes are also available.**

When people of other languages are learning English, their mistakes with English consonant clusters reflect their own languages. For example, if the word "six" is pronounced "sikis," you can guess that the cluster "ks" probably does not occur in that person's language in final position. In English, "s" also clusters readily with other consonants at the beginning of words, but in Spanish this is not the case. A Spanish speaker learning English therefore tends to add a vowel before the "s", and so "street" becomes "estreet." If people in your new community are learning to speak English, listen carefully and note any mispronunciations — this may give you some very good clues about features to watch for in your new language.

Each language has its own allowable syllable patterns. Contamination results when old habits are superimposed on the new language. For example, we "know" that the word "remember" is divided into syllables like this: re.mem.ber. However, many Africans who speak Bantu languages would probably say: re.me.mba. In their language it is more common to start a syllable with mb than to end a syllable with a consonant.

English speakers when learning to speak Bantu languages have the opposite contamination problem. In words like "to.mba" we want to break mb and say "tom.ba". The word "mba" we want to pronounce as two syllables — em.ba or m̩.ba (with a syllabic m̩). When we come upon a word like "mbe.mba" (corn, in Kikamba) we often contaminate it by incorrectly making it into three syllables: m̩.bem.ba, or em.bem.ba.

In Hausa the most common syllable pattern is CV, and there are no initial consonant clusters. As a result, Hausa speakers find English consonant clusters very hard to pronounce. The English term "screw driver" (CCCV CCVg.CC̦) is therefore often pronounced "su.ku.ru di.ri.ba" (CV.CV.CV CV.CV.CV) to better fit their common syllable pattern.

Sukurudiriba

Where does one syllable end and the next begin? In some languages it is fairly easy to hear where one syllable ends and the next begins. In other languages the syllable divisions are more blurred. If you have trouble hearing the syllable divisions in your new language, ask your helper to say some longer words *very* slowly and distinctly — you may find that he will then pause slightly between syllables. If not, you might ask him to "break the word into parts."

Pronounce the following syllables out loud. Each of these is only one syllable, and therefore has only one "beat."

First, with English clusters:

a, pa, spa, spot, spots, splots, splonts

Notice that even though the syllable length increases, each syllable still has only one beat.

Now let's do it with non-English combinations. Be careful to say the consonant clusters as they are written. Refrain from adding any other vowels between or before consonants, and do not make the consonants syllabic. The build-up should help you say the complex syllables with just one beat.

a,	la,	pla,	pla	a,	va,	bva,	bva
a,	la,	tla,	tla	a,	sa,	ksa,	ksa
a,	fa,	pfa,	pfa	a,	fa,	tfa,	tfa
a,	da,	nda,	nda	a,	la,	dla,	dla
a,	va,	mva,	mva	a,	da,	lda,	lda
a,	sa,	tsa,	tsa	a,	ta,	sta,	psta
a,	ba,	mba,	mba	a,	za,	bza,	mbza

Stress

'He will per'MIT you to get a "PERmit, or 'else trans'FER you to the "TRANSfer 'section. 'English has a 'few words like 'these in which the "meaning is 'different when the "stress is 'different. In the 'flow of 'speech of 'any 'language, "some 'syllables are 'louder than 'others. The "louder 'syllables are more "prominent and are 'called "stressed 'syllables. "Softer ones are 'unstressed. "Stressed 'syllables can be 'indicated with a 'raised 'vertical 'mark be'fore the 'syllable as in 'this 'paragraph. In "some 'languages, "sentences 'often have one or two 'syllables which are "doubly 'stressed — 'they can be 'marked with a "double 'stress mark. In your 'new 'language it will be 'very 'helpful to 'indicate the "stressed 'syllables in your tran-'scription. "Otherwise, you will for'get 'which ones are "stressed and 'which ones are "unstressed. If you 'got "the stress'es back'wards your pronun'ciation 'would sound fun"ny. After the words become old friends you will no longer need to indicate the stresses.

Practice this drill to gain flexibility with stress:

'mu	mu	mu	mu	
mu	mu	'mu	mu	
mu	mu	mu	'mu	
'mu	mu	'mu	mu	
mu	"mu	mu	'mu	
mu	'mu	'mu	mu	"mu

'mumumu'mu

Rhythm

Rhythm is a combination of a number of variables. Factors such as timing, stress, syllable patterns, frequency of consonant clusters, distinctness or slurring of speech, and lengthening or shortening of syllables. All of these together make up the distinct rhythm of a language.

You have probably had an experience like this back home. You went into a crowded, noisy room, and after a moment you sensed that someone was not talking English. You may not have been able to distinguish any words, but something about the rhythm and intonation caught your attention — it was different from English.

The rhythm of English involves **Stress Timing**. The major stressed syllables are both louder and longer than the unstressed ones. The stresses tend to come at quite regular intervals even though there may be a varying number of unstressed syllables in between. As a result, everything in between these stressed syllables tends to get compressed or drawn out a bit to preserve the rhythm.

Try this. Tap your foot or pen in rhythm with the two major stresses in the following sentences, and notice how the in-between syllables are expanded or compressed to allow the major stresses to remain rhythmic.

The "woman   w a s   "shouting.
The "woman   was   not   "shouting.
The "woman I saw was not "shouting.
The "woman I saw was not just "shouting.
The "woman that I saw was not just "shouting.

The woman was shouting

In some languages, on the other hand, the rhythm is based more on the number of syllables rather than on the stresses. We call this kind of rhythm **Syllable Timing**. In Syllable Timing each syllable gets about the same amount of time — the unstressed syllables do not get compressed or expanded. Say the previous sentences again, but this time say them with Syllable Timing. Tap your pencil for each syllable, to see that each one gets about the same amount of time.

Our rhythm habits are deeply subconscious. It is not uncommon for people to learn to speak another language very well, including excellent pronunciation of consonants and vowels — and yet their new language pronunciation is clearly contaminated by their English timing habits.

Listen specifically to the rhythm of your helper's pronunciation, and try to carefully match his timing, enunciation, and stress as you mimic.

Consonants

Englishnglish has about 30 consonant *sounds* (not letters), but you are capable of making many, many other consonant sounds with your "articulator" — your mouth. In this section we won't be exhaustive, but we will introduce you to the more common consonants. We will also show you a framework for classifying and describing them.

Stops

Make a p . Put an "ah" sound both before and after it. We will spell this "apa". Feel the way your lips stop the air for the p sound. A p stops the air, and is therefore called a **stop**. Any consonant that completely stops the air is a stop. Other English stops are: b , t , d , k , g . Say the following syllables while you feel the way the air is stopped — "apa, aba, ata, ada, aka, aga." Notice that the stops in "apa" and "aba" are both made in the same way — the air is stopped by the lips. The sounds p and b are called "bilabial" stops. Notice that the stops in "ata" and "ada" are both made by stopping the air with the tip of the tongue against the alveolar ridge (the bony ridge behind the upper teeth). So, t and d are called "tip alveolar" stops. Feel how k and g are made — the back of the tongue stops the air at the back of the mouth. We call the back of the mouth the "velar" region, so k and g are called "back velar" stops. These six sounds can be represented on a table as follows:

The big black-backed
bumblebee

TRY THE TONGUE
TWISTERS 3X EACH

	Bi-Labial	Tip Alveolar	Back Velar
Stops:	p b	t d	k g

But, how is p different from b , or t different from d ,
or k from g ? Concentrate on the consonants in the following
"sentence" as you read it aloud: "ɑpɑ ɑbɑ ɑpɑ ɑbɑ ɑpɑ ɑbɑ."
Read it again while holding your hands over your ears; again
with your hands on top of your head; and once more, with your
fingers resting lightly on your voice box (Adam's apple). Say
"ɑpɑ" while holding the p . Contrast that with "ɑbɑ" while
holding the b . Do it out loud. Notice that there is vibration
on the b sound — the "motor" in the voice box is running for
b , but not for p . (You probably also felt the vibration on
the ɑ sound.) We say that p is voiceless (because the vocal
chords are not vibrating) and b is voiced. "Voicing" also
enables us to differentiate between t and d and between k
and g . Experiment with these sounds until you can feel the
difference that voicing makes on b , d , and g : "ɑpɑ ɑbɑ, ɑtɑ
ɑdɑ, ɑkɑ ɑgɑ." Be sure you are fully voicing the voiced stops —
b , d , g — since in English we often barely voice them. If
you have trouble hearing the difference, it might help to hold
your hands on your ears, head, or voice box while humming:
"*hmmmmm*." You can feel the vibration because the cavities of
the head act as resonating chambers and amplify the vocal
chord vibrations.

Hold your hands
over your ears

In English, a voiceless stop is usually pronounced with a
small puff of air following it. Hold the back of your hand close
to your mouth while you say: "pɑ, tɑ, kɑ." Repeat these syllables and feel the puff of air that blows on your hand after the
stop. This little puff of air is called *aspiration*, and so a stop
with this puff is called an "aspirated" stop. Aspiration is
symbolized with a raised "h" after the stop symbol — p^h, t^h, k^h.
(In English we do not have aspirated *voiced* stops.) In English
when p , t , or k follows s , the puff of air is usually
omitted. Hold the back of your hand near your mouth while
repeating the words "pan, span." As you repeat the words,
notice the puff of air after the p in "pan", and the absence of
the puff after the p in "span" (though you may feel some air
on the s sound). Experiment with the words "tan, Stan" and
"can, scan," to begin to become aware of the difference between
aspirated and unaspirated stops. (Notice that the sound spelled
with "c" in "can" and "scan" is the same sound that is spelled
with "k" in "kill" or "skill" — we will represent that backvelar
stop with "k" in phonetic spelling.) Spanish, along with various
other languages, has only unaspirated stops. If the stops in
your language are unaspirated, your English habits will tend
to cause you to incorrectly substitute aspirated stops. You can
find out if the stops in your language are aspirated or unaspi-

A kritikal
kriket kritik

rated by holding your hand or a small strip of paper in front of your helper's lips while he says words which have sounds like p , t , k . Some languages have both aspirated and unaspirated stops — a word with an aspirated stop can have a different meaning from a similar sounding word with an unaspirated stop. Practice the stops in your language with Pronunciation Differential and Substitution drills, so you can learn to produce these as they are produced by the native speakers of your new language.

Flexibility in producing and omitting aspiration can be drilled with the following exercise. The first and third colums are the normal pronunciation for English. The fifth column repeats the first. The second column puts aspiration where English does not, and the fourth leaves aspiration off where you would normally put it.

To drill, first contrast Columns One and Two, reading the *pairs* across. Concentrate on adding a robust puff of air after the stop of the second column. Keep the back of your hand at your lips so you can feel the aspiration.

Next, contrast Columns Two and Three, aspirating all stops. Column Three represents the normal English pronunciation, even though we normally spell as in Column Four.

Next, contrast Columns Three and Four, being careful to remove all aspiration in Column Four.

Then contrast Columns Four and Five. Don't aspirate any of these stops.

Finally, read across all five columns.

Exasperated stop

1	2	3	4	5
span	sp^{h}an	p^{h}an	pan	span
spin	sp^{h}in	p^{h}in	pin	spin
spool	sp^{h}ool	p^{h}ool	pool	spool
stan	st^{h}an	t^{h}an	tan	stan
stone	st^{h}one	t^{h}one	tone	stone
stool	st^{h}ool	t^{h}ool	tool	stool
skin	sk^{h}in	k^{h}in	kin	skin
skate	sk^{h}ate	k^{h}ate	kate	skate
sketch	sk^{h}etch	k^{h}etch	ketch	sketch

Sometimes English speakers make a voiced stop instead of a voiceless unaspirated stop. In other words, when they try to make unaspirated p , t , and k , they make b , d , and g instead. Here is a drill with words from Thai to help you check yourself. Read across the columns in sets of three. The words of each column must sound different or the meaning will be confused. (Notice that the stops in the second column are unaspirated.)

bit	pit	pʰit
"twist"	"to close"	"wrong"
baw	paw	pʰaw
"light"	"to blow"	"to burn"
bet	pet	pʰet
"fishhook"	"duck"	"peppery"
dam	tam	tʰam
"black"	"to pound"	"to make"
dok	tok	tʰok
"fertile"	"fall"	"to skin"
dak	tak	tʰak
"to ensnare"	"draw water"	"to braid"

Big black bug's blood

There is one more stop sound in English. "Oh-oh!" Say that again. What is that sound you put in the middle of the word where the hyphen is? Say it again — feel how the air is stopped in your throat. Up to now, we have seen how the lips and tongue can stop the flow of air. If the vocal chords are closed, the flow of air is also stopped. Closed vocal chords can't vibrate, so the sound is voiceless. Another name for the vocal chords is the glottis. This consonant is therefore called a *glottal stop*. Phonetically, it is written as a question mark without the dot under it — ʔ (The glottal stop is almost always unaspirated in English.) English is full of glottal stops, but the glottal stop almost never causes a difference in meaning between words, with perhaps one exception — "mhmm" without a glottal stop means "yes", but put a glottal stop in it ("hmʔmm") and it means exactly the opposite. The natural place in English for the glottal stop is at the beginning of words which start with a vowel. Say "I" and feel the stop in your throat before the vowel. Say it again and hold the stop, releasing it with a slight explosion into the vowel. Say "oh-oh" again. Before, you noticed the glottal stop between the vowels, but if you listen carefully you may notice that you also made a glottal stop before the first vowel. You can learn to say vowels without the initial glottal stop by thinking the sound "h" (without actually saying it) before the vowel, or by slightly breathing in with your throat open before saying the vowel. Practice with: a a a, o o o, u u u."

Release it
into the vowel

Say "my elbow." Did you hear a glottal stop between the two words? Practice putting it in and leaving it out between the words. Similarly practice the following phrases: "blue ink,"

Pretty ear

"my eye," "so awful," "dirty iron," "go up," "pretty ear," "every apple." Put in the glottal stop; leave it out. Put it in; leave it out.

In many languages (American Indian languages, for example), the glottal stop is a regular consonant like k or s. In these languages, if you use a glottal stop out of habit, without being aware of it, you may be saying a different word than you intended to say. Other languages, like Spanish, rarely use glottal stops either consciously or unconsciously — foreign accent is spotted by the presence of glottal stops before words beginning with vowels.

Our chart for STOPS can now be more complete:

		Bi-Labial	Tip Alv.	Back Velar	Glottal
Stops:					
Vl.	Aspirated	p^h	t^h	k^h	
	Unaspirated	p	t	k	?
Voiced		b	d	g	

Notice that each sound is differentiated from each of the others. Each stop can now be defined with a specific description which separates it from all other sounds:

p	—	voiceless bilabial stop
b	—	voiced bilabial stop
t^h	—	voiceless aspirated tip alveolar stop
t	—	voiceless tip alveolar stop
k	—	voiceless back velar stop
g	—	voiced back velar stop
?	—	glottal stop

How would you describe d? You are right if you said: Voiced tip alveolar stop. The *four basic questions to be answered in a consonant description* are:

1. Is there sound coming from the voice box when that consonant is being produced?

A voice box

Voicing. All consonants can be classified as being either voiced or voiceless. We say that a sound is voiced when the voice box (the vocal chords) vibrates — b, d, g are voiced sounds. We call a sound voiceless when the vocal chords are not vibrating — p, t, k are voiceless sounds.

2. What moves to produce the consonant?

> **Articulator.** We use the term "articulator" to describe the part of the mouth that moves to make the sound. The articulators we have seen so far are the lower lip (p), the tip of the tongue (t), and the back of the tongue (k).

3. Where in the mouth is the consonant being produced?

> **Point of Articulation.** The points of articulation are the places along the upper part of the mouth where sounds are made. Notice that t and d are made at the "alveolar" point of articulation; k and g are made at the "velar" point of articulation; p and b are made at the "labial" point of articulation — when we combine the name of the articulator with that of the point of articulation for these labial sounds, we call them "bilabial," rather than "lip labial." Slowly say the following syllables and feel how the articulators move to the points of articulation: "atʰa, aga, apʰa, ada, aba."

The flow of air
is stopped

4. What happens to the air when the consonant is produced?

> **Manner of Articulation.** The manner refers to what happens to the flow of air as the sound is being made. The flow of air for p , b , tʰ , k , etc., is stopped when the consonant is made, so these sounds are classified as stops. You will soon be introduced to fricative, nasal and lateral manners of articulation.

> (When describing voiceless stops, we must also say whether they are aspirated or unaspirated. An aspirated stop has a little puff of air after it, while an unaspirated stop doesn't have the puff of air after it.)

When you know these four facts about a consonant, you have the basic information necessary to identify and produce it. For example, if you are told to produce between vowels a "voiced back velar stop," you should make the sound g between vowels — "aga." Try it yourself — produce the following consonants between vowels (concentrate on each one before going on to the next one):

Voiceless bilabial aspirated stop
Voiced tip alveolar stop
Voiceless back velar aspirated stop
Voiced bilabial stop.

(If you have trouble with any of these, refer to the chart on page 260.) You should have said "apʰa" "ada" "akʰa" and "aba."

Here's a broadside split-half view of your head. You'll note that all of the points of articulation are on the upper side of the oral cavity, and the articulators are on the lower side of the oral cavity.

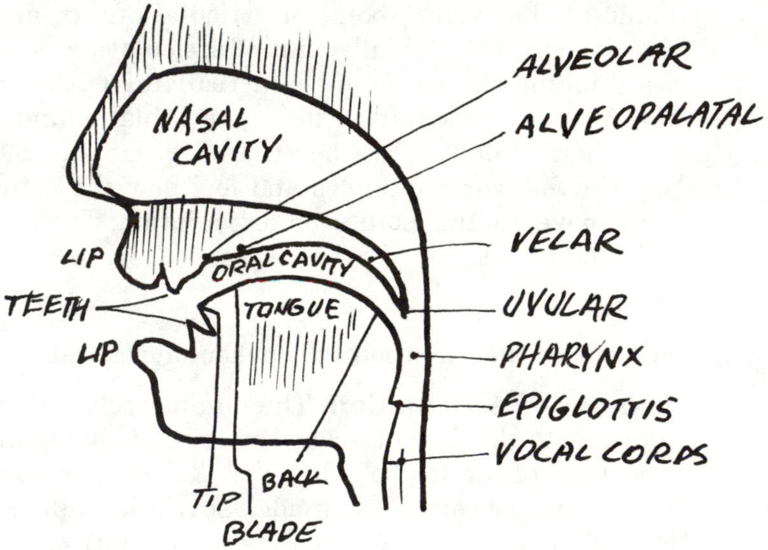

NOTE: Each paragraph between here and page 289 introduces a different sound or feature. We do not recommend that you speed-read this section. Dwell on each paragraph long enough to say each new sound distinctly with an understanding of its articulation characteristics, then go on to the next paragraph.

We don't expect our readers to become skilled phoneticians by reading this chapter! We *do* expect you to become aware of the variety of sounds in human language. This awareness should condition your *attitude* toward the sounds of your new language. You will accept the sounds of the language, rather than insisting on English sounds. We also expect that you will be able to identify, classify, and with practice, *accurately* produce each of the sounds of your new language.

If one of these sounds seems to be particularly difficult for you to produce, check with your helper to see if it is in your new language. If

you won't need it, then don't spend a lot of time on it. If you do need it, make a note about it, and come back frequently until you master it.

Fricatives

Say "f ew" and "v iew." Say them again and lengthen the initial consonant in each word. These consonants — f and v — do not stop the flow of air. They only restrict it, causing friction. We call this the "fricative" *manner* of articulation. Slowly say "afa" and contrast it with "ava." Feel your ears, head or voice box to determine which of the consonants is voiced and which is voiceless. What is the articulator for f and v ? It is the same as for p — the lower lip. But the point of articulation is different than for the p . Say "afa" and feel where the lower lip moves to. We call this the "dental" point of articulation. We can now describe these two fricatives:

Feel where
the lower lip moves

> v — voiced labio-dental fricative
> f — voiceless labio-dental fricative.

Say "th y th igh." Repeat these words slowly, listening carefully to the fricatives at the beginning of each of these words. Notice that the sound spelled by "th" in "thy" is different from the sound spelled "th" in "thigh." Say these until you can hear and feel the difference. By now you have probably guessed that the difference between these two sounds is that one is voiced and the other is voiceless. We will call the voiceless one (the one in "thigh") by the Greek term "theta" (the initial sound in "theta" is this same voiceless fricative). We write this sound with the Greek symbol θ . The voiced "th" sound (like in "thy") can be phonetically written as a "d" with a bar through it (đ), and is called "barred d." (The bar through the đ will identify it as a fricative.) English spelling does not show the difference between these two sounds — they are both spelled "th." The foreigner learning English simply has to memorize the fact that he must voice the fricative in words like: *thy, that, the, they, bathe* and *lathe*. And he must learn to leave the voicing off the fricative in words like: *thigh, think, thing, tooth,* and *bath*. It would be easier

I thought a thought.
But the θought I θought
wasn't ð̵e θought
I θought I θought.

if the different sounds were represented by different symbols. (Similarly, it will be helpful for you to use different symbols to represent sounds that are different in your new language.)

Notice that the point of articulation for ð̵ and θ is the same as for f and v — dental. Say "thy," and feel the articulator for the fricative — it is the tip of the tongue. Both ð̵ and θ are tip dental fricatives. One is voiced, the other is voiceless.

Notice also that the "h" consonant, as in the words "ha" and "hat," is not at all related to the "h" in the "th" spelling. The h is a slightly fricative sound made in the throat — we can call it a glottal fricative.

Say " s ee C aesar." The initial consonant in both words is the same sound, even though it is spelled differently in English. Only one symbol is needed to represent this sound — we will use the symbol "s."

As you say the word " s ei z e" notice that there are two fricatives which restrict the air at the alveolar point of articulation (the same point of articulation as d and t). The difference between the two fricatives of *seize* is voicing — the first is voiceless, and the second voiced. Say " s ei z e" until you really feel the difference. Speak up, or the second fricative will sound voiceless. Notice that the letter "z" in sei z e" represents the same sound that the letter "s" represents in "Cae s ar" — we will use the symbol z for this sound. It is important for you to become aware of the differences between sounds and spellings. Remember that in phonetic writing we represent each sound by one symbol.

Pay attention
to the tongue

Pay attention to your articulator — the tip of the tongue — as you say the fricatives in "seize." Is the tip of your tongue down by the lower teeth, or is it up behind the upper teeth? Some English speakers make this sound with the tip of the tongue up and others make it with the tip down. If it is made with the tip of the tongue down, then the friction is caused by an area of the tongue behind the tip, called the "blade" of the tongue, and the sound is called a "blade alveolar fricative." For convenience, we will refer to s and z as tip alveolar fricatives. Try to see if Kino makes these sounds with the tip of the tongue up or down.

The Gileadites captured the places where the Jordan could be crossed. When any Ephraimite who was trying to escape would ask permission to cross, the men of Gilead would ask, "Are you an Ephraimite?" If he said, "No," they would tell him to say "Shibboleth." But he would say "Sibboleth," because he could not pronounce it correctly. Then they would grab him and kill him there. (Judges 12:5-6. Good News Bible.)**

The word "shibboleth," which meant "ear of corn" was an effective password because the Ephraimite dialect apparently did not have voiceless fricatives that were made at the alveopalatal point of articulation. The alveopalatal area is just behind the alveolar ridge, and in front of the soft palate. English words spelled with "sh" are usually made by friction with the blade articulator at the alveopalatal point of articulation. It is cumbersome to write one sound with a combination of two letters, so we will write the "sh" sound as an "s" with a wedge over it — š — and call it "s wedge." A word like "show" could be written phonetically — šow.

The sixth šeik's
sixth šeep's
sick.

Pronunciation contamination, like "sibboleth" instead of "shibboleth" has been used various times to tell friend from foe. The Italian language has the "ch" sound, but French doesn't. The French, under Charles of Anjou, had occupied Sicily for many years during the thirteenth century, and many Frenchmen had learned the Sicilian dialect of Italian almost well enough to pass for natives — except for this one phonetic feature. They used "sh" instead of "ch." The Sicilians finally revolted against their French oppressors and quite a massacre resulted. If the Sicilians were in doubt about the nationality of a suspect, they asked him to say "Cicero Ceci." If they got "Sheeshero Sheshee" instead of "Cheechero Chechee," there was one less Frenchman.

The English spelling "ch" denotes a consonant cluster, but the spelling is misleading. If you take apart the two consonants of the cluster you will discover that the sounds are t and š. English spelling would more clearly show this cluster if it were spelled "tsh" — tshurtsh (church!). Cicero Ceci phonetically is tšitšero tšetši; but the French failed to make the cluster, and šišero šeši resulted. (The tš cluster can also phonetically be written č.)

There are not many words in English which add voicing to the blade alveopalatal fricative, but it does occur in words like:

leisure, pleasure, azure, measure, and in "Zsa Zsa" (Gabor). Phonetically this sound is written with a "z wedge" — ž .

Practice saying the following syllables to make sure you can distinguish these four fricatives: "asa aza aša aža," "aša asa aža aza."

The word "judge" has one consonant cluster that is spelled in two different ways — the "j" and the "dge" both represent the cluster dž . If you say the word "judge" slowly, you can feel the clusters. Another way to feel this consonant cluster is to slowly say "did you"; then say it fast, and it becomes "didžu." Notice that the words Jim and George both start with this dž cluster. The dž cluster can also phonetically be written ǰ.

The ability to pronounce this ǰ sound was once used as a life-or-death password during the nineteenth century. The Egyptians, under the leadership of Ibrahim Pasha, invaded the Turkish-held province of Syria. Ibrahim had recruited widely for the Egyptian army, and his ranks even included many Syrians. In Syria, the Egyptian army was unexpectedly routed by the hard-fighting Druses, and many were captured. The Druses wanted to spare any of their fellow Syrians, but when the prisoners found this out they all claimed to be Syrian! Of course Arabic was the common language for the Syrians and Egyptians but there were dialectical differences. The captives were compelled to say the word for "camel" — Egyptians said "gamal" while the Syrians pronounced it "ǰamal." Only the "ǰamal" speakers were allowed to live.

Next we will give a table of the consonants you now know; but first, let's take a "note break."

NOTE: English speakers have also been faced with pronunciation "passwords." American and Canadian draft-dodgers during the Second World War would try to get lost on the opposite sides of the border. The immigration authorities couldn't tell the difference, so suspects were simply requested to recite the alphabet. For Americans the last letter is "zee," while Canadians (and British) finish with "zed" — foiled again!

(We are indebted to Mario Pei for most of this information about language "passwords." For more, read his book *What's in a Word*, Hawthorn Books, New York, 1968.)

A table with the sounds we have discussed so far looks like this:

	Bi-Labial	Labio-Dental	Tip Dental	Tip Alveolar	Blade Alveo-palatal	Back Velar	Glottal
Stops:							
Vl. Asp.	pʰ			tʰ		kʰ	
Vl. Unasp.	p			t		k	ʔ
Voiced	b			d		g	
Fricatives:							
Voiceless	◯	f	θ	s	š	◯	h
Voiced		v	đ	z	ž		

Notice the location of the two circles on the chart.

English has stops, but not fricatives for the bilabial and back velar articulations. However, many languages have fricatives made at these points.

Play a comb

Let's "play a comb" to learn how to make bilabial fricatives. Wrap a piece of thin paper around a comb and hold it against your lips while you hum. Be sure your lips are open enough to let air go out against the comb. Smile while you hum. If you are doing it properly, your lips should begin to tingle before you reach the end of your tune. After you have done this, begin to "hum" the same tune in the same way but remove the comb and paper. Be sure not to let your lips close. Think about the articulation. As you hum, the voice box "motor" is running, so the sound you are making is voiced. The articulation is bilabial — the lower lip is causing friction along the upper lip. Instead of a bilabial stop (b), you are making a bilabial fricative. This sound is represented by drawing a bar through a "b": ƀ. We call this a "barred b." Practice saying "aƀa", being careful not to let the lips completely touch each other to stop the air while you are making the barred b. You will need to practice this since English bilabial consonants normally are stops. Be careful not to round your lips, or you may be just saying "awa", instead of "aƀa". Be sure there is friction between the lips. The correct sound of "aƀa" will be very similar to "ava". Be sure, however, that in saying "aƀa" the lower lip is causing friction against the upper lip rather than against the upper teeth. Get a small mirror so you can watch yourself as you practice. OK, now practice for a while.

Smile slightly while blowing on the back of your hand. Look at your lips in the mirror and think about the articulation. Air is being forced between the lips with voiceless friction,

Look in the mirror
while you practice

so the manner is fricative, and of course it is bilabial. Yet, this sound is different from the bilabial fricative we just wrote as ƀ . This one is voiceless (like the bilabial stop p), so we will write it ᵽ (barred p). Practice saying "ƀƀƀ ᵽᵽᵽ ƀƀƀ ᵽᵽᵽ ." Don't move your lips at all — hold the bilabial fricative steady while you turn the voicing on and off. Now try: "aƀa, aƀa, aᵽa, aᵽa." Look in the mirror while you practice. Now, say "ƀaby" and "ᵽaper". Make sure there is friction, and don't let your lips completely close — if your lips close, it becomes a stop, and if there is no friction it is no longer a fricative.   ◦§

Imitate a cat

Some languages make fricative sounds at the point of articulation where English makes k and g . These fricatives could be written ꝁ and ǥ (barred k and barred g). Some people make the ꝁ sound when they imitate a cat hissing at a dog. This fricative can also be produced by "whistling" a tune with the back of the tongue. To make a barred g (ǥ), simply turn on your voicing as you "whistle" with the back of your tongue — i.e., by humming while you whistle with the back of your tongue, but don't close your lips to hum. Practice: "ꝁ ꝁ ꝁ ǥ ǥ ǥ ꝁ ꝁ ꝁ ǥ ǥ ǥ ." If your new language has one or both of these sounds, listen to Kino and practice mimicking him. Set up a Pronunciation Substitution drill as demonstrated on pages 62-65. Practice by listening, mimicking, and producing, until you can produce these sounds satisfactorily. It might be helpful to note that English speakers tend to stop the air before making the fricative, resulting in a consonant cluster — aka is thus incorrectly pronounced ak ꝁ a: and aga is similarly mispronounced ag ǥ a.   ◦§

Here are some exercises to help you drill these new sounds. First read down each column; then drill by contrasting the pairs in adjacent columns. Build up until you can read all the way across the rows.

V o i c e d						**V o i c e l e s s**				
b	ƀ	v	bƀ	ƀƀ		p	ᵽ	f	pᵽ	ᵽᵽ
ba	ƀa	va	bƀa	ƀƀa		pa	ᵽa	fa	pᵽa	ᵽᵽa
bo	ƀo	vo	bƀo	ƀƀo		po	ᵽo	fo	pᵽo	ᵽᵽo
bu	ƀu	vu	bƀu	ƀƀu		pu	ᵽu	fu	pᵽu	ᵽᵽu
aba	aƀa	ava	abƀa	aƀƀa		apa	aᵽa	afa	apᵽa	aᵽᵽa
obo	oƀo	ovo	obƀo	oƀƀo		opo	oᵽo	ofo	opᵽo	oᵽᵽo
ubu	uƀu	uvu	ubƀu	uƀƀu		upu	uᵽu	ufu	upᵽu	uᵽᵽu
ab	aƀ	av	abƀ	aƀƀ		ap	aᵽ	af	apᵽ	aᵽᵽ
ob	oƀ	ov	obƀ	oƀƀ		op	oᵽ	of	opᵽ	oᵽᵽ
ub	uƀ	uv	ubƀ	uƀƀ		up	uᵽ	uf	upᵽ	uᵽᵽ

	V o i c e d					**V o i c e l e s s**			
g	ǥ	ž	gǥ	gg	k	ꝁ	h	kꝁ	kk
ga	ǥa	ža	gǥa	gga	ka	ꝁa	ha	kꝁa	kka
go	ǥo	žo	gǥo	ggo	ko	ꝁo	ho	kꝁo	kko
gu	ǥu	žu	gǥu	ggu	ku	ꝁu	hu	kꝁu	kku
aga	aǥa	aža	agǥa	agga	aka	aꝁa	aha	akꝁa	akka
ogo	oǥo	ožo	ogǥo	oggo	oko	oꝁo	oho	okꝁo	okko
ugu	uǥu	užu	ugǥu	uggu	uku	uꝁu	uhu	ukꝁu	ukku
ag	aǥ	až	agǥ	agg	ak	aꝁ	ah	akꝁ	akk
og	oǥ	ož	ogǥ	ogg	ok	oꝁ	oh	okꝁ	okk
ug	uǥ	už	ugǥ	ugg	uk	uꝁ	uh	ukꝁ	ukk

Nasals

So far, we have considered two manners of articulation of consonants — stops and fricatives. Another manner of treating the air stream is to allow the air to go through the nose. Sounds which are made with the air going through the nose are called "nasals." English has a bilabial nasal (m), a tip alveolar nasal (n), and a back velar nasal which is usually spelled "ng" in English (phonetically it is written ŋ). In English, m and n can occur at the beginning, middle, or end of words; however, the velar nasal — ŋ — does not occur at the beginning of English words. A word like "longing" has the velar nasal in the middle and at the end. Since the velar nasal is always preceded by a vowel in English, English speakers want to put a vowel before initial ŋ in other languages. For example, the Vietnamese name "Nga" (ŋa) might be mispronounced as "eŋa" or even "eŋga." If your new language has ŋ at the beginning of words, you might practice as follows: Repeat the word "longing"; leave off the "l" and continue repeating "onging"; now, pause after the first vowel, so you are saying "o - ŋiŋ"; now, leave off the first vowel and say "ŋiŋ." Practice saying it with different vowels — "ŋa ŋo ŋu."

Say "cannon." Now say "canyon." Lengthen the nasal sounds in the middle of these two words, so you can feel what you are doing. Now, as you say "canyon," concentrate on holding the tip of your tongue down and the blade up as you say the sound spelled "ny". The sound can be written phonetically — ñ . It is a

Lemony liniment

Hold the tip
of your tongue down

blade alveopalatal nasal. Practice: "aña oño uñu, ña ño ñu, añ oñ uñ." As you practice, be sure you are saying ñ with your tongue tip down behind your lower teeth.   ✍

NOTE: Occasionally learners think the alveopalatal region is the soft palate. As you say "canyon" with your tongue tip down, you will note that the blade of the tongue (just behind the tip) is touching the roof of the mouth far forward of the soft palate. That is where all alveopalatal sounds are made. The name we use for the soft palate is "velum," and sounds which are made there (like k) are called "back velar" sounds.

You have just seen how a nasal sound can be made at the alveopalatal point of articulation. You can also make an alveopalatal stop. Say "ada". Say "aña". Now say "ada" but keep your tongue tip down for the stop — you have just made a voiced alveopalatal stop, which can be written " đ ". You can also make a "t" sound by keeping your tongue tip *down* as you say something like "ata" — it will become "aⱦa." Practice the following: "aña ađa aⱦa, aña aⱦa aña ađa."   ✍

Say the affirmative: "mhmm". Look in a mirror. Notice that your lips are closed all through this word. The sound represented by an "h" in this word is quite different from the "h" in "hum". The middle sound in "mhmm" is actually a voiceless bilabial nasal! The articulation (bilabial nasal) is the same as for "m", but there is no voicing; the vocal chords are not vibrating. Say "mhmm" slowly and lengthen the voiceless part so you really feel what is going on. You have your lips closed and you are blowing air through your nose. (Hold your fingers under your nose to feel the air.) This voiceless nasal is written with a capital letter — M . The word "mhmm" could be phonetically written: m̥'Mm̩. Now, practice saying the other nasals with their voiceless counterparts in a similar fashion — "n̥Nn̩ ŋ̥Nŋ̩ ñ̥Ññ̩" — letting the air blow through your nose for the voiceless nasals. The sequence "n̥Nn̩" will sound like "mhmm" except your lips will be open and your tongue will be in the n position. Say the following modified English sentences, putting a voiceless nasal before each voiced nasal: "merry mice make merriment" (Mmerry Mmice Mmake MmerriMmeNnt); "nobody never knows nothing" (Nnobody Nnever Nnows NnothiŋN).   ✍

A chart of all the sounds we have studied so far looks like this:

	Bi-Labial	Labio-Dental	Tip Dental	Tip Alveolar	Blade Alveo-palatal	Back Velar	Glottal
Stops:							
Vl. Asp.	pʰ			tʰ	t̰ʰ	kʰ	
Vl. Unasp.	p			t	t̰	k	ʔ
Voiced	b			d	d̰	g	
Fricatives:							
Voiceless	p̶	f	θ	s	š	k̶	h
Voiced	b̶	v	d̶	z	ž	g̶	
Nasals:							
Voiceless	M			N	Ñ	N	
Voiced	m			n	ñ	ŋ	

Laterals

Feel the flow of air for aθa ad̶a asa aša. For these sounds the air goes over the tongue. But, when we pronounce the "l" in "ala," the air goes around the sides of the tongue. Consonants that are made with this manner of articulation are called "laterals." Many different laterals are possible — English itself has at least three different "l"s. You thought English had only one, didn't you? The English "l" varies depending on the surrounding sounds. Listen carefully as you contrast the "l" sound in "lee" with the "l" in "law." Lengthen the "l"s and feel the way your tongue rests in your mouth. You will find that when making the "l" in "lee" the back of your tongue is higher than it is when you say "law." Some languages, like Spanish, use only high tongue "l." Other languages use both, but use them differently than we do in English. Say the following words as you concentrate on keeping the back of the tongue *high* for the laterals (these will probably sound different from the way you normally say them): "lˆaw, lˆow, lˆa, lˆap, lˆuck, allˆ, Alˆ." Did you keep the tongue high for all of them? Say the following words while you concentrate on keeping the back of the tongue *low* (these also should sound a little odd to you): "lˇeap, lˇip, lˇoose, lˇook, lˇet, lˇate, illˇ, coolˇ." Now say each of the words from both lists, first with high tongue and then with low tongue.

Old oily Ollie
oils oily autos

English speakers also make a voiceless "l". This occurs after aspirated stops. A voiceless "l"? Yes. Some other languages have voiceless laterals too. The articulation is the same as for a voiced l — air comes out laterally around the tongue, but the vocal chords are not vibrating. This sound can be symbolized phonetically with a capital letter — L . (In phonetic writing, various of the less common voiceless sounds are symbolized with capital letters — the voiceless nasals you just practiced were written with capitals: M, N, Ñ, and N). Now, let's make a voiceless L — lengthen the aspiration after the p^h or k^h in the following words and you will hear the voiceless L: play, clay, clump, plump, pleat, cleat. (Actually, in English, after voiceless stops the "l" has both a voiceless and voiced part and could be symbolized "Ll".)

Lengthen
the aspiration

Remember the alveopalatal nasal (ñ) you practiced? You can make an alveopalatal lateral in a similar fashion — put your tongue tip down behind your lower teeth, and use the blade of the tongue against the alveopalatal area. The alveopalatal "l" is written l̃ . Say: "aña al̃a aña al̃a, ña l̃a ña l̃a, añ al̃ añ al̃." Keep the tongue tip down for these, and don't let it come up.

In some languages, like Navaho, tip alveolar laterals are made with lateral friction. These are called "lateral fricatives." Lateral fricatives can be voiced or voiceless. The voiced one sounds similar to z or ž. Sometimes people who speak English with a lisp use the voiced lateral fricative instead of z and the voiceless lateral fricative instead of s. Say "pLa." If you blow extra hard while making the voiceless lateral, you will probably be making the voiceless lateral fricative — "pɫa." (The lateral fricative is symbolized with a line through the letter just as it was for b .) You can make the voiced fricative in a similar way — say "bla" and force the air out as you say the lateral — bɫa. Experiment until you feel some friction on the lateral (you may have to raise the sides of the tongue a little in order to create more friction).

Raise the sides
of the tongue

If your new language has any of these variations of laterals, develop drills with Kino. Practice until you can say the laterals accurately in the context of words and phrases.

Here is a chart of the laterals we have just seen:

	Tip Alveolar	Blade Alveopalatal
Laterals:		
Voiced High tongue	l̂	l̃
Voiced Low tongue	ľ	
Voiceless	L	
Voiceless Fricative	Ł	
Voiced Fricative	ł	

Thrills of Trills (Flaps and Trills)

In many languages, some of the tip alveolar consonants are made with a very rapid motion — the tip of the tongue flips up to the alveolar ridge and back down rapidly. The sounds t , d , l , n , can all be made with this quick flip of the tongue, and are then called "flaps." If you rapidly say the words "ladder" and "latter," you probably are making a flapped d (ď) and a flapped t (ť) respectively. The words "lilly" and "Minnie" when produced quickly will give examples of flapped l (ľ) and flapped n (ň). (Isn't it strange that English spelling writes the consonant twice when it only takes half as long to say it?) Watch the r's in your new language and learn how they are made — they may be flapped, and therefore will be different from your English r's. The flapped r (ř) will sound like the flapped d or flapped t, but will have a slight "r" quality. If your language has ř it will probably be spelled "r", but it is not at all like the English glided r . (In Swahili, part of the greeting is spelled "habari." Phonetically, the "r" in this word represents ř . One learner thought she couldn't make this sound, but her problem was resolved when she began to think of the spelling as "habatti.") Look back at page 63 for an example of a Substitution drill on ř .

ř-ř-ř

"That's a quality r"

Some languages have what is called a trilled r. This is symbolized phonetically as an r with a tilde over it — r̃ . It is made by allowing the tip of the tongue to rest easily against the alveolar ridge while the passing air causes the tip of the tongue to flap quickly two or more times in succession. Many times boys playing with cars will simulate the sound of the car's motor by making a trilled r̃. In Spanish, children play with the trilled r̃ by saying this tongue twister in which each of the r's are trilled: *Rápido corren los carros del ferrocarril* (The train cars run fast). As you practice trilling, you will discover that it is possible to make the trilled r̃ both with and without voicing. The voiceless one can be written with a capital letter — R̃ . Practice this: "ar̃a aR̃a, r̃a R̃a, ar̃ aR̃."

Open your mouth and look in the mirror. In the back of your mouth you have a little finger-like thing hanging down — this is called the "uvula." Sometimes when gargling (or playing with cars) people allow the uvula to rest on the back of the tongue so that the passing air causes an uvular trill. French uses this back trill in words such as *beurre* (butter) and *au revoire*. The uvular trill can also be voiced or voiceless. Phonetically it is written as an "r" with a dot under it to denote that it is in the back of the mouth, and a tilde over it to signify that it is trilled — ṛ̃ (voiced), or Ṛ̃ (voiceless).

Uvula

Additional Features
For Consonant Analysis

On page 260, four questions were given that provide basic information needed when classifying a consonant. These questions pinpoint the following features — 1) *voicing,* 2) the *articulator* that moves, 3) the *point* to which it moves, and 4) the *manner* of air flow.

However, some consonants are not completely described in terms of the four features above. One example is the contrast that is made between aspiration and no aspiration on voiceless stops. Here are some other possible variations:

Fronted and backed consonants. We have talked about consonants as though they occurred at exact points of articulation. For example the alveolar point of articulation. Say "ɑtɑ." Feel the point where your tongue touches. Now say "ɑtɑ" but move your tongue forward to the teeth — in other words, a fronted "t". Phonetically this is written with a small "tooth mark" under the t — ṭ . Now say "ɑtɑ" but make the "t" with your tongue tip far back in your mouth (this is called "retroflexed"). This sound is written with a dot underneath — ṭ . Back velar sounds can also be made a little forward or a little back in the mouth. Say "keel, call." Feel how both of the "k" sounds are made with the back of the tongue, but the k in "keel" is farther forward than the one in "call." Now try it the other way around — say "keel" with a backed k (ḳ) and "call" with a fronted k (ḳ̭).

Practice going back and forth on the following Differential drill:

Fronted	Mid	Backed
ɑṭɑ	ɑtɑ	ɑṭɑ
ɑḓɑ	ɑdɑ	ɑḍɑ
ɑḽɑ	ɑlɑ	ɑḷɑ
ɑṉɑ	ɑnɑ	ɑṇɑ
ɑṣɑ	ɑsɑ	ɑṣɑ
ɑḵ̭ɑ	ɑkɑ	ɑḵɑ
ɑḡɑ	ɑgɑ	ɑgɑ

Goats graze
in groves on grass
which grows in grooves
in groves

Many languages have both fronted and backed consonants.

274

Lengthened Consonants. In some languages, certain consonants are held for a longer time than others. Try it — say "ɑmɑ" but hold the m extra long. Lengthened consonants can be indicated with a raised dot after the letter: m·. Almost any consonant (except flaps) can be lengthened. Say these: ɑp·ɑ, ɑb·ɑ, ɑl·ɑ, ɑs·ɑ, ɑn·ɑ, ɑʔ·ɑ.

Double Consonants. In some languages, especially in West Africa, two consonants can occur simultaneously, rather than sequentially. If your new language has this kind of double consonants, you can learn to make them by imitating the cackle of a chicken. That's right! Go ahead and try it — loud enough for your neighbors to hear. Now think about the articulation while you do it. You are making a stop, but you are stopping the air both with the back of the tongue and with the lips at the same time — a **double stop.** It is voiceless, so it is a combination of p and k released simultaneously. It can be written ᵏp. As you imitate cackling, you should be saying "ᵏpɑ ᵏpɑ ᵏpɑ." Now practice it again at normal speaking volume. Be careful not to say "cuppa cuppa cuppa."

Double stop

Now, if you add voicing, you can pronounce "ᵍbɑ ᵍbɑ ᵍbɑ." Do you remember the Igbo people of Western Nigeria (Biafra)? Their tribal name was usually spelled Ibo in American newspapers since outsiders seldom correctly pronounce the double consonant. You can pronounce it correctly if you say Iᵍbo — be careful not to just say Ibo, or Ig-bo.

Stop!

A **double nasal** also occurs in some of these West African languages. You have practiced the velar nasal (ŋ) and learned to say it in initial position in a word like " ŋɑ ." The velar ŋ can be made simultaneously with m . Practice it. Be careful not to start either sound before the other, and also be careful to release them at the same time — "ᵑmɑ ᵑmɑ ᵑmɑ, ᵑmu ᵑmo, ɑᵑm oᵑm uᵑm."

Clicks. Smooch! Sma-ack! A kiss is a click that is more fun with a special someone else. A kiss is a bilabial click (with someone else it is quadrilabial). Try a bilabial click with a vowel after it. Since this click is bilabial and voiceless it can be symbolized with a modified "p" — p←. Try this: "p←ɑ p←o p←u." Now, put it between vowels — ɑp←ɑ, op←o, up←u. Next, put it at the end of some words: bɑp←, op←, up←. Some of the languages in the southern part of Africa have a variety of clicks for consonants.

A fun click!

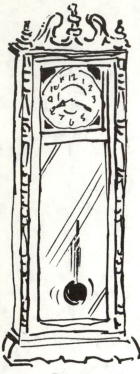

The English spelling "tsk tsk" often represents a click which is made by the tip of the tongue. Another kind of click is made by the sides of the tongue, the way you might call a squirrel, or giddyap a horse. A fourth kind of click can be made when the whole tongue pops as it leaves the roof of the mouth. You might imitate the tick-tock of an old grandfather clock this way.

Hum while kissing. This is called a nasalized click. Practice making each of the clicks while humming.

If you make a g simultaneously with the click, then you will further enhance your repertoire with what is called a voiced click. Practice making each click simultaneously with a g .

There are phonetic symbols for each of these clicks, but languages which have clicks have their own spelling to represent each of these sounds and you can begin using those spellings if you are learning Zulu, SiSwati, or Hottentot.

The Air Stream Source and Direction. Almost all speech sounds are made with lung air coming out. This is called **egressive lung air**. A few languages have consonants that are made with **ingressive** rather than egressive air. The air is either pulled in with the glottis or with the tongue. When air is pulled in by the back of the tongue, it is called **ingressive mouth air**. The consonants made in this manner are the clicks you have just practiced. You can feel the ingressive air by lengthening a kiss sound for two or three seconds as you feel your mouth fill up with air drawn in from the outside.

Tick-tock

Many North American Indian languages have consonants made with the air stream initiated at the glottis. This produces sounds with an explosive characteristic. Make a glottal stop and hold it — " ? ". While you are holding your glottis closed it is impossible to breathe. You normally "hold your breath" by closing your glottis. Now, while holding the glottis closed, make and release a p with your lips. You can feel a puff of air when the p is released. This produces an explosive "popping" sound. Since this consonant is made with the glottis closed, it is called a **glottalized consonant.** It can be written phonetically with a raised glottal stop after it — p? . Hold a long glottal stop and make three or four p's in quick succession while still holding the glottis closed: "p? p? p?."

Make a ? and hold it

The glottis closes the vocal chords, then moves up when you close your lips for the p? . Some air is then trapped between your lips and the vocal chords. As the glottis moves up, the trapped air is compressed in your mouth. When you release the p? with your lips, the puff of air is the compressed mouth-air escaping. You can pretend you have a small piece of grass on the tip of your tongue. This compressed air would then be what you would use to blow it off. The p? sounds about the same, except that your tongue is not peeping out.

You can also make t's and k's in the same way. Each has this unique explosive characteristic: "t? t? t? k? k? k?."

Make a series of glottalized p's: "p? p? p?," while lightly resting your fingers on your voice box. With practice you can feel what is happening. The glottis is moving upwards. Repeatedly say "heehaw" — you can feel the glottis go up on the "hee" and down on the "haw." When the glottis is closed, this up and down action is like a piston — it moves the air column up and down. When your mouth is closed, the upward action of the piston compresses air that can be used for the glottalized consonants p? t? and k? . The downward action of the piston creates a vaccuum in the closed mouth. If the lip closure is released, then air rushes in from the outside to fill the vaccuum. The result is called an **implosive consonant.** Implosive consonants are written with a hook over the consonant: ɓ, ɗ, ɠ.

Alternate rapidly between p? and ɓ while holding the same glottal stop: "p? ɓ p? ɓ p? ɓ." Touch your voice box with your fingers, and you will feel the piston action as your glottis moves up and down.

Practice the implosive "t" by alternating between t? and ɗ as above. Do the same with k? and ƙ . The implosive ƙ is the sound some people make when they are imitating the sound of water pouring from a bottle — "ƙ ƙ ƙ."

Many West African languages use implosive consonants — especially voiced ones: ɓ , ɗ and ɠ . Some people make the ɠ when imitating a frog — "ɠ ɠ ɠ."

If your new language uses implosive sounds, listen to Kino and mimic him. Set up pronunciation Differential drills like the following to contrast the implosive sounds with their regular counterpart.

b	ɓ	d	ɗ	g	ɠ
ba	ɓa	da	ɗa	ga	ɠa
bo	ɓo	do	ɗo	go	ɠo
bu	ɓu	du	ɗu	gu	ɠu

Drill as explained on page 81.

Rubber
baby buggy bumpers

The following chart shows consonants which are common to English. Make a similar chart for the consonants in your language. A blank chart is prepared for your use on page 306. Any entries that are different from English will indicate sounds that you will need to develop new habits for. You will also need new habits if your language uses these consonants in environments that are not common to English.

Consonants Common to English

	Bi-Labial	Labio-Dental	Tip Dental	Tip Alveolar	Blade Alveo-palatal	Back Velar	Glottal
Stops:							
Vl. Asp.	pʰ			tʰ		kʰ	
Vl. Unasp.	p			t		k	ʔ
Voiced	b			d		g	
Fricatives:							
Voiceless		f	θ	s	š		h
Voiced		v	đ	z	ž		
Nasals:							
Voiceless	M						
Voiced	m			n		ŋ	
Laterals:							
Voiceless				L			
Vd. High				lˆ			
Vd. Low				lˇ			
Flaps:							
Voiceless				ř ň			
Voiced				ḓ ľ			
Glide:							
Voiced				r	y	w	

Let's conclude this section on consonants with a table that displays symbols for each of the sounds you have been introduced to. If you find a consonant in your new language which you can't quite mimic to Kino's satisfaction, look at the following table and try saying some of the sounds which are near neighbors to the sound you think you are hearing. Try a near-by point of articulation. Try a different manner at the same point of articulation. Try lowering or raising your tongue slightly. By experimenting, you should be able to hit on the sound you are searching for.

Hit the sound
you are searching for

Summary of Consonant Symbols

	Bi-Labial	Labio-Dental	Tip Dental	Tip Alveolar	Retro-flexed	Blade Alveo-palatal	Back Velar	Glottal
Stops:								
Vl. Asp.	pʰ		t̪ʰ	tʰ	ṭʰ	t̃ʰ	ḵʰ kʰ ḳʰ	
Vl. Unasp.	p		t̪	t	ṭ	t̃	ḵ k ḳ	ʔ
Voiced	b		d̪	d	ḍ	d̃	g̱ g g̣	
Fricatives:								
Voiceless	ꝑ	f	θ ș	s	ṣ	š	ꝁ	h
Voiced	ƀ	v	đ ẓ	z	ẓ	ž	g̵	
Nasals:								
Voiceless	M		N̦	N	Ṇ	Ñ	Ŋ	
Voiced	m		n̦	n	ṇ	ñ	ŋ	
Laterals:								
Voiceless				L				
Vd. High			ļ	lˆ	ḷ	ĺ		
Vd. Low				lˇ				
Fric. Vl.				Ł				
Fric. Vd.				ł				
Flaps:								
Voiceless				t̆				
Voiced				d̆	ř			
Nasal Vd.				ň				
Lateral Vd.				ĺ				
Trills:								
Voiceless				R̃			R̰	
Voiced				r̃			r̰	
Double:								
Voiceless	ᵏp							
Voiced	ᵍb							
Nasal Vd.	ⁿm							
Clicks:								
Voiceless	p←			t←				
Glottalized:								
Voiceless	pʔ			tʔ			kʔ	
Implosives:								
Voiceless	ꝑ			t			ƙ	
Voiced	ɓ			ɗ			ɠ	
Glides								
Voiceless						Y	W	
Voiced	(w)				r	y	w	

279

I NEVER HEARD OF AN ENGLISH WORD WITH "W" FOR A VOWEL!

Vowels

English has five vowels — a, e, i, o, u and sometimes w and y — right? Wrong!

The different vowel sounds in the following words demonstrate that English itself has about eleven different vowels (some dialects have more).

1.	beat	eat
2.	bit	it
3.	bait	ate
4.	bed	Ed
5.	bat	at
6.	bus	us
7.	box	ox
8.	bought	ought
9.	boat	oat
10.	books	oops
11.	booze	ooze

Read out loud the above list of words that begin with the letter "b." Then, read the list of words which begin with vowels. Notice that the vowel is the same for the two words on each line. Finally, go through the words saying the vowels alone, without initial or final consonants.

In English, often we have different vowel sounds spelled alike. For example, the spelling *-ough* is used for at least five different vowel sounds:

through	(who)
though	(hoe)
bough	(how)
hiccough	(up)
rough	(huff)
cough	(off)

(The *-ough* word rhymes with the word in parenthesis beside it.)

NOTE: Not only does English represent many different sounds with one spelling, but it can also represent one sound with many different spellings. Notice that the vowel sound of the following rhyming words is

the same, though it is spelled differently: to, two, too, through, new, you, Sue, Sioux, Sault (Ste. Marie, Michigan), coup, suit, lute. (Fortunately, most other languages represent each vowel sound with one consistent spelling.)

In English there are more than the traditionally-believed five vowels, and in other languages there can be even different vowels. Vowels may have different characteristics as well. For example, they may be nasalized or breathy or whispered, or formed with rounded lips, etc. With all the possible variations, there are well over a hundred potential vowels.

Let's begin to explore vowels by putting the English sounds on a vowel chart.

	Front	Central	Back
High	eat [1] it [2]		ooze [11] oops [10]
Mid	ate [3] Ed [4]		oats [9]
Low	at [5]	us [6] ox [7]	ought [8]

Ed's ox ought eat oats.
Oops,
It ate at us — ooze!

Read around the chart out loud, repeating each of the vowels and omitting the consonants.

The same vowels are on the chart below, using phonetic symbols.

	Front Unrounded	Central Unrounded	Back Rounded
High Lower High	i [1] ɪ [2]		u [11] ʊ [10]
Mid Lower Mid	e [3] ɛ [4]		o [9]
Low Lower Low	æ [5]	ʌ [6] ɑ [7]	ɔ [8]

ɛdz ɑx ɔtʰ itʰ owts.
ʊps,
ɪtʰ eytʰ ætʰ ʌs — uz!

Read around this phonetic vowel chart, producing the same vowels as before.

Each of these written symbols has its own distinct sound and name. As we discuss each of these vowels, refer to the charts. Learn to associate each symbol with its own distinct sound.

NOTE: Different dialects of English use different vowels. (English consonants are relatively stable across dialects.) The following explanations of vowels are based on Standard American English which is

common (with a few regional exceptions) from the West Coast to mid New York state, and is also widely used on radio and television.

The LAMP demonstration cassette tape gives examples of all the sounds of Chapter Four. You may find it especially helpful for the vowels.

The numbers on the chart will provide an easy way for us to refer to the specific sounds in the following paragraphs.

1) The first vowel, i , sounds like the "i" in "machine" or the "ee" in "see." It is simply called "I." ✑

2) Number two is written without a dot, and with a hook at the bottom — ι . It is called "iota." The iota is pronounced like the vowel in "it, in, and is." ✑

3) The third vowel is written and called e , and is pronounced like the "e" in "they." English usually uses "a" to spell this sound, like in "bait, rake, ate." Unfortunately, these and other English words with this sound do not have a "pure" e vowel sound. In English, this vowel is characteristically followed by a glide created by a slight closing of the mouth (or raising of the tongue) during the vowel. This glide is called a "y" glide. The above words, then, written phonetically are: beyt^h, reyk^h, and eyt^h. Say the vowel in these words slowly so that you hear both the vowel and the glide. Many English speakers when attempting to take the "y" glide off this vowel end up saying vowel #4 — which in English does not have the "y" glide. You can practice making a pure vowel by stopping the vowel in the middle with a glottal stop. Try it with the word "ate": eʔeʔeʔeʔeʔeʔeyt^h. ✑

Stop the vowels with a glottal stop

4) Number four is written as a backwards "3" — ɛ . It is called "epsilon" and is pronounced as the vowel in words like "Ed, said, and deck." These words spelled phonetically would be: ɛd, sɛd, and dɛk^h. Some dialects of English, especially in the southern United States, let the tongue glide back in the mouth, which results in the ɛ being followed by an "uh" sound. Be sure to say "sɛd", not "sɛ-uh-d." ✑

5) This vowel is called "digraph," which in Greek means "two writings." By practicing a little, you can learn to write it with a single stroke by following this pattern: ɔ ɔ̄ ɚ æ . Practice writing it. This is the vowel sound in words like "at, cat, and bat." Written phonetically: æt^h, k^{h}æt^h, bæt^h. ✑

Is there a plɛzn̩t pɛzn̩t prɛzn̩t?

6) The sixth vowel is called "caret" and looks like an upside down v — ʌ . It sounds like "uh" and it occurs in words like "us, but, and bus." Written phonetically: ʌs, bʌt^h, bʌs. ✑

aaah

7) This one is called "a" and is pronounced like the vowel you have been using with all of the consonants. It is like the sound the doctor has you say when you stick out your tongue — "aaah." For this sound, the mouth is wide open. It occurs in words like "pa, ma, hop, pot and spot." Written phonetically these words would be: pʰa, ma, hapʰ, pʰatʰ, spatʰ.   ᥴ

8) Number eight is called "open o" and is written as a backwards "c" — ɔ. It is pronounced like the vowel in the words "bought, ought, and taught." Some dialects of English say these words without rounding their lips or holding the back of their tongue very far back. To pronounce the ɔ correctly, be sure your lips are rounded and your tongue is well back. The above words spelled phonetically are: bɔtʰ, ɔtʰ, tʰɔtʰ.   ᥴ

Pure o's

9) The ninth vowel is called "o". This is another vowel which rarely occurs as a pure vowel in English. While saying this vowel we tend to begin to close our mouth and round our lips more tightly, causing a glide. This glide with lips rounded is called a "w" glide. Watch your lips in a mirror and you can see this extra lip rounding. Learn to hear and say a pure o rather than the English ow. Words like "boat, oats, no" would be spelled phonetically: bowtʰ, owts, now.   ᥴ

10) This vowel is named after the Greek "upsilon." It is written as a "u" without a tail — ʊ. It is the sound in words like "book, look, soot, oops, and put." Be sure to round your lips tightly for this vowel. These words spelled phonetically: bʊkʰ, lʊkʰ, sʊtʰ, ʊps, and pʰʊtʰ.   ᥴ

11) Number eleven is called "u" and written u. It is the vowel sound in words like "boot, ooze, loose." These words spelled phonetically: butʰ, uz, lus. Notice that u is never pronounced "you." "You" would be phonetically spelled: yu.   ᥴ

The following chart does not have the numbers on it. Orally read around the chart until you have the distinct sound attached to each symbol. Then read the symbols in random order to make sure each is firmly lodged in your mind.

	Front Unrounded	Central Unrounded	Back Rounded
High	i		u
Lower High	ɪ		ʊ
Mid	e		o
Lower Mid	ɛ		
Low	æ	ʌ	ɔ
Lower Low		ɑ	

Examine the top
and the sides

By examining the top and side notation of the vowel chart we can learn about the categories which are helpful in distinguishing the vowel sounds. The three main columns indicate that for some sounds the tongue is forward, for some it is central, and for others it is back. Say these pairs and feel your tongue as it moves back and forth: i u i u i u i u; e o e o e o e o; æ ɔ æ ɔ æ ɔ.

Not only does the tongue move forward and back on a horizontal plane, it also moves up and down, as indicated by the positions at the side of the chart, from "high" to "lower low." Say the following pairs to feel the tongue (and jaw) moving up and down: i æ i æ i æ; u ɔ u ɔ u ɔ.

A glance at the above chart reveals some "holes" — places where other vowels are possible. In the lower low front unrounded hole goes the so-called "Boston a." It is written a and called "printed a." Imitate a Kennedy Boston accent and say "Park your car in Harvard yard." (Phonetically: pʰakʰ yʌ kʰa ɪn havʌd yad.) Many southern United States dialects use this a sound. We have heard Southern belles use this sound when they say "bye-bye" — phonetically: baba.

Practice going up
the central column

The lower mid central unrounded vowel is called "shwa" and written phonetically with an upside down "e" — ə. This is the sound we make in English when we are pausing or stalling for time, "uh". (It should not have any "ɑh" quality. The caret, on the other hand, is low enough to have some of the quality of the lower low "ɑh".) Practice going up the central column: ɑ ʌ ə, ɑ ʌ ə, ɑ ʌ ə. If you say "uh" with your teeth closed you will be producing another vowel above the shwa. This lower high central unrounded vowel is often symbolized ɨ, and is called "barred i." With practice you can learn to distinguish four vowels in the central column: ɑ ʌ ə ɨ.

Here is a chart that includes these vowels:

English Vowels

	Front Unrounded	Central Unrounded	Back Rounded
High Lower High	i ɪ	 ɨ	u ʊ
Mid Lower Mid	e ɛ	 ə	o
Low Lower Low	æ a	ʌ ɑ	ɔ

It happens that all front and central English vowels are made without rounding the lips, and all back vowels are made with lips rounded. Of course, just the opposite is possible. Try it. Hold your lips tightly rounded as you read down the front column: i ɪ e ɛ æ; i ɪ e ɛ æ. Now, smile broadly as you read down the back column: u ʊ o ɔ; u ʊ o ɔ. For practice purposes, it will be easy to indicate this change from the English pattern by an umlaut — two dots over the symbol — ï.

"Try these persimmons for those front rounded vowels"

NOTE: It is, of course, ethnocentric to use English as the basis and to indicate changes from English by the umlaut. But, for learning purposes it is better this way. If your new language has rounded front or central vowels, or unrounded back vowels, it will symbolize these sounds in a different way. For that matter, each language decides for itself how it will symbolize each of the sounds it uses.

The front rounded column could be symbolized: ï ï ë ë æ̈; and the back unrounded could be symbolized: ü ü ö ö.

By the one modification of lip-rounding the number of vowels you can produce is doubled! Charted, they look like this:

	Front		Central		Back	
	Unrounded	Rounded	Unrounded	Rounded	Unrounded	Rounded
High	i	ï			ü	u
Lower High	ɪ	ï	ɨ	ɨ	ü	ʊ
Mid	e	ë			ö	o
Lower Mid	ɛ	ë	ə	ə̈		
Low	æ	æ̈	ʌ	ʌ̈	ö	ɔ
Lower Low	a	ä	ɑ	ɑ̈		

Practice the pairs of the chart back and forth: i ï i ï; ɪ ï ɪ ï; e ë e ë; etc. Nothing should move except for the rounding and unrounding of your lips. The quality of the vowel should remain the same except for the rounding effect. Think about your tongue and be sure it doesn't move while you round your lips.

High rounded sounds, whether in the back u or in the front ï should have the lips tightly rounded. Practice repeating: u ï u ï u ï, while holding your finger against your lips. You should not be able to feel any lip movement, but your tongue will move from back to front, back and forth as you alternate between the two vowels.

Alternate between the front and back mid rounded vowels, while again holding your index finger against the edge of your lips to be sure they stay rounded. Don't let your lips move. Only the tongue moves — back and forth. Round tightly: o ë o ë o ë o ë.

"The rounded vowels in my language are far out!"

Give each vowel
its own beat

Likewise drill the unrounded vowels. Smile broadly and say i . Now alternate between the two high unrounded sounds i and ü : i ü i ü i ü i ü i ü. Place your finger on your lips as you say these to be sure you keep smiling without rounding. Watch yourself in the mirror — it might also help. Again, only the tongue moves.

Vowel Clusters

In a vowel cluster each vowel carries its own beat and is therefore a separate syllable. Practice the following vowel clusters, giving each vowel its own beat — be careful not to put glottal stops between the vowels: o.e, i.ʌ, ɛ.o, æ.i, ə.ʊ, ʊ.ɹ, e.a, etc. (The dot between the vowels indicates syllable division.)

Rearticulated and Lengthened Vowels

Sometimes a vowel is said twice in succession. When there is a cluster of two identical vowels with syllable beats we call this **rearticulation**. It is a vowel cluster of two identical vowels. Practice the following rearticulated vowels: di.i, pɪ.ɪ, be.e, sɛ.ɛ, gæ.æ, tʰa.a, fɑ.ɑ, lʌ.ʌ, mə.ə, kʰɨ.ɨ, šɔ.ɔ, žo.o, hʊ.ʊ, ku.u.

Many languages lengthen some vowels. A lengthened vowel has only one beat; even though it is held longer it is only one syllable. Lengthening is symbolized with a raised dot after the vowel. Read around the chart using lengthened vowels: i· ɪ· e· ɛ· æ· a· ɑ· ʌ· ə· ɨ· ɔ· o· ʊ· u·. Now go around the chart, contrasting lengthened vowels with rearticulated vowels: i.i i·, ɪ.ɪ ɪ·, e.e e·, ɛɛ ɛ·, etc. Do it once more, but this time with a three-way contrast of short, long, and rearticulated vowels: i i·i.i, ɪ ɪ·ɪ.ɪ, e e·e.e, ɛ ɛ·ɛ.ɛ, etc. (An extra-long vowel can be symbolized with a colon after the vowel — i:, e:, u:.)

Pure Vs. Glided Vowels

We have already mentioned that English e and o are usually glided. When a vowel is glided toward the high front position, it is called a "y" glide. English e usually has this y off-glide. Feel it as you slowly say these words: "aim" (phonetically: eym), "bake" (beykʰ), "name" (neym). Now say them leaving off the glide: em (not ɛm), bek, nem. They don't quite sound like English without the glide, do they? But if your new language has e it won't sound right if you always pronounce it ey .

It's not the same
without the glide!

Any vowel can have a y off-glide. The word "I" or "eye" is an English example of an off-glide after ɑ — ɑy . (In Southern dialects this would probably be ay .) Drill around the vowel chart adding a "y" off-glide to each sound. Be careful to avoid making two syllables. ◄§

A noyzi noyz
annoyz an oyster

The English "o" is almost always glided toward a high back rounded position — toward u . This is called a "w" off-glide. Spanish and many other languages that have o do not characteristically have ow . Our English word "no" has the w off-glide (now), while the Spanish equivalent is an unglided "no." At first you can practice making the pure o by stopping it with a glottal stop: oʔoʔ.

Read around the chart putting the w glide after each of the vowels: iw, ɪw, ew, ɛw, æw, aw, ɑw, ʌw, əw, ɨw, ɔw, ow, ʊw. Don't make two syllables, for then you would be saying: i.u, ɪ.u, e.u, ɛ.u. ◄§

In addition to gliding toward the high front and high back positions, vowels can also glide toward a mid-central position — towards "uh" (this glide is sometimes indicated with a raised shwa — ə). Many people say ɛ with a slight "uh" after it. Read around the chart putting this glide after each of the vowels: iᵊ, ɪᵊ, eᵊ, ɛᵊ, æᵊ, ɑᵊ, ɔᵊ, oᵊ, ʊᵊ, uᵊ. ◄§

A regal rural ruler

One more glide is the "r" glide. You might be interested to know that linguists have a continuing discussion as they try to decide if the r sound is a consonant or a retroflexed vowel. It doesn't have a point of articulation like other consonants. For our purposes it doesn't really matter. Here are some words with an r glide at the end: ear, air, ere, err, are, or poor. (You may feel your tongue tip retroflex as you say these.) ◄§

Glides can also preceed a vowel. In this case they are called on-glides. Feel the on-glides and the off-glides in the following pairs.

On-glides		Off-glides	
few	[fyu]	fooey	[fuy]
yoke	[yokʰ]	coy	[kʰoy]
yea	[yey]	yea	[yey]
yon	[yɑn]	nigh	[nɑy]
wad	[wɑd]	Dow	[dɑw]
wap	[wap]	pow	[pʰaw]
wow	[wɑw]	wow	[wɑw]

Which is the witch
that wished
the wicked wish

re	[ri]	ear	[ir]
ray	[rey]	air	[er]
rot	[rɑtʰ]	tar	[tʰɑr]
row	[row]	wore	[wor]

Now, read around the vowel chart being careful to say each vowel as a pure vowel, not gliding at all.

Vowel Modifications

Opening
the nasal passage

Whisper as you read a couple sentences. Whispering demonstrates that vowels can be voiceless. **Voiceless vowels** are written phonetically with capital letters. Whisper as you read around the chart to practice producing voiceless vowels. In many languages the final vowels after voiceless consonants can be voiceless: dikI, dɪkɪ, dekE, dɛkƐ. Try it between voiceless consonants: ditIti, dɪtɪtɪ, detEte, Etc.

Another vowel modification is nasalization. Some vowels of French and Portuguese are nasalized while others are not. If your new language has some **nasalized vowels**, you will need to produce a clear distinction between "oral" vowels (not nasalized vowels), and "nasal" vowels. Nasalized vowels are made by opening the nasal passage and allowing air to escape through the nose as well as through the mouth. Phonetically, nasalized vowels can be written with a little hook underneath: i̧ ɪ̧ ȩ ɛ̧ æ̧ a̧ ɑ̧ ʌ̧ ə̧ i̧ ɔ̧ o̧ ʊ̧ u̧ etc. Practice nasalizing all the vowels.

Do you know what a
polite ghost says?

You can also modify vowels by making them "breathy." Marilyn Monroe talked with **breathy vowels.** In English, given certain circumstances, they tend to add an air of pseudo sensuality. A few people also add a breathy quality when praying in public. Phonetically, breathy vowels are written with a plus mark under the vowel (indicating a surplus of air) — e̟ . When we make breathy vowels, only a part of the vocal chords is vibrating, the rest is open to let air pass. Practice breathy vowels i̟ ɪ̟ e̟ ɛ̟ a̟ ɑ̟ ʌ̟ ə̟ i̟ ɔ̟ o̟ ʊ̟ u̟ etc.

Vowels can even be made with the tongue tip pointing up and back. These are called **retroflexed vowels** and are written with a dot underneath — ẹ . As you say these, it might sound like you have some peanut butter stuck on the roof of your mouth: i̩ ɪ̩ e̩ ɛ̩ æ̩ a̩ ɑ̩ ʌ̩ ə̩ i̩ ɔ̩ o̩ ʊ̩ u̩.

Did you ever notice how your voice seems to have an extra catch or vibration just after you wake up in the morning? Listen for it as you stretch and say "I'm so-o-o-o-o slee-e-e-epy." The distinct quality of these vowels is caused by a trill of the glottis. The vowels are called **laryngealized vowels**, but you might think of them as "glottalized." These vowels are written with a glottal mark over the vowel symbol — ĕ̓. People sometimes use laryngealized vowels to imitate sheep bleating. Try these: ĭ̓ ɪ̓ ĕ̓ ɛ̓ æ̓ ă̓ ɑ̓ ɔ̓ ŏ̓ ʊ̓ ŭ̓ ʌ̓ ə̓ ɨ̓.

As we conclude this section on vowels, it should be pointed out that the classifications on the chart are not fixed points. Rather, each merges into its neighbor. Any of these sounds can be made a little higher or lower, or a little more forward or back than the basic English positions we have been working from. You will probably need to modify some of these positions for the vowels in your new language.

On page 307 is a vowel chart framework for you to fill in with the vowels of your new language. Fill in the chart in pencil because your guesses are still tentative at this point. You should revise your hypotheses about the sounds as you become more familiar with the language. The Application section will help you further resolve your hypotheses.

Flexibility in both mouth and attitude will ensure your ability to mimic and produce each of the new sounds you meet. You may encounter sounds that have not been discussed in this chapter — like the Arabic vowel with the root of the tongue pulled back, or the Kikamba highly rounded w , or the Korean "tight-lips" (fortis) p , or the Shona rounded s . Watch your helper's mouth carefully to determine what is happening as the sound is made. Ask him to say other words which have this same sound — you may find it easier to hear the sound when it is in a stressed syllable. Try to determine what moves, where it moves to, what is the manner, and the voicing. Make up a symbol for it, perhaps by modifying the symbol for a similar sound. Mimic your helper, then gather words with this sound for use in Substitution or Differential drills. Time invested in pronunciation practice will pay rich, long-term rewards, as you gain confidence in the accuracy and clarity of your pronunciation.

Gather words

Tone

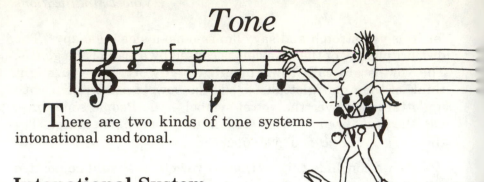

There are two kinds of tone systems—intonational and tonal.

Intonational System

All languages have an intonational system which is an integral part of every utterance. Intonation can superimpose an additional meaning on the overall phrase beyond the meaning expressed by the words themselves. Notice for example the difference between "You're my friend." and "You're my friend?" Or, "What is that in the road ahead?" and "What is that in the road, a head?"

We cannot talk without intonation.

The English intonation system carries a large number of important distinctions. Emotion, for example, is often expressed through intonation.

Notice how intonation alone can change the meaning of the word "what" in the following interchanges:

> "I just ate it."
> "What?" (Slightly rising intonation — i.e., Repeat your statement.)
> "I just ate it."
> "What?" (Slightly falling intonation — i.e., What did you eat?)
> "The caterpillar."
> "What?!" (Extra high intonation — i.e., Surprise or disbelief.)

From the beginning of language study it is important to mimic the intonation patterns to the best of your ability, and thus build new habits. Intonation lines can be drawn above your transcription to help you remember the general pattern. They can be drawn with block form,

> The blonde's name is Patty Richardson.

or like this,

> The blonde's name is Patty Richardson.

Unfortunately, a common mistake of English-speaking people when they learn another language is to neglect the intonation, and unconsciously superimpose their old English intonational habits. This can cause not only poor accent, but also confusion of meaning. Continued subconscious use of English intonation in your new language will reinforce bad habits which can become nearly impossible to break.

Pay close attention to intonation patterns:

> How do questions differ from statements?
> How is surprise or emphasis shown by intonation?
> How is the tone of voice used to convey emotions — joy, anger, sadness, irritation, sarcasm, amusement?
> What intonation indicates the end of a sentence?
> What intonation indicates a mid-sentence pause?

We have a friend who has learned English very well, but his intonation occasionally causes problems. He has a habit of saying the word "no" with an intonation that in English denotes disgust, although he has no intention of being offensive — he is just carrying the intonation of his language over into English.

Your English intonation habits are deeply ingrained, so you will need to pay special attention to the intonation patterns of your new language, especially during the first few weeks of language learning.

Listen to a tape of an English speaker and notice the intonation patterns just before each pause. What happens in mid-sentence pauses — does the pitch tend to rise, drop, or to remain level? How about the loudness — does the voice get louder, softer, or remain the same before a pause? What about length — do the syllables just before the pause tend to be longer, shorter, or equal in length to the other syllables in the phrase? How is this different from pauses at the end of other kinds of sentences like questions or exclamations? What kinds of pitch, timing, and volume are used when counting or listing? Is the last item in the list said with different intonation from the rest?

Now listen to some of your recordings of Kino and ask these same questions about your new language. Notice the differences in pitch, timing and intensity between your new language and English. Practice mimicking intonation while paying special attention to the pitch, timing and volume just before each pause.

Here is a practice technique that is especially helpful in learning intonation and rhythm patterns, though it is also helpful in practicing consonants and vowels. It is a technique called **tracking**. Play a tape of some new material in the language and mimic it while the tape is running. Try to stay not more than a couple of syllables behind the tape. When you first try this it may seem pretty tricky, but with practice you will rapidly become proficient. Try tracking tapes, radio, and television. (When you track TV, mimic the gestures and facial expressions as well.) Don't try to track people aloud — most people find it quite irritating. You can, however, *mentally track* conversations. Whenever you are in a situation where language is going on that you don't understand, or that doesn't concern you, mentally track it for a while. Tracking takes quite a bit of energy, so it is better to track for various short periods a day rather than for one extended period. When you track, pay careful attention to the rhythm and intonation of what you are mimicking.

Tonal System

Probably about half of the world's languages are tonal languages. In these languages, the tone level of each syllable is just as important as the consonants and vowels. Tone languages are particularly common in Africa and Asia. Except for Swahili and one or two other languages, almost all of the approximately 1500 languages of Sub-Saharan Africa are tonal. Many Oriental languages are well-known for their tonal characteristics — Vietnamese and various of the Chinese languages are examples. Some Indian languages of the Americas are also tone languages.

In a tone language, a word can have a variety of meanings depending on its tone level. The tone for a syllable may be level or glided. Some languages have only two levels: Low and High; others have three levels: Low, Mid and High; a few languages have four levels. Glides can rise or fall. A few tone languages have combined glides of fall+rise or rise+fall.

In Vietnamese, not only the direction of the glide is important, but also the length of the glide and its starting point. The "length" of a glide does not refer to the length of time it takes to say it, but rather to the relative distance between the beginning and end points of the rise or fall. For example, a fall from a high tone to a low tone is a "longer" fall than one from a

Long fall

Short fall

mid tone to a low tone, even if both take the same amount of time to say. In other words, you might think of a tone glide length as a measurement in a vertical plane, while vowel length is a measurement on the horizontal — time — plane.

There are five words spelled "ma" in Vietnamese. The difference in meaning between these words is indicated solely by tone:

mā — said on a level tone means "ghost"

má — said with a short rise that begins on a high tone means "cheek"

mạ — said with a long rise that starts on a low tone means "tomb"

mạ — said with a short rise starting on a low tone means "rice"

mạ — said with a short fall starting on a low tone means "but".

mạmá

Don't give up on tones just because they are different or difficult. Even people who think they are musically "tone deaf" can and do pick up tone languages by investing some effort. If you find words in your language which are distinguished only by tones you will need to pay careful attention to the tone patterns. Don't just ignore the tones feeling they are relatively unimportant. They won't go away. In a tone language the tones are just as important as the consonants and vowels. Iv you iknore the donez you gan brotuze as much gonvuzion as iv you iknoret the foizet-foizelezz tizdingtion on gonzonandz. (To unravel the "nonsense", substitute the voiced or voiceless counterparts for the stops and fricatives.)

If you have trouble identifying tones, focus first on careful *mimicry*. You don't have to have the tones analyzed in order to mimic — don't get the cart before the horse. You will find that you can more easily identify the tones of words and phrases which you have first mimicked carefully, and even memorized. (You will soon learn the very useful technique of sorting words into piles which have the same tone patterns — you can learn to classify tones even if you have some difficulty identifying them.)

It is often possible to train your helper to move his hands in a way that corresponds to the tones as he speaks. His feeling about how the tone goes should be accepted as a hypothesis, however, not a fact. Although speakers of a tone language automatically use tones correctly and are immediately aware when they hear a word pronounced with the wrong tone, they may not be able to describe the tones or explain how the tone is

Train your helper to move his hands

wrong, since their knowledge about the use of tone is at a subconscious level. Likewise, the knowledge that an English speaker has about his use of voiced and voiceless consonants is also subconscious — he knows when a word is pronounced wrong, but to describe the correct articulation would be beyond him.

Be sure to include tone markings as you transcribe your material. Unfortunately, many tone languages do not write the tones. For the native speaker the context usually carries the sense of the meaning when reading, but the learner needs the written tones just as much as the learner of Hebrew needs to write the vowels (though Hebrew vowels are not normally written).

There are various ways to indicate the tones in writing. A common way is to:

> indicate each hígh tone with a mark pointing up (´)
>   over the vowel;
> indicate each lòw tone with a mark pointing down
>   (`) over the vowel;
> and leave mid tones unmarked.

If there are only two levels, then only the least common one needs to be marked. A glide can be marked by a slash through the syllable from left to right in the direction of the glide: rise, fall.

Another system of indicating tones is to use numbers: High[1], Mid[2], Low[3], Lower Low[4]. (You could just as easily consider the lowest tone to be [1] and the highest one [4] — just be consistent.) A glide can be indicated by showing its starting and ending points: Long Fall[14], Long Rise[41], Short Low Fall[34], Short High Fall[12], etc. (See also page 299.)

Maybe the easiest way to indicate tones (providing you double space your material is to put short lines over and under the syllables: High, Mid, Low, Extra Low. (You could leave the mid tones unmarked.)

Here is a sentence written all three ways (it means "The boy quickly rides the horse, and the dog runs alongside."):

> nì.sí ndí dza tsè, bá na.sí tsé mà.fa.
> ni³.si¹ ndi¹ dza² tse²³, ba³¹ na².si¹ tse¹ ma³.fa¹⁴.
> ni.si ndi dza tsè, bá na.si tse ma.fa.

(The dots within words indicate syllable divisions.)

Some language learners find it best to first use a wavy line to indicate the general pitch pattern (see the example on page 290) and then gradually tighten up the markings as they tune their ears to the language.

As you study the tones of your language, one way to begin is to collect a number of two-syllable words and write each one on a separate slip of paper or card. Arrange all of these cards in piles according to your tentative hypotheses of the tone and stress patterns. Then check them with your helper. Continue regrouping them until all members of each pile have the same tone pattern.

Check with your helper

We were recently working in a Kenyan language. A step-by-step description of our initial procedures might provide an example which you can follow.

At the end of our first week of language learning we looked through our practice and text materials and collected out all the two-syllable words. We wrote each word on a slip of paper — like this:

nyũnyi [ñṹñì] "bird"	nyũnyi [ñúñí] "greens"	ndengu [ndéŋgù] "small green beans"
mbevo [mbévò] "cold"	mboso [mbòsò] "beans"	nthee [ndèè] "wild pest"
mũtĩ [mùtɨ] "tree"	ngũkũ [ŋgúkũ] "chicken"	nguku [ŋgúkù] "termite"

nyũnyi
[ñú.ñì]

We wrote the words with regular KiKamba spelling so our helper could read them easily, and then we put the phonetic spelling in brackets for our own use. Since tones are not indicated in the regular spelling of the language, our helper couldn't distinguish some words in isolation (like nyũnyi and nyũnyi above), so we wrote the English meaning on the card to help distinguish the identically spelled words. (If he had not been bilingual we could have accomplished this with drawings, or by writing synonyms in his language on the card, or by writing a short sentence in which the word is used in context.)

Our first hypothesis was that there were two levels, high and low. Under this hypothesis, two-syllable words would have to fall into one of four categories, based on the tones of the syllables. So we separated our cards into four piles:

High-High	*High-Low*	*Low-High*	*Low-Low*
ŋgú.kú	ñú.ñì	mù.tí	mbò.sò
ŋgí.yá	ì.tù	nzè.lé	ndè.è
nzá.má	ŋgú.kù	kì.wá	mù.tù
nzé.é	mbú.à	kì.wú	
ŋgí.ŋgó	ñá.mà	lù.má	
mbá.ké	ŋgá.ì	ù.tá	
	ví.ñà	ñè.kí	
	yú.à	kù.tú	
	mbé.mbà	kì.kó	
	mú.ndù	ŋgà.í	
	ndú.ŋgù	ì.vú	

Then we asked our helper to read all the words of the High-High stack. Some words didn't seem to have the same two tones as the others, so they were removed to a residual pile. Our helper then read the words of each of the other three stacks of cards. Again in each stack some words were clearly classified correctly, while some didn't quite have the same tones as the rest. Our residual pile grew.

Our residual pile grew

Now our data looked like this:

High-High	*High-Low*	*Low-High*	*Low-Low*
ŋgú.kú	yú.à	kù.tú	mbò.sò
ŋgí.ŋgó	mbú.à	kì.wú	ndè.è
ŋgí.yá	ŋgá.ì	ù.tà	
nzé.é		ì.vú	

Residue:			
nza.ma	ñʋ.ñi	ñe.ki	mʋ.tu
mba.ke	ndʋ.ŋgu	kɪ.ko	
	vi.ña	lʋ.ma	
	ŋgu.ku	mʋ.tɪ	
	mʋ.ndʋ	nze.le	
	mbe.mba	kɪ.wa	
	ña.ma	ŋga.i	
	ɪ.tu		

We weren't sure about the tones of residue words at this point, but we hypothesized that a Mid tone might enable us to classify them. The additional possible categories for two-syllable words were: Mid-Mid, Mid-High, Mid-Low, High-Mid, Low-Mid.

We asked our helper to read each residual word again while we made a guess (hypothesis) about its tones and put it in one of the five piles. When they were all classified we asked him to read each set to help us confirm whether all of the words in each pile shared the same tone pattern. Whenever there was doubt, we had our helper contrast a word with similar words from neighboring patterns. We now had nine piles of two-syllable words — the four piles previously listed plus the following five piles:

We had nine piles

Mid-Mid	*High-Mid*	*Mid-Low*	*Low-Mid*	*Mid-High*
nza.ma	ñú.ñi	ñʋ.ñì	ñè.ki	lʋ.má
mba.ke	ndʋ́.ŋgu	ŋgu.kù	kì.ko	nze.lé
	ví.ña	mʋ.ndʋ̀	mʋ̀.tɪ	
	mbé.mba	ña.mà	kì.wa	
		ɪ.tù	ŋgà.i	
		mʋ.tù		

By now, our helper was becoming pretty sophisticated himself. We asked him to read all the words in a pile and try to think of any other words that might fit the same pattern. We also asked him to experiment with various words by saying them with different tones. In this way we discovered more words which were spelled alike but had different tones and different meanings. We made cards for each of these new words, as they would be especially helpful for use in Differential drills.

At this point we felt that our hypotheses enabled us to classify most two-syllable words according to tone patterns (although we still had questions about how tone was affected by stress, sentence intonation, and vowel length). To recheck the accuracy of our hypotheses, we shuffled the piles and then asked two other people (one at a time) to read the words and help us reclassify the cards. Both times we ended up with the same categories as before. As we continued to encounter new two-syllable words in texts and communication time we found that they seemed to fit into one of these nine tone patterns.

Shuffling the piles

The classification of tones was not an end in itself. That was only analysis. Now we needed to *do* it. We needed practice to help us learn to hear and say the tones correctly.

Our first step was to practice Pronunciation Substitution drills. We drilled the words of each set following the basic model for pronunciation substitution practice. We spread the cards from one pile, forming a "column" on the table in front of our helper so that he could read the words. We had already done quite a bit of listening, so we went to the mimicry stage, mimicking each word three times. Next, we produced each word as we read down the column, and had our helper correct

High-High

as needed. Then we produced the words at random as he pointed to any card in the set. We followed this procedure for each set.

We were now ready to do Differential drills between each closely related pair of tone patterns. The various differential drills contrasted words with the following patterns:

High-High vs. Mid-Mid	Low-Low vs. Mid-Mid	Mid-Mid vs. Mid-High
High-High vs. High-Mid	Low-Low vs. Mid-Low	Mid-Mid vs. High-Mid
High-High vs. Mid-High	Low-Low vs. Low-Mid	Mid-Mid vs. Low-Mid
High-Low vs. High-Mid	Low-High vs. Low-Mid	Mid-Low vs. High-Mid
High-Low vs. Mid-Low	Low-High vs. Mid-High	Mid-High vs. Low-Mid

(If you think that tones are not your forte, you may wish to start out by doing Differential drills which contrast opposite patterns, or patterns that are not quite as closely related to each other: High-Low vs. Low-High; High-Mid vs. Mid-High; High-High vs. Low-Low; etc.)

Mid-Mid

We felt that if we could master the distinctions between these combinations, we would become much more at ease with the tones of the language. We set up Differential drills by spreading the cards of the two contrasting patterns into two adjacent "columns" on the table. Then we could follow the basic procedures for Pronunciation Differential drills (pages 81-82). The Differential drill contrasting High-Mid versus Mid-Low tones used this data:

High-Mid	*Mid-Low*
ñú.ñi	ñʋ.ñì
ndú.ŋgu	ŋgu.kù
mbé.vo	mʋ.ndʋ̀
ví.ña	ña.mà
ndé.ŋgu	kɪ.kò
mbé.mba	mʋ.tù

In your language you will find that you can drill a couple of tone Differential drills a day, and each day briefly review the ones you have previously drilled. Concentrate on the meaning of the words as you drill. Your goal should be to accurately produce the tones of any words you encounter, and to classify the words according to their tone patterns.

NOTE: This technique of sorting words into piles that have one feature the same can be used for other features besides tones. You can sort words that have a set of similar consonants you have trouble distinguishing, or words that have very similar yet different vowels, rhythm,

Low-Low

or stress patterns. You will probably find that it is easier for you to hear the differences than to identify them phonetically — but once you have worked with the sounds, sorted and drilled them, the identification and analysis will come easier. In other words, it is often easier to first learn to hear if two sounds are the same or different, and then later determine what the difference is.

If, in your language, the residual words have glides, then the next step would be to sort them into categories. Do some glides fall and others rise? If so, you need at least two glide categories. If your language had High and Low level tones and simple rise and fall glides, each syllable could have one of four patterns: High, Low, Fall, or Rise. Two-syllable words could have one of the following sixteen patterns:

High-High	High-Low	Low-High	Low-Low
Fall-Fall	Fall-Rise	Rise-Fall	Rise-Rise
High-Fall	High-Rise	Low-Fall	Low-Rise
Fall-High	Rise-High	Fall-Low	Rise-Low

For some languages the length of the glides may also vary. If so, the glides may need to be further sub-divided. The falling glides might include: High to Low, High to Mid, and Mid to Low. While the rising glides could be: Low to High, Low to Mid, and Mid to High.

You might also find that on some single syllables there are two combined glides, resulting in this, or this.

They mutiply rapidly

Clearly the number of options for tone pattern combinations can multiply rapidly. Level tones can occur on as many as four levels: Low, Mid, High and Extra High — Let's call them levels 4, 3, 2 and 1. Single glides could then possibly have the following length distinctions:

1 Extra High
2 High
3 Mid **(Rises:)** 43, 42, 41, 32, 31, 21. **(Falls:)** 12, 13, 14, 23, 24, 34.
4 Low

Four levels and 12 glides for a total of sixteen possibilities for a one-syllable word! Theoretically, two-syllable words could then have 16×16 or 256 tone patterns. We have heard that a Liberian language uses 9 of the 16 possibilities, which means that up to 81 two-syllable combinations would be mathematically possible. That's a lot! But, there is no reason to believe that a language must have all of the patterns that are mathematically possible. In the example on page 294, the only falling tones occurred at the ends of phrases. If this pattern were consistent in the language, it might prove to be the result of phrase intonation. Even tone languages have intonation patterns on phrases and sentences. In some Bantu languages, for example, the high tones at the end of a sentence are lower than the high tones at the beginning, and the other tones are lowered accordingly.

A minimal pair

How many of the possible combinations of tones in your language are really significant? Well, some will make a difference in the meaning of words and cause confusion if you mix them up, and others will only cause accent if you produce one pattern instead of another. Some are "phonemically" different, while others are only "allophonic" variations of one phoneme. When you find two words that are spelled identically but have different meanings when said with different tones, that is called a "minimal pair" and demonstrates that the two tone patterns are both necessary. — Well, we're getting ahead of ourselves. The next section will show you how to identify phonemes and their corresponding allophones. The principles will apply to consonants, vowels, and to tones (if your language is tonal).

If the syllables of your language have many tone possibilities, you may find it easier to begin drill with single syllable words, rather than two-syllable words. But there is a problem — it is harder to identify the pattern when only one tone is spoken in isolation. To overcome this problem you need to classify and drill the one-syllable words in the context of short "frame" sentences.

Make up a card for each single-syllable word, and follow the previously described procedures for classification and drill. As you follow the procedures, have Kino say each word in the frame sentence. As mentioned before, up to sixteen tones are possible — a separate pile of one-syllable words should be developed for each tone represented in your language. The language of the following example has only four tones:

High	*Low*	*Fall*	*Rise*
káŋ "deny"	ŋàn "dry out"	ŋâŋ "mail"	kǎn "sell"
bét "await"	bàk "buy"	bâk "carry"	běk "sit on"
wák "multiply"	nwàn "sacrifice"	wât "kick"	ŋǎt "pump"
bók "care for"	bòk "receive"	bôk "push"	bǒk "read"
sák "laugh at"	sàk "bite"	sât "lift"	sǎt "squeeze"
fík "coerce"	bùk "bury"	fîk "throw"	fǐt "press"
dúk "enter"	dùk "eat"	dûk "seal"	dǔt "boil"
tík "praise"	tìk "hit"	tîk "cook"	tǐk "drink"

All of the above event words (verbs) are in the command form and can fit into the following sentence frames:

_____ kù bì kɑ́. ("Don't _____ it today.")

tɛ́ _____ bì kɑ́kɑ́. ("Plan to _____ it tomorrow.")

Frames can also be helpful in drilling two-syllable words. In a frame sentence context you can learn how the intonation of a sentence affects its individual words. Frames can precede the slot, follow the slot, or surround the slot. For example, in English the frame "They were _____ " is a preceding frame, " _____ was here" is a following frame, while "They _____ yesterday" is a surrounding frame. You may find a short surrounding frame the most helpful.

Finding a frame

Try to find a frame in which one pitch is high enough that no substitution word has a higher pitch — this will give you a stable point against which to compare the upper pitches. Similarly, try to find a frame in which one of the pitches is low enough that no substitution word has a lower pitch — this will give you a stable point for comparing the lower pitches.

Sometimes the tones of the frame can affect the tones of the substitution words, or vice versa. Try a variety of frames — preceding, following, and surrounding frames — to find frames in which the tones remain most stable.

Be sure not to just analyze the tones — *practice* them. Listen, mimic, and learn to use them correctly. Practice the words in the frames and in isolation.

You will probably need to have different sentence frames for object words, event words, and quality words. Here are some examples of possible sentence frames for *object* words:

I want _____.

That is the _____ I saw.

That _____ is nice.

That is called _____.

Frame sentences for *events* can include:

He _____ every day.

I want to _____.

Did you _____ already?

Frames like the following can work for substituting *qualities* that relate to objects:

It is _____.

The _____ table is here.

Occasionally you can use a general frame into which a variety of words can fit. Perhaps the most general one is:

I said " _____ ."

NOTE: Whether or not your language is tonal, the frame technique can also be useful in studying other features such as vowels, consonants, rhythm, and stress. When working with vowels, pick a frame which has vowels you are quite sure of, and use these as stable points against which to compare the vowels you are unsure of.

To get a feeling for rhythm and stress, arrange words in sets according to the number of syllables in the words: one syllable words, two syllable words, three syllable words, four syllable words, and words with more than four syllables. Listen to the sets and then further subdivide each set into piles of words which are identical in stress and rhythm. For two syllable words, for example, you might have the following piles: "__ __,, "__", "__'__, and '__"__. Don't be content just to organize the piles. *Practice* them to develop a feel for the rhythm of the language. Choose one or two piles to practice each day until you have practiced them all. Practice the piles in isolation, and then practice them in frames to see if any of the frames cause a difference in the stress or timing of the substitution words.

As your knowledge about the language deepens, you should be able to hypothesize "rules" about the way tone, intonation, stress, and syllable structure work together. Rules about these features in the Hausa language might go like this:

1. Hausa syllables can be CV, CV·, CVg, CVC, or CC̣ (CC̣ is always ʔn̩).
2. There are three tones: High, Low, Fall.
3. High and Low tones can occur on all syllable patterns.
4. A Fall is usually on CVC syllables, but can also occur on CV· and CVg (not on CV).
5. Sentences generally have a "downdrifting" intonation.

But in a question, the final high tone becomes a fall, and the final short vowels are lengthened.

6. A question that can be answered with a simple "yes" or "no" does not have any downdrift intonation. It ends with an extra high tone on the last high-tone syllable, and even the low tones stay high after that extra high tone.
7. Some words can carry a stress for emphasis. They become louder, but the tone is not changed.

Rum & Bored
House Rules

1. ———
2. ———
3. ———
4. ———
5. ———
6. ———
7. ———

Application

We've talked about a lot of sounds — Syllables, Stress, Consonants, Vowels, Intonation, Tones. Now we want to help you determine which of the sounds you need to master for your new language. So far, we have presented a broad phonetic framework which works for all languages. But you are not learning "all languages," so you need principles to help you sort from the broad general framework and make specific application to your new language.

Your goal, of course, is to develop good pronunciation habits. What you learn about the sound system of the language will help you build specific pronunciation drills which you can practice in order to move toward your goal.

In each language, *certain pairs of phonetically similar sounds* are considered *different enough* to cause a difference in the meanings of words. For example, the sounds s and z in English cause a difference in meaning in words like "sip" and "zip," "sue" and "zoo," or "price" and "prize." If a learner of English made a mistake and used one sound instead of the other, his hearers would be amused, confused, or perturbed. These sounds that are significantly different to the native speaker because they cause a difference in meaning are called *phonemes*. (We write phonemes between slant lines — /s/, /z/.)

Keep your goal in mind

On the other hand, in each language there are *sets of sounds* which are considered to be so closely related that they are *only variants of each other*. Often these variants can be used interchangeably without causing any difference in the meaning of words. For example, in English the sounds p and pʰ can be used interchangeably at the end of a word, like "stop." Variants, however, are not always interchangeable, for sometimes their use is conditioned by their position in a word. In American English when a "t" occurs in the middle of a word (like "letter") it is flapped, but when it occurs at the beginning of a word (like "tea") it is aspirated, yet in both cases it is still a "t" to us. Sounds that are variants are called *allophones* (from the Greek words, "allo" other, and "phones" sounds). We will write allophones in brackets — [t], [tʰ], [ť].

The sound system of every language is different from the sound system of other languages. For example, in English the sounds /s/ and /z/ are different phonemes — they cause a difference in the meanings of words. On the other hand, in Latin American Spanish the sounds [s] and [z] are allophones, or variants of one sound. When the letter "s" occurs before a voiced consonant (as in the word "desde") it is pronounced [z], otherwise it is pronounced [s].

Although in English the sounds [p] and [pʰ] are just variants, in the Thai language these two sounds are separate phonemes. They cause a difference in the meanings of words. For example, the Thai word /pèt/ means "duck," while the word /pʰèt/ means "peppery."

In tone languages, tones are phonemes. In English the basic dictionary meanings of words are not affected by tone levels — you can say the word "book" with any tones and it still means "something to read." In the Amoy language of Taiwan, the word /bāk/ (with a mid tone) means "to defile," but the word /bāk/ (with a high tone) means "wood." In the Mano language of Liberia, the syllable gɛ has five different meanings depending on its tone:

gɛ̄ (mid level tone)   — "cotton tree"
gɛ̄ (high level tone)   — "green snake"
gɛ̀ (fall from high to low) — "Gio tribe"
gɛ̌ (rise from low to mid) — "devil"
gɛ̀ (fall from mid to low) — "rattle"

How can you tell which sounds are significantly different to the native speaker and which ones are just variants? The spelling system of many languages will give you some clues about the phonemes of the language, but you will usually have to find out the variants — the allophones — on your own.

NOTE: There are systematic procedures which can be followed to help you analyze the sound system of your new language — these are called "phonemic" procedures. By following phonemic procedures you can identify the specific sounds and their variants. A brief guide to phonemics — *Programmed Phonemics* — can be ordered from Lingua House. $3.50x.

What sounds should you practice?

A basic principle is to practice any sounds which you have trouble producing or distinguishing.

Take a close look at your English pronunciation habits. You have practiced English pronunciation for many years now, and you have developed habits which are deeply ingrained. Because of this, you will have a tendency to impose these English habits on your new language. On page 306 is space for you to prepare charts of the Consonants and Vowels *you* use in your dialect of English (look at the sample charts on pages 278 and 284). On 307 you can chart the sounds of your new language (look at the charts on pages 279 and 285). When you have completed the charts of English and your new language, carefully compare them. Any differences will indicate sounds you can expect to have difficulties with due to your English habits.

There are three basic areas where a knowledge of your English habits, combined with a knowledge of the sounds of your new language, *will help you know what sounds to practice:*

1. *Sounds which occur in the new language but do not occur in English.*

As you compare the charts of English with the charts of the sounds of your new language, note any sounds in your new language which do not occur in English — sounds like clicks, alveopalatal stops, implosives, trills, rounded front vowels, unglided vowels. When your new language has a sound not found in English, your tendency will be to substitute the nearest English sound. You can anticipate this interference from your English habits, and prepare drills that will help you develop new habits. Make a point to practice these new sounds until you can correctly produce and hear them.

2. *Sounds which have different variants in your new language than in English.*

In speaking, you will unconsciously want to substitute English variants in the words of your new language. For example, in your dialect of English the phoneme /l/ probably has three variants: [lˆ] only occurs before high vowels; [L] only occurs after voiceless aspirated stops; [lˇ] occurs elsewhere — you will have a tendency to substitute these variants of /l/ in the same environments in your new language, even if the distribution of the variants should be different. You will need much practice to

Consonant Chart
Your Dialect of English

	Bi-Labial	Labio-Dental	Tip Dental	Tip Alveolar	Blade Alveo-palatal	Back Velar	Glottal
Stops:							
Vl. Asp.							
Vl. Unasp.							
Voiced							
Fricatives:							
Voiceless							
Voiced							
Nasals:							
Voiceless							
Voiced							
Laterals:							
Voiceless							
Vd. High							
Vd. Low							
Flaps:							
Voiceless							
Voiced							
Glide:							
Voiced							

Vowel Chart
Your Dialect of English

	Front Unrounded	Central Unrounded	Back Rounded
High / Lower High			
Mid / Lower Mid			
Low / Lower Low			

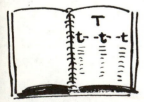

Notebook

Begin now to collect words that have each of the sounds on your charts. Perhaps in a small notebook you could designate a page for each sound. Begin collecting and writing down words which have the sound in initial position, in medial position, and in final position. Your lists of words will help you in making up pronunciation drills

Consonant Chart
Your New Language

	Bi-Labial	Labio-Dental	Tip Dental	Tip Alveolar	Retro-flexed	Blade Alveo-palatal	Back Velar	Glottal

Vowel Chart
Your New Language

	Front		Central		Back	
	Unrounded	Rounded	Unrounded	Rounded	Unrounded	Rounded
High Lower High						
Mid Lower Mid						
Low Lower Low						

develop new habits. Set up and practice *Pronunciation Substitution Drills* to help you become consciously aware of which variants you should be using, and to help you develop these new habits.

3. *Pairs of sounds which are separate phonemes in your new language but are variants in English.*

In English, fronted [ḳ] and backed [ḵ] velars are variants of /k/, but in the Meo language they are separate phonemes, and cause a difference of meaning in words. An English speaker learning Meo finds it difficult at first to hear any difference between these sounds, and has a tendency to substitute the one for the other when speaking, thus causing confusion to his listeners. Whenever a pair of sounds which are variants in English are separate sounds in your new language, you will need to set up and practice *Pronunciation Differential Drills* to help you hear the contrasts and use the sounds correctly.

Here are some questions to ask yourself as you determine what sounds you need to practice:

How is each consonant articulated in my new language?
 (Write out the description of each consonant.)
Which consonants are different from English?
What consonant clusters occur in my new language?

What are the characteristics of each vowel?
Are the vowels glided as in English?
Are some vowels short and others lengthened?
What vowel combinations are possible?

What are the common syllable patterns and where do syllable divisions come?
How are these different from English?

What syllable is generally stressed in words?
What word is generally stressed in sentences?
What words are generally unstressed?

What are the normal phrase and sentence intonation patterns:
 For statements?
 For questions?
 For requests and commands?

"You just have to ask questions, Watson."

How many tone levels are there?
Which glides are used?
Are the glides distinguished by length or starting point?

In the final analysis, you would profit from practicing most of the sounds in your new language, for almost every sound will have at least a slight difference in pronunciation or environment from your English habits. As you practice Substitution and Differential drills, keep a running list of the sounds you have practiced so that you will know where your needs are. Don't forget to practice tones, rhythms, length, and clusters, as well as consonants and vowels.

A running list

After you have done Substitution drills on individual sounds, and Differential drills on pairs of sounds, it is a good idea to practice a drill on all the sounds with one manner of articulation — all the stops in one drill, all the nasals in another, the fricatives, the vowels, the modifications of vowels. These drills should be like Differential drills except that you might have three to five columns rather than just two.

How should you practice?

Remember that there are two basic types of pronunciation drills: Differential Drills, and Substitution Drills.

Differential Drills. Some sounds in your new language may be so similar that you don't always hear the difference — yet you know that they are different to native speakers because they make a difference in the meaning of words. Whenever you have trouble contrasting such sounds in your new language, you need to prepare and practice Differential Drills to help you hear and produce the difference. Let's say that you had the following data which showed that in your new language there was a significant difference between /p/ and /pʰ/:

1. 'pan   "bread"   4. 'pʰɑ.so   "pidgeon"   7. 'ɑ.pi   "garlic"

2. 'o.pʰi   "leeks"   5. sɑ.'pɑ.lo   "cut"   8. 'e.pe   "soon"

3. 'pɑ.lo   "go"   6. ɑ.pɑ.'go.mɑ "tie"   9. 'pʰɑn   "house"

For the Differential Drill, arrange the words for maximum focus on the difference between /p/ and /pʰ/. Put similar pairs across from each other. It is a good idea to have the shortest, easiest words first.

```
┌─────────────────────────────────────────────────────────────┐
│  Pronunciation Differential Drill          July 1            │
│  /p/ vs. /pʰ/                                                │
│                                                              │
│         /p/                           /pʰ/                   │
│         pan                           pʰan                   │
│         páso                          pʰáso                  │
│         ápi                           ópʰi                   │
│         sápalo                        apʰagóma               │
└─────────────────────────────────────────────────────────────┘
```

(The words should probably be written in the writing system of
the language so that Kino can read them easily.)

Practice the drill following the instructions on pages 81
and 82. Be sure to check your ability to hear the difference —
have Kino read words at random and you identify whether they
are /p/ words or /pʰ/ words. Then check your ability to clearly
produce the difference — you say the words at random and see
if Kino can easily identify the columns.

Substitution Drills. Whenever you are having trouble
correctly producing the variants of a sound, prepare and practice a Substitution Drill. You need to learn to automatically
use the correct variant in the appropriate environments, so *the
columns of the Substitution drill should correspond to the environments* which affect the variants. For example, you might
encounter a language in which the phoneme /a/ has three
variants: [ɔ] only occurs in stressed syllables before a syllable-
final consonant; [a] only occurs in stressed syllables which do
not have syllable-final consonants; [ʌ] occurs elsewhere (i.e., it
never occurs in a stressed syllable). The columns of your data
should then correspond to these three environments.

itá

```
┌─────────────────────────────────────────────────────────────┐
│  Pronunciation Substitution Drill          July 3            │
│  /a/                                                          │
│                                                              │
│     [ɔ]                 [a]                 [ʌ]              │
│     pán                 pá                  ópa              │
│     otán                itá                 ótan             │
│     ikámso              ikáso               íkas             │
└─────────────────────────────────────────────────────────────┘
```

From now on, when you set up your Substitution drills,
don't be content with just getting the sounds in initial, medial,
and final positions — try to set up the columns of the drill to

correspond to the environments which affect the variants. In this way, you will be reminding yourself of the environments as you practice. Practice the drill following the instructions on pages 63 and 64. Your aim is to begin to use the variants automatically in their appropriate environments so that your speech will sound natural to the native speakers.

After practicing the individual words in these drills it is helpful to practice the sound you are focusing on, by putting the words in sentences. In this way you can check your ability to say the sound correctly in longer stretches of speech in which there is more to think about.

Don't be content to just practice a drill once and then go on to another sound. If the sound is at all difficult for you, you will need various practice periods spaced at two or three day intervals. The first time you practice a sound you may just be beginning to become aware of the sound. It may take various practice periods before the sound is really yours. Don't try to "master" a really difficult sound at one sitting — you will tend to get frustrated and may even develop a mental block. Work on the sound for a while and then make a note to come back and practice it again in a couple of days. In between practice periods with Kino, you might play a drill tape of the sound a couple of times as a listening exercise to keep the sound in your mind. Plenty of practice and review is necessary if you are to develop new skills.

Pronunciation should be in focus from your first day of language learning, and should remain in focus for a number of weeks. You will no longer need to spend part of Practice time on these drills when (and only when) your pronunciation satisfactorily approximates the native speaker's in each of these areas — syllables, rhythm, consonants, vowels, intonation, and tones. Don't be satisfied to allow your pronunciation to settle at a plateau that is less than satisfactory. Once you stop focusing on it, your pronunciation may never further improve — these habits will become unconscious, for your attention will be focused on words and meaning. Don't underestimate the positive contribution that your life can make when it is evident to everyone that you have cared enough about them to learn to pronounce their language accurately.

Don't settle on a plateau

When you care enough to do your best

Higgledy-Piggledy,
Pygmalion's Higgins
Loved his phonetics, and
Masterfully taught it.

Soon that old "Rain in Spain's"
Pronunciability
Changed the girl's life, hearing
"By George, she's got it!"

'hɪ.gl̩.di 'pʰɪ.gl̩.di
'bru.str̩ ænd 'bru.str̩
'rɑy.tʰɪŋ ænd 'stɑy.lɪŋ ænd
'θɪŋ.kʰɪŋ ʌv 'yu,

'fɛltʰ ðætʰ sʌm 'vr̩.sɪ.fɑyd
'ɪm.pʰɛ.tšu.'ɑ.sɪ.tʰi
'hæd tʰu bi 'rɪ.tʰɛn ænd
'ðɛn wid bi 'θru!

CHAPTER **5**

How to Master
The Structures
Of Your Language

Communication is the goal of language learning. In any language people communicate by using words in ways that are natural for that language. These "natural ways" are usually referred to as the grammatical structures of the language. You need to learn to use these structures comfortably and automatically in order to be a good communicator.

If your language growth were confined to saying just what you have learned for your texts and practiced in Fluency Practice, that would simply be growth by addition. It would take an infinitely long time to learn the infinite number of possible sentences that way. But, fortunately, the speakers of each language use a limited number of *patterns* to talk about their entire world. In Accuracy Practice you learn to use each of these patterns to express a wide variety of messages. The result — multiplication! By building new sentences on the basic patterns, you will be able to participate in extended conversations, and you will no longer be limited to the specific material you have memorized in your texts.

In Accuracy Practice each day, you should practice Structure Substitution and Differential drills to multiply the usefulness of each pattern and structure you encounter. Remember to keep the focus on learning to communicate, so always be thinking of the *meaning* as you drill. (By the way, don't delay practicing a particular structure just because you don't fully grasp the meaning of all its subparts. There

Communication
is the goal

313

will be grammatical features which at first you will not completely understand. By practicing these features in Structure Practice, you will develop a "feel" for their use, and your understanding will grow.)

A native speaker's understanding of the structures and grammatical features of his language is usually intuitive and subconscious. He automatically uses the appropriate word order and structures to communicate what he wants to say, but he may not be able to explain *why* he says things the way he does.

You learned English by using it. Later on, after you spoke English quite well, you went to school and learned how to talk about some of the grammatical features of English, and learned some rules about English grammar.

Unfortunately, many people have had a bad experience with grammar in school. If you have suffered from the "I-can't-learn-a-foreign-language" syndrome, it might be because you feel that you don't understand grammar. Cheer up! There is hope! In fact, you *do* "know" English grammar. You use the various English grammatical constructions when you speak, and you know when you hear an incorrect sentence. If you heard someone say, "Here are my key," you would know it was wrong, and you would know how it should be said correctly. As a language learner, you need the same kind of comfortable ability to use the new language and to spot your own errors.

You first need to learn to *use* the language to say what you want to say. The "rules" and "why's" can wait until you feel comfortable doing it correctly. In other words, you need to spend time practicing and using the structures of the language more than you need to spend time memorizing rules about them. Rules try to give you a cognitive understanding of the structures, but they are seldom the means of gaining fluency in the language. Only plenty of practice and use of the language can do that.

One of the problems you face is the fact that no language arranges the parts of its sentences exactly like another language does. For some languages, the verbs come first; in others, the verbs come last. Modifiers can come before or after whatever is being modified. Tenses may be indicated by a separate word (like "will" for future tense in English) or by a part of a word (like "-ed" for past tense in English). This part might be tacked on to a verb or even on to a noun, and it could occur at the front, middle, or end of the word. Tenses might even be marked by tone.

In every language, the parts of the sentence are arranged in a particular order. Words are never arranged in a random order. 10Be 3were 4in 14anything 2they 6order 11able 8would 5random 1if 13understand 12to 9not 7we. Each language decides for itself how it will arrange the parts of its sentences. There is no external logic that determines the arrangement of the parts or the relationships between them.

Let's focus on the arrangement — the word order — for a moment. The following are fairly literal translations of various types of sentences from different languages. Notice the variation in word order from one language to the next. (If two words are hyphenated in the translation, it indicates that the meaning is expressed by one word in that language.)

English: *The brown house is very big.*
Hopi: Brown house very big.
Vietnamese: The house color brown is very big.
Farsi: The house brown very big is.

English: *This house is not big, it is small.*
Hopi: This house negative big, very small.
Vietnamese: The house this is not big, it small.
Korean: This house-(subject) big-not, small.

English: *Go away! Go inside the house.*
Swedish: Go away! Go into in house-the.
Hopi: You away-future. House-inside-future.
Farsi: Away go! Inside the house go.
Senoufo: Go away, go house the inside.

English: *She uses the stick to stir the fire.*
Korean: She fire-(object) stir-in-order-to stick-(object) use-present.
Farsi: She the fire uses the stick to stir.
Senoufo: The stick, she uses the fire stir.
Swedish: She uses stick-the for to stir around in fire-the.

English: *Give the food to the girl.*
Korean: The-girl to the-food-(object) give.
Senoufo: The food, give girl to.
Farsi: The food to the girl give.

English: *I washed the child.*
Swedish: I washed child-the.
Korean: I child-(object) give-washing-to-past.

English: *When I awoke this morning I looked out the door and saw one man following another man down the street.*
German: As I today early up-woke and by the door away-out looked, saw I a man the street away-under going and one other man followed him.
Hopi: I now awakened-when opening-toward-through looked some men-two one-behind-another trail-along walking-plural.
Korean: Today's morning I-woke door-outside looked-out road-down one-man-(subject) another man-(object) after-going-him so.
Farsi: This morning when I woke I out the door looked and one man saw another man down the road following.

The stick, she uses the fire stir.

We speak with English sentence arrangements, while others use their own arrangements and relationships. If an English arrangement is used in another language, confusion can result, just as confusion could result if English were spoken with some of the above arrangements.

In Fluency practice you learn to use full sentences in normal ways without thinking about the complexities of structure and arrangement. In Structure Accuracy practice you gain a deeper understanding of those structures and learn to use them to communicate a variety of meanings. *This order is important* — learn to *use* sentences fluently in texts and then practice making substitutions in the patterns. Don't try to understand all the structural relationships before gaining fluency.

The rest of this chapter is divided into three major sections:

1. The first section deals with **how to practice**. Come back to this brief section from time to time for help in practicing.

2. The second section (page 322) — **What to Practice** — is the one you will want to spend most of your time in. By working through it, you will discover the simple and non-simple sentence types of your language, and you will learn how to modify these and gain flexibility in their use.

3. The third section (page 350) describes some common grammatical structures and helps you begin to **analyze** the structures of your language. You should be able to spontaneously *use* the various types of simple sentences before trying to work on *analysis*.

NOTE: Throughout this chapter, we have tried to explain grammatical relationships as simply as possible, and we have tried to keep the technical vocabulary to a minimum, since most of our readers are neither grammarians nor linguists.

So, let's start.

Section 1
How to Practice

You learned in Chapter One that there are two very basic kinds of structure drills — Substitution drills and Differential drills. A Substitution drill helps you practice *one* structure or pattern. A Differential drill helps you focus on the relationship or contrast between *two* (or more) related patterns. These two basic drills can be used to practice a wide variety of features of the language. (In this chapter, you will also learn to use another kind of drill — a Consistency drill.)

Substitution Drills

The parts of each sentence you use in your daily texts are organized according to a system — a pattern. By using Substitution drills you can practice the *pattern* and learn to say a variety of other sentences based on the same pattern.

Make a habit of developing and practicing a Structure Substitution Drill for each new sentence pattern you encounter. Use the new sentence as the "Pattern" sentence, and identify the slots where you can substitute other words.

Structure Sub. Drill		June 11
Pattern Esther	likes	potatoes.
Paul	wants	yams.
Jonathan	eats	peas.
David	dislikes	carrots.
Leilani	enjoys	porridge.

(left margin label: F i l l e r s)

Eating a dog

In preparing a substitution table, try to use words that are *compatible* with each other. If in the previous substitution table you were to substitute "dogs" for "potatoes," you would probably find an American helper reluctant to help you practice the statement "Esther eats dogs," although most of the other combinations would be compatible. You could either omit the word "dogs," or else just avoid the word when drilling sentences with the verb "eats."

In Substitution drills, beware of any substitution which would require a change in some other part of the sentence. If you were to substitute the word "children" for "Esther" in the above drill, you would need to change the verbs from singular to plural. Be careful to only substitute items which are similar enough not to cause other changes.

Instructions for practicing Substitution drills are given on page 47. Instructions for taping them are on page 66.

Differential Drills

In any language, there are *closely related* sentence patterns which can best be learned by practicing Differential drills. You can use a Differential drill to practice patterns that you tend to confuse. You can also use it to practice a new pattern that is related to a pattern you have already practiced. In this case, you would be building on what you know and working from the known to the unknown.

Differential drills can help you practice features such as:
Singular vs. plural (The boy walks. The boys walk.)
Present vs. past (The boy walks. The boy walked.)
Verb forms for different persons (He walks. You walk. I walk.)
Sentence modifications (See page 326.)

You may find it helpful, especially in the early stages of language learning, to practice a Substitution drill on one or both sentence patterns before combining them into a Differential drill.

Instructions for practicing Differential drills are on page 83, and instructions for taping them are on page 97.

These two basic drills, Substitution and Differential, can be used to practice a wide variety of structural features.

Some Hints for Practice

Before describing what to practice, we would like to give you some hints on getting the most out of your Structure practice.

● Your drill materials should be interesting, useful, and varied.

● Drills should progress in difficulty, and should be suitable for your level of language ability. Build drills on what you already know so you can move from the known to the unknown.

● It is very important that you keep the meaning in mind as you practice. If you drill without thinking of the meaning, you may just be wasting your time. On the other hand, don't get into the habit of thinking about the meaning in English — that will slow down your learning. Make a commitment to yourself to refuse to think in English when drilling. This means that you will have to be creative in finding ways to keep the meaning in focus as you drill. In the early stages, you can make extensive use of objects, stickfigures, pictures and acting out. You don't have to be an artist to sketch objects and activities for your drills — your sketches will serve the purpose as long as you and Kino both know what they mean. (By the way, if your helper can't read, you will find it especially necessary to use visual means of cueing your drills.)

Be creative
as you drill

Here is an example of a drill cued with drawings. The basic sentence pattern is "The boy saw the dog."

Pattern:	El niño	vió	el perro
	La niña	tocó	el gato
	La mujer	llamó	el cochino

● Your Structure Practice each day should focus on the needs you feel. Generally these felt needs will grow out of your texts and your Communication times. You can build Structure drills in response to mistakes you have made, similar sentence patterns you tend to confuse, or a pattern which you tend to contaminate from your English habits. You should also develop drills around new structures you find you need, and structures you encounter in texts. By responding to mistakes, needs, and opportunities which you yourself recognize, your practice will be more relevant and interesting.

Focus on needs

Each day, stretch yourself in practice and make a conscious effort to master a previous difficulty. Don't stop once you are able to make yourself fairly well understood. Keep stretching and learning. Make a point to listen to native speakers as they talk with each other. Listen for the structures they use that you may not have been aware of, or which you tend to avoid.

● Don't spend a lot of time memorizing rules about the language — focus your time on drilling the structures until they become automatic, and you can use them fluently in communication.

● Some of you have studied a language before and found yourself memorizing paradigms of verb conjugations or noun cases. Remember the Latin:

amo (I love)	amamos (we love)
amas (you love)	amatis (you plural love)
amat (he loves)	amant (they love)

Don't spend time practicing paradigms like this — they have virtually zero communicative value. Always practice grammatical structures in complete sentences. Put the verbs or nouns into slots of complete sentences and use the context of the sentence to remind you which form to use.

You might first practice a Substitution drill on each form:

Substitution Drill Sept. 5 *Subject "He"*		
He	loves	Mom.
	calls	Doris.
	likes	Shari.
	sees	Susan.

Substitution Drill Sept. 7 *Subject."They"*		
They	love	Mom.
	call	Doris.
	like	Shari.
	see	Susan.

When the individual forms come easily to you, you are ready to put them together in pairs as a Differential drill: he/they; he/you; singular nouns/plural nouns; etc. Later you may also choose to practice a Consistency drill.

Put them together
in pairs

● If there is a sentence pattern with a grammatical relationship word (a word like of, a, or) that you keep forgetting to use or which you tend to put in the wrong position in the sentence, prepare a substitution table in which that word is used in each of the sentences.

Substitution Drill *Focus on "i"*				August 16
Pattern: Meri	i wokabaut	long haus.	(The girl walks in the house.)	
Ol	i go	long stua.	(They go to the store.)	
Man	i wok	long gaden.	(The man works in the garden.)	

As you practice the drill, consciously think about the relationship word (function word) each time you say it, to reinforce it in your mind. You might then prepare and practice a Differential drill between a sentence pattern in which the word occurs and a related sentence pattern in which the word does not occur. This will help you develop a feel for when it should be used and when not.

Differential Drill	August 18
Focus on use of "i"	
Meri i wokabaut long haus.	Yu wokabaut long haus.
Ol i go long stua.	Yumi go long stua.
Man i wok long gaden.	Mi wok long gaden.

Think of the meaning
as you drill

● Here's another way to draw your attention to function words. Have Kino dictate a short story to you while you write it down. You may find that you tend to omit the function words in your transcription since they are generally unstressed. Have Kino check your transcription to see if anything was omitted. This will help focus your attention on the proper use of these words.

We might remind you that the Fill-in-the-Blanks drill (page 61) can also help you focus on function words.

● **Boredom** or **frustration** in practice times should not be ignored. They may be symptoms of poor progression in the difficulty of your drill material or of inefficient drill habits.

If you are **bored**, it may mean that you are not challenging yourself enough in your drill material. Try using more new vocabulary in your substitution tables. Try speeding up the cadence of the drill so that you have to respond more rapidly.

Perhaps you are bored because you are doing the drill mechanically without really thinking of the meaning or without focusing on the *pattern* behind what you are drilling. Maybe you have been working for too long without a break. Perhaps you are using vocabulary that is uninteresting or not useful for you. Or maybe you just need a change of scenery. Try doing some informal drills with Kino while going for a walk or while acting it out in your study room. Be creative — drill is not synonymous with dull, unless you let it be.

Frustration is usually caused by tackling more than you are ready to handle. Are you trying to work on a complex sentence before mastering simple sentences of the basic pattern? Are you jumping to multiple triggers before really being able to handle single triggers?

Put drills on tape

Maybe you need to back up and listen or mimic more before going to production. (Remember to really focus on the meaning and on the patterns as you listen and mimic. Otherwise, you will probably not be ready for production as quickly — if at all.) If you get frustrated easily in Structure practice, you may wish to have Kino put drills on tape for you. Only do the mimicry and listening stages initially. After Kino leaves, you can listen and mimic more until you feel you really have the hang of the drill. Then, when Kino comes the next day, you can do the production stage of the drills you mimicked the day before (and tape a new drill or two for the following day).

Perhaps you are trying to accomplish too many things in one drill. Maybe you are frustrated because you are trying to learn new sentence patterns, new vocabulary, and new sounds all at the same time.

Another major cause of frustration for Kino and for yourself is lack of clear, concise directions. Be sure you explain clearly to Kino what you want to accomplish, and how you would like to do it. A little time spent in explaining to him can save a lot of practice time in the long run.

● Don't be content to practice a particular structure once and then put it in your "completed" file and ignore it. Review previous drills from time to time. If you encounter a difficult pattern, build two or three drills on it using different vocabulary. Practice it informally, using the suggestions given below. *Most important – don't avoid it in speaking*. Instead, make a conscious effort to *use it at every opportunity* and to get correction if you say it wrong. This is *very* important. The more you avoid a structure for fear of making mistakes, the less opportunity you will have to really learn it.

● Once you have practiced a pattern, you are ready for informal practice and communication. Here are five ways to get extra practice *informally:*

Getting the hang of it

1. Drill yourself mentally after you begin to get the hang of a new pattern. As you walk down the street, you can mentally describe each thing you are seeing or doing. Then change each sentence to the past tense, to a negative form, or to a question. Make a habit of "subvocalizing" in the language whenever you have the opportunity. This is more than worth the extra effort.

2. Get neighborhood children or young people to drill you by making a game of language with them. Informally practice the structures you have been practicing formally. Be creative in inventing ways to play language games with them. It is quite possible that there are various language games they can teach you. Take advantage of these to increase your mastery of the language in fun and natural ways. (See page 127 for more specific ideas on language games.)

3. If you are learning the language with someone else — a friend, mate, co-worker — take turns giving each other cues for drills when you are engaged in other activities that do not require mental work. (Be sure to only drill each other on patterns that you both are already somewhat familiar with.)

4. If your tape recorder has an automatic shut-off, you can play your Practice drill tapes at night as you go to bed and in the morning as you dress. (If others are around, it might be a good idea to use an earplug.)

5. Spend time talking with people. Make a conscious effort in conversation to use the structures and patterns you are learning. If you make a mistake, learn from it. Jot it down and use that as a springboard for further Accuracy practice with Kino.

The more you experiment, the more you will find other equally good ways to practice informally. Let your personal style develop naturally.

On the following pages we will give you samples of different sentence types that you need to begin learning and using. The first part of this section deals with various types of *simple* sentences. Practice them before going on to the second part — *non-simple* sentences. In your daily texts you will probably encounter most of the basic sentence types of your language. In your Accuracy Practice time, drill the simple and non-simple sentence patterns you encounter in your texts. *Also* begin working systematically through this section by practicing with Kino the sentence styles described.

Simple Sentences

There are many definitions of simple sentences, but let's use a non-technical description, and say that for practice purposes *a simple sentence is one in which one actor (or one group of actors) engages in one activity or state of being.* Under this definition, the following sentences would qualify as simple:

Simple

> Mamabear cooked the porridge.
> The house is red.
> Sally is running.
> The boys are in school.
> The big bully hit the little boy.

(Some of these sentences are easier or shorter than others, but all are "simple.")

The following sentences would *not* qualify as simple:

> Once upon a time there were three bears who lived in a house in the forest.
> Goldilocks went inside and saw the porridge on the table.
> While staying at a friend's house, I broke my arm.
> The ladies fixed dinner and the men ate it.
> The car that's parked out front is mine.

In each of these sentences there is more than one activity or state of being, so the sentences are not "simple."

Non-simple

A **minimal** simple sentence is one in which there are no extra words, and no necessary words are left out. Of the simple sentences above, most are minimal sentences. Which one isn't minimal? Why?

The fifth simple sentence is not minimal — it has extra words that are not necessary for a complete sentence. A minimal sentence would be "The bully hit the boy." Notice that we couldn't shorten it any more and still have a complete English sentence — "Bully hit boy." That doesn't quite sound right for English (though it could be correct for another language).

Start first by practicing the minimal simple sentence patterns in your language. Once you have the basic minimal patterns under your belt, you are ready to work on the modifications of simple sentences.

BASIC TYPES OF SIMPLE SENTENCES

In any language, there is a limited number of basic simple sentence types. The following sentence types are common to most languages but are not an exhaustive inventory. When you can use these simple sentence types fluently in your language, you will be able to carry on conversations easily at a basic level. You can then use what you know to discover and master any other sentence types your language may have.

Patterns
under your belt

There are *seven basic simple sentence types* that are very common. In your new language, the patterns of each of these sentence types may be quite different from each other (and, of course, also different from English).

Read the descriptions of each type and try to think of sentences from your texts that would correspond to each of these types. If you haven't encountered a sentence of a particular type, try to elicit one from Kino. Try to find a way to use the pattern in a text so that you will have more opportunities to practice it in communication time.

NOTE: Be sensitive when eliciting new sentence patterns. Your new language may not use all of these sentence types. But Kino (especially if he is school-educated) may be able to "make up" a sentence to fit your request, though such a novel sentence would never actually be used by native speakers in normal conversation. Emphasize to Kino that you want to learn to speak the way people normally speak.

Select a pattern sentence for each of the simple sentence types in your new language and work with Kino to identify the slots and get fillers for each slot. Practice these Substitution drills until the various minimal sentence patterns are comfortable and automatic.

Type 1. Someone (or something) does an activity. This is
often called an *intransitive* sentence. It includes sentences like:

The bears were walking.	They yelled.
Goldilocks sat down.	She is crying.
Charles coughed.	The puppy awakened.
You will jump.	I fainted.
The dog sleeps.	The volcano erupted.
Rachel yawned.	The book fell.

In intransitive sentences, there is one actor or group of actors engaged in a particular activity.

Doing its activity

Jason
is swiping a cookie

Type 2. Someone (or something) does an activity to another person or object. This is often called a *transitive* sentence. It includes sentences like:

Goldilocks opened the door.
She tasted the porridge.
The porridge scalded her.
She broke the chair.
The boy ate the cookies.
The dog is biting Phil.
I saw Rachel.
You will meet Martha.
They read the book.

In transitive sentences, there is one actor or group of actors acting on something or someone else.

A sub-type of this is a sentence in which someone or something is acted upon. This is often called a *passive* sentence. In a sense, it can be thought of as the reverse of the previous sentences. It includes sentences like:

Phil's getting bit!

She was scalded by the porridge.
The chair was broken by her.
The cookies were eaten by the boy.
Phil is being bitten by the dog.
Rachel was seen by me.
Martha will be met by you.
The book was read by them.
A good time was had by all.

In passive sentences, the true actor is often not stated. You can say: "Phil is being bitten." That is a complete sentence in English, even though we don't know who or what is doing the biting.

Type 3. Someone (or something) acts on himself. This is sometimes called a *reflexive* sentence. It includes sentences like:

She washed herself.
The baby hit himself.
He shaved himself.
Dwight fed himself.
That parakeet hurt itself.
The tape recorder turned itself off.

In the previous three kinds of sentences, there was an activity or event. Prepare and practice Substitution drills for each of the *event* sentence types in your new language.

The following four types are not activity sentences, and in some languages these types do not have verbs.

Type 4. Someone (or something) is identified. This type of sentence is sometimes called an *equative* or *classification* sentence. It includes sentences like:

This is Babybear.

The man is the vice-president.
Samuel is a man.
An oak is a tree.

In classification sentences, one object is equated with another:
man = vice-president; oak = tree.

Type 5. Someone (or something) is described. This is some-
times call a *descriptive* sentence.

Babybear was little.
The chair was hard.
Hannah is pretty.
The house will be red.
Fido is cute.
I was fat.
He is old.

The house will be read

In descriptive sentences, a quality of the person or object is stated.

Type 6. Someone (or something) is possessed. This is called a
possessive sentence.

The bed was his.
The shirt is mine.
The book is Ron's.
The baby is Ramona's.

Type 7. The location of someone (or something) is stated.
This can be called a *locative* sentence. It includes sentences like:

Goldilocks was in the bed.
The letter will be in the mailbox.
The house is on the corner.
She is at the store.
Norman is under the car.

Prepare and practice Substitution drills for each of the *non-event* sentence types in your new language.

These groupings of sentences into seven different types are based on the *relationships* between objects (or people), events, qualities, and locations. The basic types probably apply to most languages, but the actual examples which we have given here may not apply in some languages. For example, in English, "I am hungry" is a descriptive sentence, but in another language it might be expressed as a transitive sentence — "I desire food." The sentence, "He washed his face," is a Type 2 (Transitive) sentence in English — someone acts on something. But in Spanish a comparable sentence would be: "Se lavó la cara" (He washed himself the face). This is a Type 3 (reflexive) sentence — someone acts on himself.

For each of these seven basic sentence types in a language, there is likely to be a specific *order* for the arrangement of the words and a

He washed
himself the face

specific *relationship* between the various parts of the sentence. Practice Substitution drills on each of the basic sentence types in your new language.

Got that?

Next, we will give you some techniques for multiplication and flexibility, so that you can get the most mileage out of these basic simple sentences.

MULTIPLY THE BASICS!

Once you can handle the basic statement sentence types in your language, you are ready to begin practicing modifications of them. There are four very common modifications that can multiply the usefulness of the basic sentence types. These modifications are: *negation, question, emphasis,* and *instructions.* You can practice each modified sentence pattern in Substitution drills first and then in Differential drills between the basic statement and its modification.

Multiply by Negation

Multiple negations

One very common modification of a simple sentence is to make it negative. In English, all of the basic sentence types can be made negative:

The bears weren't walking.	(Intransitive — Type 1)
Goldilocks did not taste the porridge.	(Transitive — Type 2)
She wasn't scalded by the porridge.	(Passive — Type 2b)
She didn't wash herself.	(Reflexive — Type 3)
This isn't Babybear.	(Classification — Type 4)
Babybear is not little.	(Descriptive — Type 5)
The bed is not his.	(Possessive — Type 6)
Goldilocks wasn't in the bed.	(Locative — Type 7)

Practice making all of the basic sentence types into negatives. When practicing negatives, find out if double negatives can be used, and what they mean. In English, double negatives, such as in the sentence, "I don't want to do nothing," are not generally acceptable to educated native speakers. But in Spanish, the equivalent sentence, "*No* quero hacer *nada,*" is acceptable and grammatical, since in Spanish, negatives are combined to emphasize the negation.

Multiply by Questions

Simple statements can usually be modified into two kinds of questions.

One common kind of question asks for a "yes" or "no" answer.
Yes/no questions can include sentences like these:

Were the bears walking?	(Intransitive)
Did Goldilocks taste the porridge?	(Transitive)
Was she scalded by the porridge?	(Passive)
Did she wash herself?	(Reflexive)
Is this Babybear?	(Classification)
Was Babybear little?	(Descriptive)
Was the bed his?	(Possessive)
Was Goldilocks in the bed?	(Locative)

Practice changing all the basic sentences from statements to yes/no questions.

A second major kind of question asks for various kinds of information.

Information about the *objects* or *people* involved:

Who was walking?	(Intransitive)
Who ate the porridge?	(Transitive)
What did she eat?	(Transitive)
Who was there?	(Locative)

Information about the *event:*

What happened?   (Any of the event sentences — Transitive, Intransitive, or Reflexive.)
What did Babybear do?   (Any event sentence.)
What did Goldilocks do to the chair?   (Transitive)

Information about *identification:*
Who is that girl?

Descriptive information:
What is she like?
What size was Babybear?

Information about *possession:*
Whose was the bed?
Whose book is this?

Information about *location:*
Where was she?

(Questions for other kinds of information will be discussed under "Expansion," page 333.)

Practice changing sentences from statements to information questions.

There may also be a special question form for *Rhetorical questions* — questions that a speaker asks without really expecting an answer.
When will you ever learn?
What's the matter with me?
And, children, you know what happened next?

Find out when rhetorical questions are appropriate, and practice them.

Multiply
by Emphasis or Exclamation

Most of the basic simple sentences can be modified to make them emphatic or exclamatory. Some English examples include:

My, how you are growing!	(Intransitive)
What a lot of porridge that girl ate!	(Transitive)
How that girl can eat!	(Transitive)
What a guy!	(Classification)
What a big house!	(Descriptive)

Practice making the basic sentences emphatic. Learn to use them in appropriate contexts.

Multiply
by Instructions or Commands.

Simple sentences can often be made into instructions which ask someone to do something. (This is also called an *imperative* modification.) You have probably been responding to imperative sentences in all of your Comprehension exercises. Here are some examples of instructions in the various English sentence types:

Walk.	(Intransitive)
Eat the porridge.	(Transitive)
Wash yourself.	(Reflexive)
Be a man.	(Classification)
Be brave.	(Descriptive)
Be mine.	(Possessive)
Be there at eight.	(Locative)

Lettuce commands

In some languages, an instruction given to a group of people has a different form than an instruction given to an individual. There may be a difference between instructions to a friend and to a stranger. There may also be ways to express commands to "us" (in English, this is often expressed with the phrase "Let us . . .").

Practice changing sentences from statements to instructions. Practice them within an appropriate broader context so that you learn how to give instructions to different types of people (See pages 150-151). The topics of Chapter Three can provide you with lots of ideas.

Multiple Modifications

Changing a Statement
to an instruction

You may find that two or more of these modifications can be combined. Here are some examples of combinations in English.

Negative and command:
Don't walk.
Don't throw that away.

Negative and question:
She didn't eat the porridge, did she?

Didn't she eat the porridge?
She ate the porridge, didn't she?

Notice how these questions in some way imply the answer that the speaker expects. Find out what answers are implied by the different question forms in your language. Practice the question together with the appropriate answers.

Question and exclamation;
(Child — "I just traded my bicycle for a frog.")
Mother — "You what?!"

Exclamation and command:
Get out!
Shut up!
(In English, the tone of voice helps indicate whether it is a neutral command or an exclamatory command.)

Use Differential drills to practice each of the modifications with each of the simple sentence types.

Now let's try something more elaborate.

GAIN FLEXIBILITY!

You can further multiply the usefulness of the patterns you know by four flexibility operations: Replacement, Expansion, Deletion, and Rearrangement.

You can **replace** sentence parts with other kinds of words.

You can **expand** the basic sentence by adding modifiers and other phrases.

You can **delete** through contractions and omitting "understood" phrases.

You can **rearrange** the sentence by interchanging the order of some of its parts.

NOTE: We are indebted to Donald N. Larson and William A. Smalley for the conceptualization of these four operations. See *Becoming Bilingual,* pages 119 and 245.

Most of the basic sentences or modified sentences can be used as patterns for each of the flexibility operations. Always work with complete sentences when practicing flexibility operations.

When any of these four flexibility operations are carried out on a basic sentence, a closely related sentence results. In general, related sentence pairs are best practiced with a Differential drill, although you may first practice each sentence pattern with a Substitution drill before combining them into a Differential drill. (We will also be introducing two new types of drills in this section — Expansion drills and Consistency drills.)

Flexibility
through Replacement

Flexibility through Replacement: *Replace a word of one grammatical form with a word of a different grammatical form.*

There is a variety of features you may be able to practice by replacement. Here are a few examples:

A singular noun replaced by a plural noun:

The *boy* chops the *tree*.   The *boys* chop the tree.
                               The boy chops the *trees*.

A noun replaced by a pronoun:

The boy chops *the tree*.   *He* chops the tree.
                               The boy chops *it*.

A noun replaced by a name:

The boy chops the tree.   *Roy* chops the tree.

A noun replaced by a question word:

The boy chopped the tree.   *Who* chopped the tree?

An article replaced by a demonstrative or number:

The boy chops the tree.   *This* boy chops the tree.
                             One boy chops the tree.

A present tense verb replaced by a past tense verb:

The boy *chops* the tree.   The boy *chopped* the tree.

A completed action verb replaced by a continuing action verb:

The boy *chopped* the tree.   The boy *was chopping* the tree.

Third person replaced by first person:

He chops the tree.   *I chop* the tree.

A definite verb replaced by an indefinite verb:

The boy *will chop* the tree.   The boy *might chop* the tree.

Notice that in some of these sentences, a replacement of one item will require a change in some other part of the sentence. For example, if you wanted to replace the singular "boy" with the plural form in the following English sentence, what other changes would be required?

A boy is chopping the tree.

Obviously you can't just say "A boys is chopping the tree." Both the word "A" and the word "is" must also be changed:

Some boys are chopping the tree.

NOTE: The difference between Substitution and Replacement is that in Substitution, one word is substituted for another word of the same kind; while in Replacement, one type of word is replaced by a word of a *different grammatical form*. In Substitution, an object word is substituted for a similar object word, or an event word is substituted for a similar event word. In Replacement, an object word may be replaced by a pronoun, or an event word of present tense may be replaced by an event word of past tense.

Tenses can be practiced by replacement. After practicing Substitution drills on one or both of the tenses in focus, you could practice the replacement of tenses by Differential drills. Here is an example of a Differential drill in which present tense is replaced by past tense:

Differential Drill	*July 4*
Present vs. Past	
The boy chops the tree.	The boy chopped the tree.
The man locks the door.	The man locked the door.
The girl mops the floor.	The girl mopped the floor.
The dog licks the boy.	The dog licked the boy.

Practice another Differential drill between present tense and future tense:

Differential Drill	*July 8*
Present vs. Future	
The boy chops the tree.	The boy will chop the tree.
The man locks the door.	The man will lock the door.
The girl mops the floor.	The girl will mop the floor.
The dog licks the boy.	The dog will lick the boy.

You can also practice similar drills for the relationship between completed action sentences (The boy chopped the tree) and continuing action sentences (The boy was chopping the tree). Or between definite action (The boy will chop the tree) and indefinite action (The boy might chop the tree).

(If Kino seems resistant in giving you a sentence with a certain verb tense or other grammatical feature, you should be aware of the possibility that it may not exist in his language. On the other hand, you should also be on the look-out for tenses and other features in the language which have no directly corresponding forms in English.)

In addition to changes for tense, in many languages the form of the verb changes depending on whether the *actor* is singular or plural, or whether the actor is first person, second person, or third person. Sometimes there is even an alternative third person form (called "fourth person") that is used when there are two third person actors in a story, to help keep them separate in the hearer's mind.

NOTE: The grammatical terms "first person," "second person," and "third person," are somewhat egocentric. First person is "I" or "we" (singular or plural). Second person is "you" or "you plural." Third person is "he" or "they" (or any nouns — woman, men, bear, Charlie, etc.).

Changes in the *person* of the verb, or between singular and plural can be practiced as replacements with Substitution and Differential drills as described above.

Past

Present

Future

Trigger forcing change

There is another type of drill which is helpful for some types of replacement — let's call it a **"Consistency Drill."** In many languages, it is necessary for the verb to be consistent with the actor or with some other part of the sentence. In a Consistency drill, Kino gives you a trigger that forces you to make a change in some other part of the sentence to keep the sentence consistent. Here is an example of a Consistency drill for changing the actor.

Pattern: <u>He is running in the street.</u>

Kino:		*Learner:*
You	-	You are running in the street.
She	-	She is running in the street.
We	-	We are running in the street.
I	-	I am running in the street.
They	-	They are running in the street.

In the Consistency drill, the triggers that Kino gives require a change in another part of the sentence. In this case, "is" needs to be replaced by "are" or "am," depending on the trigger. If you were learning English, you would probably first need to practice each form with a Substitution drill before combining them into a Consistency drill. In the Consistency drill, have Kino rapidly give the triggers in random order until you are quickly responding correctly to all of them. If you have trouble with one or two forms, Kino should frequently come back to them.

If a similar sentence were practiced in Spanish, there would be a greater variety of forms to choose from in the Consistency drill:

Pattern: <u>El corre por la calle.</u>

Kino:	*Learner:*
Ella (she)	Ella *corre* por la calle.
Usted (you formal)	Usted *corre* por la calle.
Tu (you informal)	Tu *corres* por la calle.
Ustedes (you plural)	Ustedes *corren* por la calle.
Nosotros (we)	Nosotros *corremos* por la calle.
Ellos (they)	Ellos *corren* por la calle.

In other languages, there might be additional forms for masculine vs. feminine or human vs. non-human (it).

In some languages (Rundi, for example), in a sentence like "I see you," the verb must be consistent *both* with the actor (I) *and* with the person seen (you). You might need to practice a Consistency drill in which you first change just the actor and keep the recipient steady:

Pattern: <u>I see you.</u>

Triggers: He
He
She
We
They

And then another Consistency drill in which you keep the actor steady and just change the recipient:

Pattern: <u>I see you.</u>

Triggers: Him

Her

Us

Them

You might then be ready to practice changing *both* parts of the sentence. Kino could first give you a trigger to cause a change in the actor and then one to cause a change in the recipient. He could soon be giving them in random order and you would say the correct sentence.

Keeping the actor unsteady

In some languages, there are various *noun classes,* and the verb must be consistent with the noun. For example, in most of the Bantu languages there are noun classes, and the class of the subject noun affects the whole sentence. Prefixes of the modifiers and the verb must be consistent with the noun class. In a situation like this, after you have practiced the individual noun classes in sentences by Substitution drills, you could combine various noun classes in a Consistency drill. Have Kino cue you by giving the noun as the trigger, and you respond by saying the complete sentence using the prefix that will make the verb and modifiers consistent with the class of noun.

SEE YOU AFTER YOUR NOUN CLASS

NOTE: In discussing each of these flexibility operations, we give examples of features of English structure that a foreigner could practice when learning English. You will be able to practice some of these same features in your new language when focusing on this flexibility operation, but some other features will have to be practiced by focusing on a different flexibility operation. For example, in English, the difference between a sentence with a noun and one with a pronoun is a difference of replacement. But in some languages, the noun is always used in combination with a pronoun — "The boy *he* is cutting the tree." In this case, the difference between a sentence with a noun and a sentence with only a pronoun would be a difference of Deletion.

In no sense are we suggesting that English structures should be the norm for other languages. Please don't try to get Kino to invent sentences to "match" our English examples.

Flexibility Through Expansion: *Expand the minimal sentence by adding modifiers or other words.*

There are many things that can be added. Also, there are often questions which can be asked about the part that is added. Here are some examples of different kinds of expansions, and questions that can be asked about the expansions.

Adding **Modifiers of the people or objects:**

The boy ran.   The *little* boy ran.

Which boy ran?

What kind of boy ran?

Flexibility through Expansion

The boy cut the tree.

The boy cut the *cherry* tree.
Which tree did he cut?
What kind of tree did he cut?

Adding **Modifiers of the event:**
The boy ran.

The boy ran *quickly*.
How did the boy run?

Adding **Time words:**
The boy ran.

The boy ran *for three hours*.
How long did the boy run?

The boy cut the tree.

The boy cut the tree *yesterday*.
When did the boy cut the tree?

Adding **Location or Direction words:**
The boy ran.

The boy ran *to the store*.
Where did the boy run to?

The boy cut the tree.

The boy cut the tree *in the park*.
Where did the boy cut the tree?

Adding **Accompaniment.**
The boy ran.

The boy *and his sister* ran.
Who did the boy run with?

The boy cut the tree.

The boy cut the tree *and the bush*.
What all did the boy cut?

Adding **the Instrument:**
The boy cut the tree.

The boy cut the tree *with an axe*.
What did the boy cut the tree with?

Adding **Numbers:**
The boy cut the trees.

The boy cut the *three* trees.
How many trees did the boy cut?

Adding **the Person benefited:**
The boy cut the tree.

The boy cut the tree *for his father*.
For whom did the boy cut the tree?

Adding **the Name of the person spoken to:**
Cut the tree.

George, cut the tree.

"I cannot tell a lie."

You can practice expansions with Substitution drills, so go back through your texts and select a wide variety of sentence patterns to practice in this way.

Substitution Drill Expansions				Dec. 4
Pattern: The	little	boy	ran	quickly.
	tall	man	walked	slowly.
	big	girl	jumped	jerkily.
	young	woman	strolled	gracefully.

If there can be more than one modifier of an object word, practice sentences with **multiple modifiers,** to develop a feel for the usual order of these. After you have practiced Substitution drills with multiple modifiers, Kino can say a sentence with one modifier and then say another modifier, and you say the sentence with the modifiers in correct order.

Kino: The big apple fell from the tree.
        Red.
You: The big red apple fell from the tree.

Kino: The handsome stranger appeared.
        Tall.
You: The tall, handsome stranger appeared.

Kino: The old house collapsed.
        Large.
You: The large old house collapsed.

Kino: White.
You: The large old white house collapsed.

A cute little rabbit appeared

(Notice that in English, combinations such as "the red big apple," or "the handsome tall stranger," or "the white old large house," wouldn't feel right.)

Find out if *modifiers* can have modifiers, and practice them.

She is a pretty girl.   She is a *very* pretty girl.
He ran quickly.   He ran *too* quickly.
That is a blue dress.   That is a *bright* blue dress.
He walked slowly.   He walked *quite* slowly.

Another way to practice the relationship between expanded sentences and minimal sentences is to have Kino give you a sentence with various expansions and you say the *unexpanded* form:

Kino: The little boy ran quickly.
You: The boy ran.

Kino: Yesterday the tall boy cut the huge
        tree with a little pocket knife.
You: The boy cut the tree.

Then you could change roles. Kino could say a very simple sentence, and you could embellish it with various expansions. (Also see page 235.)

Embellished with modifications

If modifiers must be consistent with the object words they modify in number (singular/plural) or noun class, you may need to practice Consistency drills in which the object word is used as a trigger. Respond by saying the sentence using the correct form of the modifier.

Pattern: Yo veo una casa blanca.   (I see a white house.)

Kino: *Learner:*
Cordero (lamb)   Yo veo *un* cordero *blanco.*
Casas (houses)   Yo veo *unas* casas *blancas.*
Corderos (lambs)   Yo veo *unos* corderos *blancos.*

Find out if double *possessives* are commonly used in your new language. If so, you may want to practice an expanded Substitution drill such as:

Pattern: I saw	her	uncle's	house.
	my	son's	book.
	your	friend's	mother.
	his	cousin's	wife.

In some languages, possessives for body parts and relatives are different from possessives for other objects. If this is true in your new language, first practice them separately. Then practice a Consistency drill with a pattern like "That is my . . . " Have Kino name different objects, body parts, and names for relatives, and you say the sentence using the appropriate form of the possessive.

Location or *direction* words are common expansions. You may find that there are different kinds of location words that can only go with certain event words. Verbs that imply a change of location (walk, run, move, crawl) may take a variety of direction words like: toward, away from, through, into, out of, across, over, under, around, beside. Activity verbs that don't imply a change of location (cut, read, make) might only go with a few location words, such as: at, beside, near, in. Location sentences (The pencil is _____ the box) may take another group of location words.

Practice Substitution drills on each of these types of location sentences. You may wish to act out the relationships you are practicing. If you have already practiced Comprehension drills on these relationships (see "Space Relations," page 233), the Substitution drills can proceed quite rapidly.

Space relationships

Pattern: The pencil	is under	the book
paper clip	beside	box.
bookmark	near	shoe.
ribbon	inside	drawer.

Pattern: I	am walking	into	the kitchen.
	running	through	bedroom.
	moving	toward	living room.
	crawling	out of	study.

You might be able to take advantage of *time expansions* in practicing tenses. After practicing tenses by using Substitution drills and Differential drills (for each pair of tenses), you can practice a Consistency drill in which Kino says a time word, and you say the sentence using the correct form of the verb.

Pattern: <u>He saw Juanita yesterday.</u>

Kino:		*You:*
Tomorrow	-	He will see Juanita tomorrow.
Now	-	He sees Juanita now.
Before	-	He saw Juanita before.
Later	-	He will see Juanita later.
Next year	-	He will see Juanita next year.

After you get the hang of it, you can make the drill more challenging by having Kino give you a trigger to change the person as well as the time.

Pattern: <u>He saw Elnora yesterday.</u>

Kino:		*You:*
I . . . now	-	I see Elnora now.
He . . . tomorrow	-	He will see Elnora tomorrow.
They . . . before	-	They saw Elnora before.
You . . . yesterday	-	You saw Elnora yesterday.

Make the drill
more challenging

You may be able to expand the *verb* part of the sentence with relationships like the following:

<u>I eat.</u>　　　　　　　<u>I want to eat.</u>
　　　　　　　　　　　　　have to
　　　　　　　　　　　　　wish to
　　　　　　　　　　　　　like to
　　　　　　　　　　　　　ought to

or:　　　　<u>I eat.</u>　　　　　　<u>I should eat.</u>
　　　　　　　　　　　　　must
　　　　　　　　　　　　　could
　　　　　　　　　　　　　can
　　　　　　　　　　　　　shall
　　　　　　　　　　　　　will

(Or even sentences like: "I am eager to eat." "I am anxious to eat.")

If *multiple expansion* can be put on one sentence, practice combining them to develop a feel for the order in which they are usually used. (Sometimes the order may be quite free, while in other languages there may be a fixed order in which the expansions must occur.) Try adding various expansions such as time, location, instrument, and modifiers.

The boy cut the tree.

Yesterday the boy cut the tree.

Yesterday the boy *quickly* cut the tree.

Yesterday the boy and his father quickly cut the tree *with a chain saw.*

Yesterday the *young* boy and his *aged* father quickly cut the tree *in the park* with a chain saw.

(You may be able to construct long simple sentences like the last one with Kino, but *listen* to people conversing to see whether such sentences commonly occur in natural speech. Sometimes sentences with many expansions are possible but are rarely used in speaking.) Use a wide variety of the sentences you've already practiced, and now practice expanding them by adding common expansions.

Be aware of the fact that each of the basic types of simple sentences may take different expansions. One type may add the expansion at a different place than another type. Practice expansions on each of the simple sentence types in your language.

Build on previous drills as much as you can. If you have practiced Substitution drills on each of the simple sentence types, you can use those same patterns as the starting points for your Expansion drills. This will reinforce your previous practice and save time in drill preparation.

Build on old drills

Flexibility through Deletion: *Delete appropriate parts of basic sentences.*

Flexibility through Deletion

In English, *answers* to questions can often be deletions.

Where did you go?	(*I went*) To town.
What are you doing?	(*I am*) Shopping.
What are you making?	(*I am making*) A boat.

You could practice the complete answers and the deleted answers in a Differential drill. As the last step of the drill, Kino could ask a question and then say in his language, "long" or "short" to indicate which answer you should give.

After you have practiced complete answers and deleted answers, keep your ears open for questions and answers as you are in the community. In what settings do you often hear deleted answers? When are complete answers given? Do workmen answer their bosses with deleted answers or with complete answers? How do children answer adults? In a formal meeting, which kind of answer is more commonly used?

Ask Kino or other friends in the community about your tentative observations, to see if you are on the right track. They may have different ideas about the appropriate settings and relationships for deleted answers.

On the track

Deleted *questions* are also common in conversations, either to ask for more information or to ask for a repetition of some previous information.

Agnes went skiing.		What (*did she do*)?
I saw Kay.		(*You saw*) Kay?
	or:	Who (*did you see*)?
Hilda went to town.		Where (*did she go*)?
		How (*did she go*)?
		With whom (*did she go*)?
		Why (*did she go*)?

Practice deleted questions in the same way you practiced deleted answers. Find out what the appropriate answer is — it may be that a deleted question automatically calls for a deleted answer. Here is a possible five-stage sequence for practicing complete and deleted questions and answers.

Stage A. Substitution drill on the *complete answer*.

Pattern: The	girl	gave	the ball	to the boy.
	man	threw	frisbee	child.
	athlete	loaned	towel	coach.
	lady	handed	flag	player.

Stage B. Substitution drills on the *complete questions* that focus on each of the four major parts of the pattern sentence.

Focus on the *actor:*	Who gave the ball to the boy?
Focus on the *event:*	What did the girl do to the boy?
Or:	The girl did what to the boy?
Focus on the *object:*	What did the girl give to the boy?
Or:	The girl gave what to the boy?
Focus on the *recipient:*	The girl gave the ball to whom?
Or:	To whom did the girl give the ball?

After practicing Substitution drills on each question pattern, you can practice these questions by having Kino point to the part of the sentence which you are to ask a question about. If Kino points to "the girl," you can ask, "Who gave the ball to the boy?" If Kino points to the part that says "gave," you can ask, "What did the girl do to the boy?" If Kino points to "the ball," you can ask, "What did the girl give to the boy?"

Stage C. Practice answering each of the questions in Differential drills in which you *contrast* the long answer and the short answer.

Actor in focus

Actor in focus:	Who gave the ball to the boy?
Complete answer:	*The girl* gave the ball to the boy.
(Or:	*The girl* gave it to him.)
Deleted answer:	The girl.
(Or:	The girl did.)

NOTE: In English, if we were to answer with the complete answer, we would probably say the phrase "the girl" louder to emphasize that this was the most relevant part of the answer. In other languages, this emphasis might be accomplished by a rearrangement of the sentence or by adding an emphasis word or marker instead of by loudness. Find out what the correct way is in your new language and practice it.

Event focus:	What did the girl do to the boy?
Complete answer:	The girl *gave the ball* to the boy.
(Or:	She *gave the ball* to him.)
Deleted answer:	Gave him the ball.
(Or:	Give him the ball.)

You could work out similar answers for the other focuses.

Stage D. Practice asking *deleted questions* with each pattern and answering them.

Actor focus:	The girl gave the ball to the boy.
Deleted Question:	Who did? (Or: Who?)
Answer:	The girl did. (Or: The girl.)

Kino could give you a variety of sentences from your substitution table from Stage A. You ask the appropriate deleted question and answer it for each sentence.

Event focus:	The girl gave the ball to the boy.
Deleted Question:	She did what?
	(Or: What did she do?)
Answer:	Gave him the ball.
	(Or: She gave him the ball.)
Object focus:	The girl gave the ball to the boy.
Deleted question:	Gave what?
	(Or: What did she give?)
Answer:	The ball.
Recipient focus:	The girl gave the ball to the boy.
Deleted question:	To whom?
Answer:	The boy. (Or: To the boy.)

Event focus

Stage E. Kino can ask questions at *random* in either deleted or complete form, and you answer using the correct form of the answer.

Another use of deletion in English is the *contractions* used in rapid or informal speech.

I am eating.	I'm eating
I did not go.	I didn't go.
She is pretty.	She's pretty.
They will not go.	They won't go.
Let us go eat.	Let's go eat. Or even: Skweet!

Here's another possible deletion. In some languages, the *actor* doesn't have to be mentioned after the first sentence, since the person is part of the verb. In Spanish, you can say:

Full Sentence	*Deleted Sentence*
Yo voy al mercado.	Voy al mercado.
(I am-going to market.)	(Am-going to market.)
El está aquí.	Está aquí.
(He is here.)	(Is here.)

Flexibility through Rearrangement: *Rearrange the words of a sentence to form another sentence which has essentially the same meaning.*

This is sometimes done in English to make the sentence *emphatic* or *exclamatory*:

Flexibility
through Rearrangement

He fell down.	Down he fell!

Another English use of rearrangement is to *focus* on one part of the sentence.

This book is mine.	This is my book.
This house is large.	This is a large house.
My father is the vice-president	The vice-president is my father.

In some languages, what is first in the sentence receives most emphasis, while in other languages, what is said last is most emphasized. Learn how your language shows emphasis or focus. (In some languages, emphasis is shown by adding a focus word, or by adding a focus marker to the word in focus, rather than by rearrangement.)

In addition to emphasis and focus, rearrangement is used in English for *stylistic* and *poetic* variations.
"Then like an orator, impressively he rose."

Impressively he rose

In Spanish, the modifier usually comes after the noun, but when it is rearranged and placed before the noun, it often has a different *shade of meaning*.

Este hombre pobre desea limosna.	This poor (not rich) man wants alms.
Este pobre hombre desea limosna.	This poor (unfortunate) man wants alms.

Some *question* forms in English are accomplished by rearrangement (and the statement-intonation pattern is also replaced by a question-intonation pattern).

The book is big.	Is the book big?
The boy is running.	Is the boy running?

Try rearranging various parts of sentences in your language and find out what meaning results. (You may just get a puzzled look from Kino!) Practice the rearrangements that you discover.

A puzzled look

NOTE: In English, the relationship between "Olga taught the class," and "The class taught Olga," is not just rearrangement. The basic meaning of the two sentences is diametrically different.

Systematically practice Replacements, Expansions, Deletions, and Rearrangements on each of the basic sentence types and their modifications. You may also find that combinations of these flexibility operations can occur in a sentence.

We are now in the middle of Section 2 — **What to Practice.** You have discovered and practiced the various types of simple sentences in your new language. You have learned to modify these basic sentences into Questions, Negations, Instructions and Emphatic sentences. You have also gained flexibility with simple sentences through the operations of Replacement, Expansion, Deletion and Rearrangement. You now have a solid foundation from which you can accurately generate new simple sentences in just about any situation.

But, people don't always speak in simple sentences. In fact, the normal speech of most languages intermingles simple sentences with non-simple sentences. So, now you are ready to begin systematically combining simple sentences to form non-simple sentences. Of course, you have been using non-simple sentences in your texts from the beginning of your language learning, but this systematic practice will broaden your understanding and increase your confidence.

Non-simple Sentences

By way of introduction, simple sentences can be *combined* in a variety of ways to form non-simple sentences. The sentences to be combined can have the same actor or different actors. The events can occur at the same time, sequentially, at very different times, or even interrupting each other. The simple sentences can be linked together with little, if any, change; one sentence can become the main part of the new non-simple sentence, and the other can become "dependent"; they can be mixed together with one sentence embedded in the other; or one can even be reduced to a phrase in the other.

Combined
in a variety of ways

In the following pages we will help you systematically work through these various kinds of non-simple sentences.

FORMING NON-SIMPLE SENTENCES BY SIMPLE LINKING

Start practicing non-simple sentences by having Kino simply link sentences that have **different actors and different events** happening at about the same time. There are three basic ways that sentences are often linked together:

Equivalent relationship –
Simple sentences:
    Martha cleaned the house.   Stephen washed the car.
Non-simple sentence:
    Martha cleaned the house *and* Stephen washed the car.

Contrast –
Simple:
    John studied.   Ethan played soccer.
Non-simple:
    John studied *but* Ethan played soccer.

Alternatives–
Simple:
   In November I will visit Tim.   He will visit me.
Non-simple:
   In November I will visit Tim *or* he will visit me.

In English, we use linking words — and, but, or — to show these three relationships. Some languages don't use linking words or affixes, but they can still link simple sentences. In these languages, simple sentences are linked into non-simple sentences by intonation and/or juxtaposition. Let us again caution you *not* to work from translations of these English sentences. Try to find sentences in your texts that have similar *relationships*.

You never want to practice a sentence whose organization is forced or unnatural. Be a careful listener to find out how they express equivalent relationships.

Here's an excellent technique which is unfortunately often ignored by language learners. But it really isn't very difficult. Simply record a variety of 5 to 10 minute stretches of speech and then transcribe them. By studying the transcriptions you can identify common sentence types and gain all kinds of insights. (You already have some transcriptions from Comprehension Practice, pages 166 and 240.)

Practice linking all the various types of simple sentences with Differential drills in which the simple sentences are combined into a non-simple sentence.

Differential Drill
Simple Sentences vs. Non-simple Sentences – Equivalent Relationship

Simple sentences:	**Non-simple sentences:**
Maria cooked the cake.	Maria cooked the cake, *and*
Juana fixed the vegetables.	Juana fixed the vegetables.
Pancho chopped the firewood.	Pancho chopped the firewood,
Pablo mended the fence.	*and* Pablo mended the fence.
Tico played the flute.	Tico played the flute, *and*
Moncho sang a folksong.	Moncho sang a folksong.

To practice this drill . . .

Listen: Listen as Kino says the simple sentences. Kino then reads the column of non-simple sentences. Next, he can read each pair of simple sentences, followed by the related non-simple sentence. Finally, he says each non-simple sentence followed by the related simple sentences.

Mimic: Follow the same sequence while you mimic Kino.

Produce: Kino says the simple sentences, and you combine them into a non-simple sentence. Then Kino can say the non-simple sentence, and you say the related simple sentences. Don't read as you produce (production is producing, *not* reading). Finally, Kino can say either a non-simple sentence or the two simple sentences, and you respond with the opposite.

After learning to link sentences which have different actors, have Kino help you link sentences in which the **same person (or object) is the actor of two different events.** Again try to focus just on sentences that simply link, without intermingling.

Equivalent relationship –
　　I cooked the cake.　　　　　　　*I* fixed the vegetables.
　　I cooked the cake *and* fixed the vegetables.

Contrast –
　　The *clock* fell.　　　　　　　The *clock* didn't break.
　　The clock fell, *but* it didn't break.

Alternative –
　　Mary must sweep the floor.　　*Mary* must wash the dishes.
　　Mary must sweep the floor *or* wash the dishes.

Alternatives

(Often when combining sentences that have the same actor, the second part of the sentence will either have a pronoun or may not even have the actor stated at all since it is the same as for the first event.)

Practice these with Differential drills as you did for the two-actor combinations. Practice combining all of the various types of simple sentences and their modifications.

Find out if three or more sentences are commonly combined in a series. If they are, practice them also.
　　Chuck washed the car. Joel mowed the lawn. Nathan trimmed the
　　　　hedges.
　　Chuck washed the car, Joel mowed the lawn, and Nathan trimmed
　　　　the hedges.
　　I fixed my lunch. I ate my lunch. I washed the dishes.
　　I fixed my lunch, ate it, and washed the dishes.

FORMING NON-SIMPLE SENTENCES BY DEPENDENT COMBINATIONS

Now, work with Kino to learn how to combine sentences in which there is a distinct time relationship between the sentences, or a relationship like purpose, cause and effect, condition, or desire. First combine sentences that have different actors and different events.

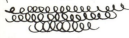

Dependent combinations

　　　　　　　He came. She left.
　　Time:　*After* he came, she left.

	He ate. She sang a song.
Time:	*While* he was eating, she sang a song.

	Steve bought it. Suzette is happy.
Purpose:	Steve bought it *so that* Suzette would be happy.

	Amanda cried. Carl fell.
Cause and Effect:	Amanda cried *because* Carl fell.

	You catch a bear. You let me know.
Conditional:	*If* you catch a bear, let me know.

	You came. I baked a cake.
Conditional:	*If* you had come, I would have baked a cake.

You might give your helper a few of these examples from English. Then turn him loose to exercise his creativity in combining a couple of familiar simple sentences in a variety of ways natural for his language. In sentences like these, one event is often somewhat "dependent" on the other. In some languages, there are different verb forms for the dependent verbs or different pronouns in the dependent part of the sentence.

Practice the dependent combinations as you did the other non-simple sentences. Be aware that some of the combinations will require changes in the verb or in other parts of the sentence. (Notice the second conditional sentence in the English examples above.) The ones that cause changes will need extra practice.

When you are handling the different combinations quite well, choose a couple of simple sentences and have Kino tell you a variety of different ways to join them. Your Consistency drill might go as follows:

Simple sentences: Brutus came.   Caesar left.

Brutus came.
Caesar left.

Kino:	*You:*
And —	Brutus came and Caesar left.
But —	Brutus came but Caesar left.
But . . . not —	Brutus came, but Caesar didn't leave.
Either/or —	Either Brutus came or Caesar left.
After —	After Brutus came, Caesar left.
Because —	Because Brutus came, Caesar left.
If —	If Brutus came, Caesar left.
	(Or: If Brutus had come, Caesar would have left.)
While —	While Brutus was coming, Caesar was leaving.
So that —	Brutus came, so that Caesar could leave.
Although —	Although Brutus came, Caesar left.

NOTE: Your new language may combine a variety of simple sentences without using joining words such as these. In English you could tell a hitchhiker, "*When* we get to the place where you are going, tell me *and* I'll stop *so* you can get out." A similar sentence in Mende would be expressed without the connecting words: "Place you are going, we reach there, you say, I stop, you get out." Learn to form non-simple sentences in locally natural ways.

You can do a similar drill with *one-actor* sentences. Notice that again some of the combinations will require changes in other parts of the sentence. Of course, your new language won't change these sentences in just the same ways English does.

Simple sentences: She ate. She went to bed.

Kino:	*You:*
And —	She ate and went to bed.
But . . . not —	She ate, but she didn't go to bed.
Not . . . but —	She did not eat, but she did go to bed.
Either/or —	Either she ate, or she went to bed.
After —	After she ate, she went to bed.
	(Or: After eating, she went to bed.)
When —	When she had eaten, she went to bed.
If —	If she ate, she went to bed.
	(Or: If she had eaten, she would have gone to bed.)
So that —	She ate so that she could go to bed.
Because —	Because she ate, she went to bed.
	(Or: She went to bed because she ate.)

You could practice a similar drill with multi-actor *single event* sentences.

Simple sentences: Romeo sang. Juliet sang.

Kino:	*You:*
And —	Romeo and Juliet sang.
	(Or: Romeo sang and Juliet did too.)
But . . . not —	Romeo sang, but Juliet didn't.
Either/or —	Either Romeo sang or Juliet did.

Continue in this fashion.

They sang

A special form of multi-actor sentences is one in which one person causes or influences the other's action:

Elizabeth went.	I	caused	Elizabeth to go.
		wanted	
		encouraged	

(In some languages this might be expressed as two separate clauses: "I encouraged her, and so she went." In others there may be just a single verb with one or more causative markers which can be attached to it.)

FLEXIBILITY OPERATIONS WITH NON-SIMPLE SENTENCES

The flexibility operations of Replacement, Expansion, Deletion and Rearrangement can often be practiced on non-simple sentences.

Flexibility through Replacement

Practice replacing the tenses or persons in non-simple sentences. Remember that a change in one part of the non-simple sentences will likely cause a change in another part, so watch for it.

Flexibility through Expansion

Find out if both parts of a non-simple sentence can be expanded, or if just one part is commonly expanded. Practice expanding non-simple sentences as you did simple sentences.

Basic form: When the man plays the organ, the monkey dances a jig.
Expansion: When the old organ-grinder man plays the hand organ, the cute little monkey dances a lively jig in the middle of the sidewalk.

Flexibility through Deletion

You may have already found that when one-actor sentences are combined, the *actor* of the second sentence may be deleted.

Simple sentences:	She danced. She sang.
Non-simple sentence:	She danced, and she sang.
Deleted non-simple sentence:	She danced and sang.

In multi-actor sentences, if the *event* is the same, it may be deleted.

Simple:	He eats his carrots. I will eat my carrots too.
Non-simple:	If he eats his carrots, I will eat my carrots too.
Deleted:	If He eats his carrots, I will too.
	(Or: . . . so will I.)

Simple:	He eats. A pig eats.
Non-simple:	He eats like a pig eats.
Deleted:	He eats like a pig.

In single-actor, single-event sentences, *both* the actor and the event may be deleted.

Simple:	I read the review. I read the book.
Non-simple:	I read the review and then I read the book.
Deleted:	I read the review and then the book.

Flexibility through Rearrangement

Often the two parts of non-simple sentences can be rearranged.

Before you called, I woke up.   I woke up before you called.
I left because he came.   Because he came, I left.

In some languages, there is a distinct preference to express the parts in the order they happened. The second sentence in each of the previous pairs is in the order in which the events happened (I woke up *and then* you called. He came *and then* I left.).

Find out if people commonly arrange their sentences in chronological order in your new language. If rearrangement is possible, find out

Chronological preference

whether it is done for emphasis, stylistic variation, or for some other reason.

FORMING NON-SIMPLE SENTENCES BY EMBEDDING

Another way that sentences can be combined is to "embed" one inside the other. Often this is done by making one sentence modify part of the other sentence—it becomes a modifying clause. Here are some examples of non-simple sentences with embeddings.

Modifying the *actor* –
Simple sentences:	The *man* is walking down the street. The man helped my father.
Non-simple:	The *man* walking down the street helped my father.

Modifying the *recipient* of action —
Simple sentences:	Babybear discovered the *girl*. The girl was sleeping in his bed.
Non-simple:	Babybear discovered the *girl* who was sleeping in his bed.

Modifying the *location* –
Simple sentences:	You are standing *here*. The mighty Zambezi begins here.
Non-simple:	You are standing *where* the mighty Zambezi begins.

I'D RATHER BE SHOT IN THE FIELD THAN THE HEAD!

Modifying the *subject* –
Simple sentences:	You said something. *It* hurt me.
Non-simple:	*What* you said hurt me.

Find out from Kino how your language puts sentences inside others like this. Practice expanding simple sentences into embedded non-simple sentences by adding these types of modifying clauses.

Simple sentence:	The man shot the elk in the field.
Expanded into non-simple:	The man, *whom I saw yesterday,* shot the elk *with the broken antler* in the field *that belonged to Caleb.*

Practice expanding just one slot at a time, but build up to as many expansions as are commonly used in the language.

Sometimes a whole sentence may even be reduced to a phrase.
Simple sentences:	Blanche is playing the piano. Frank is pleased.
Non-simple:	*Blanche's playing* pleases Frank.
Simple:	The child was laughing. The child danced down the street.
Non-simple:	The *laughing* child danced down the street.

Expand
one slot at a time

FORMING NON-SIMPLE SENTENCES BY INCLUDING QUOTES

A special kind of sentence combination involves words like "say," "tell," "think," "ask." Some languages prefer to express what is said, thought, or asked as a direct quote, others as an indirect, and in others both are used.

Direct quote	*Indirect quote*
I said, "He is not here."	I said that he wasn't here.
I thought, "He will work."	I thought he would work.
	I thought about his working.
I told you, "He will work."	I told you he would work.
	I told you about his working.
I asked him, "Will you go?"	I asked him if he was going.
	I asked him about his going.

Practice the sentence form that is most commonly used with verbs of this type.

You have now discovered and practiced the great majority of non-simple sentence types in your language. There may be a few other types which you have not yet discovered. But with the foundation you now have, you can find them as you continue using the language and listening to others.

As you listen to people talk, notice especially how they use non-simple sentences. Are non-simple sentences common? What type of combinations seem to be most common? What types of combinations seem to be least common? Do educated people use non-simple sentences more often than less educated people? Are non-simple sentences used more often in formal speeches or in informal conversation?

Also, record and transcribe (with Kino's help) a public speech, a discussion between two or three people, and a story. Classify each sentence according to simple and non-simple sentence types. Note the frequency with which each type is used in each of the three transcriptions.

Section 3
How to Analyze Further

Keep your cycle
in balance

In this section, we will give you some questions to consider as you practice the structures of your language. A little analysis tied in with your practice can be an asset in helping you verbalize relationships — *but don't let analysis sidetrack you from practice and communication.* Keep your Learning Cycle in balance.

In analysis, you become *aware* of a certain feature or relationship (like a tense-marker or a particular word order), and you may verbalize a hypothesis about it. In practice, you learn to *use* the feature and develop *habits*. You may do some analysis as you set up the drill, and/or you may do some analysis in the form of hypothesis-making after you have practiced a drill and begun to develop a feel for the structures involved. After you have formed a hypothesis, try it out on sentences you generate and have Kino tell you if the sentences are correct. If they are incorrect, you may need to revise your hypothesis.

Remember, though, that while hypotheses may help you verbalize various grammatical relationships, they cannot help you speak fluently — only sufficient practice and use of the language can accomplish that. Analysis can help you become consciously *aware* of patterns and relationships — practice helps you develop *habits* so that your use of the patterns becomes automatic and subconscious.

The main values of analysis are to help you become aware of new features and to help you verbalize what you are learning about relationships. Analysis can also help you see the big picture and enable you to identify any features you may have previously missed.

Words and Their Parts

I SAID: "AN-TID-IS-EST-ABL-IS-HMEN-TA-RIA-NIS-M"

DO YOU MEAN: "ANTI-DIS-ESTABLISH-MENT-ARIAN-ISM"?

Before we present some questions that you can ask about the structures of your new language, here are some definitions and descriptions of things you can expect.

Morpheme

Morphemes are the smallest bits of speech that carry a meaning in the language. Here are some morphemes in English:

boy dog liquid of a -s (plural) -ed (past tense) un- (negative). Some morphemes are complete words, while others are just pieces of words (we call these pieces "affixes"). Some morphemes have a concrete meaning (like "boy" or "say"), while others basically indicate a grammatical relationship (like "a" or "of").

How many morphemes are there in the following sentence?
The boy is sawing logs with a sharpened saw.

Let's separate the morphemes so you can see them more easily:

The boy is saw-ing log-s with a sharp-en-ed saw.

How can you identify morphemes in another language? The best way is by comparing sentences which are quite similar in meaning and seeing which morphemes indicate a *change* in meaning. Look at the following sentences and take a guess at the meaning of the morphemes.

1. El perro no canta.   "The dog doesn't sing."
2. El perro ladra.   "The dog barks."
3. El gallo no ladra.   "The rooster doesn't bark."
4. El gallo canta.   "The rooster sings."
5. El gallo cantó.   "The rooster sang."
6. El perro ladró.   "The dog barked."

By comparing the similar sentences, determine which morphemes have the following meanings:

_____ "dog"   _____ "negative"

_____ "rooster"   _____ "present tense"

_____ "sing"   _____ "past tense"

_____ "bark"

There are certain morphemes whose meaning you can't determine from this data. For example, there are few clues in this set of sentences as to the meaning of the morpheme "el"; nor can you tell if it was just coincidental that both nouns ended in "-o," or whether that is a morpheme whose meaning is not obvious from this set of sentences. The morphemes whose meaning was discoverable from this set of sentences are:

perro	"dog"	no	"negative"
gallo	"rooster"	-a	"present tense"
cant	"sing"	-ó	"past tense"
ladr	"bark"		

One caution — the full meaning of the morphemes is not really discoverable from this small number of sentences. You can discover only the meaning that the words have in this specific, limited context. But there will be other contexts in which the meaning of these words will be different. Think for a moment of a simple word like **dog** in English:

I have a dog named Fido.   My dogs are killing me.

I like hot dogs.   He's in the doghouse.

Hot diggity dog!   This is a dogwood tree.

These are dog days.   He has gone to the dogs.

Don't dog my steps.   She likes to put on the dog.

The planes had a dogfight.   She dog-eared the page.

The fairway has a dogleg.   He was dog trotting.

A doggie bag is for people.   See the Dog Star?

It would be unwise to assume that the word "perro" covered any of these meanings except the first, but it *would* be safe to assume that the word "perro" has its own variety of meanings in other contexts.

Root

The root of a word is its basic core. What is the root of the word "unspecialized" in English? The root, the basic part, of this word is "special." The other morphemes, un-, -ize, and -ed have been added to this root.

Occasionally a word may be a compound word made up of two or more roots — classroom, housekeeper, shoebox.

Affix

An affix is a morpheme that can be added to a root. An affix is not a core part of a word.

Sometimes an affix comes before the root. This is called a prefix. Some examples of English *prefixes* are:

en- *en*courage (makes a verb from a noun)
un- *un*tidy (makes the word negative)

An affix can come after the root. This is called a suffix. For example:

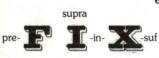

-s   cat*s* (makes the noun plural)
-s   walk*s* (makes the verb third person singular)
-ed bait*ed* (makes the verb past tense)

When an affix is added in the middle of a root, it is called an *infix*. This is less common than affixes that come before or after the root.

A change in the tone or stress of the root is a special kind of affix called a *suprafix*. Here are some examples in English where a change in stress causes a difference in the function of the word:

'permit - per'mit   (noun - verb)
'object - ob'ject   (noun - verb)

There is another specialized kind of affix in which part of the root itself is replaced. This happens in words like:

tooth - teeth   louse - lice   was - were

Occasionally, rather than adding an affix, part or all of the root is repeated (reduplicated). English rarely does this except in words representing sounds — toot-toot, choo-choo, bow-wow. (The Indonesian language makes nouns plural by reduplicating the root.)

A couple of househouse

Another term that is often used for affixes is the word "marker." So, we could describe the plural affix as a *plural marker*. Similarly, the past tense affix could be called a *past tense marker*.

By the way, in many languages it is possible to make individual words negative by adding an affix to the word. You could practice these opposites by a Differential drill such as:

Differential Drill
Opposites — un-

He tied the knot.	He untied the knot.
She caged the bird.	She uncaged the bird.
He capped the pipe.	He uncapped the pipe.

SHE SAID IT'S INVALUABLE — DOES THAT MEAN IT'S WORTHLESS?

You should be aware that there may be more than one way to negate words in the language. In English, for example, there are various ways to form opposites: tie, *un*tie; regard, *dis*regard; *il*legal; efficient, *in*efficient; technical, *non*technical. (There may also be pairs which look as though they should be opposites when they actually are not: loose, unloose; flammable, inflammable.)

Some languages tend to have words that are made up of a root plus a variety of affixes. Other languages tend to string many shorter words together.

Look at the following sentences and try to determine what the roots and the affixes are.

1. Hon jasas — "Now I see."
2. Kas jasas — "Today I see."
3. Kas jakos — "Today I call."
4. Kas sikos — "Today he calls."
5. Kas sijamkos — "Today he calls me."
6. Kas jasimkos — "Today I call him."
7. Kas lojasimkos — "Today I don't call him."
8. Kas losijamkos — "Today he doesn't call me."
9. Kas jasimtokos — "Today I want to call him."
10. Kas jasimtosas — "Today I want to see him."
11. Kas lojasimtosas — "Today I don't want to see him."
12. Kas losijamtosas — "Today he doesn't want to see me."
13. Kas jasimbikos — "Today I need to call him."

By comparing the *first four* sentences, determine which morphemes mean:

today _____   I (subject) _____
call _____   now _____
he (subject) _____   see _____

Now compare the *following four* sentences and determine the morphemes that mean:

me (object) _____   negative _____
him (object) _____

Finally, compare the *last few* sentences and find the morphemes which mean:

desire _____   need _____ .

Look at the sentences and state the order in which the various parts of the verb occur: _____

_____ .

Your statement of the order of the parts of the verb might be something like this:

Negative*, Subject-marker, Object marker*, Desire/Necessity*, Root.

(An asterisk* indicates affixes that are optional — i.e., affixes that don't have to occur every time. A slash / indicates that one or the other can occur, but not both.)

NOTE: Do you want to check to see if you isolated the morphemes correctly? Here they are:

kas	"today"	ja-	"I (subject)"	kos	"call"
hon	"now"	si-	"he (subject)"	sas	"see"
lo-	"negative"	jam-	"me (object)"	to-	"desire"
		sim-	"him (object)"	bi-	"need"

If a word can have a variety of different affixes, don't try to memorize a paradigm of all the possible combinations of affixes. Instead, practice the basic *patterns*. Learn the various affixes and the order in which they can occur, and practice them. You can then begin to generate other combinations based on these patterns you've practiced.

If a word can have two or more affixes at the same time, you may be able to clearly tell which part represents tense, which negative, which subject-marker, etc., as in these words. On the other hand, two or more affixes may clump together so that it is difficult to split them. For example, the Spanish verb "cantó" is composed of two parts — "cant" which is the root ("sing") and "-ó" which indicates past tense, third person, singular, and completed action.

Sounds of the roots

Don't be surprised if you find more than one form for the affix which indicates plural, negative, or some other relationship. Often a change in the form of the affix is related to the sounds of the root to which it is attached. For example, how many different ways do we indicate plural in English? Well, one common way is to add an affix which sounds like /s/ — cats. Another common way is by adding an affix which sounds like /z/ — dogs (don't let the spelling throw you off; say it aloud). A third common way is to add an affix which sounds like /iz/ — roses (say it aloud). If you were to look carefully at the sounds of the roots of many English words and at the forms of the plural affix that go with each, you would find a pattern emerging. You might state the pattern like this:

The plural marker sounds like /iz/ after roots ending in alveolar fricatives (/s/, /z/), or alveopalatal fricatives (/š/, /ž/). For example: boxes, roses, bushes, and garages (focus on the *sound* of the words, not the spellings).

The plural marker sounds like /s/ after roots ending in any other voiceless consonants. For example: cats, wicks, mops, and cuffs.

The plural marker sounds like /z/ after roots ending in vowels or any voiced consonants except /z/ and /ž/. For example: mobs, doves, lids, rags, and tubas.

If a person learning English had done some phonemic analysis of English, he would have concluded that /s/ and /z/ are, in fact, different English sounds (phonemes), since words like sip and zip, sue and zoo, and price and prize have different meanings. For the plural markers, however, he would just need to recognize that a variety of sounds can be used to indicate plurality.

When there is more than one form of a morpheme (whether an affix or a root), the various forms are called *allomorphs*. (In Chapter 4, you learned that allophones are variants of phonemes. In parallel fashion, allomorphs are variant forms of morphemes.)

In the example cited above, the form of the allomorph was conditioned by the manner of articulation and the voicing of the final sound of the root. Allomorphs are often conditioned by the sounds they follow or precede. Here are some of the features that can condition the form of the allomorph: point of articulation, manner of articulation, syllable shape, tone, tongue height, tongue position, voicing, or lip rounding.

Changes in the form of an affix are not always due to the surrounding sounds. Sometimes they are due to noun classes. For example, there may be one form of the plural affix for use with masculine nouns and a different form for use with feminine nouns. Or there may be an occasional "irregular" word that takes an irregular affix. In English the words ox, tooth, and mouse are "irregular," in their plural forms — they don't follow the patterns for English plurals which we just described.

Oxes' tooths

Speaking of irregular forms, all languages have some irregularities. This is just a fact of life that you must accept. There is no natural language which is totally regular and logical. The following poem highlights some of the irregularities of English plurals.

Why English Is So Hard

We'll begin with a box, and the plural is boxes;
    But the plural of ox should be oxen, not oxes.
Then one fowl is goose, but two are called geese;
    Yet the plural of moose should never be meese.

You may find a lone mouse or a whole lot of mice;
    But the plural of house is houses, not hice.
If the plural of man is always called men,
    Why shouldn't the plural of pan be called pen?

The cow in the plural may be cows or kine,
    But the plural of vow is vows, not vine.
And I speak of a foot and you show me your feet,
    But I give you a boot — would a pair be called beet?

If one is a tooth and a whole set are teeth,
    Why shouldn't the plural of booth be called beeth?
If the singular is this, and the plural is these,
    Should the plural of kiss be nicknamed kese?

Then one may be that, and three may be those,
Yet the plural of hat would never be hose.
We speak of a brother, and also the brethren,
But though we say mother, we never say methren.

The masculine pronouns are he, his, and him,
But imagine the feminine she, shis, and shim!
So our English, I think you will all agree,
Is the trickiest language you ever did see!

(Anonymous poem. Quoted from *Learning A Foreign Language* by Eugene Nida, page 14.)

Changing word categories

In many languages, it is possible to make nouns out of event words, modifiers out of object words, verbs out of quality words, etc. Often when this happens there are specific ways of showing the change in category — either by position in the sentence or by adding an affix to the word to indicate its change of category.

Following are some examples from English. Perhaps by sharing some of these examples, you can stimulate Kino to think of how category changes are indicated in his language.

A verb
changing to a noun

He plays
with a playful dog

Event to noun:

-tion	After you subtract, check your *subtraction*.
-or/er	He acts like an experienced *actor*.

Event to modifier:

-ive	That *attractive* gal attracts the fellows.
-ful	The child plays with the *playful* dog.

Object to verb:

-ize	This magnet *magnetized* my screwdriver.
en-	He was in the gulf when the water nearly *engulfed* him.

Object to modifier:

-y	The wind blows hard on a *windy* day.
-ish	That girl has kept her *girlish* figure.
-ic	This magnet points to the *magnetic* North pole.

Modifier to noun:

-ity	The *Pomposity* of the pompous man astounded them.
-ness	*Holiness* is expected of a holy man.

Modifier to verb:

-en	If you want soft hands, *soften* them with lotion.
-ize	This modern furniture will *modernize* your home.

Function Words

You will run across little "grammatical" words (called *function words*) or affixes whose meaning will elude you. If you ask Kino what the meaning is, he may tell you that it means nothing, or that it makes no difference if you use it or not. This should tell you that you are probably dealing with one of those morphemes (like "of, as, and") whose main function is to indicate relationships.

The secret for learning the meaning or function of these little morphemes is to watch how they are used and to practice sentence patterns in which they occur. Some linguists feel that you may need to use a function word in up to 100 different sentences and contexts before you really develop a feel for its use and meaning.

Dealing with function words

If there is a little word or affix that puzzles you, write down examples of its use. Whenever you hear someone use it, write down the sentence and a brief description of the setting and of the speaker's apparent frame of mind. Watch for its use. Look at the transcriptions you have made (see pages 343 and 349) and make note of the use of the function word. Once you have a number of examples, you can study them to see what the similarities are. The morpheme might be a hesitation marker ("uh"); it might be a grammatical relationship indicator ("of"); it may indicate respect or formal speech; it may be an expression of surprise; it may even be a warning that what was just said was hearsay. By keeping track of the sentences in which it is used and the social context in which it is spoken, you will eventually be able to discover the function or meaning of the marker word.

The total number of function words and affixes in any language will be relatively small, *yet their use is extensive*. For example, there are only three articles in English — a, an, the — and yet it is a rare sentence that doesn't use one or more of them. In fact, they account for over 10% of the words in the previous two paragraphs.

Make a point to focus quite a bit of attention and practice on the use of function words in sentences. You should be aware that these words are almost always unstressed, so your focus on the words should not cause you to overstress them. Since most every sentence has some function words, and since there is only a limited number of them, your practice here can pay large dividends. As you learn to recognize and use these words, you will rapidly expand your ability to get the gist of conversations and to speak correctly even though your vocabulary may not be very extensive yet.

Questions for analysis

Now for some questions you can ask yourself about the patterns, structures, and relationships in your new language. We suggest that, for the most part, you ask *yourself* these questions rather than trying to ask Kino. Kino uses his language to communicate, but he probably cannot describe the structures nor talk about the grammatical relationships of his language. Besides, you will probably learn more if you allow yourself to *discover* the answers rather than just letting someone else tell you the answers.

As you carefully consider each question, you will probably need to review quite a few of your previous texts and practice materials. Don't hurry. Be thorough. When a question applies to your language, you may want to spend most of your Accuracy Practice time for a day or two, practicing it with the different sentence types it applies to.

In a notebook, write down your tentative answers. Save plenty of space between them, because as you learn more, you will find that some of your answers are incomplete or even incorrect. Consider them to be tentative hypotheses — keep your eyes and ears open for other data that confirms, expands, or negates your hypotheses. Along with each answer, write three or four sentences as examples of the structure, pattern, or relationship.

As you read the following questions, you will probably find some questions about structures or patterns which you haven't encountered or practiced. This will give you ideas for further areas to explore and practice. Remember that your Accuracy Practice can focus both on mistakes that you make, and also on opportunities — new structures and relationships that you become aware of. Make a point to keep stretching yourself in Accuracy Practice.

WORD AND PHRASE LEVEL QUESTIONS

Let's first give you some questions about word classes and short phrases.

Object words (and other nouns)

Feminine class

Are there various **classes** of nouns? Are these classes based on gender (masculine, feminine, neuter), on the shape of the object (long, cylindrical, rope-like), on the distinction between human and non-human, on some other classification, or on an arbitrary grouping? How many classes are there?

Masculine class

Are there affixes to indicate **singular** and **plural** object words? Are there also affixes to indicate two (dual) or three? Are there different forms of the plural affix for different classes of nouns? Are there nouns that take irregular plural markers (or other affixes)?

Are there sentence patterns in which a plural noun would be redundant and a singular noun would be more appropriate even though you are talking about more than one object? (In one language, you can say a sentence like "The dogs were fighting," using the plural "dogs." But if you add a number word, you don't use the plural form because it would be redundant — you would say something like: "The two dog were fighting.")

Are there affixes to show the **possessor** — "the dog's bone?" Are there affixes to show that the object is possessed? Are some object words (like terms for relatives or body parts) always said in the possessed form? Are the possession markers for objects that are always possessed the same as those for objects which may or may not be possessed? Are the possession markers similar in form to the person markers on the verbs?

Is there any change in the form of the object word if it is used as the **actor** in a sentence or if it is used as the **receiver** of the action?

Are there affixes to indicate **location** (at, in, under, etc.)?

Is it possible to indicate **tense** as part of the object word?

Are there any affixes indicating **size** — dog*gie*? Is there a way to indicate endearment, respect, or honor as part of the noun?

What *other affixes* go with object words?

Pronouns

Pronouns are words like "he, she, it, we, you," that can be used in place of object words. Many of the previous questions about object words also apply to the pronouns. In addition, review your previous material and ask yourself the following questions:

Are there different pronouns for first person, second person, and third person? Is there also a pronoun for fourth person (another "he" for use when there are two "he's" in a story)? Are there different forms for singular and plural?

Is there a first person plural which *includes* the person spoken to (i.e., we and you), in contrast with a different first person plural which *excludes* the person spoken to (i.e., we but not you)?

Are there some pronouns for use with friends and others for use with strangers or more formal acquintances? Are there special *respect* pronouns for times when you want to show honor to the person you are speaking to (or about)?

Is there a set of **possessive** pronouns (my, your, his, her) or comparable affixes?

Are different pronouns used for the actors in **transitive** sentences than for actors in **intransitive** sentences?

Are the pronouns in the **dependent** part of a non-simple sentence the same as those used in other sentences?

Exclusive

Is there any difference in the form of a pronoun when it is used as the **actor** in the sentence (I), the **receiver** of the activity (me), or the **indirect receiver** of the activity?

Are any **modifiers** ever used with pronouns?

Inclusive

NOTE: If the pronouns of your new language are quite complex, you might want to fill them in on a chart like the following. Don't feel that you must fill in each space. On the other hand, you may need to indicate additional distinctions. (Following the blank chart is a sample chart of English pronouns.)

The chart will help you see if you have a well-rounded view of the pronouns, but don't spend time memorizing the chart after you have filled it in. Instead, practice the various pronouns in sentences using Substitution, Differential, and Consistency drills.

Pronouns *Transitive Set*

			Actor	Receiver	Indirect Receiver	Possessor
First Person Masculine	Singular					
	Dual	Exclusive				
		Inclusive				
	Plural	Exclusive				
		Inclusive				
First Person Feminine	Singular					
	Dual	Exclusive				
		Inclusive				
	Plural	Exclusive				
		Inclusive				
Second Person Masculine	Singular	Formal				
		Informal				
	Dual	Formal				
		Informal				
	Plural	Formal				
		Informal				
Second Person Feminine	Singular	Formal				
		Informal				
	Dual	Formal				
		Informal				
	Plural	Formal				
		Informal				
Third Person Masculine	Singular					
	Dual					
	Plural					
Third Person Feminine	Singular					
	Dual					
	Plural					
Third Person Neuter	Singular					
	Dual					
	Plural					
Fourth Person	Singular					
	Dual					
	Plural					

English Pronouns

		Actor	Receiver	Possessor	
				Poss.Sents.	Other Sents.
First Person	Singular	I	me	mine	my
Masc./Fem.	Plural	we	us	ours	our
Second Person Masc./Fem.	Sg./Pl.	you	you	yours	your
Third Person	Masc.Sg.	he	him	his	his
	Fem.Sg.	she	her	hers	her
	Neut.Sg.	it	it	its	its
	M/F/N Pl.	they	them	theirs	their

Modifiers of Objects

Many of the questions relating to object words also apply to their modifiers. In addition, you may also want to ask yourself the following questions.

How is **comparison** indicated ("Dan is tall*er* than Alice")? How are **superlatives** indicated ("Brian is *the tallest.*" "Matthew is the *most* advanced student.")?

Is it possible to indicate **degrees** of the quality (very little, some, very much)? How is this done?

Indicate degrees

How is the quality **negated** (*un*careful/care*less*/*not* careful)?

Are there affixes which must be added to the modifiers to make them **consistent** with the noun class of the noun they modify?

What are some of the common **kinds** of modifiers — size, color, age, smell, taste, cost, etc.? When two or more modifiers are used together, in what order do they usually occur (for example: color before size; or, age, then cost, then taste, etc.)? How many modifiers are usually used together?

Are there some modifiers that can be **affixed** to the noun, rather than being separate words?

Is a **noun** ever used as a modifier of another noun (for example: house pet, boat trailer, book stand)? Does the modifying noun then take the same kind of affixes as the regular modifiers do?

Event words

Are there verb **classes?** How many? Are these classes based on a distinction between verbs that act upon an object ("See the tree"), and those that don't act act upon an object ("Come here")? Are there seemingly arbitrary verb classes?

How is **tense** indicated? How many tenses are there (for example: past, long past, present, future, far future)? (By the way, there are some languages that don't have tenses in the sense of strictly time

relationships. For example, in one language, there are two forms — one for "present" meaning both here [space] and now [time]; and another form for remote, meaning distant in space or distant in time [whether past of future]). Are there different tense markers for different classes of verbs? Is tense always indicated, or is it sometimes optional? Is there a common way to indicate tense in relation to some other point in time (had gone, has gone, will have gone)?

Are there morphemes to indicate the **kind of action** — completed, incomplete, habitual, continuing? Are these affixes, or separate words?

Do the verbs have affixes to indicate singular and plural actors? How about two or three actors?

Are there affixes indicating the **person** of the **actor** (first person, second person, third person, fourth person)? Are these forms the same for all types of verbs and for all tenses?

Are there affixes indicating the **receiver** of the activity? (In some languages there are different verb affixes for sentences like: He *hit-her.* He *hit-them.* He *hit-me.)* Are there affixes indicating the benefactor or indirect receiver of the action ("I read the book *to him."* "I read the book *for her.")*?

NOTE: If the various person-marker affixes are complex or numerous, you may wish to prepare a chart similar to the one for pronouns (see page 360). The chart would serve to help you become aware of the various forms and help you see if you have a full picture of all of them. By examining your chart you may see patterns emerging that will help you remember the forms better. Remember to practice the verb forms in full sentences.

What affixes or additional words are used to indicate the speaker's **mood** or relationship to what he is saying? These may fall into one or more of the following categories (or continuums):

● Fact, opinion, inference, hearsay

● Desired (wish), indifferent, not desired

● Fact ("I went and got it for you."), potential fact ("Since I am going, I will get it for you."), conditional ("If I go, I will get it for you."), contrary to fact ("If I were a bird, I'd fly there to get it for you.")

● Definite, indefinite (maybe)

Are there affixes to indicate **direction** (up, down, away, toward)?

Is there an affix to indicate **negation** ("Do*n't* roll that chart.")?

Are there affixes, special verb forms, or extra words to indicate **relationships** like: *active* ("Huey hit Dewey."), *passive* ("Dewey was hit."), *causative* ("Louie made Huey hit Dewey."), *reflexive* ("Dewey hit himself."), *reciprocal* ("Huey and Dewey hit each other."), or *benefactive* ("Huey hit Dewey for Louie.")?

Huey hit Dewey
for Louie

Modifiers of Events

Some of the questions relating to event words may also apply to the event modifiers. Other questions include:

Are there markers to indicate **comparison** (quick*er*/*more* quickly), and **superlative** (quick*est*/*most* quickly)?

Are there affixes or separate words to indicate *degrees* of the quality (*somewhat* quickly, *very* quickly)?

How is the quality **negated** (gracefully/*un*gracefully)?

What are some of the common **types** of event modifiers in your new language — speed, duration, manner? When various of these qualities are used in a sentence, which comes first, which second, which third?

Are **verbs** sometimes used as modifiers of other verbs ("He walked jumpingly.")? Does the modifying verb need to have any special affixes?

Are any of the modifiers generally **affixed** to the verbs rather than being separate words?

Other words

Besides object words, event words, and their modifiers, there probably are a variety of other words, some of which may be relationship words.

Are there **time** words like "tomorrow, yesterday, next month"? Where are they placed in the sentence? Do they take any affixes?

What **time relationship** words are there ("before, after, when, during")? Is their basic function to link two events together? Do they have other functions? Are some (or all) of these time relationships expressed as affixes to the verb rather than as separate words?

What **space** words are there ("here, there, yonder")? What is their usual position in the sentence?

Are there **space relationship** words ("in, under, into, beside, near," etc.) or are these relationships expressed by affixes on object words and event words?

Are there **linking** words like "and, but, or," used to form non-simple sentences?

Are there some **function words** that seem to mostly indicate grammatical relationships rather than having a great deal of intrinsic meaning? List these words and give your best hypothesis about what they indicate.

A great deal

SENTENCE LEVEL QUESTIONS

Now, let's help you double check by giving you some questions about sentence content and organization.

Simple sentences

What **types** of simple sentences have you identified in your language? What is the basic word order for minimal sentences of each of these sentence types?

In some languages, **non-event** sentences do not have a verb. The relationship, "The book is big," would be expressed "Book big." Is there a verb or linking word in the non-event sentences of your new language?

Is the weather described with a special *indefinite* sentence form? (Weather is commonly described with indefinite sentences. What does "it" stand for in the sentence: "It is raining."?)

If there are noun classes, what other words in the sentence must be *consistent* with the noun class: Modifiers? Verbs? Numbers? Other words?

Is it usually necessary to state the *subject* of the sentence, or is the subject-person marker included in the verb in some of the sentence types?

How are yes/no **questions** formed? How are information questions formed?

How are each of the sentence types **negated?**

What **instruction** or **command** forms are there? Are there different forms for informal, formal, respectful commands, for requests, and for suggestions? In what settings is each of these appropriate? When is each inappropriate? Are there command forms for plural as well as for singular? There are probably command forms for "you" (Come!). Are there also command forms for "I," "we" ("Let us go."), "he," or "they"?

Can all of the simple sentences be made **emphatic** or **exclamatory**? How is this indicated?

What *combinations of modifications* are commonly used?

What **expansions** have you found?
Time?   Duration?
Instrument (with)?   Agent (by)?   Benefactor (for, to)?
Location?   Direction?
Co-actors?
In what order do these expansions tend to occur? Which expansions tend to occur together?

What **deletions** are common?

What parts of the sentence can be **rearranged**? What is accomplished by rearrangement?

Deletion

Non-simple Sentences

Can each of the simple sentence types be combined to form non-simple sentences?

When two simple sentences are simply **linked,** how are they joined?

When two simple sentences are combined so that one is **dependent** on the other, how are they joined? What changes take place in the dependent part?

If both parts of a non-simple sentence have the **same actor,** when is the actor repeated in the second part? When is it unnecessary to repeat the actor?

If both parts have the **same event,** is the event word repeated in the second part?

How are sentences **embedded?**

When a sentence is reduced to a **phrase,** what form does it take?

How are **quotations** commonly expressed?

Which of the **flexibility operations** are commonly used with non-simple sentences?

BEYOND THE SENTENCE

A large unit of speech

People rarely speak just one sentence. Usually they say various sentences relating to a common thought or theme. Begin focusing your attention on larger units of speech. **Record** and **transcribe** a few speeches or stories — anything that would be long enough to have two or more *sub-points* or subtopics.

Paragraph or Sub-Point Level

Here's where a little extra work can go a long way.

Listen to your tapes as you read the transcription and focus your attention on the sentences within each sub-point.

How are the **nouns** and **pronouns** used within the sub-points? Is the object or person named when it is first mentioned? Afterwards, is it referred to with pronouns? How often is the noun repeated within a sub-point? How often are pronouns used? What percentage of sentences have neither nouns nor pronouns as subject words? Do some sentences have both a noun and a pronoun referring to the same object (for example: The *house, it* is big. The *girl, she* is walking.)? If there are two people in the narrative, how are they kept separate in the hearer's mind?

Listen to your recording and study your transcription again. This time focus on the **event** words. What tenses are used within the sub-point? If a particular tense is used for the first event, do the following sentences use the same tense, or do they usually use a different tense?

Listen once more, focusing on how the sentences are joined. Are there certain **transition** words that help tie sentences together? For example, some common English transitions between sentences are:

"for example, so, then, moreover, on the other hand, thus, and then, however, and so, after that." There are also some transitions in English that a speaker can use to tie a side-track into his main point — "by the way, speaking of . . . " (these can also be used by someone else who wants to jump into a conversation and take it down a slightly different track).

Another way that sentences are tied together in English is by the use of words like *"this"* and *"that"* to refer back to previous sentences — "Rachel hid Reuben's baseball. *That* angered him." Are there words that have a similar function in you new language? How often are they used? Do they refer back to the immediately preceding sentence, or to whole sets of sentences?

Change
from past to future

Now, notice the **sentence styles.** When are full sentences used, and when are deleted sentences used? How often are non-simple sentences used? Do the non-simple sentences tend to come at the end of the topic, or are they pretty well interspersed throughout?

There are two other ways to look at the relationship of sentences within a topic. One is to take one of the texts you have previously practiced and **change** some aspect of the setting so that the text will have to be modified. You could change it from a conversation to a story, from an informal discussion to a formal speech, from a first person story ("I did this") to a third person story ("He did this"), from past tense ("I did this") to future ("I am going to . . . ") or present ("I am now . . . "), from a definite ("I am going to . . . ") to an indefinite account ("I might . . . , I should . . . , I would like to . . . "). Each time you change the setting, check out the modified form of the full text with Kino. Notice carefully the changes that are needed and get a feel for the general flow of sentences.

BEFORE   AFTER

Here's another way to focus on the flow of tenses. Have your helper give you a short description (on tape) of an important *event* which will soon happen (a sporting event, a wedding celebration, birthday party, etc.). He can tell you what he expects will happen, who he thinks will be there, what usually happens, etc. Within a day or two after the event has happened, have your helper again describe the event on tape. Two or three weeks later, again ask him for a description of that event. Transcribe all three of these descriptions and then carefully look at the **sequences** of tenses in *each* of the descriptions. Is the first description mostly in future tense? Does he describe parts of it as though it is currently taking place? Does he describe a lot of what has happened in the past as he lays the background for what he expects to happen? If so, how does he indicate the change between past and future? What about the second description — is it mainly in the past tense? Does he change tenses in the description? Is any of it given in the present tense as though the event is still happening? What differences do you notice between the *sequence* of tenses in the second description and those in the third description?

From now on, as you listen to people, be aware of how sentences are connected and of the flow of sentences within a topic or paragraph.

Discourse Level

Time now to look beyond the sub-points to the whole discourse. How does a **public speech** usually begin? Does a public speaker define his goal or state his outline? Does he state that he is moving from one point to another? Does he use expressions like "next," "furthermore," "my next point," to indicate the transition between ideas? Is the closing of a public speech gradual ("My last point is . . . "), stylized, abrupt ("I have spoken")?

What kind of expression do people use to introduce a **true story** about their own experience? Do these opening remarks differ if the story is told informally? How long an introduction is usually given when telling a story? How much background information is told? How do people indicate that what they are about to say is hearsay or second-hand?

What is different when telling a **fable** or **folk story**? Is there a stylized introduction ("Once upon a time . . . ")? Is there usually a moral at the end or beginning? Is there a particular intonation for storytelling? How does a storyteller indicate that he has ended his tale? Is there a stylized ending?

Don't just note these interesting features about transitions, openings, closings, etc. Practice them and build them into your own speaking. Your use of these features will go a long way toward making your speech more clear and natural.

So, they all lived happily ever after.

We have written.

Going a long way

APPENDIX   A

Setting Your Goal
And
Evaluating Your
Progress

Where am I going? .... **Goal**
How am I doing? .... **Progress**

These two related questions are important for satisfactory progress in your language acquisition.

First, you need to decide where you want to be in your communication ability. Your purpose for learning the language should help you keep your objectives clearly in mind. We feel it is best for you to firmly establish your goals at the beginning of language learning.

If you desire just to get by for a short while, then set a goal of **Level One.** A Level One speaking proficiency will usually enable you to carry out minimal activities of daily living in the language.

If your objective is to respond to opportunities and cope with cultural stresses on an extended temporary basis of more than two or three months, then set a goal of **Level Two.** A Level Two speaking proficiency will usually enable you to interact with people in routine social situations, and for *limited* work requirements.

If your purpose is to satisfy normal social and work requirements with professional proficiency that is usually satisfactory, then set a goal of **Level Three.** A Level Three proficiency will enable you to speak the language with sufficient structural accuracy and vocabulary to meet these limited needs.

Do you want to be able to use the language fluently and accurately with vocabulary that is always extensive and precise enough to enable you to convey your exact meaning? Set your goal at **Level Four** if your purpose is to be a change-agent and you have a responsibility to communicate effectively.

If you want to consider yourself a native speaker of the language, and have native speakers react to you as they do to each other, then set a goal of **Level Five.** A Level five speaking proficiency is equivalent in every way to an educated native speaker.

Before you set a goal for your own personal achievement, let's first describe each of the language proficiency levels more fully.

NOTE: We are deeply indebted to the United States Foreign Service Institute for the concept of the Zero-to-Five rating scale, and for the concept of the self-rating check-list of speaking proficiency.

I'M AT THE ZERO LEVEL IN 5,866 LANGUAGES!

Zero Level: No ability in the language. It is estimated that there are over 5,000 languages in the world. Almost all native English speakers are at the Zero Level in all of these languages except English.

Zero Plus Level: At the Zero Plus Level, you are barely getting started. You can use at least 50 words in appropriate contexts.

One Level: The One Level indicates an *elementary speaking proficiency*. You are able to satisfy routine travel needs and minimal courtesy requirements at the One Level. You can ask and answer questions on very familiar topics within the scope of your very limited language experience. Your speaking Vocabulary is only adequate to express the most elementary survival needs.

Errors in Pronunciation and Grammatical Structure are frequent, and a wrong meaning may often be communicated. Pronunciation and Structural accuracy are usually limited to material drilled in Accuracy Practice.

Your Fluency at the One Level should be satisfactory for memorized texts and drill material. Expressions you have not previously used require obvious effort. Your general Comprehension is limited to short, simple, familiar utterances. You can understand simple questions and statements if they are repeated at a slower rate than normal speech.

At the One Level, you should be able to order a simple meal, ask for a room in a hotel, ask and give directions, handle travel requirements, tell time, be courteous, and give a simple speech to introduce yourself. You are Involved with people and can initiate and terminate conversations with strangers in appropriate ways.

One Plus Level: At this level, you are able to meet more complex travel and courtesy requirements, and your Vocabulary is increasing. Normally you can cope with social conversation, though outside of a controlled context you frequently say things you don't intend to say. Your Pronunciation is improving through Accuracy Practice. Comprehension and Fluency are still fairly limited to familiar material.

Two Level: The Two Level indicates *limited work proficiency* with the language. At this level, you can engage in superficial discussions on current events, and you can talk about yourself, your family, and your work. You can handle limited work requirements like giving simple instructions or simple explanations and descriptions, but you need help when complications and difficulties occur.

Continuing practice
to reduce

Your Pronunciation should always be intelligible, but you need continuing practice to reduce your English accent. You can handle simple sentence patterns with accuracy, but you are aware of your limitations and lack confidence with more complex patterns. You use circumlocutions in order to avoid certain patterns and to use known vocabulary.

When you were at the One Level, most of the things you could say had been specifically prepared and practiced. By Level Two, however, you can speak extemporaneously (though in a limited way) about most topics, using sentence patterns that you have previously mastered. Your Fluency in extemporaneous situations is often hesitant and your rate of speech is erratic. Your Comprehension is improving, and you can understand most conversations directed to you on everyday topics though you sometimes misinterpret or need repetition. You can seldom fully understand conversations between native speakers.

Two Plus Level: At the Two Plus Level your Rate of speech and Fluency is increasing due to your continuing Accuracy Practice with sentence structures, combined with regular communication using new topics.

Three Level: The Three Level indicates *minimal professional proficiency* in speaking the language. At the Three Level, you are able to speak the language with sufficient Structural accuracy and Vocabulary to satisfy all social and work requirements. You can handle professional discussions within a specialized field. You can participate effectively in all general conversations, and you can discuss topics of interest with reasonable ease. Your Vocabulary is broad enough so that you rarely have to grope for a word.

Your Pronunciation skill has probably reached a plateau and is almost entirely subconscious and always intelligible. If you have not been diligent in Pronunciation Accuracy practice, you may have a continuing accent that is both annoying and obviously foreign. You control all sentence structures well enough that your errors never interfere with understanding and rarely disturb native speakers.

Your Fluency is rarely hesitant, and you are always able to sustain conversation through circumlocutions. Your Comprehension is quite complete when listening to a normal rate of speech.

You are Involved with people and use the language well enough to establish close friendships. You are Independent in your cultural activities and are making a satisfactory adjustment to the culture, though some cultural stresses continue.

Three Plus Level: At the Three Plus Level, your Vocabulary is getting much broader. Your Fluency continues to improve, and you almost always understand idiomatic speech that native speakers use when talking to each other. You still make grammatical errors with some sentence patterns. You will move to a Four Level when you can use all grammatical structure patterns correctly and spontaneously.

Four Level: The Four Level indicates *full professional proficiency* in the use of the language. At the Four Level, you are able to use the language fluently and accurately on all levels pertinent to professional needs. You can understand and participate in any conversation with a high degree of Fluency and precision of Vocabulary. Your speech is always as effortless as in English, and you are always easy to listen to. Your errors of Pronunciation and Grammatical Structure are quite rare, and you correct yourself automatically and unconsciously. You can also handle informal interpreting to or from your second language.

Four Plus Level: At the Four Plus Level, you are just short of native speaker proficiency. People feel that you share their knowledge bank well enough to talk about and defend any of their beliefs or values. A specific weakness in any language or cultural area will keep you from a Five Level.

Five Level: The Five Level indicates complete *native-speaker proficiency*. Your speaking skill at the Five Level is equivalent to that of an educated native speaker. You now have complete Fluency and complete idiomatic usage. Your peak work performance is in no way hampered by language. At the Five Level, you automatically acquire whatever Vocabulary you need, and you unconsciously adapt your idiomatic style as appropriate. (It is usually necessary to receive university education in the language and live for some years immersed in the second cultural environment in order to attain this level of speaking proficiency.)

Immersed
in the environment

Evaluate your purpose for language learning and decide on the goal that will enable you to satisfactorily carry out your objectives. We suggest that you fill in and sign the following personal commitment.

"I will need to reach Level _____ in order to conscientiously fulfill my objectives and purpose in this new culture. I am determined to discipline myself to a schedule of daily learning until I satisfactorily meet this goal."

Signed _____

Now that your goal is set, you know where you want to go. To measure your progress, you need to be able to continually evaluate how you are doing. The following checklist is designed to help you evaluate your speaking proficiency on the Zero-to-Five rating scale. We recommend that you evaluate your proficiency once each month.

NOTE: You or your agency may feel that it is helpful to submit a monthly progress report. If so, you may choose to use the "Language Learning Progress Report" forms and follow the Suggested Language Learning Progression Schedule. A copy of the form and the schedule are at the end of the Appendix.

Self-rating Checklist
of Speaking Proficiency

Level Zero Plus

☐ I can use more than 50 words of my new language in appropriate contexts.

Level One

☐ (You are at Level One when you can confidently check each of the following Level One language activities.)

☐ I can initiate conversations and use appropriate leave-takings to close conversations.

☐ I can make a selection from a menu and order a simple meal.

☐ I can ask and tell the time of day, the day of the week, and the date.

☐ I can go to the market or butcher and ask for vegetables, fruit, milk, bread, and meat, and I can bargain when appropriate.

☐ I can tell someone how to get from here to the post office, a restaurant, or a hotel.

☐ I can negotiate for a taxi ride or a hotel room and get a fair price.

☐ I can make a social introduction of someone else and also give a brief speech to introduce myself.

☐ I can understand and correctly respond to questions about my marital status, nationality, occupation, age, and place of birth.

☐ I can get the bus or train I want, buy a ticket, and get off where I intended to.

☐ I can use the language well enough to assist a newcomer in all of the above Level One situations.

Level One Plus

☐ I have a One Plus proficiency because I can do all of the Level One activities and at least three of the following Level Two activities.

Level Two

(You are at Level Two when you can confidently check each of the following Level Two activities.)

☐ I can give detailed information about the weather, my family, my home and my living arrangements.

☐ I can take and give simple messages over the telephone.

☐ I can give a brief autobiography and also talk about my plans and hopes.

☐ I can describe my most recent job or activity in some detail and also describe my present role as a language learner.

I can describe the basic structure of the government in both my home and host countries. ☐

I can describe the geography of both my home and host countries. ☐

I can describe the purpose and function of the organization I represent. ☐

I could use my new language in hiring an employee and agreeing on qualifications, salary, hours, and special duties. ☐

I feel confident that my pronunciation is always intelligible. ☐

I feel confident that people understand me when I speak in the new language, at least 80% of the time. I am also confident that I understand what native speakers tell me on topics like those of Level Two. ☐

I could use my new language well enough to assist a newcomer on any of the Level Two situations. ☐

Level Two Plus

I have a Two Plus proficiency because I can meet at least three of the following Level Three requirements. ☐

Level Three

(You are at Level Three when you can confidently check each of the following Level Three items.)

I do not try to avoid any of the grammatical features of the language. ☐

I now have sufficient vocabulary and grasp of grammatical structure to complete any sentence that I begin. ☐

I can speak at a normal rate of speech, with only rare hesitations. ☐

I can confidently follow and contribute to a conversation between native speakers when they try to include me. ☐

I am able to correctly understand any information given to me over the telephone. ☐

I can listen to a speech or discussion on a topic of interest to me and take accurate notes. ☐

I can speak to a group of native speakers on a professional subject and have confidence that I am communicating what I want to. ☐

I can understand opposing points of view and can politely describe and defend an organizational position or objective to an antagonist. ☐

I could cope with a social blunder, an undeserved traffic ticket, or a plumbing emergency. ☐

I can cope
with a plumbing emergency

I can understand two or more native speakers talking with each other about a current event or issue. ☐

I could serve as an interpreter for a newcomer in any of the Level Three situations. ☐

I feel that I can carry out the professional responsibilities of my work in my new language. ☐

Level Three Plus

☐ I have a Three Plus proficiency because I can meet at least three of the Level Four requirements.

Level Four

(You are at Level Four when you can confidently check each of the following Level Four characteristics.)

☐ I practically never make grammatical mistakes.

☐ I can always understand native speakers when they talk with each other.

☐ I can understand humor and language puns, and I can actively participate in fun and humorous situations.

☐ My vocabulary is always extensive and precise enough for me to convey my exact meaning in professional discussions.

☐ I feel I have a comprehensive grasp of the local cultural "knowledge bank."

☐ I can appropriately alter my speech style for a public lecture, or a conversation with a professor, an employee, or a close friend.

☐ I could serve as an informal interpreter for a "bigwig" at a professional or social function.

☐ I feel that I could carry out any job assignment as effectively in my second language as in English.

Interpreter
for a bigwig.

Level Four Plus

☐ My vocabulary and cultural understanding are always extensive enough to enable me to communicate my precise meaning.

☐ People feel that I share their knowledge bank well enough to talk about and defend any of their beliefs or values.

Level Five

☐ Native speakers react to me just as they do to each other — I am usually considered an "insider."

☐ I sometimes feel more at home in my second language than in English.

☐ I can do mental arithmetic in the language without slowing down.

☐ I consider myself to be completely bilingual and bicultural, with equivalent ability in English and in my second language.

☐ I consider myself a native speaker of the language.

He considers himself
to be a nativespeaker

"How much time should it take
To move from one level to another?"

That is a relative question. Some people just learn faster than others. Another factor is that some languages are complex and quite different from English (like Cantonese), and therefore more time would be required than for a language that is linguistically related to English (like Spanish).

Other factors include the amount of your daily exposure to the language; your responsibilities in the language; and the amount of time that you devote to language learning. If you live in the home of a local family where no English is heard, you have an advantage; if you are able to devote full time to language learning, you have a further advantage; and if you know that you must achieve a high level of language ability or else your agency will recall you, then you have even more incentive to learn.

GOOD ABILITY
+
EASY LANGUAGE
+
MAXIMUM EXPOSURE
+
"LIVING IN"
+
FULL-TIME
+
"LEARN or ELSE"
FAST LEARNING

It takes more time to move from Level Three to Level Four than it takes to move from Level One to Level Two. In general, the advancement of each step takes a unit of time equivalent to the time units needed for the previous two steps. Let's say, for example, that it takes a one-week unit of time to move from Zero to Zero Plus and two additional weeks to advance from Zero Plus to the One Level. To advance from the One to the One Plus Level would then take about as much time as the previous two sets combined — about three weeks. The total time needed to arrive at the One Plus Level would be about six weeks.

This time projection can be charted as follows:

Levels	0	0+	1	1+	2	2+	3	3+	4	4+	5
Units of time between steps	1	2	3	5	8	13	21	34	55	89	
Accumulated units of time		1	3	6	11	19	32	53	87	142	231

If you learn at about an average rate, and you are working steadily on a moderately difficult language, then each time unit may equal approximately one week. If you don't learn as fast and you are working on Navaho or some other "toughie," then you should expect each time unit to be somewhat longer.

It is best not to worry about your *rate* of overall learning. Instead, keep moving ahead, by setting and achieving manageable goals on a day-by-day basis. Your rate of learning should then take care of itself.

Expanded Self-Rating Checklist

Here are some finer distinctions for self rating your speaking proficiency. The expanded checklist is to be used in conjuction with the information on pages 374 to 376.

Level Zero

☐ 0.2 I can use more than 20 words of my new language in appropriate contexts.

☐ 0.4 I can initiate conversations and use appropriate leave-takings to close conversations.

☐ 0.6 I can use more than 50 words of my new language in appropriate contexts.

☐ 0.7 I can confidently check 3 (any 3) of the Level One activities.

☐ 0.8 I can confidently check 5 of the Level One activities.

Level One

☐ 1.0 I can confidently check all of the Level One activities.

☐ 1.2 I can confidently check 1 of the Level Two activities.

☐ 1.4 I can confidently check 2 of the Level Two activities.

☐ 1.6 I can confidently check 3 of the Level Two activities.

☐ 1.8 I can confidently check 6 of the Level Two activities.

Level Two

☐ 2.0 I can confidently check all of the Level Two activities.

☐ 2.2 I can confidently check 1 of the Level Three activities.

☐ 2.4 I can confidently check 2 of the Level Three activities.

☐ 2.6 I can confidently check 3 of the Level Three activities.

☐ 2.8 I can confidently check 6 of the Level Three activities.

Level Three

☐ 3.0 I can confidently check all of the Level Three activities.

☐ 3.2 I can confidently check 1 of the Level Four activities.

☐ 3.4 I can confidently check 2 of the Level Four activities.

☐ 3.6 I can confidently check 3 of the Level Four activities.

☐ 3.8 I can confidently check 5 of the Level Four activities.

APPENDIX B

Getting the Most Out of Your Learning Cycles

This section is for the learner who wants to check his own *understanding* of the Learning Cycle techniques and his *skills* in implementing them. It can also be used by language supervisors as they monitor the learners they are working with.

It is important that the learner clearly understand the purpose of each of the activities of the Learning Cycle, and how to get the most out of each one. Don't let your learning efficiency be hampered due to an inadequate understanding of the purpose and distinctiveness of each of the different Fluency and Accuracy practice activities. If the strengths and limitations of each individual activity are not sorted out, it is predictable that one's use of the cycle might be mechanical or clumsy. When you understand the distinctive features of each specific drill and can skillfully implement each activity, you will sense a new freedom in adapting the Learning Cycle activities to your personality and in using them spontaneously in your own situation.

Appendix B has been designed to help you *demonstrate* your understanding of the individual parts of the Learning Cycle. (Exercises 1-4 can be completed by your second week in the language. Exercise 5 may have to wait a little longer — maybe until the second month.)

Completing Exercises
1, 2, 3, 4

Exercise 1: Learning Cycle Overview

Write out a one-page detailed *plan* of activities to guide you for a six and one-half hour day of language study. Indicate the amount of *time* to be allotted to each of the activities listed in the plan for the day.

Exercise 2: Fluency Practice Overview

On one sheet of paper, name the *Fluency* practice drills in order of relative difficulty (starting with the least difficult), then describe the *purpose* of each of these specific drills and the *relationship* of each to its more and less difficult neighboring Fluency activities.

Exercise 3: Accuracy Practice Overview

Demonstrate that you understand the purpose and distinctives of each of the following Accuracy drills by gathering appropriate data and organizing it so that your practice can be both efficient and effective.

Structure Substitution Drill
Structure Differential Drill
Pronunciation Substitution Drill
Pronunciation Differential Drill

Lay out a drill

Use a separate page for each of these four Accuracy practice drills. For each one, describe briefly the *purpose* of the drill. Then lay out an organized drill using data on a relevant feature of your new language. Write the *drill data* in the writing system of the language (Kino can help you write it if necessary), and then phonetically as best you can. Identify the *feature* in focus and briefly give directions for the stages of practice of the drill. If you are working with a supervisor, he may want you to use the back of each sheet to write a literal word-for-word English *translation* of the drill data along with a freer, idiomatic English translation.

Exercise 4: Sample Tape

Evaluate your taping efficiency

With your helper, prepare a sample practice tape by recording each of the drills listed on page 382. (It will be helpful for you to relisten to the *LAMP* Demonstration Tape.) On the left column of page 382 indicate the footage where the drill is found on your tape. The right side provides space for you or your supervisor to evaluate the taping of each of the drills and comment on anything that would make your taping, or practice with the tape, more efficient. The recorded tape should be evaluated in terms of how well it helps you to efficiently accomplish the purpose of the drill and move toward *production* of the feature. If you are working with a supervisor, he will want to review the tape along with (1) a copy of page 382, (2) a written copy of the recorded text and organized drill data for each of the Accuracy drills — written in the writing system of your new language and phonetically (as well as you can), (3) a written English approximation of your recorded text, (4) a brief description in English of the gist of the Story Comprehension material, and (5) a literal word-for-word translation of the recorded Structure drills, along with a free idiomatic translation of them.

Exercise 5: Structure Overview

Re-read *LAMP* pages 323-325. Select the simple sentences from your previous texts and classify them. Then work with your helper to elicit a variety of additional examples to illustrate each type. *List* at least 5 examples of each of the different simple sentence types in your new language. These simple sentence patterns will give you basic material for further structure exploration and Structure drills. Facility with these basic sentence patterns can be the springboard to greater proficiency in the language. Here is a suggested format for this list:

Type One — Someone does an activity

1. The sentence in the local spelling.
   Phonetic spelling of the sentence.
   A very literal translation into English.
   The gist of the meaning in idiomatic English.
2. (The second example, following the above pattern.)
3.
4.
5.

Springboard to greater proficiency

Type Two — Someone does an activity to something

1.
etc.

Tape Record Sheet

_____
(Date)

_____
(Date language learning began)

_____
(Your Name)

_____
(Target Language)

Tape footage (or cassette mark #)	Drill	OK	Re-tape	Comments
		(Do not write on these blanks)		

Fluency Practice

Tape footage	Drill	OK	Re-tape
_____	Whole Text Listening Drill	_____	_____
_____	Phrase Mimicry Drill - A	_____	_____
_____	Phrase Mimicry Drill - B	_____	_____
_____	Build-up Mimicry Drill	_____	_____
_____	Sentence Mimicry Drill - A	_____	_____
_____	Sentence Mimicry Drill - B	_____	_____
_____	Completion Production - A	_____	_____
_____	Completion Production - B	_____	_____
_____	Completion Production - C	_____	_____
_____	Alternation with correction	_____	_____
_____	Alternation without correction	_____	_____

Comprehension Practice:

Tape footage	Drill	OK	Re-tape
_____	Story Comprehension	_____	_____

Accuracy Practice:

Tape footage	Drill	OK	Re-tape
_____	Structure Substitution Drill	_____	_____
_____	Pronunciation Substitution	_____	_____
_____	Structure Differential	_____	_____
_____	Pronunciation Differential	_____	_____
_____	Consistency Drill (P. 332)	_____	_____

Your tape can best be reviewed by someone else if the following material accompanies it:

1. A copy of this page, with your tape footages indicated.
2. A written copy of the recorded text, and the organized drill data for each of the Accuracy drills — in the writing system of your new language and phonetically (as well as you can).
3. A written English approximation of the recorded text.
4. A brief description in English of the gist of the Story Comprehension material.
5. A literal word-for-word translation, plus a freer idiomatic translation, of your recorded Structure Drills.

SUGGESTED LANGUAGE LEARNING PROGRESSION SCHEDULE

Week #	Topics for Texts and Comprehension (Methodology)	Daily Drills	Pronunciation Analysis — LAMP Four
1†	Follow all the Activities described in Chapter One during your First Week.		
2	Repeat LAMP Chapter One	Substitution Drills and	LAMP Four — Phonetics, Consonants (p. 247-279).
3†	Repeat LAMP Chapter One	Differential Drills: At	LAMP Four — Phonetics, Vowels and Tones (p. 280-303).
4†	Repeat LAMP Chapter One	least one Pronunciation	Application: Chart all sounds (p. 306-307)
5†		and one Structure drill	Application: Identify sounds to practice (p. 303-309)
6†		should be practiced each	Begin implementing a systematic practice plan (p. 309-311).
7†		day.	‡Proceed with tentative Phonemic Analysis

Daily Drills (box):

Pronunciation	*Structure***
Specific Pronunciation Substitution and Differential Drills Based on Systematic Plan	Substitution and Differential Drills from Texts; and Analysis of Basic Sentences

Week #	Structure Analysis — LAMP Five
8†	List and Practice Minimal Simple Sentence Types
9†	Continue Practice: Complete Lists of Simple Types
10	Multiply Basic Types by Negation
11	Multiply Basic Types by Questions
12	Multiply Basic Types by Emphasis
13†	Multiply Basic Types by Instructions
14	Multiple Modifications
15	Multiple Modifications
16†	Write up Samples of All Multiplied Basics

Month #	
5†	Systematically Write up & Practice Each Basic & Multiplied Sentence Type with REPLACEMENT Exercises
6†	Systematically Write up & Practice Each Basic & Multiplied Type with EXPANSION Exercises
7†	Systematically Write up & Practice Each Basic & Multiplied Type with REARRANGEMENT Exercises
8†	Systematically Write up & Practice Each Basic & Multiplied Type with DELETION Exercises
9†	Practice & Write up All Non-simple Sentence Types Formed by LINKING
10†	Practice & Write up All Non-simple Types Formed by DEPENDENT COMBINATIONS
11†	Practice & Write up All Non-simple FLEXIBILITY Operations — One Operation Each Week
12†	Practice & Write up All Non-simple Types Formed by EMBEDDING and QUOTES
13†	WORDS and their PARTS: Analyze and Practice
14†	Begin Structure Analysis Through Use of QUESTIONS: *Word and Sentence Level*
15†	Complete Structure Analysis Through Use of QUESTIONS: *Beyond the Sentence*

* Topics for Texts and Comprehension drills are to be selected from Chapters Two and Three or developed in response to your felt needs. Remember that daily Communication is essential.

** Systematic **Structure** analysis begins with the 10th week. However, each new sentence structure that is encountered in daily texts should also be practiced even though that type may not be studied "systematically" until later.

† We suggest that agencies require written reports showing evidence that specific steps have been completed. These reports might be required after the activities of each week/month indicated above with a dagger. "People do what you *inspect*, not what you *expect*."

‡ *Programmed Phonemics* (by Brewster & Brewster) — a guide to help you apply phonetics to your specific language — is available from Lingua House . . . $3.50x.

Language Learning Progress Report

_____   _____
(Date)   (Your Name)

_____   _____
(Date language learning began)   (Target Language)

1. This month the speaking skills that I have in the local language are comparable to the skills described at the following speaking proficiency level:

   ___   ___   ___   ___   ___   ___   ___   ___   ___
   0+   1   1+   2   2+   3   3+   4   4+

2. I feel that I am: (check one)
   Making steady progress _____;   Making some progress _____;
   Making no progress _____;   Retrogressing _____.

3. I have been following the suggested Language Learning Progression Schedule (page 379) _____. I have now completed the steps for week/month _____. Samples are attached _____.

4. In any given 5-day week this month I have spent a minimum of _____ hours in structured language learning. My typical daily schedule for this month is outlined on the back of this sheet _____.

5. The following activities are examples of experiences I have had this month which have demonstrated to people my role as a learner of their heart language: _____
   _____
   _____
   _____

6. The following activities are _examples_ of situations I have encountered in the past month which involved me in communication, using the language of the people: _____
   _____
   _____

7. If I made the following adjustments in my life-style, I would not be as isolated from speakers of the local language and might expect to make better progress: _____
   _____
   _____

8. In my role as a language learner this month, I gained the following information about, or insights into, the culture and thought patterns of the community: _____
   _____
   _____
   _____

9. In the coming four weeks I plan to direct some of my attention to the following specific needs:

   Language Feature   Topic Areas
   _____   _____
   _____   _____
   _____   _____
   _____   _____
   _____   _____
   _____   _____

10. I communicate my text with approximately _____ people each day.

(Permission is granted for the reproduction of this page for use as a monthly report form.)